OLAUDAH EQUIANO
AND THE IGBO WORLD

OLAUDAH EQUIANO AND THE IGBO WORLD

HISTORY, SOCIETY AND ATLANTIC DIASPORA CONNECTIONS

EDITED BY
CHIMA J. KORIEH

Africa World Press, Inc.

P.O. Box 1892
Trenton, NJ 08607

P.O. Box 48
Asmara, ERITREA

Africa World Press, Inc.

P.O. Box 1892
Trenton, NJ 08607

P.O. Box 48
Asmara, ERITREA

Book design: Saverance Publishing Services
Cover design: Ashraful Haque

Library of Congress Cataloging-in-Publication Data

Olaudah Equiano and the Igbo world / edited by Chima J. Korieh.
    p. cm.
Includes bibliographical references and index.
ISBN 1-59221-664-1 (hardcover) -- ISBN 1-59221-665-X (pbk.)
1. Equiano, Olaudah, b. 1745. 2. Equiano, Olaudah, b. 1745. Interesting narrative of the life of Olaudah Equiano. 3. Igbo (African people)--Biography 4. Slaves--Great Britain--Biography. 5. Slaves--America--Biography. 6. Igbo (African people)--Ethnic identity. 7. Igbo (African people)--History. 8. Slave trade--Biafra, Bight of, Region--History. 9. Slave trade--America--History. 10. African diaspora. I. Korieh, Chima J. (Chima Jacob), 1962-
    HT869.E6O43 2008
    306.3'6208996332017521--dc22
                                    2008035309

In memory of
my father, Linus Onyegbule Korieh,
who bought me my first Igbo literature (Omenuko)
when I was 6
&
Don C. Ohadike,
for keeping the embers alive

TABLE OF CONTENTS

Foreword   ix
Emmanuel N. Obiechina

Preface   xiii

Introduction: Mapping the Igbo-Atlantic Connection   1
Chima J. Korieh

**FROM A GLASS DARKLY: OLAUDAH EQUIANO AND
THE IGBO WORLD**

1. (Re)Imagining Community: Olaudah Equiano and the
   (Re)construction of Igbo (African) Identity   23
   Maureen N. Eke

2. The Igbo Roots of Olaudah Equiano   49
   Catherine Obianuju Acholonu

3. Igbo Sense of Place and Identity in Olaudah Equiano's *The*   67
   Interesting Narrative
   Dorothy Chinwe Ukaegbu

4. Status in Eighteenth-Century Igboland: Perspectives from
   Olaudah Equiano's *The Interesting Narrative*   93
   Dorothy Chinwe Ukaegbu

5. Olaudah Equiano and the Question of African Identity   117
   Ogbo Ugwuanyi

6. Between Literature, Facts, and Fiction: Perspectives on
   Olaudah Equiano's *The Interesting Narrative*   141
   Elizabeth Odachi Onogwu

ENCOUNTERS WITH EUROPE

7. Neoliberal Tradition in Pre-colonial Igbo Society   157
   Raphael Chijioke Njoku

8. Gathering Figs from Thistles: Hinterland Slave Trade and the
   Christianization of Igboland, 1900-1950   179
   Ogbu U. Kalu

9. Gender and Class Transformation Resulting From the Atlantic
   Slave trade and Colonialism   203
   J. Akuma-Kalu Njoku

10. Episodes of Igbo Resistance to European Imperialism   219
    Felix K. Ekechi

11. Revolution and Reaction in Eastern Nigeria, 1900-1929: The
    Background to the Women's Riot of 1929   245
    Adiele Afigbo

12. Igbo Women From 1929 to 1960   269
    John N. Oriji

ATLANTIC DIASPORA CONNECTIONS

13. Igbo Ethnicity and Identity in the Atlantic Diaspora   287
    Chima J. Korieh

14. Igbo Women in the Early Modern Atlantic World: The Burden
    of Beauty   315
    Douglas B. Chambers

15. African Cultural Values: Significance of Igbo Oral Forms in
    Caribbean Poetry   333
    Hannah N. Eby Chukwu

16. African Origins of Igbo Slave Resistance in the Americas   349
    Daniel Kloza

17. Editing Race: The Mediation of Equiano's *Interesting Narrative*
    and the Correlating Black Aesthetic   369
    Ron Milland

Selected Bibliography   381

Notes on Contributors   393

Index   399

FOREWORD

EMMANUEL N. OBIECHINA

I am truly honored to be asked to provide a Foreword to *Olaudah Equiano & The Igbo World* which is a very important book devoted to the unraveling of the background of the life of this outstanding eighteenth-century African. Olaudah Equiano (Ekweano) named Gustavus Vassa in slavery was by his account born an Eboe (Igbo) in Essaka (Isseke) in what is today known as Anambra State of south-eastern Nigeria. He was taken into slavery as a boy in America and the Caribbean islands and after a very active life, much of which was spent at sea, he bought his freedom and devoted his later life in England to fighting for the abolition of the slave trade. He published his autobiography, *The Interesting Narrative of the Life of Olaudah Equiano, or Gustavus Vassa, the African. Written by Himself,* in 1789.

Equiano's Narrative, as the autobiography has come to be popularly called, has since become a classic in its own right. It has been studied by scholars and researchers as a key text of the British abolitionist literature and as a major, defining text of the African-American autobiography of the genre known as the slave narrative. Historians of the transatlantic slavery have also adopted it as a regular illustrative text portraying an individual African's journey from the African homeland to the New World of American slavery through the horrors of the Middle Passage. But so far, the African component of Equiano's tripodal life has received only scanty attention.

The first reclamation of *Equiano's Narrative* for African Studies was made by Paul Edwards of Edinburgh University who introduced it to African readers in the Heinemann African Writers Series with the title *Equiano's Travels* (1964). *Equiano's Narrative* is also a cardinal text in an anthology of the autobiographies of eighteenth and nineteenth- century

African ex-slaves edited by historian Philip D. Curtin and titled *Africa Remembered: Narratives by West Africans from the Era of the Slave Trade* (1967). The stories detail where the people came from, the circumstances of their enslavement and departure from their African homelands.

Commendable though these early efforts to reclaim Olaudah Equiano for Africa were, they appear totally inadequate in recognition of a man who called himself *"The African"* and who celebrated his African identity by going beyond the demands of conventional autobiography and introducing himself to the reader "with some accounts of the manners and customs" of his society. It is fitting at least that such a man and his work should be acknowledged and given singular treatment through greater research and scholarly dissemination. Having defended Africa and the African world at a time when the continent and its people were grossly misunderstood by the generality of the people and misrepresented by eighteenth-century European racists, it stands to reason that the continent and its scholars should return the compliment by recognizing him as one of Africa's foremost illustrious sons and by enshrining his work among the foundational pillars of its intellectual heritage.

Today's re-awakened interest in Olaudah Equiano and his narrative is indeed a necessary and important development in the context of which *Olaudah Equiano & The Igbo World* is a ground-breaking attempt to forcefully initiate a systematic and sustained discussion of Equiano's African background. What the various chapters do is to underscore, from various angles and perspectives, the reality of Equiano's African (Igbo) identity, the essentiality of him as a person writing his story with an inside knowledge of a world that produced him, a world he knew well, a world which he subsequently and regrettably left behind but which never really left him because it was stored up in his memory to be called up at the appropriate psychological moment.

It is not possible to understand Equiano's life and narrative in totality without adverting to the society and the culture within which he had his early cultural education. The reality is that Equiano was first and foremost an Igbo before he became an African, a black man, and before he became a man of the world, a Briton by adoptive citizenship, and, a Western-oriented man exposed to the ideas of the European Enlightenment.

When I gave the 1994 Ahiajoku Annual Lecture titled "NCHETAKA: The Story, Memory, and Continuity of Igbo Culture," I referred to *Equiano's Narrative* as the work of an Igbo person bred into the tradition of oral storytelling and who had successfully turned such accomplishment into an asset when he decided to write his personal story in his attempt to reclaim his identity after the tragedy of his enslavement. He reached back to the story form with which he was already familiar in his formative years. For, it was obvious to me from the intimate way he described life in his lost homeland that he lived long enough in Igboland to absorb the culture of his society, together with its various formative influences. Storytelling as the regular nursery from which the Igbo child received cultural education, cultivated basic social values and attitudes, and developed strong moral and ethical views of life became for Equiano one of the most important formative influences. I saw in his *Narrative* Equiano's ability to give global expression to what would have remained a mere local aptitude. When accompanied by other modes of traditional education, such as exposure to the world of well-informed elders like Equiano's father who was a customary court judge, then the individual was firmly set to withstand the storms and stresses of life and to negotiate the complexities of adulthood. The fact that Equiano survived the rigors of life in a new environment and to have done so in good grace must be attributed to the confidence he built up through his early cultural education in his Isseke homeland, the kind of inner strength which people enjoy from being well integrated within their way of life and which becomes the source of their best actions.

With that kind of background, Equiano was able to meet the challenges of racial slavery and to give his non-African readers a coherent view of a way of life that was alien to them, a way of life that was generally misconstrued and disparaged. He was not only able to present a factual image of his African life, but he was also successful in comparing and contrasting the African world with the world of the Europeans which he knew equally well. For the first time, his readers were given a credible image of an African society by one born within it, a society which was not romanticized, nor was it demonized, as was the image of Africa in works by non-African writers.

The significance of *Olaudah Equiano & The Igbo World* is its giving scholarly recognition to Olaudah Equiano as an authoritative voice in the cultural struggles of the eighteenth century in his defense of the integrity of the African way of life. It, thus, sets the scene for the African phase of the study of Equiano's life and narrative. It legitimizes, and, in fact, mandates scholarly researches from the African point of view. After two centuries of *Equiano's Narrative* being viewed and studied from Afro-British and Afro-American perspectives and traditions, the time has at last arrived for it to assume the centrality it has earned in African Studies through Equiano's immense intellectual foresight and commitment to Africa and its interests.

The contributors to *Olaudah Equiano & The Igbo World* have rendered invaluable service to African Studies by foregrounding this important figure whose autobiography will henceforth become a major cohesive force in the intellectual history of Africa by not only demonstrating the recuperative power of memory in the African Diaspora but also in many vital aspects providing important linkages to illuminate large issues of African scholarship in the humanities, the social sciences, and the black expressive arts and culture.

Furthermore, Equiano's relevance does not depend only on his being able to defend his Africanity and successfully critiquing the assumption of racial superiority by Europeans in his day, but he was also able to evolve techniques and strategies for doing so which were to be subsequently adopted by African thinkers, writers, and nationalists in the nineteenth and twentieth centuries in their attempts to counteract European cultural arrogance in the age of colonial imperialism. Because of Equiano's broad intellectual reaches, his *Narrative* provides a wide scope for the extrapolation of African and pan-African ideas and ideologies and a promise of expanded analytical discourse from the particular to the general, from the specific socio-cultural, eighteenth-century Igbo background to the more elaborate , inclusive universe of ideas in African Studies.

Thus, a major collateral impact of *Olaudah Equiano & The Igbo World* is the emphasis it places on Equiano's status as the forerunner of the nineteenth century African cultural nationalists and the twentieth century anti-colonial African writers. The strategy of writing back so clearly developed in the works of later African intellectuals and writers had already been used to great effect by Equiano in his narrative. Even his classic strategy of retrieving his identity by reclaiming his original African names has since become the common practice of many African nationalists and politicians in their attempt to dramatize their indigenous identity. Many of these have dropped their given foreign or baptismal names in favor of their ethnically generated names.

With particular reference to Igbo Studies, Olaudah Equiano is a pivotal figure whose description of Igbo life and culture provides enormous resonances for the appreciation of the archaeology, history, religion, language, and ethnography of Igboland. There is hardly any aspect of Igbo Studies that has not been relevantly touched by the overarching genius of Equiano's imagination, as has been amply demonstrated in the breadth and depth of the various chapters of *Olaudah Equiano & The Igbo World.*

One does not need extraordinary prescience to predict that this book would enjoy extensive readership. It has great relevance for our time and for the light the contributors bring to bear on the life and background of this unique, iconic, eighteenth-century African. For this, both the common reader and the scholarly researcher have been very well served.

Emmanuel N. Obiechina, Ph.D; FNAL
W.E.B. Du Bois Non-Resident Fellow, Harvard University

PREFACE

The idea to produce this anthology began to germinate when I organized the 4th International Conference on Igbo Studies at Howard University in 2006. The theme of the conference, which was "The Igbo and its Diaspora: Interrogating Culture, History, and Identity," was dedicated to the late prominent Igbo historian, Don C. Ohadike, who died on August 28, 2005. Curiously enough, there were not a lot of papers that dealt with the Igbo in the Black Diaspora. An invitation by Dr. Catherine Acholonu to help organize the first International Conference on Olaudah Equiano at Owerri, Imo State, Nigeria, in July 2007, fueled my interest even more. Equiano came to represent several things, including slave, abolitionist, literary giant; but most importantly Igbo tenacity. I was motivated to explore these themes in retrospect, by working back into the African background. It is my belief that the history of the Igbo, like the history of many other ethnic groups in the Atlantic Diaspora, can tremendously benefit from a trans-Atlantic perspective. This is an important step in exploring the connections and linkages among three important phases in Igbo society: the pre-European contact phase, the first phase of European contact broadly defined to include the era of the Atlantic slave trade and the impacts of this intercourse on both sides of the Atlantic, and finally, the period of European colonialism from the beginning of the twentieth century to the end of British rule. I have tried to render a summation of my own perspective in the introduction to this collection by revealing how these themes explain the forms that existed in the past and their implications for the present.

I want to thank the contributors for their enthusiasm and effort in making the publication of this book possible. While preparing this manuscript, I benefited from the advice of my friends and contributors to this volume: Raph Njoku, Douglas Chambers, and Dorothy Ukaegbu. I thank them wholeheartedly. Finally, I am grateful to the staff of the Transatlantic Research Center, Owerri, Nigeria, for typesetting the manuscript, and to Professor Emmanuel N. Obiechina, for writing the foreword, and to my research assistant, Elizabeth Dillenburg, for editorial assistance.

Introduction:
Mapping the Igbo-Atlantic
Connection

Chima J. Korieh

The recent controversy surrounding the nativity of Olaudah Equiano, the ex-Igbo slave who wrote *The Interesting Narrative of the Life of Olaudah Equiano*, is enough reason to re-examine his Igbo roots in relationship to aspects of Igbo history, culture, and identity.[1] Specifically, this book examines the Igbo speaking people, one of the largest single ethnicities in Africa, located in southeastern Nigeria on both sides of the River Niger, from a transatlantic perspective. Although they are found in significant numbers in Cameroon and Equatorial Guinea, the Igbo remain one of the only surviving coherent ethnic groups from the first set of proto-Kwa speakers to penetrate the forest areas of contemporary Southern Nigeria. The goal in this volume is twofold: The first goal is to explore the extent to which the encounter with Europeans via the Atlantic slave trade provides historical data for reconstructing the early history and social dynamics of the Igbo. This will be done through a re-examination of the picture of Igbo life painted by Olaudah Equiano in his *The Interesting Narrative*.

The second goal is to explore the impacts of this earlier encounter and the subsequent colonization of Igboland on both sides of the Atlantic. Here we offer some preliminary assessment of the ways enslaved Igbos influenced the cultures and history of the Atlantic world following their enslavement in the New World. We also want to explore aspects of the transformations that occurred on the African side as a result of the European encounter with the Igbo. The goal is to extend Igbo scholarship to the Atlantic world and to show how small places in the African world had lasting impacts on global formations and history.

European encounters with African societies from the fifteenth century led to major transformations on both sides of the Atlantic. How these encounters shaped the societies of Africa and the Americas has received considerable attention. Yet, significant aspects of the impacts of these contacts remain unexplored or fully fleshed out. The contributors address developments among the Igbo from the period of European contact and Igbo response to two hegemonic institutions—slavery and colonialism— in the African and New World contexts. The volume, by its nature, cannot explore the array of manifestations of this contact or its impact on the Igbo. Thus the book is an exploration of an African society's interconnectedness with the Atlantic world from the era of the slave trade, through later colonial encounters and the effects on the Igbo world. We begin from the premise that while the Igbo, like many other groups, were subsequently forced to migrate into the New World under bondage, they nevertheless influenced the early history and culture of the Atlantic world in important ways—ways both intellectual and cultural. Whether as groups or as individuals, the Igbo people of the Bight of Biafra hinterland helped shape the history of the world system that developed with the European explorations of the West African Coast in the fifteenth century. The intellectual contribution of one of its most famous sons, Olaudah Equiano, remains outstanding.

Understanding changes in Igbo society from the period of European contact, as well as Igbo influences in the Atlantic world, requires an examination of the pre-contact institutions and structures of the Igbo. For it is only within this context that one can understand their peculiar resistance to the institution of slavery and their history of resistance to European colonialism from the late nineteenth century. The reconstruction of the early history of the Igbo, like the history of many pre-literate societies, is bedeviled by the problem of sources, despite the important roles archeology and oral tradition have played in reconstructing the early past. Archaeological, linguistic, botanical, and anthropological evidence also suggest that the Igbo have lived in their present habitat for a considerable length of time. It is generally believed, however, that the Igbo originated in an area near the confluence of the Niger and Benue Rivers. Their shared linguistic ties with the Bini, Igala, Yoruba, and Idoma suggest a long history of habitation in their present location. This is based on the speculation that these languages may have split about five or six thousand years ago.

A considerable amount of literature has been devoted to different aspects of the history and culture of the Igbo people of West Africa.[2]

Historical and anthropological works on the Igbo, in particular, have attempted to resolve several inter-related issues: the matter of origin, pre-colonial economy and commerce, inter-group relations, and identity. With the institution of the "Ahiajoku Lecture Series" in 1989, beginning with Michael Echeruo's inaugural lecture entitled "Ahamefule: A Matter of Identity," several laureates of the series have explored aspects of Igbo society, history, culture, political, economy, religion, and worldview.[3] Yet, much remains to be explored. As often occurs in the study of pre-literate societies, scholars of Igbo studies are faced with methodological issues. First, it is difficult to generalize about the Igbo, whose cultures and history have been marked by regional variation, despite the Igbo language's centrality as a source of pan-Igbo identity.[4] The diversity in kinship structures, as well as the political institutions and the source of political authority, make any notion of a structurally defined pan-Igbo sociopolitical structure an anomaly. Geographical variations and their role in the economic life of the Igbo remained a source of diversity. Second, like most pre-literate societies, several aspects of ancient Igbo history remain informed speculations due to the lack of evidence.

Yet, this diversity did not mean the absence of a pan-Igbo identity as reflected in well-institutionalized republican political structures characterized by democratic village assemblies, a common language (Igbo), and common religious and cosmological views. Indeed, most Igbo societies had no centralized chieftaincy or political affiliations. Instead, the responsibility of leadership rested on village councils and other associations.

Although ignoring the role women and women's associations played in Igbo political life, a British colonial officer in Nigeria outlined the basic principles of the system:

> The social structure of . . . all Ibo and Ibibio peoples of the Eastern Provinces, was essentially democratic and in ancient times each village had been administered by a Council of Elders. Like most indigenous institutions, the composition of these Councils was vague and undefined and when serious matters of general concern required consideration virtually the whole community assembled in the village playground, the elders in the centre, the younger men grouped around them and the women and children often sitting quietly at discreet distance. Age was respected and, as in many gerontocracy, policy was moulded upon the decisions of the ancestors.[5]

Yet, the political institutions of the riverine Igbo communities of Onitsha, Oguta, Aboh, and Osamiri, of which Ikenna Nzimiro and Richard Henderson have written, challenge the core concept of "stateless society" often used to describe the Igbo in anthropological and historical writings.[6] The riverine communities developed traditions of monarchical institutions. Such monarchical institutions, nevertheless, still exhibited the basic principles of Igbo democratic republicanism. The basic principles of traditional Igbo political systems and institutions would have a significant impact on how enslaved Igbo responded to the destabilizing influence of the slave trade in Africa and slavery in the Americas, and to colonialism in the beginning of the twentieth century.

The Igbo economy was dominated by agriculture. Although we can only speculate on the antiquity of plant and animal domestication among the Igbo, the large variety of domesticated plants and crops would suggest a long history of agriculture in the region.[7] Demographic and environmental conditions also offer glimpses into the agricultural past. The high population concentration in the Igbo region and the large-scale transformation of the original forest by the late nineteenth century would indicate a long history of horticultural practice among the Igbo.[8] Their staple crop of yam was inescapably linked to their world view, religion, mode of production and male identity. The introduction of American and Southeast Asian crops, including certain species of yam, cocoyam, rice, and banana, provided new varieties of food crops that further transformed the Igbo economy and supported a larger population.[9]

The cultural and artistic sophistication of the Igbo is reflected in art forms of fine quality, including copper alloy castings discovered at Igbo Ukwu that date to the tenth century. The Igbo Ukwu art shows that the Igbo had already achieved a high level of technological and cultural advancement by the ninth century.[10]

The Igbo are deeply religious. They generally believe in the existence of a Supreme Being, *Chukwu/Chineke*, but practiced ancestral worship in a variety of forms. The belief in spirits and their influence among the living is powerful. As Edward Falk, an early colonial administrator among the Igbo observed, "spirits are interposed between man and the Supreme being, and the good ones may intercede on behalf of the individual before it;" a conception, he noted, that was "precisely akin to that of the Catholic Peasantry in many parts of Europe if we substitute Saints for Spirits."[11] Divination was, thus, frequently practiced among the Igbo, as they would often seek the diviner's advice to ascertain whether the auspices were favorable, to seek advice on the appropriate sacrifice to be performed in order to resolve problems, or to ascertain the appropriate place to build a new home, among others needs. Many of these beliefs have survived in one form or another despite massive conversion to Christianity, as they did in the oldest Christian countries of Europe.[12] As such, it would be redundant to speak of a pan-Igbo religion, considering the regional diversity that exits among the Igbo.

FROM A GLASS DARKLY

The recent past offers ample evidence to reconstruct the distant past of the Igbo. The task of reconstructing pre-colonial Igbo societies has benefited from indirect references by early European travelers. Igbo encounters with Europeans began indirectly in the fifteenth century, as European traders began commercial relations with the Bight of Biafra. These encounters provide some of the earliest glimpses and perspectives on the Igbo people of the Bight of Biafra Hinterland. Early European travelers to West Africa, including Portuguese geographer, Duarte Pacheco[13] and John Grazilhier,[14] provide some of the oldest accounts of the Igbos' economic relations with their coastal neighbors.

Direct Igbo connections with the outside world began with the Atlantic slave trade. Deservedly, a huge amount of literature has been devoted to the slave trade: enslavement in Africa, the Middle Passage, and servitude in the New World.[15] As part of the largest involuntary migration in human history, the enslavement of Africans from the Biafra Hinterland increased tremendously in the seventeenth century. The trade, which was largely organized by Aro middlemen, saw a large number of enslaved Igbo passing to the coast and on to the Atlantic World. From the available estimates, we know that the increased enslavement activities on the Bight of Biafra from the eighteenth century drew heavily from the Igbo population.[16] As the Igbo economy became part of a larger regional economy of the Bight of Biafra by the seventeenth century, the commercial relations that had developed prior to European contact increased with the expansion of the slave trade in the eighteenth century.

The commercial relationships that developed between the Igbo and the Europeans had important consequences for both the African world of the Igbo and the world of the Igbo in the Atlantic diaspora. The enslavement of thousands of Igbo people in the Americas provides an unusual, but rare and important glimpse into the Igbo world before European colonization in the last decade of the nineteenth century. The accounts of these enslaved Igbo pioneers offer important sources for the reconstruction of early Igbo history and, indeed, an articulation of Igbo identity, economy, and social life in pre-colonial times. The memoirs of enslaved Igbo like Olaudah

Equiano,[17] and lesser known Igbos like Archibald Monteath among others, provide a window into Igbo society - though through a glass darkly. Igbo slave Archibald Monteath and an overseer on a property owned by John Monteath in Kep, St Elizabeth, rose to become a very important missionary among the Morovians in Jamaica. Although "Some slaves laughed at him, and derided him for learning to read the white people's book," Maureen Warner-Lewis noted, "he was fixated on literacy and would not relent." When Archibald bought his freedom in 1837, he became "a full-time worker with the Moravian Church" and "a Helper at New Carmel Moravian Church." One tribute at his funeral in 1864 described him as "the most eminent for his truly Christian character, spiritual experience and varied usefulness who, for many years past, has been a true apostle among his countrymen."[18] Like Equiano, his memoir offers glimpses into Igbo society in the eighteenth century.[19]

The most celebrated Igbo in these respect remains Olaudah Equiano (Olauda Ekwealuo).[20] Olaudah Equiano's autobiography, *The Interesting Narrative of the Life of Olaudah Equiano, or Gustavus Vassa, the African,* published in 1789, is one of the few texts written in English by a person of African descent during the eighteenth century. Its impact as an account of a journey up from slavery, written by one who personally experienced the middle passage and subsequent enslavement, has been monumental. Recent interest in Equiano has been motivated by contemporary developments, including Vincent Carretta's *Equiano, the African: Biography of a Self-Made Man.* Carretta discovered two documents that purported that Equiano was born in Carolina. The first was a baptism record from February 9 1759, in St Margaret's Church, Westminster, England, naming a 12 year old "Gustavus Vassa" born in Carolina. The second document is a muster list on a ship on which Equiano served in 1773, in which his birthplace was listed as the Carolinas. They suggest, therefore, that Equiano may never have set foot in Africa and could have "invented rather than reclaimed an African identity," and paints the narrative of his early life as fiction rather than representing his true experience. Though these discoveries raised important and legitimate concerns, Carretta's conclusions are problematic. The baptismal record was not weighed against several other factors, including who provided the information on the record. Second, the Gustavus Vassa entry was the only one listed without the corresponding name of parents. This uncertainty obviously limits the extent to which one can draw firm conclusions.

According to his autobiography, written in 1789, Olaudah Equiano (c.1745-1797) was born in Igboland. He was kidnapped and sold into slavery when he was 11 years old. As a slave to a captain in the Royal Navy, and later to a Quaker merchant, he eventually earned the price of his own freedom by careful trading and saving. Arriving in London, he became involved in the movement to abolish the slave trade, an involvement which led him to write and publish *The Interesting Narrative of the Life of Olaudah Equiano, or Gustavus Vassa, the African* (1789), a strongly abolitionist autobiography. What does Equiano's autobiography offer towards a reconstruction of the Igbo world and history? What does it offer in articulating Igbo history in an Atlantic context? We begin in Africa where it all began.

The communal ethos of the Igbo people has been well articulated in contemporaneous ethnographic writings. Some of the papers in this book re-examine Equiano's claim and his autobiography in light of contemporary evidence, critical re-assessment of the existing scholarship, and in relation to the Igbo world. Oladuah Equiano's autobiography, *The Interesting Narrative*, offers a window into Igbo life and identity in the eighteenth century, giving the earliest glimpses of Igbo community ethos and values. Maureen N. Eke's paper captures this sense of community in Olaudah Equiano's attempts to reestablish his humanity by reclaiming his identity not only as a black person, but also as an Igbo. As Eke points out, Equiano's text suggests a careful attempt to reestablish the author's Africanness by defining himself in relation to an Igbo world. But it was a world in which the notion of community was central. Equiano's image of himself and his home was often expressed in terms of "our people." Although Vincent Carreta's *Equiano, the African: Biography of a Self-made Man*[21] seems to suggest that Equiano may have not been an Igbo, Carretta's contention, Eke argues, does not alter Equiano's carefully constructed image of an Igbo world. Thus, Equiano's Igbo world can be read as a "carefully constructed world and, by extension, his identity through a mapping of various areas: culture, community/race, and place."

Catharine Acholonu interrogates recent discourses on Equiano's Igbo origins and broader implications for his identity as an Igbo, Igbo scholarship, and Igbo ethnicity in the New World. Building on her previous work, published as *The Igbo Roots of Olaudah Equiano*, and more recent evidence, she challenges the claims made by Vincent Carretta, whose book, *Equiano, the African*, casts doubt on Equiano's birth in Igboland. She argues that contemporary evidence from Isekke and the Niger Delta in the Bight of Biafra support Equiano's claim of an Igbo origin. The broader impact of Equaino's work lies in its importance as a source for contemporary academic discourse, but also that "Equiano's voice was a key instrument for Black anti-racism struggle in America, the Caribbean, Europe, and among African nationalists struggling against colonialism in the twentieth century. Equiano's poignant and proud portrayal of an African society gave

Africans born in the diaspora a sense of pride and cultural identity." Yet the paper also uses Equiano and his autobiography to explore the Igbo World and issues of identity.

In "Status in Eighteenth-century Igboland," Dorothy Ukaegbu challenges the uncritical use of European sources in reconstructing the Igbo past. In particular, she challenges Vincent Carretta's characterization of status among the Igbo. His reconstruction, she argues, uncritically used information from early explorers' accounts to reconstruct status among the Igbo, thus imposing forms of identity that do not reflect Igbo realities. She argues that ascribing Eurocentric notions of work and leisure on the traditional Igbo society of Equiano's time obscures the true meanings of Igbo cultural concepts and thus misinterprets the realities of the Igbo *ichi* bearer and status among the Igbo.

Linked to this communal essence is what Dorothy Ukaegbu examines in the context of a "sense of place" in this volume. She addresses the meaning of place and sentiments about home among the Igbo, especially as they relate to questions of identity. She focuses on Olaudah Equiano and his *Interesting Narrative* to illuminate the writer's "sense of place" in the autobiography, as well as meanings of place that can be deciphered. Scholars writing on Equiano to date have yet to properly analyze his African world with regard to the issue of his identity. In the autobiographical context, "identity is circumscribed in the representation of self and place. Human agency becomes the focal point for uniting self and place and identity. Equiano's representation of his 'self' is a story of his personhood—the meaning and significance of his name, his life as a typical child of the village, and his life experiences beyond the confines of Essaka."

Equiano's representation of himself was, in essence, a broader representation of his Igbo world. These notions of self in relation to home are articulated in the formation of home associations that expanded greatly from the colonial period. One might conclude that such articulations become more important as one leaves his or her immediate community. They emerge outside the "home" as memories of one's origin and as strategies of survival in new communities. Still significant in Equiano's reconstruction of his identity was clear identification of geographical markers in describing his home in relation to other "nations." Ukaegbu argues that in the Igbo world, "a sense of place begins with the natural environment—the land—where a person is born, and the patrilineal or matrilineal kin reside." For Equiano, like any other Igbo outside their place of birth, memory and multifarious meanings of place that exist, "are inextricably linked to a person's personal and social identities; their social relations to their fellows, gods and ancestors; and to the land to which they belonged."

Equiano's autobiography had its critics, as Equiano himself acknowledged:

> I believe it is difficult for those who publish their own memoirs
> to escape the imputation of vanity; nor is this the only disad-
> vantage under which they labor: it is their misfortune that what
> is uncommon is rarely, if ever, believed, and what is obvious we
> are apt to turn from with disgust, and to charge the writer with
> impertinence.[22]

Indeed, the boundary between fiction and fact in autobiographical writing is often blurred. Indeed, the issues of memory and autobiography have recently been explored by Paul Lovejoy in "Autobiography and Memory."[23] Here, Elizabeth Onogwu addresses the contentious issue of memory, autobiography, and literature, evaluating how much of Olaudah Equiano's *The Interesting Narrative* is fiction and how much of literature it might contain. She makes a case for re-evaluating the work in light of Vincent Carretta's argument in *Equaino the African: Biography of a self-Made Man,* acknowledging that part of what Equiano has written is not fiction, but the fact, even the truth of his life and times. Her argument views the autobiographical genre from more than one angle—as a product of lit-erature, fact, and fiction. Like all autobiographical writings, Equiano's *The Interesting Narrative*, she argues, has elements of all three categories. Yet Equiano's autobiography has a broader historical significance than most autobiographies. The connection between the different parts of the Atlan-tic world—Africa, the Americas, and Europe - makes this book unique in not only reconstructing an African society's experience of slavery, but much more importantly, creating an enduring agency for Africans when this was denied them by Europeans.

The broader implication of Equiano's work on the affirmation of African identity is immeasurable. Ogbo Ugwuanyi extends the discourse on race and African identity by exploring the role Equiano and his narrative played in affirming the existence of an African identity different from that imposed on Africans by Europe. Such imposed identity remained the source of the crisis of a true African identity. While contemporary African scholars have been addressing this crisis, which had its roots in the enslavement of Africans, such a critical African epistemology had its origin in the work of Olaudah Equiano. His writing and campaigning against slavery was a rebuttal of the degradation Europe had imposed on Africans and an attempt to regain their dignity. Through what he calls the epistemology of racism, the author high-lights the inherent problem with racism and African identity.

We must agree, however, that a close examination of Equiano's narrative and his description of Africa captured elements of contemporary Igbo culture in vivid identifiable forms, and that such detailed descriptions could only come from someone who had experienced the culture. Despite the obvious lapses that occur with human memory, certain aspects of memory are often so deeply embedded in the psyche of the individual that they are difficult to extinguish, particularly when one is violently pulled out of a familiar and nurturing environment. This is what enslavement did to Africans, and many enslaved Africans relived their African life in their memories much more than those born into slavery. Equiano's autobiography offers evidence to reconstruct aspects of eighteenth century Igbo life in ways that no other written sources have been able to provide. The greatest strength of the *Interesting Narrative* is its affirmation of African personhood and identity in a world that denied that these existed for an African.

OTHER ENCOUNTERS WITH EUROPE

The Igbo response to European influences can be understand only in the context of their traditional culture. The institutional structures of traditional Igbo society, including the political system, economic system, social dynamics, and gender ideology, provide a context from which we can examine later developments. Raphael Njoku's contribution to this volume further explores aspects of these traditional institutions and culture. Framed around the concept of neo-liberalism, Njoku argues that a basic framework of neoliberalism was already at work in traditional Igbo society before the term emerged as the catchword for economic deregulation and political decentralization in the West. He argues that concepts such as democratic values, civil society networks, the absence of totalitarianism, individualism, women's rights, human rights, and freedom of worship that predated the "protestant ethic," which emerged in Europe with the rise of the Calvinists and the Puritans of seventeenth century England," were deeply rooted in traditional Igbo society. These values and ideas played important roles in how the Igbo responded to external influences and how they attempted to sustain these values under both slavery and colonial rule.

Like other ethnic groups in Western Africa, the Igbo experienced greater and more direct interaction with Europe after the abolition of the slave trade. The social impact of the transformation of slavery and the slave trade in the region know as the Bight of Bifara and its hinterland has not been fully explored. The Igbo did not escape the Christian missions' extension of the so-called "White Man's Burden" to inner Africa following the abolition of the slave trade and the "Enlightened" fervor of the nineteenth century.[24] By the late nineteenth century, different strands of European missions were active in the task of evangelizing inner Africa. Ogbu Kalu explores the impact of abolitionism on the expansion of Christianity among the Igbo. He shows "a certain irony in the relationship when the slave traders and the slave routes became the instruments and routes for spreading the gospel." In this context, the Aro, who were the main intermediaries and organizers of the trade in the Biafra hinterland, sought the new opportunities offered by missionaries, including Western education. To their credit, they avoided the crisis of the transition era that ultimately sunk the fortunes of many who were not in a position to produce palm oil as a replacement for the trade in slaves.

The effects of Europe's encounter with Africa on gender ideology have been well noted for both the slave trade and the colonial enterprise. Ugo Nwokeji's analysis of the gender demographics of the Atlantic for the Bight of Biafra has called attention to how regional variations and African dynamics could account for such variations in numbers of men and women exported from Africa.[25] The impact of the abolition of slavery on gender followed similar patterns and variations. J. Akuma-Kalu Njoku's chapter provides a broad overview of social change and gender transformations that occurred among the Igbo as a result of the Atlantic slave trade and British colonial rule. The study focuses on the impetus for change that came with expansions in both regional and overseas trade relations that significantly changed social statuses, marriage, gender, and the class system. These relationships underwent further transformation after the imposition of colonialism on the Igbo.

The ideological underpinning of the colonial enterprises has often been blamed for transforming gender and class structures, for the colonial enterprise was undoubtedly male, even though the colonies were certainly not as Oyeronke Oyewumi has noted in her study of Yoruba gender ideology.[26] Imperial and colonial officials noted that the Tropics was not a place for European women. As F. B. Carr, a British colonial administrator in Nigeria wrote in his memoir, "there were few, if any women, for Government officials were not allowed to take wives and traders and miners seldom did so because of the climate."[27] Thus, the demographics of the colonial officials, as well as the dominant Victorian gender ideology, had important implications for conceptions of gender in the imperial context in particular. As Akuma-Kalu Njoku argues, the social and cultural transformations that occurred as the Igbo encountered Europe were the result of a combination of factors, including the imposed, rigid assimilation model; the creativity of the African population; and the new identities that emerged as a result of the interaction of these factors.

Indeed, colonialism brought the Igbo deeper into the vortex of the European political economy and social engineering in the early years of the twentieth century. But it was the arrogance of British imperialists that would eventually bring them into conflict with the Igbo. One such official, a Commissioner in the Calabar Province, noted the difficulty in implementing British rule among the Igbo in 1915:

> The problem that has to be faced is not so much one of system but that the mental caliber of the native, with but isolated exceptions, is of such a low order that to formulate a more advantageous system of administration is well nigh impossible and until such time the Chiefs or Headmen can be brought to realize their duties and responsibilities as such and their egoism stamped out no system of self administration can be a success.[28]

An avid observer of the Igbo, anthropologist Sylvia Leith-Ross recalls:

> Whether you intended it or not, you were caught up in this exuberant Ibo life, one with the long file of women going to market, hub and center of their lives; joining in the lamentations at the low price of palm oil; or rejoicing as the first yam shoots appeared. You bent low over the babies and the cooking pots and watched entranced the unique, unforgettable beauty of the women's dance.[29]

These were the same people that Mr. H. P. Palmer described a "some centuries behind the countries west of the Niger in natural development"[30] and whose articulation of their demand and framing of their protest in 1929 would baffle those who ignored the diverse structures of the societies they were called upon to govern in Nigeria.

This was certainly a society in transition and one in which the hegemonic power of the colonial state created obstacles and, at times, a dilemma for the Igbo. But it was one in which the Igbo responded in ways the British never predicted. Their massive revolt against colonial rule in 1929 was undoubtedly the most significant event in African-European relations in colonial Nigeria. Felix Ekechi traces the long history of Igbo resistance to European intrusion from the early twentieth century until the end of colonial rule in 1960. Unlike any other group in Nigeria, the British found the Igbo most intractable and were faced with several acts of revolt from the Igbo people. The pacification of Igboland and the basic principles of Indirect Rule as implemented among the Igbo ran counter to the basic principles of Igbo republicanism. Mr. H. P. Palmer, on a visit to Southern Nigeria circa 1914, noted:

> The attempt therefore to preserve Native Custom have so far resulted in steadily destroying it and among these relatively primitive peoples full Europeanized individualistic government is being introduced. The Government machine is steadily grinding to powder all that is "Native and transforming the people into black Englishmen." Secondary agents in effecting this change are the spread of missionaries and education.[31]

As Ekechi outlines, local resistance to British rule was widespread and varied. Segments of the population adopted several strategies, including military and non-military measures, "to maintain political independence and sovereignty." These early social movements, he argues, became the forerunner of modern nationalist struggles for independence in which "the Igbo educated elite were in the vanguard."

This culture of resistance culminated in one of the most stunning acts of resistance to British rule in West Africa in what is known as the "Women's Revolt" of 1929. Adiele Afigbo captures the historical origins of the 1929 Women's Revolt in his contribution to this volume. He argues that "European rule inaugurated a many-sided revolution which was in no way congenial to the temperament of the conservatives among the Igbo and Ibibio peoples of eastern Nigeria; and that the Women's Riot 1929 must be seen as one, if the most violent, of the people's reactions to this revolution." Although the Igbo embraced some aspects of the resources offered by the Europeans, their embrace was also qualified by some attempts to preserve elements of their pre-colonial culture. One District Officer recalled the Igbo attitude towards Christianity: "The old men, who are mostly pagans, may disagree violently with some of their teachings, on the question of monogamy, for example, but they are appreciative of the schools and medical facilities which they provide."[32] This sort of contradiction in Igbo response to colonialism defined women's demand for political change and enabled them to create a counter hegemonic discourse and consciousness through which they defined their relationships with other segments of colonial society.[33] As Afigbo concludes, the revolt "shattered the complacent British belief that their rule was welcome to the over-whelming majority of Nigerians." He argues that it also brought an end to "the era in which it was confidently, though unjustifiably, held that the hope of Nigerians lay in the political education of their traditional rulers for ultimate self-government rather than in listening to the so-called detribalized minority."

John Oriji's chapter also examines the Women's Revolt of 1929 and its impact in transforming the Native Administration system among the Igbo. He addresses the intellectual background of the women who led the revolt and how their leadership enhanced the social status of women in its aftermath. The end of the revolt was followed by reforms in the Native Administration system, including the appointment of women into the Native Court system. But most importantly, the revolt rekindled interest in the Igbo people, their history, and way of life, sparking a renaissance of sorts in Igbo studies that began in the 1930s with major anthropological studies. Oriji argues that the Women's Revolt served as an inspiration to those who organized subsequent social movements in Nigeria. Yet its peasant roots set it apart from other such social movements in colonial Nigeria. These traditions rooted in the Igbo culture, egalitarianism, and worldview would be important in the Igbo response to slavery and the new formations that emerged in the diaspora.

THE IGBO IN THE ATLANTIC DIASPORA

Any engagement with the making of the early history and societies of the New World must recognize the role Africa and Africans played in it. Enslaved Africans were critical in the making of the early societies and cultures of the New World. But the extent to which African cultural practices survived enslavement and slavery has been a matter of debate among scholars of slavery and the diaspora since the 1940s. Two views have dominated the literature. One side of the debate argues that the experiences of the Middle Passage and enslavement in the America were traumatic enough to wipe out the memories of enslaved Africans. Others see a greater level of retention of their Africanness and culture that eventually influenced early American history and culture. Still others have argued that what emerged in the New World was rather a hybrid of cultures that drew from both the African and European backgrounds.[34] Recent scholarship has moved us beyond the rhetoric of the early debate to identity not only the influence of Africans on the Americas, but has also mapped identifiable "ethnic" patterns that can be linked to Africa. These mappings between specific regions and people in Africa and identifiable cultural elements in the New World have added to our understanding of the broader processes of culture formation in the Americas.

The connections between the Igbo and identifiable cultural patterns in the Atlantic World are relevant for understanding ethnic patterns in the African Diaspora. For one, the large number of Igbo exiles had important consequences for the development of slavery in the Atlantic

14

World.[35] To date, much of the historical writing about the Igbo in the diaspora has centered on their reputation as bad slaves. American scholars of slavery, Michael Gomez and Gwendolyn Midlo Hall, have noted that Igbo slaves had a very bad reputation in the Americas, often choosing the path of suicide, a tendency that was obviously inimical to their master's investment. Douglas Chambers and Daniel Littlefield have made similar observations.[36] As I have noted elsewhere, the Igbo remained an enigma to slave holders and other slaves alike because of their peculiar responses to the institution.[37] Douglas Chambers' *Murder at Montpelier*, the first major work on the Igbo Diaspora in the Americas, explores the transformations of a slave community at James Madison's Montpelier, and in particular, the "Americanization of Igbo culture in the New World." The book centralizes the Igbo in the making of "African Americans" in Virginia.[38]

Some of the contributions in this volume go beyond the stereotypes that have projected a negative image of the Igbo in order to understand the Igbo question in the diaspora, and their peculiar response to slavery in the New World, from their African context. Chima J. Korieh's contribution sets out to explore Igbo identity in the New World. He presents a framework for understanding identity as flexible in both Africa and the Atlantic Diaspora. The paper emphasizes the African background in situating the changing identities of enslaved Africans in the New World. For the Igbo, in particular, their peculiar response to slavery drew on their African background, the republican political institutions that informed their world view.

Douglas Chambers explores a much neglected aspect of the African Diaspora—gendered discourses and the legacies left by Igbo women in the New World. He accounts for how Igbo women negotiated their enslavement, the issues of reproduction, and their femininity. Enslaved Igbo women negotiated slavery and created agency through the strategic manipulation of their bodies and reproductive power. Even in slavery, Igbo women negotiated their identities in ways that were not solely defined by those who held them in bondage. This, of course, provides new insights into questions of identity, power, and control within the American slave societies.

Like many societies with a strong oral tradition, Igbo life is expressed in music, art, and other forms of cultural expressions. These were transmitted in identifiable forms in the diaspora. Igbo custom survived in other ways in the culture, language, music, and diet of the African Diaspora. Hannah Chukwu examines Igbo influences in Caribbean literature. These transmissions became part of what she described as a "vibrant, functional, and strong assertion of national identity present in the Caribbean's literary production."

In extending the African background in shaping the response to enslavement and the impact of Africans in the America, Dan Kloza examines why the Igbo responded to slavery in unique ways. He argues that the republican and egalitarian structures of the Igbo were a marked contrast to the world of slavery in the Americas. While all slaves resisted their enslavement, Igbo attitude towards slavery marked them as a distinct and often rejected group. Planters hated their propensity to commit suicide or run away. Their women ran away in greater numbers than other groups.

Although hated for tendencies inimical to the enterprise of slavery, they were, nonetheless, also one of the most "reliable" groups. The ambivalent attitude towards enslaved Igbo is reflected in the ways many planters valued them for their work ethic and yet hated them for their individualistic tendencies and peculiar forms of resistance to the institution of slavery. They were associated with slave rebellions in the Americas. Their traditional democratic republicanism ran counter to the slave system, hence the unique ways the Igbo resisted enslavement.

The ultimate form of resistance was the assertion of self-worth and an authentic African identity. Here, Equiano's life as he presented it in the *Interesting Narrative* was the greatest challenge to the institution of slavery. Ron Milland's chapter asserts that slave narratives remain a source of insight into the institution of bondage, as well as material for scholarly analysis and debate. The conception of these narratives, however, was contextualized by the abolitionist movement and the emergence of new perspectives regarding humanity and the black aesthetic. This polemic of abolitionism was often employed by those who edited the slave narratives so that the completed works would suit the preconceived notions of a potentially racist readership. Accomplishing this in a way that would persuade the reading public to rally for an end to bondage required the editors to design works that both elicited sympathy for the enslaved and confined them with this new rhetorical framework – a formulaic structure that was intended to ideologically truncate their freedom and even their expressed humanity. Through an examination of the slave narratives of Olaudah Equiano and others, Milland asserts that, despite the efforts of editors to envelope their voices in multiple layers of authentication, ex-slave authors successfully express a sense of their originality, a recognition of the difficulties of racial integration, and the social and legal limitations of curtailing or abolishing slavery and enforcing freedom – thus serving to allude to the need for subsequent struggles such as desegregation and the Civil Rights movement. In this regard, Equiano's work helped to re-affirm African identity.

The question of the Igbo-Atlantic connection is so complex that this volume can only make a modest contribution to the subject. It draws attention to this neglected aspect of Igbo history and culture and the role the

Igbo played in the making of the Atlantic World. Thus, the contributions in this book should serve to stimulate more interest in African Diaspora connections from a transatlantic perspective.

NOTES

1. See Robert J. Allison, ed., *The Interesting Narrative of the Life of Olaudah Equiano* (Boston: Bedford/St. Martins Press, 1995). On the controversy, see Vincent Carretta, *Equiano, the African: Biography of a Self-Made Man* (Athens: University of Georgia Press, 2005). On response to Carretta, See also Paul Lovejoy, "Autobiography and Memory: Gustavus Vasa, Alias, Olaudah Equiano," *Slavery and Abolition* 27, issue 3 (December 2006): 317-347 and Catherine O. Acholonu-Olumba, *The Igbo Roots of Olaudah Equiano (Revised Edition with Reply to Vincent Caretta)* (Abuja: Afa Publications, 2007).

2. Seminal works include the explorations of different aspects of Igbo history and cultures. See for example, Victor Uchendu, *The Igbo of Southeastern Nigeria*, Adiele E. Afigbo, *The Warrant Chiefs: Indirect Rule in Southeastern Nigeria 1891-1929* (New York: Humanities Press, 1972). See also the collected works of Afigbo edited by Toyin Falola as *Myth, History and Society: The Collected Works of Adiele Afigbo* (Trenton: Africa World Press, 2006. For major works of synthesis, see Elizabeth Isichei, *A History of the Igbo People; Igbo People and the Europeans, Igbo World,* among many others. Samuel Ottenberg's works have explored Igbo arts and ritual life from an anthropological perspective.

3. See also Bede N. Okigbo, *Plants and Food in Igbo Culture and Civilization: 1980 Ahiajoku Lecture* (Owerri: Ministry of Information and Culture, 1980).

4. On Igbo cultural areas, see for example, M. A. Onwujeogwu, "Evolutionary Trends in the History of the Development of Igbo Civilization in the Culture Theatre of Igboland in Southern Nigeria," *Ahiajoku Lecture, 1987* (Owerri: Ministry of Information and Culture, 1987).

5. Rhodes House, Oxford University, MSS Afr. s. 1551 (hereafter RH). J. G. C. Allen "Nigerian Panorama, 1926-1966" (A District Officer from Eastern Nigeria looks back).

6. Ikenna Nzimiro, *Studies in Ibo Political System: Chieftaincy and Politics in Four Niger States* (London: Frank Cass/University of California Berkeley, 1972). See also, Richard N. Henderson, *The King in Every Man: Evolutionary Trends in Onitsha Ibo Society and Culture* (New Haven and London: Yale University Press, 1972).

7. See Okigbo, *Plants and Food in Igbo Culture and Civilization.*

8. See for example, W. B. Morgan, "Farming Practice, Settlement Pattern and Population Density in Eastern Nigeria," *The Geographical Journal* 121, no. 3 (Sep., 1955), 330.

9. Afigbo, *Ropes of Sand*, 126.

10. See Thurstan Shaw, *Unearthing Igbo-Ukwu: Archaeological Discoveries in Eastern Nigeria* (Oxford: Oxford University Press, 1977).

11. RH: Mss Afr s. 1000, Falk Edward Morris, Papers as District Officer in Nigeria, December 24, 1920.

12. Ibid.

13. Duarte Pacheco Pereira, cited by David Northrup, "The Growth of Trade among the Igbo before 1800," *Journal of African History* 13, 2 (1972), 220.

14. "Mr. John Grazilhier's voyage from Bandy to New Calabar," in John Barbot, *A Description of the Coasts of North and South Guinea* Vol. V, in Churchill's *Voyages and Travels* (London, 1746), 380-1, cited in Elizabeth Isichei, *Igbo Worlds: An Anthology of Oral Histories and Historical Descriptions* (Philadelphia: Institute for the Study of Human Issues, 1978), 10.

15. See for example, David Eltis, "Free and Coerced Transatlantic Migrations: Some Comparisons," *American Historical Review* 88 (1983): 251–80; David Eltis, "The Volume and Structure of the Transatlantic Slave Trade: A Reassessment," *William and Mary Quarterly* 58, no. 1(1991): 17-46; John Thornton, *Africa and Africans in the Making of the Atlantic World, 1400–1800* (Cambridge: Cambridge University Press, 1992); Daniel P. Mannix and Malcolm Cowley, *Black Cargoes: A History of the Atlantic Slave Trade, 1518–1865* (New York: Viking Press, 1962); Robin Law and Silke Strickrodt, eds., *Ports of the Slave Trade (Bights of Benin and Biafra)*: Papers from a Conference of the Centre of Commonwealth Studies, University of Stirling, June 1998 (Stirling, 1999); Robin Law, ed., *From Slave Trade to "Legitimate" Commerce: the Commercial Transition in Nineteenth-Century West Africa* (Cambridge: Cambridge University Press, 1995); Boubacar Barry, *Senegambia and the Atlantic Slave* Trade, trans. Ayi Kwei Armah (Cambridge: Cambridge University Press, 1998); Philip Curtin, *The Atlantic Slave Trade: A Census* (Madison: University of Wisconsin Press, 1969); David Eltis, Stephen D. Behrendt, David Richardson, and Herbert S. Klein, eds., *The Trans-Atlantic Slave Trade: A Database on CD-ROM* (Cambridge: Cambridge University Press, 1999).

16. See David Eltis and David Richardson, "West Africa and the Transatlantic Slave Trade: New Evidence on Long Run Trends," *Slavery and Abolition*, 18, no. 1 (1997); Douglas B. Chambers, "'My own nation": Igbo Exiles in the Diaspora', *Slavery and Abolition* 18, 1 (1997): 72-97. For African export figure for 1470s-1699, see, Paul E. Lovejoy, "The Volume of the Atlantic Slave Trade: A synthesis," *Journal of African History* 23 (1982), especially 478-481; for 1700-1809, see David Richardson, "Slave Exports from West

and West-Central Africa, 1700-1810: New Estimates of Volume and Distribution," *Journal of African History* 30 (1989), 3, 6-17; and 1811-1870, see David Eltis, *Economic Growth and the Ending of the Transatlantic Slave Trade* (New York: Oxford University Press, 1987), 249, 250-2.

17. See Olaudah Equiano, *The Interesting Narrative of the Life of Olaudah Equiano, or Gustavus Vassa, the African. Written by Himself* (London, 1789).

18. *Jamaican Gleaner*, "An icon of Moravian history." Interview with Maureen Warner-Lewis, 16 February 2008.

19. Archibald John Monteith's memoir was written by Reverend Joseph Horsfield Kummer in 1853. Kummer served the Moravian Mission in Jamaica and this account was edited by Vernon H. Nelson from the manuscript in the Archives of the Moravian Church, Bethlehem, Pennsylvania. See "Archibald John Monteith: Native Helper and Assistant in the Jamaica Mission at New Carmel," *Transactions of the Monrovian Historical Society* 21, 1 (1966), 30. For a new biography on See Maureen Warner-Lewis, *Archibald Monteath: Igbo, Jamaican, Moravian, Jamaican, Moravian* (Kingston: University of the West Indies Press, 2007).

20. Isekke oral accounts say that there was an enslaved boy known as Olauda Ekwealuo, and ethnographic work by Catherine Acholonu suggests that this was indeed Olaudah Equiano. See Catherine O. Acholonu-Olumba, *The Igbo Roots of Olaudah Equiano (Revised Edition with Reply to Vincent Caretta)* (Abuja: Afa Publications, 2007). See also L.O.I. Ugweze, "The Isseke Root of Olaudah Equiano (Olaude Ekweabuo) Gustav Vassa, The African," paper presented at 1st International Interdisciplinary Conference of The Olaudah Equiano Global Legacy Project, Imo State University, Owerri, Nigeria, 26-28 July 2007.

21. Vincent Carretta, *Equiano, The African: Biography of a Self-Made Man* (Athens: University of Georgia Press, 2005).

22. Equaino, *The Interesting Narrative*.

23. Paul Lovejoy, "Autobiography and Memory: Gustavus Vassa, alias Olaudah Equiano, the African," *Slavery and Abolition* 27, no. 3 (2006): 317-47.

24. On the extension of Christianity into Igboland, see also Ogbu U. Kalu, *The Embattled Gods: Christianization of Igboland, 1841-1991* (Lagos/London: Minaj Publishers, 1996); Felix K. Ekechi, *Missionary Enterprise and Rivalry in Igboland, 1857-1914* (London: Frank Cass, 1972).

25. G. Ugo Nwokeji, "African Conceptions of Gender and the Slave Traffic," *William and Mary Quarterly* 58, no. 1 (2001): 47-68.

26. Oyeronke Oyewumi, *The Invention of Women: Making an African Sense of Western Gender Discourse* (Minneapolis: University of Minnesota Press, 1997).

27. RH: Mss Afr. s. 546. Reminiscences of Sir F. Bernard Carr—Administrative Officer, Nigeria 1919-1949.

28. RH: Mss Afr s. 1873. Broocks (Robert Bernard) Reports and Papers.

29. RH: Mss Afr s. 1520. Sylvia Leith–Ross, "Reminiscence."

30. RH: Mss Afr s. 1873.

31. Ibid.

32. RH: Mss Afr. s. 1924. A. E. Cooks, "Memoir."

33. See Chima J. Korieh, "Culture, Gender, and Peasant Intellectual Protest in Colonial Eastern Nigeria," *Mbari: The International Journal of Igbo Historical Studies* 1, no. 1 (2008): 114-146.

34. See for example, Melville J. Herskovits, *The Myth of the Negro Past* (Boston: Beacon Press, 1941); Franklin E. Frazier, *Negro Family in the United States* (Chicago: University of Chicago Press, 1939); and Franklin E. Frazier, *Negro Church in America* (New York: Shocken Books, 1974); Sidney Mintz and Richard Price, *An Anthropological Approach to Afro-American Past: A Caribbean Perspective* (Philadelphia: Institute for the Study of Human Issues, 1976); and Paul E. Lovejoy and David V. Trotman, eds. *Trans-Atlantic Dimensions of Ethnicity in the African Diaspora* (London and New York: Continuum, 2003).

35. Chambers, "'My Own Nation,'" 77.

36. See Michael A. Gomez, *Exchanging our Country Marks: The Transformation of African Identities in the Colonial and Ante-bellum South* (Chapel Hill and London: The University of North Carolina Press, 1998); Gwendolyn Midlo Hall, *African Ethnicities in the Americas: Restoring the Links* (Chapel Hill and London: University of North Carolina Press, 2006); Chambers, "My Own Nation."; Daniel C. Littlefield, *Rice and Slaves: Ethnicity and the Slave Trade in Colonial South Carolina* (Baton Rouge: Louisiana State University Press, 1981).

37. See my contribution in this volume or the earlier publication, "African Ethnicity as Mirage?: Historicizing the Essence of the Igbo in Africa and the Atlantic Diaspora," *Dialectical Anthropology* 30, no. 1-2 (2006): 91-118.

38. Douglas B. Chambers, *Murder at Montpelier: Igbo Africans in Virginia* (Jackson: University Press of Mississippi, 2005).

FROM A GLASS DARKLY

OLAUDAH EQUIANO AND THE IGBO WORLD

CHAPTER 1

(RE)IMAGINING COMMUNITY: OLAUDAH EQUIANO AND THE (RE)CONSTRUCTION OF IGBO (AFRICAN) IDENTITY

MAUREEN N. EKE

Whether the love of one's country be real or imaginary, or a
lesson of reason, or an instinct of nature, I still look back with
pleasure on the first scenes of my life.

—Olaudah Equiano, *The Interesting Narrative of the Life of
Olaudah Equiano*, 1789

INTRODUCTION: WHEN EQUIANO SPEAKS

Scholars in general agree that Equiano's singular goal in publishing his
autobiography, *The Interesting Narrative of the Life of Olaudah Equiano,
or Gustavus Vassa the African* (London, 1789)[1] was to protest the slave trade
and slavery. He mapped out his life in his narrative as the exemplum of the
devastating effects of slavery on Africans, as he, Equiano served as an eye
witness to slavery's dehumanization of Africans. Most readers and schol-

ars of Equiano's narrative also note that although the narrative provides readers with a first-person eye-witness account of the Trans-Atlantic slave trade and slavery, the text is filled with gaps and ambiguities, particularly in terms of the specific voice of its author/narrator. Some critics have pointed to Equiano's involvement as a merchant on slave trading ships as indicative of his complicity in the trade, while others see his acknowledgment of such involvement in his narrative as a mask, and still others have expressed discomfort over his seeming acceptance of slavery in Africa and his advocacy for the colonization of Africa.[2]

Moreover, the publication of Vincent Carretta's biography, *Equiano, the African: Biography of a Self Made Man,*[3] only two years before the 200th Anniversary of the ending of British Slave Trade (1807), seems to have sparked off a firestorm on both sides of the debate over who Equiano really was. Carretta claims that his "[r]ecent biographical discoveries have cast doubt on Equiano's story of his birth and early years," adding, "[the] available evidence suggests that the author of *The Interesting Narrative* may have invented rather than reclaimed an African identity."[4] In other words, according to Carretta, Equiano did not live the experiences of the Middle Passage which he describes, because "the accounts of Africa and the Middle Passage in *The Interesting Narrative* were constructed—and carefully so . . ."[5] Interestingly, the epigraph which opens my paper anticipates Carretta's contention and provides us with strong authentication for Equiano's construction of such passages about his people, be those passages imaginary or real.

Whether or not Equiano was African is not currently the focus of my paper. Rather, I depart from existing scholarship to underscore the special construction of the passages about the Igbo (African) world in Equiano's autobiography. I argue that because Equiano was aware of the various (predominantly negative) discourses about slavery and Africans during his time, he chose to re-imagine his community, to re-construct it, as it were, re-stitch, piece together anew, the Igbo (African) world in his narrative in order to counter the European "othering" of Africans as a justification for their enslavement. In fact, Equiano had to deploy a rhetoric that was as carefully constructed and exaggerated as the rhetoric and images that were used to describe the continent and Africans at that time. I assert also that because Equiano was aware of eighteenth century Europe's preoccupation with enlightenment, reason, knowledge, education, and civilization, Equiano was compelled to present a parallel culture, at least, one in which Igbos, his people, who become the representatives of the African continent in his narrative, share similar ideals/ideas as Enlightenment Europe. I will focus primarily on the first two chapters of his narrative and specifically on some of those aspects of culture that Equiano emphasizes in order to humanize himself and to make his case against the enslavement of Africans. These aspects of culture and society include governance/judicial system, marriage, religion, and other cultural practices. I will also pay attention to the way in which Equiano employs language, especially in his descriptions as a means of self-location, -identification, and -construction.

A SORT OF SPACE CLEARING

Charges that Equiano fabricated his African origins, however, cannot simply be accepted without interrogation, especially in light of other claims which suggest otherwise. Catherine Acholonu,[6] for instance, claims that she has found strong evidence that suggests that Equiano was an Igbo. Despite questions about the methodology of her research, other scholars agree that some of the words in Equaino's narrative are Igbo in origin,[7] suggesting that Equiano may have been an Igbo. Indeed, Carretta is correct in pointing out that "Equiano's biographer faces many problems,"[8] but Carretta's attempt to deny Equiano his origin or right of birth and the authenticity of his work returns us to the claims of pro-slavery proponents who argued that slave narratives were simply fabricated propaganda probably written by abolitionists who did not experience the events they describe. In the case of Equiano, the implications are troubling, because Carretta's suggestion that Equiano was not an Igbo as he indicates in his narrative forces us to reexamine our understanding of the Middle Passage, since scholars have relied on the narrative for first hand accounts about the Middle Passage, and specifically about West Africa during that period. As Carretta points out, "it is difficult to think of any historical account of the Middle Passage that does not quote [Equiano's] eye-witness description of its horrors as primary evidence."[9]

Clearly, there is ambiguity in Equiano's narrative as we have already pointed out, and several scholars have addressed the fogginess and/or contradiction they see in Equiano's narrative, including the question of his voice, his acceptance of African slavery, the sources of his description of West Africa, the ideological tension between his embracing of British nationality and his advocacy for his people as an African, and finally, his seeming support for the colonization of Africa. In her essay, "Dominant or Submerged Discourses in *The Life of Olaudah Equiano (or Gustavus Vassa?)*," Katalin Orban, for instance, indicates that "some critics" might see "the *main* rhetoric as a façade, a mask for the real message." For Orban "the problem is one of authorial intention," adding, "Is the more prominent message to be taken at face value, or is it just a cover for smuggling dangerous ideas into the heads of unsympathetic readers."[10] Similarly, Wilfred

D. Samuels "wonders "what, in the final analysis . . . Equiano intended,"[11] pointing out that Equiano "confronted the difficult task of reporting his lived experiences during slavery to an audience which did not recognize him as a member of its society, and, in fact viewed him 'as an alien whose assertion of common humanity and civil rights conflicted with some of its basic beliefs.'"[12] But, Hinds concludes that Equiano's critique of slavery "takes the form of a free-trade argument." According to Hinds, "[t]rade with a free Africa, [Equiano] contends would better serve an international market."[13] However, Ide Corley reads the narrative as engaging in multiple projects simultaneously:

> As it advances an important argument against slavery, *The Life of Olaudah Equiano* produces a conscious and apparently volitional discourse of black subjectivity. It contains within that discourse an image of 'enlightened' blackness. But the attempt to speak from a stable political position despite the lack of institutional support produces enigmatic textual postures. Passages that disaffiliate the voice of the speaking subject from its 'enlightenment' assertions set the text awash.[14]

Of course, there is a problem with trying to tease out Equiano's intentions in his narrative and in trying to limit him to a singular voice. Hinds concurs that "as a representative of Anglo-America and Africa," Equiano "constructs in this narrative a four-fold self . . . a slave, a merchant, a juridical subject, and a convert to a blending of various Christian theologies."[15] In other words, Equiano speaks in multiple voices and through multiple lenses and selves. Still, critics agree in general that his narrative serves as a strong treatise against slavery.

Because autobiographies are retrospective or reflective narratives about the lives of individuals, they are constructed, fabricated, crafted from recollections or memory, specifically, from selected "key" moments in the individuals' lives. As such, autobiographies can be distorted and/or exaggerated, because memory can be faulty, making recalling exact facts about one's life problematic. Adam Hochschild concurs, acknowledging "the long and fascinating history of autobiographies that distort or exaggerate the truth."[16] "But in each of these cases," Hochschild adds, "the lies and inventions pervade the entire book. Seldom is one crucial portion of a memoir totally fabricated and the remainder scrupulously accurate; among autobiographers, as with other writers, both dissemblers and truth-tellers tend to be consistent."[17] Other slave narratives such as Frederick Douglass' *The Narrative of the Life of Frederick Douglass: An American Slave* (1845),

William Wells Brown's *The Life of William Wells Brown* (1847), Harriet Jacobs' *Incidents in the Life of a Slave Girl* (1861), and William and Ellen Crafts' *Running a Thousand Miles for Freedom* (1860) all rely on memory and the careful selection of key moments in the authors' lives to construct the narratives. In all of these, the narratives focus on select years, rather than provide us with the totality of these authors' lives or experiences. In fact, according to Nellie Y. McKay and Frances Smith Foster in their "Introduction" to the Norton Critical Edition of Jacobs' narrative, "A large part of the drama in the book focuses on the time between Jacobs' mid-teen years and her late twenties, when she was the object of James Norcom's unrelenting sexual pursuit."[18] McKay and Foster add that "[w]hen the 1973 edition of *Incidents* appeared, and for several years after, it generated a controversial debate among scholars who disputed the validity of its authorship and its authenticity as a slave narrative."[19] Certainly, Equiano's narrative cannot be an exception to scholarly questions about its structure or content. But, like the other slave narratives mentioned above, Equiano's narrative is equally constructed, fleshing out only certain details while leaving others unexplored or underdeveloped. Consequently, there are bound to be silences in the text. These aspects must also be considered in analyzing it.

Equaino's narrative has received considerable attention today, what with scholars raising questions about the author's identity and "intentions." Part of the complexity, perhaps, the problematic nature of Equiano's narrative, stems from tension between the authorial voice(s) of the adult Afro-British Gustavus Vassa or Olaudah Equiano and the narrative persona of the African child and adult Equiano. In other words, as an autobiographical sketch, the narrative has an inherent ambiguity resulting from the uncertainty of memory, as well as a dissonance between the adult self or selves of the author and the narrative persona(s). Still, Equiano's narrative remains central to any discussion and understanding of eighteenth century slavery and the Trans-Atlantic slave trade.

In the "Introduction" to his Longman edited volume of *The Life of Olaudah Equiano, or Gustavus Vassa the African*, Paul Edwards states: "Olaudah Equiano is generally agreed to be the most remarkable of the black British and American writers in the late eighteenth and early nineteenth centuries..."[20] Having manumitted himself, Equiano's task would be to recreate himself in this narrative by presenting his audience with details of his "adventures" through slavery. In doing this, he presented himself not only as an individual engaged in a quest of self-discovery but one with an important trans-cultural mission: the construction of a strong argument for the abolition of slavery and the slave trade, and through that declare his humanity and that of his people. The narrative also suggests that part of the author's project is to engage and respond to European perceptions of Africa in the late eighteenth century. In writing as an opponent of slavery and a voice for Africa and Africans, Equiano also undertakes to re-educate Europe about Africa by reconstructing the image of Africa in European consciousness. Equiano achieves this feat through his re-construction of the Igbo world, perhaps, idealized, in the narrative.

Consequently, the early chapters, primarily the first and part of the second chapter of the autobiography, focus on his life in West Africa and construct an Igbo (African) world whose values or systems seem to parallel the European/British society. In these chapters, what emerges, therefore, is an Igbo or African world defined on the basis of those values which Equiano perceives as important to Europeans and they include: political structure/government, administration of justice, agriculture, marriage, religion, beauty (art), and entertainment. As such, as an abolitionist text, the narrative undermines any arguments of racial superiority which Europeans may use to support the enslavement of Africans.

Additionally, Equiano's portrayal of Africa in these two chapters represents one of the first acts of protest by an African (Black) against the imaging of Africans in Western consciousness. One could say that Equiano's narrative (consciously or unconsciously) writes or talks back to Europe, particularly to those who perceive Africans as "other," only fit for enslavement, servitude, sale, or objects of display.[21] According to Marc A. Christophe in his article, "Changing Images of Blacks in Eighteenth Century French Literature:"

> [W]e can affirm that by the end of the eighteenth century, there was evidence in Europe, especially in Paris in the households of the nobility and of the rich bourgeois, of the existence of individuals belonging to the black race. They functioned as servants, footmen, pages and, sometimes, because of the European craze for things oriental or exotic, they were dressed in turbans and silk and used as "objets de luxe" or as conversation pieces.[22]

Christophe adds that the eighteenth century French writer Voltaire "informs us that a certain Dr. Ruysch in Amsterdam once had dissected the body of a black and discovered that, between the skin and the muscles, there existed a mucous membrane. The membrane, whose color is black, is, according to the Dutch doctor, the cause of the African's dark pigmentation."[23] Ruysch's research was not unique. He was like other European scientists who were preoccupied with the anatomy of Africans (Dr. Georges Couvier's preoccupation with the body of Sara (formerly Saartjie) Baartman comes to mind also)[24] and who employed science to justify European racism against Africans.

For Christophe, "the idea of black people, within the concept of a created, as well as a scientific world was a historical and anthropological puzzle for the European mind."[25] Africa and Africans were still mysteries or exotic to Europe. In his article, "The European Approach to the Interior of Africa in the Eighteenth Century," Robin Hallett asserts that although "Europeans had made themselves aware of the broad outlines of the Continents of Asia, Africa and America" by the "middle of the sixteenth century,"[26] of the three continents, Africa was still the least familiar to Europe. The image of Africa in European consciousness was so distorted that a "compiler of one of those massive *Systems of Geography*" Yearbooks, Hallett adds, described Africa as "burning and savage territory,' region of mystery, of poetry, of superstitious awe."[27] But, by 1789 when Equiano's narrative was published, the British public had become more familiar with Africa and the slavery debate. Again Hallett, "Never before had so many people in England thought so intensely about Africa" adding that between 1750 and 1788, the British public had become more aware of Africa than in the previous years due to traveler reports about the continent.[28] Those years also experienced increased explorations into the continent in search of more access into the hinterland. Hallett confirms that groups such as the African Association sponsored travels into the continent in an effort to encourage colonization and put an end to slavery. Like his British contemporaries, Equiano was also engaged in a process of rethinking and reconstructing Africa as his narrative shows. So, his description of agriculture in his home country could be read as a masked endorsement of colonization as an alternative to slavery and the slave trade.

Really, Equiano's narrative arrived at an appropriate moment in these debates. Equiano had been free since 1766 and had traveled through Europe, the Mediterranean, North America, and the Caribbean as a free man and witnessed the horrible treatment of blacks in captivity. Also, a number of other incidents serve as informing texts to Equiano's narrative. In 1781, the *Zong* massacre occurred in which 132 slaves were drowned on the order of the ship's captain so that the owners could collect insurance.[29] Equiano reported this incident to Granville Sharp in 1783, who tried to redress the wrong done to the Africans, after the Zong Captain was acquitted of insurance fraud.[30] Robert J. Allison in his "Introduction" to his edited volume of the *Narrative* agrees that "Equiano's narrative came at a critical moment in the British antislavery movement."[31] Carretta also agrees that "The timing of the publication of *The Interesting Narrative* was no accident. Abolition of the slave trade had become a truly popular cause only since the mid 1780's, especially after the founding in London of the Society for Effecting the Abolition of the Slave Trade."[32] For Equiano, it was necessary to address the status of Africans in England. Besides, he had lived through slavery. He, as an eye witness to slavery, was the ideal voice to confront the topic. He was the ideal subject. Robert Allison concurs:

> Equiano was uniquely qualified to write an antislavery book
> . . . . He knew the whole system of slavery, from the kidnap-
> ping of slaves in Africa, to the brutal middle passage across
> the Atlantic, to the plantations of the West Indies and the
> American mainland, to the intercolonial slave trade. He had
> experienced every part of the slave system. But he had also
> lived as a free man for twenty years. His life was more than a
> testament against slavery: it was a record of one man's survival
> of both a brutal institution and a savage age.[33]

If Equiano saw his story as the conduit for exercising some agency—pro-testing against slavery and the slave trade—then, he had to control the subject and content of the narrative. Above all, the language of such narra-tive had to be carefully deployed.

In his review of Catherine Acholonu's *The Igbo Roots of Olaudah Equiano*, O. S. Ogede states, "[i]ntentionally cast in the voyage form, Equiano's story employed romantic colouring principally to build a more positive image of the African than was allowed in the society of his day."[34] Clearly, since Europe had created Africa as its foil, as blankness and the "other" unto which Europe projected its nightmares, fears, and neurosis, Equiano had to counter this "othering" by presenting Africa as Europe's equal, or at least, almost like Europe. In his narrative, therefore, Equiano strategically deploys binary opposition—juxtaposing Africa to Europe. Ironically, Equiano is bound by the very language of representation that he attempts to challenge, because he also replicates it in his own con-struction of Africa. So, in confronting the European rendering of Afri-cans as "other," he produces a new "good" "other" by appropriating what he may have perceived as European positive images of Africans. Indeed, an Africa that is like Europe or shares attributes with Europe undermines any European sense of racial and cultural superiority and finally affirms Equiano's claim of human rights, freedom, and equality for Africans. One does not suggest that the experiences Equiano describes in his narrative are false. My contention, however, is that the discursive strategy of binary opposition—good/bad African, lazy/hardworking African, barbaric/noble savage—problematizes Equiano's attempt to construct an African identity that is free of idealization or distortion, and ultimately disrupts the narrative. In other words, Equiano cannot escape such Manichean relationship, even as he struggles to counter it.

Interestingly, eighteenth century Enlightenment by its "Declaration of the rights of man" asserted the universality of human rights. Ironically, those rights were not extended to nations and cultures outside Europe, in this case Africa and the colonies or economic outposts in the Americas and elsewhere. Hence, while Europe was proclaiming the "rights of Man," it was simultaneously denying them to Africans and exporting them because they were not necessarily seen, read, or defined as "men," human beings. Also, affected by this ironic application of European enlightenment values were blacks in the New World and the indigenous peoples of the Americas and Caribbean. Even when those ideas were extended to Africans, they were still defined as "other," and particularly in terms of the "noble savage." Indeed, the ideals of enlightenment Europe were contradictory and Equiano's narrative occupies a space where the tensions are clearly manifested—the extension of the "rights of man" or human rights to Africans (free and enslaved).

According to Paul Edwards, "African slaves had been reclassified between the years 1600 and 1700, from human beings under *Habeas Corpus*, to items of trade under the *Navigation Act*."[35] Edwards further states that "in 1701, an Englishman's will could declare of his African servant, 'I take him to be in the nature of my goods and chattels,'"[36] adding that in "1745, the year of Equiano's birth, Lord Hartwicke announced his legal decision that slaves 'are like stock on a farm.'"[37] There is no indication that slaves were reclassified in the following years. So, the dehumanization of Africans created by their commodification or objectification would inform attitudes towards Equiano and other blacks who found themselves in Britain before the abolition of the slave trade in 1807.

FROM MARGINAL LAND TO KNOWN CONTINENT: CLAIMING CULTURE/LOCATING AFRICA

Part of Equiano's strategy in constructing his narrative is to locate Africa by framing it within a context that eighteenth century Europe understood. In other words, he would engage in an act of racial and cultural recuperation. T. Carlos Jacques in his article "From Savages and Barbarians to Primitives" contends that "Africa was framed by the Enlightenment *philosophes* within a body of knowledge that defined its place adjacent to the knowledge of Europe and the other regions of the world."[38] The continent served only as the source of raw materials (humans included) for

European commercial interests and exotic desires, as well as the object onto which Europe in the same manner as with the Orient projected its negative visions, desires, fears, and nightmares. Geographically, Jacques adds, "the continent was little more than a series of coasts and its people, more often than not, were simply listed along with the other traded commodities."[39] These "Orientalist" perceptions, as Edward Said would name Europe's relationship with the Orient, further underscore the contradictions inherent in Enlightenment attitudes towards those seen as "other." In fact, in his work *Orientalism*, Said locates the starting point for "Orientalism" in the late eighteenth century. According to Said:

> Taking the late eighteenth century as a very roughly defined starting point Orientalism can be discussed and analyzed as the corporate institution for dealing with the Orient—dealing with it by making statements about it, authorizing views of it, describing it, by teaching it, settling it, ruling over it: in short, Orientalism as a Western style for dominating, restructuring, and having authority over the Orient.[40]

Europe's application of Orientalism as a style or process was not limited to the Orient. It also extended to Africa and Africa was lesser known to Europe than the Orient. Because Africans were denied full humanity, and therefore, seen as incapable of reason, Africans and their continent were also seen as inferior to Europe. Even when Africans were humanized, they were rendered as childlike, naïve, noble savages who could only be Christianized, therefore, saved and civilized by Europe. Such placement of Africa does not provide any middle ground—both representations are negative. Equiano was writing and responding to those perceptions and their implications for any black (African) person in Britain at the time.

In chapter one of his narrative, Equiano locates his country or birth place geographically, carefully placing it within the context of what Europeans knew of the (West) African landscape and cultures at the time. He writes:

> The part of Africa known by the name of Guinea, to which the trade for slaves is carried on, extends along the coast above 3400 miles, from Senegal to Angola, and includes a variety of kingdoms. Of these the most considerable is the kingdom of Benin, both as to extent and wealth, the richness and cultivation of the soil, the power of its king, and the number and warlike disposition of the inhabitants.[41]

Here, Equaino underscores his knowledge of geography, at least, of the West African landscape known to Europe. According to Hallett, "on the Upper Senegal the French had by 1750 successfully maintained for half a century a trading post over four hundred miles from the sea."[42] But the English, the primary audience of Equiano's narrative, did not necessarily possess such knowledge or control of the West African inland that Equiano describes in his narrative. Besides, African rulers and populations were also resistant to European intrusion into the hinterland. Again, Hallett asserts, "there was another, and more potent, form of obstruction to be overcome, the unwillingness of African societies to allow Europeans to travel freely in their midst."[43] In fact, Equiano comments on the absence of European presence in his community, when he says, "I had never heard of the white men or Europeans, nor the sea,"[44] signaling his people's distance from the coast. Moreover, his village, he states, is too remote to feel the reach or authority of the reputed kingdom of Benin,[45] which Europeans knew.

In these early passages, Equino uses known information not only to authenticate his identity as an Igbo (African), and as one who knows the landscape better than his English audience, but also to present an African landscape that is both familiar and unfamiliar, yet non-threatening to Europeans. Critics who point to Equiano's use of other sources for these passages as indicative of Equiano's invention of an imagined identity miss the point. Clearly, Equiano, the author, had to rely on other sources to locate his country geographically, especially since the child Equaino could not possibly have had the privilege of a map or knowledge of cartography (to guide his kidnappers and his enslavers!). How else would he accomplish the task of locating his homeland for an audience that did not know the territory well? In their essay, "The Path Not Taken: Cultural Identity in the Interesting Life of Olaudah Equiano," Robin Sabino and Jennifer Hall contend that these questions about the authenticity of Equiano's narrative were "largely predicated on the elitist assumption that an Igbo could not acquire sufficient competency in English language and culture to author such an acceptably English text."[46] Simply put, Equiano, like his abolitionist contemporaries and later slave narrators, was very aware of his audience. But, Equiano was also aware of his audience's limited knowledge of the subjects (Africa and Africans) of his narrative. Therefore, his narrative maps out these unfamiliar landscapes for his audience.

As indicated in Hallett's article, by the end of the sixteenth century, Europeans had established long-standing trading relationships with Africans. But, their activities were limited to the coast. In his article, "European Explorations and Africa's Self-Discovery," Ali Mazrui asserts that "Africa was indeed a dark continent, in the sense of being relatively unknown outside itself. To eighteenth-century Europe, little more than the coastline of Africa was known."[47] Then he adds, "North Africa, very much part of the Islamic world, was almost inaccessible to Christians at that time. There had been a few European adventurers who had disguised themselves in Arab dress and travelled up the Nile from Cairo."[48] In other words, the African hinterland was relatively unknown to Europeans, a fact which Equiano underscores in his "the interior part of Africa to a distance hitherto I believe unexplored by any traveler."[49] Carretta agrees that "[t]he slave trade debate reminded the [English] public how little they understood about much of Africa and its peoples."[50] At its publication, Equiano's narrative drew even more attention to that knowledge gap, to his humanity and to that of Africans, who were the subject of that debate. Really, Equiano's use of existing knowledge reveals his mastery of a society that had marginalized him. His act challenges his audience's claim of intellectual superiority. Interestingly, in a society that valued literacy (education, the arts) as indicative of refinement, Equiano's acknowledgment of his sources in his narrative demonstrates his acquisition of education/knowledge (literacy), and ultimately, his refinement, just like his audience. As an African writing in the late eighteenth century, Equiano was modeling the society that had "produced" him, but he was an African!

Through his autobiography, Equiano would engage in an act of racial and cultural retrieval and (self) re-authentication by describing in detail what he saw as key aspects of his society. His description of government among his people cannot be overlooked, because the narrative in this section has been constructed to counter any suggestions of African lack of political structures. Europeans were familiar with African chiefs, for afterall, some of these chiefs were at the center of the slave trade or trade with Europe. Equiano's reference to the king of Benin points to an existing relationship with Europe. But, Europeans simultaneously conducted business with African chiefs while refusing to acknowledge African political structures. If anything, they saw these structures as inferior, paying attention to them only when they affected trade. As Philip D. Curtin states in his work, *The Image of Africa*:

> Since Europeans mainly came to the Coast for trade, they reported with an eye to matters of commercial importance. An elementary knowledge of political structure was essential for traders, who had to deal with the African authorities. Certain aspects of material culture and the African economic systems were equally crucial, especially when they concerned the slave trade in the interior or the market demand for European goods.[51]

Clearly, Europeans were not interested in learning about or understanding African cultures, their political systems or personhood. Besides, because these political systems were often not seen as formalized within the European contexts, they were seen as irrelevant or only useful if they affected commerce. For his late eighteenth century British audience, Equiano's narrative was an eye-opener, an adventure into the African hinterland that was previously unknown to his audience, and such adventure included an exposition on governance and the application of justice among his people. His narrative presented his audience with a group that possessed a cohesive system of governance and one in which he, Equiano had first hand knowledge, because it involved his father.

Since Europeans already knew about the kingdom of Benin in West Africa, Equiano uses that knowledge as a framing device to locate his community. Thus, in the narrative, he defines his birth place by its relationship to Benin. According Equiano, although the king of Benin ruled the entire kingdom, Equiano's community's contact with Benin was "nominal," "for every transaction of the government . . . was conducted by the chiefs or elders of the place."[52] Then he introduces his father, telling us later: "My father was one of those elders or chiefs I have spoken of, and was styled Embrenche; a term, as I remember, importing the highest distinction, and signifying in our language a *mark* of grandeur."[53] He carefully draws his audience's attention to the hierarchy of power and the exercise of authority among his people. Perhaps, his audience would recognize such structure, for his African people share a political structure that is similar to that found in his adopted country. The Embrenche have power to administer justice, including issue death sentences or slavery depending on the offence. And, contrary to European assumptions about African disorderliness, ignorance, and indolence, Equiano's society is organized, cohesive, orderly, well-managed and dynamic; people work. Really, he tells his audience, "You see, we are like you!"

Similar objectives inform his comparison of "'the manners and customs of [his] countrymen and those of the Jews, before they reached the Land of Promise, and particularly the patriarchs while they were yet in the pastoral state which is described in Genesis.'"[54] In drawing these parallels between his people and the Jews of the Old Testament, Equiano seems to highlight a commonality with an ancient culture that his audience recognizes. How can his audience reject his culture and religion without implicitly rejecting that of the Jewish people of the Old Testament? In addition, the analogy serves especially to emphasize a parallel between the experience of the Jewish people, the children of Israel in the Old Testament, and those of Africans in captivity. So, like the children of Israel, favored by the God of the Old Testament and delivered from bondage by that God, the Africans also will be delivered from captivity.[55]

Despite his people's similarity with Europeans and Jews, Equiano tells us that he comes from a "people who have little commerce with other countries"[56] and whose manners are "generally very simple." T. Carlos Jacques indicates that the French philosopher Abbé Demanet, for instance, described Africans as "possessing only the most rudimentary arts and industry."[57] Equiano seems to be appropriating some of that language and representation here, but, his depiction of his people also suggests that such simplicity can be deceptive as he reveals a complexity of social roles, relationships, and processes within his culture. Critics, including Carretta, wonder why Equiano does not delve into more details in this area. Equiano has provided enough geographical and cultural information to locate his people and that information serves as a conduit for a larger project—Equiano's presentation of himself as a representative of these people and as human. In other words, part of his strategy is to suggest that "if you know me, you will also know my people; I am, therefore, they are." Also, one has to acknowledge that the adult author can only remember what the child persona knows or retains. How much of his culture did he know before he was kidnapped at age eleven? He tells us that he had not matured to learn all the intricacies of his culture before he was kidnapped into slavery. "I was also *destined* to receive [the *Embrenche* mark] by my parents,"[58] he informs us. This sentence like the passage about his father is significant because it provides Equiano with an occasion to inform his audience that he was of noble (elite) birth or parentage. Slavery robbed him of his nobility, his family, community, and rendered him an object, chattel. In other words, Equiano would claim, therefore, that slavery rendered him socially dead as Orlando Patterson has suggested.[59]

In fact, in the next chapter, Equiano reinforces his point about the destructiveness of family and community by slavery. Recalling his experience of the Middle Passage, he describes how Africans were brutalized, dehumanized and battered, destroying any sense of community or familial relationship. "In this manner, without scruple, are relations and friends separated, most of them never to see each other again,"[60] he writes. Let us not forget, he was separated from his sister,[61] and a final time, after a brief encounter during the Middle Passage.[62] Of course, we can now understand his famous apostrophe: "O ye nominal Christians! Might not an African ask you, learned you this from your God, who says unto you, Do unto all men as you would men should do unto you?"[63] Who would not ask such a question? And to underscore his claim that slavery destroys familial bonds and social relationships, and that he and his people have been wronged, he adds: "Is it not enough that we are torn from our country and friends to toil for your luxury and lust of gain?"[64] Clearly, we cannot miss the force of this rhetorical question. Equiano wants to make a point: slavery is evil and partaking in it is equally evil! And if his language evokes sympathy or guilt from his audience, so be it!

Another aspect of culture that Equiano addresses in his narrative is marriage. In describing the institution of marriage, Equiano counters European stereotypes of supposed African promiscuity or sexual laxity, therefore, African barbarity. Nudity was seen as further indication of African moral degeneracy. In fact, Europeans did not recognize African customary marriages[65] and polygamy was seen as evidence of sexual deviancy on the part of Africans. So, one way to restore the image of Africans and interrogate European claims of African sexual deviancy is to clarify the culture to those who do not fully understand it by underscoring similarities with European or English cultural practices. Equiano's presentation of marriage as a sacred relationship among his people serves that purpose. He writes: "so sacred among them is the honour of the marriage bed, and so jealous are they of the fidelity of their wives."[66] To emphasize the importance and high regard his people have for marriage, he tells us that adultery by women is considered so serious a crime that it is punishable even by death, and he gives us an example of one such case, although mercy is shown to the woman because "it being found, just before her execution, that she had an infant in her breast; and no woman being prevailed on to perform her part as a nurse, she was spared on account of her child."[67]

Furthermore, in this section of the narrative, Equiano presents marriage not only as a liaison between the bride and groom, but also as a family and communal event, one to which members of the community are called upon to bear witness to the sealing of the relationship between the man and the woman. The act of witnessing also serves as a deterrent to other members of the community. The groom stands "up in the midst of all their friends who are assembled for the purpose," Equiano writes, and "declares she is thenceforth to be looked upon as his wife, and that no other person is to pay any address to her."[68] This image is contrary to the image of Africans as promiscuous.

On polygamy, Equiano states, "the men, however, do not preserve the same constancy to their wives, which they expect from the; for they indulge in a plurality, though seldom in more than two."[69] Of course, these representations of Igbo communal life and culture suggest an organic and well-structured society with values that govern human relations and social actions; specifically, Equaino suggests that social mores deter women from being sexually lax and female chastity is preserved. Similarly, the men do not liaise with more than two women, if they engage in "plurality." Equiano's choice of language in this section, and especially, to describe polygamy is interesting. He refers to polygamy as "plurality" rather than adultery which may appear morally charged. "Plurality," I believe, is non-threatening and seemingly non-judgmental. Perhaps, Equiano chooses this word in an attempt not to appear critical of such practices among his audience or of those who have sexual liaisons with African women in the West Indies.[70]

In addition, Equiano speaks about the "fidelity of their wives," acknowledging patriarchy and male "ownership" of wives, a point which he stresses by describing the symbolic act of claiming ownership, performed when the bride is taken to her groom's: "her parents then deliver her to the bridegroom, accompanied with a number of blessings, and at the same time they tie round her waist a cotton string of the thickness of a goose-quill, which none but married women are permitted to wear: she is now considered as completely his wife . . . "[71] A few sentences later, Equiano emphasizes the social status of the bride as "the sole property of her husband."[72] Might Equiano also be drawing a parallel between the social status of Igbo brides and that of English wives or brides at the time? A rather savvy Equiano understands the limits of his position. As we have established, part of his rhetorical strategy is to underscore parallels between his culture and that of his audience.

For many Europeans, African social structures were meaningless and Equiano's narrative endows them with meanings and "logic." Indeed, his narrative re-constructs an African, here Igbo, identity that challenges the myths about Africans. As stated earlier, to correct those distortions, Equiano also appropriates other myths, specifically, the myth of "the noble savage," which to him may appear seemingly positive. Because his narrative is informed by the manichean relationship between Europe and Africa, Equiano's counter representation appears idealized or exaggerated. Critics have pointed out his ironic employment of the "noble savage" myth in his narrative. But it is important to note that Equiano did not write in a vacuum. He was influenced, not only by the travel narrative convention, but also by the language of the humanitarian and abolitionist politics of his time. Philip Curtin correctly confirms that the convention of the noble savage "helped to form a vague and positive image of the 'good African,' and it was widely used by the anti-slave trade publicists for exactly this purpose."[73]

Indeed, the image of the noble savage in an Edenic environment helps Equiano underscore that the slave trade and slavery have disrupted the peaceful and simple co-existence of his people within their natural environment. In other words, the slave trade is evil! Curtin adds, "Since the slave traders claimed African life so 'degraded' that even slavery in the West Indies was preferable, the humanitarians had to provide an answer,"[74] and so did Equiano. If Englishmen who were not personally invested or transformed by the slave trade and slavery could respond by producing seemingly "positive" counter images of Africans to confront those presented by the slavers, why would not an African who had been degraded, dislocated from his people and transformed by slavery?

Equiano had cause and he would employ several strategies, including the rhetoric of difference that had been effective for the abolitionists. His strategy includes underscoring the simplicity of his people to draw attention to the destructive nature of the slave trade: "As our manners are simple, our luxuries are few."[75] His people are so simple that they "are totally unacquainted with strong or spirituous liquours."[76] In highlighting the pristine nature of his people's culture he writes: "Our manners of living are entirely plain; for as yet the natives are unacquainted with those refinements in cookery which debauch the taste."[77] In another section, he says, "As we live in a country where nature is prodigal of her favours, our wants are few and easily supplied,"[78] and almost as an after thought, he adds, "of course we have a few manufactures."

Clearly, Equiano is engaged in a carefully mapped out refashioning of Igbo (African) identity in those passages discussed. For sure, his remembrance of his homeland will be tainted by nostalgia. It is also not surprising that he may have borrowed (as critics have suggested) passages or the language of representation from other travel narratives and reports to flesh out descriptions of West Africa.[79] By the late eighteenth century, humanitarians, abolitionists, and travelers, especially those advocating colonization had developed increasing interest in the geography of Africa, especially its fauna, in an attempt to promote the idea of agriculture as part of colonization. Philip Curtin concurs. "By the eighteenth-century," Curtin states, "a full-fledged myth of tropical exuberance had been created."[80] He adds,

> Eighteenth-century travelers or publicists described the Guinea Coast in rapturous terms. John Wesley believed it was 'one of the most fruitful, as well as the most pleasant countries in the known world,' a place where: 'the soil is in general fertile, producing abundance of rice and roots. Indigo and cotton thrive without cultivation; fish is in great plenty; the flocks and herds are numerous and the tree loaded with fruit.[81]

How could Equiano not use this language to his advantage? Recall his introduction of his birth place: "a charming fruitful vale;"[82] later, he states, "we live in a country where nature is prodigal."[83] Still later, he adds, "Our land is uncommonly rich and fruitful, and produces all kinds of vegetables in great abundance. We have plenty of Indian corn, and vast quantities of cotton and tobacco. Our pine apples grow without culture; they are about the size of the largest sugar-loaf, and finely flavoured."[84] Equiano's language in these passages clearly echoes John Wesley's. Curtin confirms that "[s]imilar ecstatic reports figured in the works of almost every traveler to West Africa, and the witnesses before the Committee of Privy Council in 1789 told the same story of agricultural wealth."[85] Really, Equiano would be an exception if his narrative did not tell a similar tale. Besides, he was simply employing the language to make concrete images of a landscape that he knew quite well.

CLOSING

As stated, part of Equiano's strategy in his autobiography is to engage some of the rhetoric, if not the totality, of European discourse on Africa and to help the abolitionist cause. If some eighteenth century European "liberal" humanitarian philosophers and opponents of slavery perceived Africans as natural "man" or "noble savage," Equiano activates that representation in sections of his narrative to highlight how European enslavement of Africans displaced Africans from their natural Edenic environment. Consequently, one would surmise that Equiano seems to suggest, as did some abolitionists, that Africans' loss of innocence and natural rights can only be attributed to the presence of Europeans. Therefore, Equiano, speaking through his narrative as an African and for Africans, claims that the slave trade and slavery have wronged him and his people, even, if he regards himself *"a particular favourite of Heaven."*

George E. Boulukos in his article, "Olaudah Equiano and the Eighteenth-Century Debate on Africa," states that Equiano's representation of himself and his identity is informed by "the possibilities and the stakes of competing African and national or political identities within eighteenth-century British discourse, and particularly in relation to the slavery debate."[86] Boulukos, therefore, suggests that Equiano cast himself as a British political subject while insinuating an "African cultural identity." In other words, Equiano was British and African simultaneously. Like Boulukos, Suzan M. Marren in "Between Slavery and Freedom: The Transgressive Self in Olaudah Equiano's Autobiography," claims that Equiano "wrote in response to two imperatives: on the one hand, an internal compulsion to establish himself as a speaking subject and, on the other hand, an external compulsion to serve the antislavery movement."[87] While Boulukos and

Marren are correct in their assessment, one should also consider a third imperative: the need to carefully craft an image of Africa that challenges or undermines its negative representation in western consciousness. Perhaps, for Equiano, only an authentic African, a true child of the continent, could achieve such a feat. Equiano saw himself as that subject and that may also explain the appendage of his African name to his slave name of Gustavus Vassa. Olaudah Equiano, the African who is also British speaks with a loud voice. His names Gustavus Vassa or Olaudah Equiano, the African would signify his true identity, an Afro-British and true son of Africa. As a son of Africa, he was living his name by his action. As he informs us in his narrative, his name, *Olaudah* in his language "signifies vicissitude or fortune . . . one favoured and having a loud voice and well-spoken."[88] Writing his autobiography is an act of speaking, talking back with a loud voice and through it Equiano fulfills his name.[89]

Equiano wrote his autobiography to strike a blow against slavery. But the narrative also confronts the perceptions of Africans by eighteenth century Britain (Europe). Consequently, Equiano employs a strategy, where Africa is portrayed as a parallel to Europe, not as a foil or other, but a land with a people whose values, beliefs, and customs are like those familiar to the British (Europeans). Africans are humanized, even if it means romanticizing them to the degree that Europeans romanticize themselves, fashioning them as Ogede has suggested in "a more positive image . . . than was allowed in the society" of Equiano's day. Equiano even acknowledges that he may be romanticizing or idealizing his home country, stating, "whether the love of one's country be real or imaginary, or a lesson of reason, or an instinct of nature, I still look back with pleasure on the first scenes of my life,"[90] then adding to remind his reader of his loss, "though that pleasure has been for the most part mingled with sorrow."

The author Equiano was conscious of his audience and so is the narrative persona, and lest he be accused of arrogance at introducing himself and his country with such exuberance, he pleads for his reader's indulgence: "I hope the reader will not think I have trespassed on his patience in introducing myself to him with some account of the manners and customs of my country."[91] He then defines his act as one of cultural recovery because "the manners and customs of my country . . . had been implanted in me with great care, and made an impression on my mind, which time could not erase."[92] He continues, "all the adversity and variety of fortune I have since experienced served only to rivet and record," as if to respond to those who may suggest that slavery had robbed him of the memory of his country. This demonstration of humility, an act of self-effacement is one that Equiano employs at various moments in his narrative.

In the opening paragraph of his letter to the British Parliament written on October 30, 1790[93] introducing his narrative, Equiano signals his awareness of his social status as marginal and "other" in British society, in spite of his manumission. Humbling himself before his audience, he pleads: "Permit me, with the greatest deference and respect, to lay at your feet the following genuine narrative; the chief design of which is to excite in your august assemblies a sense of compassion for the miseries which the Slave-Trade has entailed on my unfortunate countrymen."[94] In these few words, Equiano effaces himself enough to dispel the perception of potential threat from this "private and obscure individual, and a stranger too." Paul Edwards describes Equiano's act as "authorial pseudo-modesty."[95] But, Equiano's letter signals the nature of the narrative—a narrative that is gravely aware of its audience and which has to be carefully constructed if it is to achieve its central project: to promote "the interests of humanity." It is through this narrative that Equiano will begin a process of recasting himself, other Africans or Blacks, re-construct his Igbo community, in particular, and Africa in general in human terms. To engage in this project, Equiano deploys a rhetoric that carefully articulates his opposition to slavery without belligerently confronting a society that refuses to recognize his humanity. Like the European travelers, from whom he borrowed material, Equiano also wrote to "please [his] audience as well as inform," to use Phillip D. Curtin's language. As such, language becomes important in his narrative—the only tool or weapon with which to dismantle slavery or objectification and through which a bartered and battered community can be re-constituted, reclaimed, and reinvested with humanity and subjectivity.

NOTES

1. For the purpose of this essay, references will be to: Robert J. Allison, ed., *The Interesting Narrative of the Life of Olaudah Equiano* (Boston: Bedford/St. Martins Press, 1995) and Paul Edwards, ed., *The Life of Olaudah Equiano of Gustavus Vassa the African* (New York: Longman, 1996).

2. See Wilfred D. Samuels, "Disguised Voice in the *Interesting Narrative of the Life of Olaudah Equiano or Gustavus Vassa, the Africa*," *Black American Forum* 19, no. 2 (Summer 1985): 64-69; Susan Marren, "Between Slavery and Freedom: The Transgressive Self in Olaudah Equiano's Autobiography," *PMLA* 108, 1 (Jan, 1993): 94-105; Katalin Orban, "Dominant and Submerged Discourses." *The Life of Oaludah Equiano (or Gustavus Vassa?), African American Review* 27, no. 4 (Winter 1993): 655-664; Elizabeth Jane Walls Hinds, "The Spirit of Trade: Olaudah Equiano's Conversion, Legalism, and the Merchant's Life," *African American Review* 32, no. 4 (1998): 635-47;

and Vincent Carretta, *Equiano, the African: Biography of a Self-made Man* (Athens, GA: Georgia University Press, 2005) for discussions of Equiano's narrative self/selves.

3. Carretta, *Equiano, the African.* Carretta claims in his book that baptismal records he has located and a ship's log provide evidence that Equiano was not a native-born African and as such he could not have experienced the Middle Passage or experienced the Igbo culture the author describes in his narrative.

4. Carretta, *Equiano, the African*, xiv.

5. Ibid.

6. For a discussion of Equiano's Igbo roots, see Catherine Obianju Acholonu, *The Igbo Roots of Olaudah Equiano* (Owerri: Afa Publications, 1989). Acholonu has identified Isseke in Ihiala, Anambra State, Nigeria as "the most likely transcription of the word Essaka" in Equiano's narrative. O. S. Ogede in his review takes issue with Acholonu's assertions, claiming that they are guided by Igbo nationalist intentions, although Acholonu does not necessarily make such claims. See O. S. Ogede's review, "The Igbo Roots of Oladah Equiano," *Journal of International African Institute* 61, no 1 (1991): 138 – 41.

7. See Paul Edwards, "Textual Notes to the *Narrative,*" *The Life of Olaudah Equiano*. According to Edwards "embrenche" in modern Igbo is *mgburichi*. Edwards cites John Adams as saying "that the Ibo word for gentleman is *Breeché*" in *Sketches Taken during Ten Voyages to Africa* (London, 1822), 41–2.

8. Carretta, *Equiano, the African*, xv.

9. Ibid., xii.

10. Orban, "Dominant or Submerged Discourses," 657.

11. Samuels, "Disguised Voice," 66.

12. Ibid., 64.

13. Hinds, "The Spirit of Trade," 636.

14. Ide Corley, "The Subject of Abolitionist Rhetoric: Freedom and Trauma in 'The Life of Olaudah Equiano,'" *Modern Language Studies* 32, no. 2 (Autumn 2002), 142.

15. Hinds, "The Spirit of Trade," 636.

16. Cited Carretta, *Equiano, the African*, xvi.

17. Ibid., xvi.

18. Harriet Jacobs, *Incidents in the Life of a Slave Girl*, eds., Nellie Y. McKay and Frances Smith Foster (New York: Norton, 2001).

19. Ibid., xiii.

20. Edwards, *The Life of Olaudah*, vii.

21. Africans served as objects of European curiosity or gaze in the late eighteenth century and even in the early nineteenth century. The most famous example is the case of Sara (Saartjie) Baartman, a South African woman of Khoisan background, who was taken to London in 1810 and because of her

unusually large buttocks, a condition referred to as steatopygia, was placed on display as a curious object in England and France. In France she would become known as the "Venus Hottentot" or "Hottentot Venus." Ironically, she was exhibited in London just a few years after the ending of the Trans-Atlantic Slave Trade (1810). Baartman died in France in 1816; she was only 25, and after her death, her body parts were placed on display at the Museum of Mankind (Musée de l'Homme) in Paris until 1974. In 1994, President Nelson Mandela made a plea to the French government for the return of Sara Baartman's remains. Her remains were finally returned to South Africa in 2002 and buried in the Gamtoos River Valley in the Eastern Cape. See Suzan Lori Parks' play, *The Venus* (1996) for a dramatic exploration of the life of Baartman. See also the Saartjie Baartman Centre for Women and Children at http://www.saartjiebaartmancentre.org.za/. [Accessed April 20 2008]. *The Life and Times of Sara Baartman "the Hottentot Venus"* A film by Zola Maseko (1999). See http://www.frif.com/new99/hottento.html; see also www.vgallery.co.za for Diana Ferrus, "A Poem for Sarah Baartman" which has been described as being so powerful that it moved the French Parliament to release Baartman's body for its return to South Africa. See also http://www.Southafrica.info. [Accessed April 20 2008].

22. Marc A. Christophe "Changing Images of Blacks in Eighteenth Century French Literature," *Phylon* 48 no. 3 (3rd Qtr. 1987), 184.

23. Ibid.

24. After Baartman's death in 1816, Dr. Georges Cuvier made a cast of her body before dissected it, removing her skeleton and brain, which he then preserved with her genitalia and placed on display at the Musée de l'Homme.

25. Christophe, "Changing Images," 185.

26. Robin Hallett, "The European Approach to the Interior of Africa in the Eighteenth Century," *Journal of African History* IV, 2 (1963), 191.

27. Here Hallett cites several texts, including C.T. Middleton, *A New Complete System of Geography* (London, 1779): 11, 241 and *Other Systems of Geography* complied by Bowen (1747), Fenning (1765), Miller (1782) and Bankes (1787). See Hallett, "The European Approach," 193.

28. Hallett, "The European Approach," 532.

29. On September 6, 1781, the British slave ship, the Zong, left West Africa overstocked with slaves heading for Jamaica. Faced with illness and disease, Luke Collingwood, the ship's captain, ordered 132 (Allison cites 132 other sources indicate 133) Africans to be drowned so that the ship's owners could collect the insurance rather than absorb the loss if the Africans were to die. After the ship's captain was acquitted of "insurance fraud," Granville Sharp tried to bring a charge of murder against the captain and crew. The Zong massacre is famous for being one of the strongest evidence for the abolition

of the slave trade. Equiano reported this incident to Granville Sharp in 1783. See Robert Allison's chronology in *The Interesting Narrative*, 198.

30. See www.gloucestershire,gov.uk [Accessed 20 April 2008] for a discussion of the "Zong Incident," Equiano's role in drawing public attention to the incident and the abolitionist movement, as well as Granville Sharp's letter to William Baker regarding the incident and Sharp's attempt to seek justice for the Africans.

31. Allison, *The Interesting Narrative,* 15.

32. Carretta, *Equiano, the African,* 2.

33. Allison, *The Interesting Narrative*, 14.

34. O. S. Ogede, review of Catherine Acholonu's, *The Igbo Roots of Olaudah Equiano,* 140.

35. Edwards, *The Life of Olaudah,* xviii.

36. Edwards cites the *Will of Thomas Papillion,* 1700-1, Kent Archives V.1015. T.44.

37. Edwards, *The Life of Olaudah,* xviii.

38. T. Carlos Jacques, "From Savages and Barbarians to Primitives: Africa, Social Typologies, and History in Eighteenth-Century French Philosophy," *History and Theory* 36 no. 2 (1997): 190-215.

39. Ibid., 198.

40. Said, *Orientalism,* 3.

41. See Edwards, *The Life of Olaudah Equiano,* 2.

42. Hallett, "The European Approach," 190.

43. Ibid., 194.

44. Edwards, *The Life of Olaudah Equiano,* 2.

45. Edwards suggests that Equiano exaggerates the size of Benin in this section and that ["t]his may reflect the fabulous reputation of Benin, possibly encouraged by Equiano's reading of Benezet and other travel literature." See Edwards' "Textual notes to the *Narrative*," (171). Carretta also suggests that the volume of publications which focused on Africa during the late eighteenth century reveals a growing increase in the subject, adding that Equiano had access to these publications and records.

46. Robin Sabino and Jennifer Hall, 5-6.

47. Ali Mazrui, "European Exploration and Africa's Self-Discovery," *The Journal of Modern African Studies* 7, no. 4 (Dec., 1969), 665.

48. Ibid.

49. Edwards, *The Life of Olaudah Equiano,* 2.

50. Carretta, *Equiano, the African,* 7.

51. Philip D. Curtin, *The Image of Africa: British Ideas and Action, 1780 – 1850* (Madison: The University of Wisconsin Press, 1964), 23.

52. Edwards, *The Life of Olaudah Equiano,* 2.

53. Ibid.
54. Ibid., 14.
55. Equiano's references to the children of Israel in the Old Testament are not unusual as African captives in the new world also saw themselves within a similar context as revealed in the African American spirituals and slave narratives. See also Paul Edwards. Edwards reminds us that "this kind of analogy with the release of Israel from bondage is to become a commonplace of black literature, particularly in the American slave narratives, and black song" (14). Edwards also indicates that in this section, "Equiano goes so far as to suggest that his 'Eboe' people may have been originally Hebrew, and proposes interbreeding as the reason for their darker complexion" (14). Equiano may have been prescient since Igbos would refer to themselves as the children of Israel or modern day Jews in Nigeria during the Biafran (Nigerian) Civil War (1966-1970). Also, other Africans, particularly the Fallasha Jews of Ethiopia in the twentieth century would declare themselves as descendants of Israel in a diaspora, dislocated by the Biblical exilic experience of the Jews. See The Centre for Intercultural Learning, Canada at http://www.intercultures. ca/cil-cai/intercultural_issues. [Accessed 20 April 2008]. See also Carretta, *Equiano, the African* (xviii) for Achebe's suggestion that "the consciousness of the Igbo identity that Equiano asserts is a far more recent phenomenon."
56. Edwards, *The Life of Olaudah Equiano*, 2.
57. Jacques, "From Savages," 200.
58. Edwards, *The Life of Olaudah Equiano*, 2.
59. See Orlando Patterson, *Slavery and Social Death: A Comparative Study* (Cambridge, MA: Harvard University Press, 1982).
60. Edwards, *The Life of Olaudah Equiano*, 27.
61. Ibid., 16.
62. Ibid., 18.
63. Ibid., 27-28.
64. Ibid., 28.
65. In fact, even as late as the twentieth century, African couples who were married under traditional or customary laws were often told by the missionaries that those marriages were not legal, and generally coerced into church sanctioned marriages. Tsitsi Dangarembga's *Nervous Conditions*, (1989) addresses this issue critically.
66. Edwards, *The Life of Olaudah Equiano*, 3.
67. Ibid.
68. Ibid.
69. Ibid.
70. There is strong substantial and undisputable evidence of sexual liaisons (willing and forced) between whites and African/Black women in the New

World. African American slave narratives and literature in general address this phenomenon. The most famous is the Thomas Jefferson-Sally Hemings story. For details of the Jefferson/Sally Hemings story, see http://www. monticello.org/plantation/hemingscontro/hemings-jefferson_contro.html [Accessed 10 March 2008].

71. Edwards, *The Life of Olaudah Equiano*, 3.
72. Ibid.
73. Curtin, *Image of Africa*, 51.
74. Ibid., 53.
75. Edwards, *The Life of Olaudah Equiano*, 4.
76. Ibid., 5. Also, historians tell us that one of the items of trade in the slave trade was liquor—spirits—such as rum. This point was also highlighted for me by one of the docents at the Fort at El Mina, Ghana during my visit to the Fort in 2006. Equiano's comments here can be read almost tongue-in-cheek.
77. Edwards, *The Life of Olaudah Equiano*, 5.
78. Ibid., 6.
79. Scholars have suggested that Equiano borrowed his material from other travel narratives; most critics point to Benezet.
80. Curtin, *Image of Africa*, 60.
81. Curtin cites John Wesley, *Thoughts Upon Slavery* (London, 1872), 60.
82. Edwards, *The Life of Olaudah Equiano*, 2.
83. Ibid., 6.
84. Ibid., 7.
85. Curtin, *Image of Africa*, 61.
86. George E. Boulukos, "Olaudah Equiano and the Eighteenth-Century Debate on Africa," 2.
87. Suzan M. Marren, "Between Slavery and Freedom: The Transgressive Self in Olaudah Equiano's Autobiography," *PMLA* 108, no. 1 (Jan, 1993), 94.
88. Edwards, *The Life of Olaudah Equiano*, 11.
89. See Paul Edwards, "Textual Notes to the *Narrative*," (173) for more explanation. See also bell hooks' discussion of black people's assertion of voice as an act of resistance in *Talking Back: Thinking Feminist, Thinking Black* (Cambridge: South End Press, 1989).
90. Edwards, *The Life of Olaudah Equiano*, 15.
91. Ibid., 15.
92. Ibid.
93. See Allison, *The Interesting Narrative*.
94. Edwards, *The Life of Olaudah Equiano*, 30.
95. Ibid., xix.

CHAPTER 2

THE IGBO ORIGINS OF OLAUDAH EQUIANO

CATHERINE OBIANUJU ACHOLONU

The Trans-Atlantic Slave Trade, which began in the fifteenth century, saw millions of Africans transported in slave ships across the Atlantic Ocean to the Americas, and was in its boom from the sixteenth to the late eighteenth centuries. With the connivance of some local chiefs and individual profiteers on the African side, African men and women were traded as commodities for over four hundred years. By 1750, England, Holland and France had become leading slave traders, surpassing Portugal. By 1776, there were slaves in every American colony from New Hampshire to Georgia. By the 1780s, "the Atlantic Slave Trade was a well-established mercantile system connecting Africa, Europe and the Americas in a web of (illicit) commerce."[1] Slavery became the mainstay of European and American economies, as well as the main domestic workforce, until the middle of the nineteenth century. The United States prohibited the slave trade after 1808, a year after Britain outlawed slavery.

   Much has been written about the role of Europeans in the abolition of the slave trade, but no corresponding attention has been paid to the role of Africans in the abolition agenda. However, the role of Olaudah Equiano, the Igbo ex-slave whose autobiography contributed to the abolition course has been noted. My concern in this paper, however, is the recent discourse on Equiano's Igbo origins and the broader implications of that for his identity as an Igbo and his impact on Atlantic world history. This analysis will be placed in the context of my previous findings on the subject published under the title *The Igbo Roots of Olaudah Equiano*, and more recent evidence that further confirms his Igbo roots.

EQUIANO AND THE ABOLITION OF SLAVERY IN BRITAIN

While the fire of abolition was raging in North America, the slave trade remained deeply entrenched in Great Britain. It was against this backdrop that Olaudah Equiano, himself an African from the Igbo ethnic group in what is today Nigeria, took up the struggle to abolish slavery from England as a personal challenge. His journeys through the Americas as a slave and later as a sailor's boy had exposed him to the horrors of slavery in that part of the world, but it had also fired him with the flame of the American anti-slavery movement. In 1781 when Luke Collingwood, captain of the slave ship *Zong*, ordered 133 sick slaves drowned in order to claim insurance benefits, Equiano broke the story to the British public, causing national outrage and subsequently giving teeth to the abolitionist movement in Great Britain. The most notable abolitionists who were strengthened by Equiano's anti-slavery activism in the wake of the *Zong* massacre were Thomas Clarkson, a college student at Cambridge; the prolific Reverend James Ramsay; William Wilberforce, the powerful orator and parliamentarian; and Olaudah Equiano himself.[2]

In 1785, a damaging statement by a London slave-merchant, James Tobin, one of abolitionism's harshest critics, incensed Equiano, who hitherto had been operating from behind the scenes, into making a public statement in condemnation of slavery. Tobin, in a vitriolic attack on Reverend Ramsay's *Essay on the Treatment and Conversion of Slaves in the Sugar Colonies* (1874), had insisted that blacks who were not slaves would not work, and that "out of the whole of this number, those who are not in livery are in rags; and such as are not servants, are thieves or mendicants." Tobin's argument that blacks were fit only to be slaves infuriated Equiano into firing back from what had been his apparent anonymity. The argument was becoming personal because it raised questions about the personal integrity and character of the black man. Equiano responded and called Tobin "an invective fibber" in a letter to London's *Public Advertiser*. He apologized for having to descend to Tobin's level in order to give him the reply he evoked.[3]

From this point on, there was no more going back for Equiano. Having lived in slavery for ten years and known twenty years of freedom, and having been born on the African continent, Equiano saw his own life as a testament of slavery on the one hand, and on the other hand, a witness to the integrity, civility and humanity of the black man that were being called to question. Having experienced every aspect of slavery on the three continents—Africa, the Americas, and Europe—Equiano embarked upon his autobiography, using his own life-story as an instrument to demonstrate the reality, the horror and the savagery of building an entire civilization upon human merchandize and upon man's enslavement of his fellow man. He and another former slave, a fellow Igbo living in London, Ottabah Cugoano, organized an intellectual war on slavery. Ottabah Cugoano's book published in 1787, *Thoughts and Sentiments on the Evils of Slavery,* was his attempt to expose the evils of slavery. His was the first such contribution by an African to the debate.

Two years after the publication of Ottabah Cuguano's work, Equiano's autobiography was published under the title *The Interesting Narrative of the Life of Olaudah Equiano, or Gustavus Vassa, The African, Written by Himself* (1789). In the book, Equiano presented himself not only as a victim of slavery, but more importantly, he gave the first detailed description of socioeconomic, cultural and political life in an African village from the point of view of an African and an ex-slave.

In the United States of America, *The Interesting Narrative* is recognized as the first great African-American slave narrative. Equiano was the only slave author who gave detailed insight into his native African nation, culture and lifestyle, including the lifestyles of the peoples among whom he traversed on the African continent. This gave his work the stamp of authenticity and even so was his impact on the English, American, and global society. His *Interesting Narrative* became an international bestseller, with eight English editions published before Equiano died in April 1797. The book also had an American, a French, a Dutch and a Russian edition, a feat no other work by an African or a Black had attained. In the United States and Britain, the book continued to be a political tool for the abolition of slavery and racism against Blacks well into the early nineteenth century. Equiano's fame and popularity continued to grow, and the records indicate that, eighty years after his death, he was still remembered as an influential abolitionist. The inscription "Olaudah Equiano, the African," was found on the tombstones of his daughter and son-in-law.

Equiano's voice was a key instrument for the Black anti-racism struggle in America, the Caribbean, Europe, and among African nationalists struggling against colonialism in the twentieth century. Equiano's poignant and proud portrayal of an African society gave Africans born in the Diaspora a sense of pride and cultural identity. Indeed, an African-American author and veteran of the Harlem Renaissance noted the "whispered pride" with which African-Americans trying to reclaim their own history cited Equiano's *Narrative*.[4]

EQUIANO'S IGBOLAND AND ISSEKE IN PERSPECTIVE

In the first and introductory part of *The Narrative*, Olaudah Equiano gave some details about the customs and socio-cultural lifestyles of the natives of his country. His geographical description of the part of Africa where he was born indicates that he was born in West Africa, somewhere between Senegal and Angola, among a people he named "Eboe" (Igbo) in a town he spelt "Essaka" and situated a "very considerable" distance from the Kingdom of Benin. Equiano concluded that any subjection of his people to the kingdom of Benin must be "little more than nominal, for every transaction of government . . . was conducted by chiefs or elders of the place."[5] Equiano's description of the Kingdom of Benin is interesting. Benin, prior to the time of Equiano's birth, was already trading with the Portuguese. Equiano says that the kingdom was considerable in its extent, wealth, riches, agriculture, and the power of its king, as well as the number and warlike disposition of its inhabitants. Yet its influence was hardly felt in his own "Eboe" homeland of Essaka.

About the Igbo system of government, Equiano had written: "Those *Embrenche*, or chief men, decided disputes and punished crimes, for which purpose they always assembled together. The proceedings were generally short, and in most cases the law of retaliation prevailed."[6] In this short and cryptic description, Equiano demonstrated two different types of government found in pre-colonial Africa: namely, monarchy as in the case of Benin; and republican democracy as in the Igbo case, where elders deliberated together on affairs of the community and took decisions collectively.

Equiano described Igbo customs that existed, and still exist, among the Igbo people in Nigeria in detail. These include belief in one Supreme God, the creator of all, who lives in heaven; Igbo harvest festivals and offerings; as well as Igbo customs regarding marriage, housing, architecture, agriculture, and gender relations. Others include the Igbo system of government, legislature, language, commerce, medical system, military system, slavery, the involvement of the Aro in slavery, as well as the methods of enslavement and of protecting citizens from slavers. He described the Igbo social system, cuisine, dressing, the Igbo belief in reincarnation, et cetera - all or most of which have been corroborated through field work by scholars, including myself, who traced his claims to his home in Essaka.[7] He described the flora and fauna of the rainforest region where Igboland is located, emphasizing the oil-palm tree, a tree that produces wine, nuts and oil, which is specific to Nigeria and environs and whose general usage differs from one group to another. He highlighted, accurately, its diverse uses in the Orlu part of Igboland where Isseke has been located.

Interestingly, Isseke possesses some peculiarities of customs, known to Equiano, that also add to its identification as Equiano's actual homeland. They include female militancy and *ichi* scarification as a mark of manhood for boys, as the greatest symbol of nobility among elders, and as a prerequisite for joining the council of senators and judges. He noted Isseke as a nation of dancers and music-makers and a community of master smokers, where men, women, boys and girls indulge in pipe-smoking as a favorite pastime. Other customs include a militia community and a community of craftsmen and women: molders of pottery, spinners and weavers of cotton, blacksmiths and smelters of iron who produce their own ammunition and tools of tillage out of iron. Of great importance to Equiano and to any reading and apprecia-tion of his work is his overweighing emphasis on the Igbo facial scarifica-tion, *Igbu Ichi*, which he called "Embrenche." He described the customs of his native community of "Essaka," supplying minute details that have been found to tally with an uncanny exactitude with the customs of the little known town of Isseke in Ihiala, Anambra State, located on the Eastern side of the River Niger.[8] Equiano goes to such infinitesimal details as to correctly describe the color of Isseke earth, which is red, and the arrangement of the houses in their homesteads. He named the common crops and agricultural products of Isseke, indicating those that grow with and without culture. He described Isseke musical instruments and farming implements, mentioning details that would elude anyone but a native.

For a period of over two and half years, between 1986 and 1989, I conducted fieldwork in Isseke, verifying Equiano's claims (and again in 2006/2007) after Vincent Carretta claimed that Equiano was probably not born in Africa.[9] My findings confirmed that Equiano had first-hand knowledge of Isseke customs as indicated in *The Narrative*, a few examples of which are cited here: the number of offerings made after harvest before the new yam is eaten (two offerings); the kind of spices used in these particular offerings—bitter herbs, which Isseke people and their neighbors call *onugbu* and *utazi*; the Isseke common practice of marrying no more than two wives; veneration of the python; and Isseke traditional cloth of calico, usually dyed blue, that is spun, woven and dyed by Isseke women and which is still in use among Isseke elders. He also noted the act of kissing eatables and drinks before a buyer to erase the suspicion of poisoning, the absence of any river or spring in Isseke and the preponderance of wells in the town.[10]

Equiano had written that his name "Olaudah" signifies in Essaka language "vicissitude, or fortunate; also one favoured and having a loud voice and well spoken." Indeed the name Olaude is a common name in Isseke and means "a ring with a vibrating or loud sound, a fortunate person; it also implies a person with a loud voice and a person who will touch lives/go places (vicissitude)." Igbo names have prophetic meanings and the subsequent course of Equiano's life proved true to his native Igbo name. He wrote in *The Narrative:* "my father was one of those elders or chiefs I have spoken of, and was styled *Embrenche*, a term, as I remember, importing the highest distinction, and signifying in our language a mark of grandeur."[11] Olaudah thus revealed that he was descended from an Igbo noble family. As it was rare for sons of noblemen to be sold into slavery in Igboland and in Isseke, and as there was and still is only one Isseke noble family with a similar surname to that borne by Olaudah, our search quickly turned up the family of Ekwealuo (also pronounced Ekweanuo), a family of nobles and *Embrenche* whose name portrays that war-like disposition of Isseke people described by Olaudah. Ekwealuo means "when-we-mutually-agree-we-go-to-war."

Of recent, more light has been thrown on the name of Equiano's hometown. In his autobiography, he called it Essaka, which has been identified by various scholars as Isseke. More than that, Equiano, in a letter to the members of the British Senate dated 9 June 1788, wrote that he hoped to return to his "estate in Elese, in Africa." Dorothy Ukaegbu has identified Elese as a short form for Ala-Isse, "land of Isse," formed from a joining of two words, "'Ala' and 'Isse."[12] This is in tandem with the explanation given to me by the traditional ruler of Isseke, His Highness Igwe Emma Nnabuife, regarding the origin of the word Isseke. "Isseke," he said, "is a short form for Isi-Eke-Ise. Over the years, the word was shortened to Isi-Eke and then to Isseke."[13] Equiano's privileged knowledge of the etymology of the word 'Essaka' is added proof that he was indeed a native speaker. *Isi-Eke-Ise* means, 'Head-of-Five-Eke.'[14] Igwe Emma Nnabuife explained further that there are five leading *Eke* deities in Isseke. The deity that has its shrine in Isseke is the leading deity of the five. Its name is *Ogwugwu*. It is because of this deity that Isseke earned its name *Isi-Eke-Ise* (Head-of-Five-Deities).

Accordingly, the Isseke market, which is held daily (one of the very few daily markets in traditional Igbo-land), does not function on *Eke* day, which is regarded as the day spirits and powerful wizards and god-men from all over Igboland buy and sell at the market. *Ala-Ise*, "Land of Five," misspelled by Equiano as *Elese*, would thus be a native code name for the hallowed Land-of-Five Deities that has come to be known as Isseke, a code-name known to and only used by indigenes. The fact that Equiano used this native code word in a letter he personally made out to the British Parliament is further proof that he was a veritable son of *Ala-Ise* (Isseke) soil.

Bright Nwabueze Ekwealu who possesses the unique Ekwealuo head and facial features. © *Catherine Acholonu*

Olaudah Equiano

Fidelis Ekwealuo © *Catherine Acholonu*

All through the two and half years during which I undertook the field work of searching out Olaudah Equiano's Igbo roots, I had thought the most I could do would be to make a likely identification of his town by virtue of the instances of customs he described in his book. I hardly believed that I would actually find members of his family. Therefore, nothing prepared me for the shock of getting to Isseke and coming face to face with actual living family members who not only bore the same surname with him, Ekweanuo/ Ekwealuo, but actually had the same facial features: a fourteen year old boy named Bright Ekwealuo whose facial features were the same as those of young Equiano preserved in the latter's portrait at the Royal Albert Memorial Museum, Exeter, UK; Fidelis Ekwealuo, a grand nephew of Olaudah; and Oliver Ekwealuo, another cousin of Fidelis. My meeting with Fidelis Ekwealuo was my confirmation that I had found Olaudah Equiano's family.

Further enquires revealed that Olaude Ekwealuo was a prince, for he belonged to one of the two ruling houses of Isseke. Ekwea*l*uo is also pronounced Ekwea*n*uo. The shift from -*l*- (used in Orlu dialect) to –*n*- (used in Onitsha dialect) might have been affected by Olaudah himself. This kind of shift is common when Orlu Igbo encounter a larger Igbo community. To this day, whenever this happens, dialectal differences usually shift in favor of Onitsha, which is considered sweeter to the ear.

ISSEKE RESEARCH AND A GRAND CONSPIRACY AGAINST *THE IGBO ROOTS*

During the years while my research was going on, I was publishing my findings in the local newspapers. When they were published in *The Guardian* newspaper, with the pictures of Bright Ekwealuo and Olaudah Equiano, the Nigerian public was highly impressed by them. An article titled "The Home of Olaudah Equiano: A Linguistic and Anthropological Search," followed in the *Journal of Commonwealth Literature*.[15] The editor of the *Journal of Commonwealth Literature* considered the results so important that he made contact with Paul Edwards, the European authority on Equiano, and with the British Council, recommending that my research be supported. Between 1987 and 1989, I continuously shared my findings with Edwards. Edwards' personal letters to me affirmed my conclusions.[16]

He proposed a joint project that would result in a book on Equiano from three angles—part I, Equiano in Africa (by me), part II, Equiano in America and part III, Equiano in Britain (by Edwards) who had undertaken to invite Henry Louis Gates, then at Cornell, to do the American section. He hoped that this project would give my work the attention it deserves "I think your case is very persuasive," he wrote.

Paul Edwards did make good his promise to bring me to the Commonwealth Literature Conference and arranged for the British Council to organize a lecture tour of universities and culture centers in Britain for me to share my findings with the academic and cultural community as part of the *Olaudah Equiano Bicentenary Celebrations* in Britain in December 1989. Between November 19 and December 6, I delivered talks at the Commonwealth Institute, London; the University of London, School of Oriental and African Studies; the University of Exeter; the University of Hull; the University of Reading; the University of York and at the East London Polytechnic—all thanks to Paul Edwards.

At this same period, the *Olaudah Equiano Bicentennial Celebration* was going on in the USA. The United States Information Service (USIA), with the support of Henry Louis Gates Jr., invited me and sponsored my trip to the USA under the *American International Visitors' Program* to share my findings with scholars there. I gave the Keynote Speech at the *Olaudah Equiano Bicentennial Symposium*, University of Utah. I visited and shared my findings and research materials with the Library of Congress; the Moorland Spingarn Collection and Afro-American Research Center, Howard University; the Afro-American Historical Museum and the Charles Blockson Afro-American Collection, Temple University, Philadelphia. I also gave an interview to the *Voice of America*. I gave lectures to staff and students at the Africana Studies and Research Center at Cornell University, Ithaca. I gave a talk to a class at Harvard University. In January 1989, on the advice of the USIS (US Information Service), Nigeria, I had written to Henry Louis Gates Jr. informing him about my work. The USIS, which was sponsoring the trip, had scheduled a TV discussion program in Lagos on Equiano for Henry Louis Gates and me. On February 2, 1989, Henry Louis Gates wrote me, indicating clearly that Paul Edwards had informed him that I had indeed found Equiano's birthplace. Gates wrote that he had read my work and was impressed.[17] Louis Gates did not eventually join the planned excursion to Isseke. He and Edwards had been harangued into changing their minds about my work.

During my trip to the UK, the widely read *West Africa* magazine published in Britain carried an interview with me on three full pages of the magazine. When the issue came out, Paul Edwards, my major supporter, suddenly turned against me through people like Olu Oguibe. Oguibe attended my "Olaudah Equiano Roots Research" workshop at the Royal Albert Memorial Museum, Exeter UK and distracted the proceedings for more than forty minutes by engaging me in a word duel, arguing that I had done nothing new because Chinua Achebe was the first to mention that Equiano's "Essaka" was Isseke and that the credit for that discovery should go to him. Then came Paul Edwards' two articles: one in *The Guard-ian* (Nigeria) and the other in *Research in African Literatures*, in which he simply "dismissed" my work! In the hurried review of my book that he pub-lished in *Research in African Literatures* 21, (1990), 124-28, he stated that in two letters written to him by Chinua Achebe twenty-six years earlier (in the early sixties), Achebe had told him that "Equiano's birthplace might be "a village called Iseke in the area I have always suspected to be the home of Equiano. The village is dead on the Onitsha-Orlu boundary, about six miles from Ihiala ...." One would have thought this would lend credence to my own conclusions, but Paul Edwards termed my work "a pioneering attempt to map out the Igbo world of Equiano, a task which can only be carried out adequately by Igbo scholars." He went on to say, "We have in fact discussed together the matters I raise here and she knows that I am as hopeful as anyone that she is on the track of valuable information." This was false, as all his letters to me clearly reveal. He continued, "The fact that a widely read journal of some standing (meaning the *West Africa* magazine) gives lengthy but uncritical consideration to this book, confirms for me the need to examine it more closely if students in the field are not to be misled."[18] Some even went to the extent of accusing me of plagiarizing Achebe and Edwards, all in the bid to discredit my work.

For the avoidance of doubt, Chinua Achebe has never done any research on Equiano; he had merely expressed a personal feeling that he did not substantiate. Even so, I had listed Achebe among those who had "contributed constructively to the debate about Equiano's (Isseke) home-land."[19] No one can accuse me of not giving due credit to Achebe and to other Igbo scholars, who, like him, had speculated on the likelihood of Essaka being the same as Isseke.

Attacks were suddenly coming from the most unexpected angles. Henry Louis Gates, whom I was meeting for the first time at the Olaudah Equiano Bicentennial Symposium at the University of Utah, where I gave a Keynote Address, after listening to my speech, stood up and tried to dismiss my presentation and my findings. Shortly after all this, Paul Edwards had a stroke and died soon afterwards, and I was not in any mood to launch a counter attack on a dying man. I was also convinced that Paul was under pressure by forces he could not afford to ignore. I decided that time alone would reveal the truth.

OLAUDAH EQUIANO'S IGBO ROOTS AND THE CARRETTA CONTROVERSY

Until recently, the contributions I made towards Equiano research published in *The Igbo Roots* and in a number of journal articles removed the question of whether Olaudah Equiano is from Isseke from the realm of speculation. However, by defacing my work, Achebe apologist Paul Edwards inadvertently brought the matter of Equiano's Igbo origin back to the realm of speculation. Vincent Carretta, intent on sensationalizing the whole matter, argues:

> Recent biographical discoveries cast doubt on Equiano's story of his birth and early years. The available evidence suggests that the author of *The Interesting Narrative* may have invented rather than reclaimed an African identity . . . Baptismal and naval records say that he was born in South Carolina around 1747. If they are accurate, he invented his African childhood and his much-quoted account of the Middle Passage on a slave ship.[20]

This question is summarized in a recent article titled, "Autobiography and Memory: Gustavus Vassa Alias Olaudah Equiano, The African" by Paul E. Lovejoy.[21] Lovejoy writes, "Vassa was engaged in so noble a cause as the freedom and salvation of his enslaved and unenlightened countrymen. If he was not born in Africa, then he lied, perhaps with noble political motives." In the same article Lovejoy presents a most poignant case against taking the baptismal record seriously, revealing through his own research that the South Carolina entry emanated from Equiano's god-mother, Mary Guerin, most probably against Equiano's will, and that notwithstanding this entry, the same Mrs. Guerin testified on more than one occasion to the veracity of Equiano's African birthplace. Accordingly, Lovejoy asks, "Are we to believe the testimony of his god-mother in St. Margaret's church at the time of his baptism or her later testimony confirming his African birth? . . . Why doubt Vassa's own account of his birth rather than what is registered" in these controversial records and "muster books."[22] One can only concur that, going by the facts of the case, where there is a lie in the case of the baptismal record, it is not to be attributed to Equiano, but rather to his godmother. Going by this Guerin example, we must conclude with Lovejoy that the *Racehorse*/muster record might equally have been influenced and contrived by some one or other who felt that a birthplace outside Africa was "more respectable." This is the more sensible and objective approach to the issue.

The question of "if" has been answered by the fact that the South Carolina birthplace may have been fabricated at the time of young Equiano's baptism by his overbearing godmother, Mrs. Guerin, and is being carried forward by default. This ought to have been the end of the matter, but unfortunately, it is not. Equiano spent more than twenty of the last years of his life telling everyone he was "*Olaudah Equiano, the African,*" signing his signature as "*Olaudah Equiano/Gustavus Vassa, the African.*" This is evident in the sample of Equiano's signature written in his own handwriting.[23] Even his tombstone/epitaph and obituary and those of his wife and children, including that of a son-in-law who never met him, still bore the allusion to their relationship to "*Olaudah Equiano, The African*" more than eighty years after his death.

Surely the records Carretta claims to have discovered cannot be more legitimate than Equiano's own handwritten identification of himself, his authorized epitaph, the knowledge of members of his own immediate family, and other existing official and personal records that say unequivocally that Equiano was born on the African continent. He referred to Africa as his birthplace in his autobiography *The Interesting Narrative* and in letters to the British parliament. Carretta himself has published most of these memoirs. Why then should he or anyone single out the few, the very few, records that just happen to say the contrary? By questioning Equiano's African origin and as such bringing his overall credibility to question because of questionable records, all "Middle Passage" experiences have been brought to question. Until a matching South Carolina birth record and actual birth certificate, as well as an actual birthplace and existing relatives in South Carolina, are located, Carretta's conclusions will remain mere speculations. If Equiano was born in the USA, whether under the name of Equiano or Vassa, the family records would still be there since African slaves were never allowed to retain their African names. In the case of slaves born in the USA, it would have amounted to grave peril for parent and a child of slave parents to bear African names. A slave going by an African name (Olaudah) and surname (Equiano) could not have been born in the USA.

Moreover, Carretta's much touted baptismal record of a South Carolina birthplace was judged by those who investigated it physically as very vague and lacking in vital facts that would have made it authentic. Lovejoy argues that "the entry in the baptismal registry is curious and deviates from the other entries in the records, which give full name of child, . . . as well as the first names of father and mother and the date of birth or age if not an infant."[24] A baptismal entry that is lacking in such vital details as full name of the child, names of mother and father, and date of birth should actually not be worth anyone's second look, unless of course, that someone is an *enfant terrible* hungry for fame, with loads of vested interests and ulterior motives. In fact, all that the Equiano baptismal certificate discovered by Carretta says is "A black born in South Carolina 12 years old."[25]

What I am saying, is that we must have proof beyond all reasonable doubt, for this is what scientific research is all about. Nothing less will suffice. For this to be acceptable, the new evidence must also disprove Equiano's very elaborately illustrated and long-drawn claim to an Eboe (Igbo)/Essaka (Isseke) homeland. In the final analysis, such research must consider Igboland and must disprove the mounting evidence of Equiano's Igbo/Isseke heritage. Carretta should further research in, failing which his findings cannot be taken as conclusive.

Equally worrisome is the fact that Carretta's description of the Igbo, in his choice of words, sources and quotations, exhibit evidence of ethnic profiling of the Igbo people to a point that suggests that the major problem that these scholars have with Equiano is that he was an Igbo man. Carretta's heaping of invectives on the Igbo has no bearing on the issue in question and could only have been employed as a means of giving a dog a bad name to hang it. Igbo people are well known around the world since Pre-colonial times. The fact that their sense of self-worth, character, dignity, industry and enterprise is hardly matched by any other African group is also well known. Their homegrown democratic system of governance, highly organized social systems, modes of worship, customs and ways of life popularized in Equiano's works and in the world-famous novels of Chinua Achebe have in no small way been a source of pride to all Africans in the home continent and in the Diaspora. Yet, leaning on obscure and questionable historical sources, Carretta highlights, without criticism Brian Edwards (1793) descriptions of the Igbo as "the lowest and most wretched of all the nations of Africa," repeating that "their despondency of mind; which are so great as to occasion them very frequent to seek in a voluntary death, a refuge from their own melancholy, ... the Eboes are in fact more truly savage than any nation of the Gold Coast."[26]

These conclusions about Igbo ways of life are easily recognizable as falsehoods. For Carretta often uncritically employs questionable evidence, such as Granger's (1764) claim that "the teeth-fil'd *Ibbos* . . . as they are more commonly called . . . make good slaves when bought young; but are in general foul feeders, many of them greedily devouring the raw guts of fowls, they also feed on dead mules or fowls."[27] In fact, Equiano had written about a people who filed their teeth and ate without washing their hands. He described them as savage even in their sexual behavior, concluded that he was appalled at their way of life, which he said was at variance with that of his Igbo native country, and stated that they spoke a language he did not understand![28] Researchers have generally concluded that these were the Ibibio. Yet Vincent Carretta called them Igbo. For the avoidance of doubt, I quote Equiano's account of these people in full:

> All nations I had hitherto passed through resembled our own in their manners, customs and language; but I came at length to a country, the inhabitants of which differed from us in all those particulars. I was very much struck with this difference, especially when I came among a people who did not circumcise, and ate without washing their hands. They . . . fought with their fists among themselves. Their women were not so modest as ours, for they ate and drank and slept with their men . . . The people ornamented themselves with scars, and likewise filed their teeth very sharp. They wanted sometimes to ornament me in the same manner, but I would not suffer them; hoping that I might some time be among people who did not thus disfigure themselves, as I thought they did.[29]

The reasons given by Carretta as to why Igbo slaves were unpopular, and postulations as to why some would take their own life rather than live in slavery, are also false and contrived. The true reason, which has been stated in many texts, not the least of which was Hugh Crow's (1790), is that the Igbo, especially the *ichi* bearers, were noblemen, gentlemen, and sons of noblemen, "and having seen better days, would not suffer themselves to be enslaved."[30]

Equiano's knowledge of the Igbo language, for which reason he was deployed while serving under the slaver Dr. Irving to recruit and manage slaves of Igbo origin (referred to as "his own countrymen"), has been amply emphasized by Paul Lovejoy. He argues that Equiano's selection for this venture is proof that Equiano was of Igbo birth, since the success of the project depended on his fluency in the Igbo language and the ability to interact in the native language and gain the confidence of fellow Igbo fresh from the home continent. Lovejoy argues that Equiano could never have acquired his proficiency in Igbo in South Carolina "where there were few Igbos."[31] What I can add here is that this bit of information supplies proof that Equiano was a fluent speaker of the Igbo language and was conversant with Igbo ways of life. More than that, the records refer to Igbo slaves as Equiano's "own countrymen." I do not think we need more proof than these that Equiano was an Igbo. How many African-Americans speak any African language fluently? The speaking of vernacular African languages among slaves was forbidden in the USA by slave owners and attracted severe penalties. Therefore, Equiano could not have acquired proficiency in Igbo in any part of the United States.

Equiano insisted he was born *in* Africa, gave the name of his African family and that of his hometown, described accurately and in detail the customs of his native African village and of the Igbo group, was accepted among Igbo slaves as a fellow Igbo and spoke Igbo fluently. In fact, the missing bits of information on the Carretta baptismal record actually lend credence to the fact that Equiano was born in Africa because children born in Africa before the introduction of written records (which commenced around 1850) had no recorded birth-date, contrary to what would obtain in South Carolina at the same period. If Equiano had been born in South Carolina, he would certainly know his birth date and his parent's first names; and his parents would have had two names each in the baptismal record. The fact that his parents did not have "first names," indicating that they had one name each instead of two, is again strong proof of his African Isseke/Igbo birth, for in Igboland married men possess only single names and do not bear surnames. In the Orlu area of Igboland, where Isseke is located, it is customary for wives to drop their first given names after marriage and to be renamed by their husbands. The names given them by their husbands are pet names or romantic names such as *Ukwudiya* (Husband's Legs), *Obidiya* (Husband's Heart), and *Ihudiya* (Husband's Face). These names replace the woman's real name. Equiano could not have known his mother's real name and would have been hard put to give his father's pet name for his mother in the Baptismal record. The fact that the Baptismal record did not have a name for Equiano's mother is yet further proof that Equiano was born, not in America, but in Africa.

Equiano's very detailed and knowledgeable description of the process of *Ichi* scarification and its meaning and importance to the Igbo nation is also strong evidence of his Igbo origin, for Equiano's was the first recorded description of the process of *ichi* scarification in history. His description tallies very closely with that given to me in elaborate form by Isseke elder Igwe Agabaka,[32] which again is in tandem with that rendered by eminent Igbo anthropologist, M. A. Onwuejeogwu, illustrating the process of *ichi* scarification among the Nri people who are important custodians of Igbo culture.[33] The accounts given by Isseke elders, Onwuejeogwu and Chinua Achebe agree with Equiano's that *ichi* (which in most instances is synonymous with the *ozo* title) is the title of greatness and well-being borne by the rulers/elders/senators/judges/*ndi-ichie* of the land, that it is facilitated by rich men for their teenage children, and that it is the symbol of manhood and dignity. Within the same period that Equiano wrote his book (1790s), other authors like J. Wilson and Hugh Crow made some mention of *ichi* scarification, but without the graphic details of the process Equiano provided. Hugh Crow wrote that, "The *Breeches*, so called from the word *Breche*, signifying gentleman ... or son of a gentleman ... undergoes the operation to distinguish his rank by having the skin of his forehead brought down from the hair so as to form a ridge or line from the temple." Crow's *Breeche*, contrary to Lovejoy's opinion, is actually a transcription of the Igbo word *Mgburichi* (Equiano's *Embrenche*) which when pronounced goes with a double [i] sound, a sound, which in English Alphabet is represented by the letter /e/. The Igbo letter and sound /gb/, which does not exist in the English language, is usually rendered with the letter /b/, as we also find in Equiano's transcription of the word "Igbo" as "Eboe." I have reason to suspect that Hugh Crow's "Breeche" might have been coined directly from Equiano's *Embrenche* and that the phenomenon might only have attracted his keen interest after Equiano's book was published and was commanding national, even global attention.

Another proof of Equiano's Igbo origin and actual experience of the Middle Passage is the fact that he knew about a very remote and, until recently, unknown town of Tinimah (which he called Tinmah), where he claimed to have been bought by a widow. His description of the geographical location of Tinimah and the landscape of the place have been found to be accurate.

Only recently did Dorothy Ukaegbu locate Tinimah in Bonny in the Niger Delta, Nigeria. I have confirmed her findings. Tinimah and the twin town of Finimah attracted media attention only recently when the Nigerian government cited a Liquefied Natural Gas project in this Niger Delta community and had to move the communities to another location. That was how Tinimah and Finimah first drew public attention. Other than that, Tinimah has remained unknown and unheard of to many outsiders except in Equiano's *Narrative*. Here again, Equiano's description was accurate, including the creeks, which he called rivulets; the cocoanut trees that formed and still form the vegetation of Tinimah; and the Ijaw coastal-dwellers of Bonny who still live, eat and sleep in their canoes. Equiano noted that the family who bought him in Tinimah spoke his language and treated him as their equal. Indeed, many of the inhabitants of this area of the Niger Delta were descended from former Igbo slaves, including the famous King Jaja of Opobo, who rose from the rank of a slave to become king of Opobo and one of the most famous monarchs of pre-colonial Nigeria. Here again is undisputed evidence that Equiano's middle passage was experienced and not fabricated.

CONCLUSION

This paper examined the Igbo roots of Olaudah Equiano, focusing on the cultural and ethnographic data from contemporary Isseke in present day Nigeria. The paper challenges the recent claims made by Vincent Carreta, whose book, *Equiano The African,* cast doubt on Equiano's birth in Igboland. We argue that contemporary evidence from Isekke and the Niger Delta of Nigeria support Equiano's claim of an African origin.

NOTES

1. Robert J. Allison, "Introduction," *The Interesting Narrative of the Life of Olaudah Equiano* (Boston and New York: Bedford/St Martin's, 1995).
2. For a fictional account of the Zong massacre, see Fred D'Aguiar, *Feeding the Ghosts* (New York: Harper Collins, 2000).
3. Allison, *The Interesting Narrative,* 12.
4. Ibid., 22.
5. Ibid., 34.
6. Ibid., 34-5.
7. See Catherine O. Acholonu-Olumba, *The Igbo Roots of Olaudah Equiano (Revised Edition with Reply to Vincent Carretta)* (Abuja: Afa Publications, 2007).
8. See Acholonu-Olumba, *The Igbo Roots,* 27ff.
9. Vincent Carretta, *Equiano, The African: Biography of a Self Made Man* (Athens: University of Georgia, 2005).
10. Acholonu-Olumba, *The Igbo Roots.*
11. Allison, *The Interesting Narrative,* 34.
12. *Isse* or *Ise* means "five." See *Las Vegas Review Journal,* 18 December, 2006.
13. Interview with His Highness Igwe Emmanuel Nnabuife, 2 January 2007.
14. *Eke* is the name of a leading deity in Equiano's part of Igbo-land: the deity associated with the *Eke* market day. (The Igbo have four market days, which make up the Igbo four-day week: *Eke, Orie, Afor and Nkwo.*
15. Catherine Acholonu, "The Home of Olaudah Equiano: A Linguistic and Anthropological Search," *Journal of Commonwealth Literature* 22, no. 1, (1987): 5-16.
16. These letters are published unedited and in their original form in the revised edition of *The Igbo Roots of Olaudah Equiano,* under Appendix iv.
17. See Figure 5 in Acholonu-Olumba, *The Igbo Roots,* revised edition, 308.
18. Paul Edwards, review of *The Igbo Roots of Olaudah Equiano* in *Research in African Literatures* 21 (1990): 124-28.
19. Acholonu-Olumba, *The Igbo Roots,* 1.

20. Carretta *Equiano, The African*, xiv and in "Why Equiano Matters," *Historically Speaking*, 2006.
21. See Paul Lovejoy, "Autobiography and Memory-Gustavus Vassa Alias Olaudah Equiano, The African," *Slavery and Abolition*, 27, 3 (2006): 317-347.
22. Lovejoy, "Autobiography," 17.
23. *The Igbo Roots*, 297. This was mailed to me by Paul Edwards.
24. Lovejoy, "Autobiography," 86.
25. Ibid., 6.
26. Carretta, *Equiano The African*, 311-312.
27. Ibid., 311.
28. Equiano, *The Interesting*, 53.
29. Allison, *Olaudah Equiano*, 53 (*emphasis mine*).
30. See Lovejoy, "Autobiography,"13.
31. Ibid., 13-14.
32. Acholonu-Olumba, *The Igbo Roots*, 197-200.
33. M. A. Onwuejeogwu, *An Igbo Civilization Nri Kingdom and Hegemony* (London and Benin City: Ethiopie Publishing Corporation, 1981), 80-1.

Chapter 3

Igbo Sense of Place and Identity in Olaudah Equiano's Interesting Narrative

Dorothy C. Ukaegbu

INTRODUCTION

The controversy pertaining to the nativity of Olaudah Equiano, a problem with many facets, reflects a deep vacuum in the halls of modern scholarship and academia. According to his 1789 autobiography, *The Interesting Narrative of the life of Olaudah Equiano, Gustavus Vassa, Written By Himself,* he was born in 1745 in Essaka, the present day Isseke, in Anambra State of Nigeria. According to Vincent Carretta, and later Paul Lovejoy, baptismal and naval records show a 1747 birth in South Carolina.[1] As a result, Equiano's claim of African birth is challenged.

This chapter examines the meanings of place and sentiments about home among the Igbo, especially as they relate to questions of identity. It focuses on Olaudah Equiano and his *Interesting Narrative* to illuminate the writer's senses of place, as well as meanings of *place* that can be deciphered, beyond a mere geographical location to include a sense of belongingness, and the philosophical, emotive, ideological, and contingent uses of place. It employs Paul Ricouer's hermeneutic principles of textual analysis,[2] and the phenomenological approaches used by Feld and Basso in their analysis of senses of place.[3] Sense of place and the meaning of home are particularly important at this time, in lieu of the controversy surrounding Equiano and his Igbo origin. It is important also in the context of African continuities in the Atlantic Diaspora, where the Igbo constituted a large proportion of enslaved Africans from the Bight of Biafra Hinterland. This paper argues that Equiano's ultimate goal in writing the narrative transcends his desire to end slavery; he sought to memorialize his African birth place, and in the process, reclaim his identity. Alluding to our common humanity by noting fundamental similarities shared by all cultures, including kinship, family, law, ways of governing and wresting a living from the environment, aesthetic sense, a belief in the supernatural, a system of communication, the use of cultural symbols, doctors, magicians and medicine men, etc, Equiano tried to show that slave and master inhabit a common place - the universe - and have equal rights to live as free human beings upon it. However, he affirmed that the Igbo occupy a specific niche in that universe, and Equiano was determined to recapture his "stolen" identity. Despite the similarities, Equiano also stressed the differences between his Essaka and other places, differences that would help identify his Eboe geographical place—the homeland. Indeed, the authenticity of a narrative does not depend on access to "total memory"—a recollection of all that occurred in a person's life. Equiano's inclusion of unique, identifiable symbols in the Igbo tradition of sense of place is sufficient credible evidence to support his claim of Igbo identity. In doing so, Equiano's narrative offers an opportunity to engage the issue of Igbo identity generally.

CHALLENGES TO EQUIANO'S AFRICAN ROOTS

There has been major disagreement over where Equiano was born, and the disagreement is of long standing. Some scholars and commentators contend that he was not born in Africa,[4] while others have supported his African birth.[5] There are also African scholars who believe that he was born in Africa, but squabble over where in Africa Equiano hails from. The first to challenge Equiano's African nativity were enemies of the abolitionist movement in Britain during his lifetime. Two London newspapers, the *Oracle* and the *Star*, charged that Equiano was born in the Danish Island of Santa Cruz, in the West Indies, rather than in Africa.[6] Equiano recognized that these attacks were racially motivated and warded off the attackers by reaffirming his African birth.[7]

The next wave of scrutiny came from contemporary Africanist historians, anthropologists, literary critics and other scholars, who in due course reached the consensus that his birthplace was Africa, although the exact location was unknown. Some were inclined to think it was the kingdom of Benin of the Edo cultural group of modern Nigeria because of Equiano's claim that his home was under the influence of Benin.[8] In *Facts into Fiction*, Steven Ogude challenged Equiano's Igbo origins, asserting that Equiano created "the fiction of the beautiful Essaka." He argued further that, "It is possible . . . that Essaka and Tinmah, the only two African towns specifically mentioned in the *Interesting Narrative* may have disappeared from the face of the earth." Initially, Ogude gave more credibility to Equiano's accounts about the Kingdom of Benin.[9] Nonetheless, in a 2003 conference held in the United Kingdom, Ogude conceded to Equiano's Igbo origins, but denied his Isseke birth, choosing Ikwuano, another Igbo territory in the present-day Abia state of Nigeria, as the place of Equiano's origin.[10]

According to L.O.I. Ogueze, however, oral accounts from Isseke and surrounding Igbo areas suggest that:

> Isseke was never under Benin Kingdom. However the fame of Benin was known even beyond Onitsha and other riverine communities like Atani, Ogbaru and Ossomari which claimed relationship of a kind with Benin and whose trading influence extended to Isseke . . . folkstories of Isseke and neighboring communities often spoke of *idu na oba* (stories about the Oba of Benin). It is therefore possible that Olaudah could have come to think of his Essaka as one of the districts of the great kingdom whose influence was limited to the folktales and moonlight stories.[11]

Yet for some Igbo areas, Benin influence was "real." According to the oral history of Ogwa, mercenaries from Benin who inhabited a section of Ogwa in the eighteenth century, during Equiano's time, led the Ogwa people in a decisive battle with other neighboring communities.[12] The role of Benin migrants in inter-clan wars could have led the Igbo to speak of Benin influence and dominance, and the young Equiano to declare that "our (Essaka) subjection to the king of Benin was little more than nominal."[13]

The disagreement over Equiano's nativity reached a climax when Vincent Carretta announced that he had discovered a baptismal record that stated that Equiano was born in South Carolina and a ship's muster roll that also mentions South Carolina.[14] Carretta argued that these discoveries cast doubt on the truthfulness of Equiano's *Interesting Narrative* and the belief that his family was actually located in the Southeastern region of Nigeria. Carretta's "evidence" is problematic. The content of the ship's muster roll raises more questions than answers. A Gustavus Weston rather than Gustavus Vasa was listed on the ship, *Racehorse*. According to Lovejoy, Gustavus Vasa indicated in the narrative that he was aboard the ship. But a Gustavus Weston claimed a South Carolina identity. Could there have been another individual with the same first name on the *Racehorse*?

The publication of Vincent Carretta's *Equiano the African: Biography of a Self-Made Man* rekindled the debate on Equiano's place of birth. In his article, "Autobiography and Memory: Gustavus Vasa, Alias Olaudah Equiano, the African," the Africanist historian Paul Lovejoy delved deeply into the question of Equiano's nativity through analysis of the narrative and found corroborative evidence from other historical sources that support Equiano's African birth. In his response to Lovejoy's article, Carretta maintained his stance. Lovejoy cited evidence from Hugh Crow's memoir, which states that slave traders who went to Bonny in the 1790's were averse to buying slaves who bore the *ichi* scarification marks of nobility with which Equiano was familiar.

Carretta's discoveries further exacerbated the controversy by impugning ethnographic research results. Catherine Acholonu's ethnographic findings that point to Isseke as Equiano's birth place were ignored. Carretta's unfamiliarity with the inner-workings of Igbo culture led him to view negatively Equiano's attempts at restoring his sense of place; and so, Carretta reduced Equiano's biography to a mere work of fiction.[15] Thus, the vacuum in scholarship on Equiano emanates from the failure of scholars to understand the African world he described. Equiano's values, his assertions and perceptions, sense of "place" and "belongingness" were not grasped as scholars groped for the substance of his account. The result of this dilemma has been contention from many perspectives, most of which do not sustain a coherent angle of consideration.[16] One angle that merits consideration is the criticism of Acholonu's work in terms of methodology. Among Carretta's criticisms is the issue of the longevity of the subjects upon which Acholonu relied for evidence. According to Carretta, it is not feasible for a person to live to be one hundred and fifty years old as Acholonu had calculated in the genealogy of her Isseke data.[17] This constitutes a methodological issue—one that calls for a reexamination of Equiano's genealogy.

Yet there is evidence of Equiano's African origin. Equiano's godmother, Mary Guerin; her brother; and friends attested to Equiano's lack of English when he arrived in Britain. When he was chosen to manage Irving's plantation, he planned to rely on his fluency in Igbo in his handling of Igbo slaves.

Lovejoy noted that Equiano disliked the slenderness of English women. Lovejoy's observation regarding Equiano's opinion is culturally significant in that it was a candid assessment by a person who grew up in the Biafran interior where fat was considered beautiful. Going into the fattening house, intended as part of a girl's rite of passage into womanhood, was common in the Niger Delta and some parts of Igboland. As a native, Equiano exhibited his cultural eye for beauty.

Another aspect of this debate is methodological. Carretta apparently disregarded *the validity of Africa's oral traditions*, particularly[18] the oral history of the Dimori kindred of Isseke that alludes to a little boy, Olaude, who was enslaved during the Atlantic slave trade. This omission is a return to a time when Africa's oral traditions were not admitted as a valid source of historical knowledge, and the continent was written off as a people with nothing but conjectural history.[19] Indeed, it appears that the proponents of Equiano's South Carolina identity are bent on dismissing any perspectives corroborating Equiano's African Identity and reasons why Equiano might have chosen to suppress his Igbo identity at any point.[20] It is also possible that Equiano, having lost all hopes of ever returning to Essaka, chose to list the Carolinas as a "new home base," the place he visited frequently. Although Equiano had bought himself out of slavery at the time of the muster roll, freedom for a slave did not necessarily mean security or immunity from re-enslavement and could have motivated him to distort his identity.[21]

The final part of this puzzle is the problem of translation and interpretation. First, Equiano's *Interesting Narrative* told of how he came to learn the English language. In his lifetime, Africa had no written languages nor had any of its languages been translated into English for him to use as resource. What Equiano did was to render from his Igbo memory the English equivalents of his African concepts while using "African" words for the Igbo terms that have no direct English equivalents, such as "Ah-Affoe-way-cah" and "embrenche"[22] This fact lies at the heart of the inability of non-Igbo scholars to understand Equiano's use of the English language to render cultural meanings from his Igbo world. For example, Alexander Byrd admits to finding Equiano's use of the terms, "Eboe," "country" and "nation," as well as other sections of the narrative dealing with his African life, to be "opaque" and "ambiguous."[23]

EQUIANO'S AFRICA AND ISSUES OF IDENTITY

Scholars writing on Equiano to date have yet to properly analyze his African world with regard to the issue of his identity. In the process of seeking his "place" and identity in Africa, Equiano's random usages of "Eboe," "country" and "nation" may have led to semantic misconceptions about their meanings and usages. His *Interesting Narrative* alludes to three interpretive contexts or worlds within which the semantic usages are rendered meaningful, his life experiences understood, and the multiple ways "place" was rendered in the text, as well as how they are tied to identity, are uncovered. The contexts include the world of the text as products of Equiano's memory; the New World in which he lived; and the world of the Igbo external to Equiano's active memory. This Igbo world has dual facets, one of which lives in Equiano's passive and unconscious memory and is inscribed in the text, and the other, the world of the Igbo outside of the text, involving cultural elements and symbols that Equiano did not include in the text nor remembered, but are nonetheless apparent.

In the European world in which Equiano lived, "nation" meant a relatively large group of people closely associated with one another by common descent, history, and language that set them apart as a distinct race of people.[24] In this earlier usage, the racial idea was stronger than any political affiliations. Equiano recognized the presence of different nationalities that lived in Britain, including Turks, Danish Islanders, Jews, and others. In contrast, "country" was a territory demarcated by topographical features, or the land of one's birth or citizenship.

In the Igbo world external to Equiano's memory, multifarious meanings of place existed and were inextricably linked to a person's personal and social identities, as well as to the social relationships with other members of the group, gods and ancestors, and to the land to which they belonged. Among the Igbo of the eighteenth century, *the "clan" was the country*. It was a distinct geopolitical unit with a unilineal descent system, characterized by consanguinity and shared residential grouping. It was one's own taproot or place where social identity was confirmed. This concept of clan puts in perspective Equiano's cognitive map in relation to his Igbo identity and his construction of the narrative. He used this geographical arrangement of Igbo territories to articulate Igbo social structure, and he applied it to other areas of the hinterland in his itinerary.

According to anthropologists, a sense of place begins with the natural environment—the land—where a person was born, and where the patrilineal or matrilineal kin—dead and living - reside.[25] For the Igbo, the land (*ala*) is the source of life - the center of one's existence. As a deity, *ala* is the custodian of the social and moral order.[26] She is revered as a goddess of fertility, who is also responsible for the production of crops and ensures the continuity of life by assisting barren women. Memories of the Igbo homeland included the environment: its people, inanimate objects, plant and animal life. Hence a person's personal identity is fixed by the environmental objects that reinforce one's attachment to the land.[27] According to Feld and Basso, these ethnographic features "register a full range of discursive and non-discursive modes of expression through which everyday and poetically heightened *senses of places* are locally articulated."[28]

A sense of belonging to the land is legitimized through the homestead (*mbara ezi*); this consisted of a cluster of houses placed to form a circle, with an open centre that allowed all kinds of social interaction. To be born in a homestead is to have a place, an identity. The homestead is the symbolic *Ama*, or the smallest family unit. The Igbo concept of *Ama* fits into the patrilineal ideology: the continued existence of a man's *Ama* is contingent upon the birth of a male offspring who would carry on his bloodline, the ultimate source of his social identity.

Anthropologist Uchendu notes that the underlying denominator in Igbo social relations is "human interdependence." This, he says, lies in "the realization that no individual or spirit is self-sufficient. Thus, human interdependence is a constant theme in the folklore of the Igbo,"[29] and is reflected in how Equiano presented his narrative. Through socialization, an Igbo child learns human interdependence by associating first with his *ikwu* (members of the homestead)—the in-group relations. Beyond the imme- diate *ikwu* kin group are higher level kin-group segments: the *umunna* (children of the same father) polity, and the *Oha* (general assembly), made up of several *umunna* polities. The clan as a whole corresponds to the *Oha*. The entire *Oha* can refer to themselves as *umunna* if the referent is the clan ancestor. Sometimes, based on contingency, the Igbo as a whole can refer to themselves as the *Oha*. "An Igbo without *umunna* is without citizenship both in the world of man and in the world of the ancestors."[30] In my view, all these units function as *psychological and social places* for the Igbo. They are emotive and provide a niche in the social and cultural arrangements, giving one a sense of place.

On the opposite side of the *ikwu* is the concept of *ibe*, defined as "the related outside body in the Igbo polity," that can include the whole world and expands or contracts as relationships shift. Njaka writes: "One of the main characteristics of the Igbo is to defend any *ikwu* member, whenever and wherever he is in trouble."[31] To be at home with oneself and with the Igbo, is to be in harmony with one's *ikwu*. This sense of belonging was the vehicle of social relations between Equiano and other slaves, as reflected in the *Interesting Narrative*.

Furthermore, there are other presences in the Igbo landscape—"things unseen"—gods and spirits;[32] an awareness of their presence enables the Igbo to have a sense of place. In contrasting the world of man and the world of spirits, Victor Uchendu writes:

There is the world of man peopled by all created beings and things, both animate and inanimate. The spirit world is the abode of the creator, the deities, the disembodied and malignant spirits, and the ancestral spirits. It is the future abode of the living after their death.[33]

These ethnographic features are linked to other aspects of sociocultural life and constitute the cultural core of understanding upon which the interpretation of the *Interesting Narrative* and possible confirmation of Equiano's identity hinges.

EQUIANO'S AGENCY, PLACE AND IDENTITY IN THE NARRATIVE

In the autobiographical context, identity is circumscribed in the representation of self and place. Human agency becomes the focal point for uniting self and place, notions of belonging, and identity. From a literary perspective, Balogun's work on *Self and Place in Equiano's Narrative*, is an analysis of how the "biographical or fictional self exists within the identified space."[34] Equiano's representation of his "self," his agency, is a story of his personhood: the meaning and significance of his name, his life as a typical child of the village, and his life experiences beyond the confines of Essaka. Balogun identifies the three social spaces or places in which Equiano's self-hood was played out. "Place" was discussed in phases, covering the period he lived as a free man in his homeland, Essaka, and the contexts in which his enslavement and liberation occurred. A number of social identities emerged out of these "places" and served as products of his self-creation. He defined himself as a native African, and transformed himself into a sailor, military aide, and a crew member on a scientific expedition. In Balogun's rendition, Equiano alternated between these social identities as a result of the specific situation in which he found himself.[35] Mieko Nishida notes that most enslaved Africans in the new world, in their attempts to re-create identity, capitalized on shared memories of freedom in their homelands in Africa, and used them to "construct and reconstruct their individual notions of freedom in their daily experiences of oppression and exploitation in the New World."[36] Equiano reconstructed traditional markers of manhood in his homeland by adopting similar social roles in the New World. The role of military aide, for example, corresponded to the role of warrior or protector he would have attained had he remained in Essaka. This work differs from Balogun's work by revealing the manner in which human agency is deployed in the construction of identities.

Indeed, notions of self and place are crucial in the construction of cultural identities. The merging of self, place, and identity is an interactive process that illuminates the salient features of identity (as revealed by Equiano's agency) and the non-salient features of identity in the *Interesting Narrative* (the unconscious representations of one's self and accompanying indices of cultural identity) in his rendering of a real or imagined Eboe place.

The narrative style of the *Interesting Narrative* indicates that Equiano considered his sense of bearing as paramount in tracing his Eboe identity. For him, Eboe, and finding Eboe's geographic place, were the key to the restoration of his identity. It is possible that Equiano used the terms "Eboe," "country," and "nation" as equivalents of geographical reality of his native land, a skill derived from his knowledge of Western geography. When Equiano said that he came from Abyssinia, he was aware that some referred to 'negroes,' especially Ethiopians[37] as members of the continent located at the other side of the hemisphere. At that time, the name Africa was also in use, and Equiano also referred to himself as an African in the *Interesting Narrative*. What became problematic for Equiano was where to situate Eboe in the vast continent of Africa. Equiano's perceived difficulty[38] in the use of "Eboe" was due in part to the lack of definable national/geographical enclaves in Africa during this period.

Equiano's numerous references to "Eboe" indicate that he developed a sense of a collective identity for enslaved Igbos.[39] Despite differences in dialects and other cultural traits, Igbo language was preeminent in the development of a collective identity. "Collective identity," Mieko Nishida argues, "emerges only when some individuals successfully recognize their common traits as a group, beyond differences, and connect with one another in opposition to others."[40] Given the multiplicity of languages from the various parts of Africa, and the English language of the New World, Igbo slaves spoke Igbo among themselves.[41] When Equiano assisted his masters in purchasing slaves, he spoke Igbo to the new arrivals as a means of identifying fellow Igbos. External appearance in the form of facial scarification marks of the Igbo and certain unifying cultural behaviors and attitudes fostered a sense of pan-Igbo identity; collective identity is an inevitable phenomenon in the face of adversity. Equiano's visits to the Carolinas are indicative of attempts to maintain social ties, although the details of his relationship with the Igbo slaves there were not emphasized in the narrative. Britain, the Danish Islands of the West Indies, and the Carolinas represented *imagined social places*, re-visioned by Equiano to 'replace' the Igbo place of Essaka.

Karen Leonard writes that collective identities are also shaped in the new country when immigrant populations create new representations of their new communities by seeking and elaborating upon similarities between their homeland and the new country.[42] In her view, "space and the "otherness" of the host society can be bridged by a continuing connection with and sense of one's own society."[43] The plantations became a re-visioned geographical landscape to represent farms in the old country. Similarly, in an effort to reconstruct the homeland, people whose sources of cultural identity reside outside the host country construct "new sites of memory"[44] based on shared cultural symbols. Expressions of connectedness to the sites of memory shape collective identities.

Among the cultural items brought to the New World by slaves were their religious symbols, gods and goddesses. In the West Indian environment in which Equiano lived, slaves built shrines for gods to reflect their African religions. Although a form of religious syncretism developed among African slaves, for the Eboe slaves, the cult of *Amadioha* was symbolic of their shared experience. It functioned as a psychological and literal place of solace for seeking retributive justice wherever they were, as Equiano showed in the narrative.[45] When the Igbo was faced with a serious infraction at the hands of others, they called down curses on their enemies—"May *Amadioha* strike you!" One of the roles of *Amadioha* was to exercise judicial functions. As the executor of justice, *Amadioha* was swift in punishing offenders by striking them with lightning. Anyone struck with lightning was believed to have committed an offense no one knew about, of which *Amadioha* alone was cognizant. Equiano sought divine intervention when faced with a rueful plight on a voyage to Santa Cruz. Three bags of fruit belonging to him and his companion (another slave), which they intended to sell, were taken away by two white men who also threatened and swore at them. Equiano narrates:

> In our consternation, we went to the commanding officer of the fort…but we obtained not the least redress . . . I now, in the agony of distress and indignation, wished that the *ire of God* in *his forked lightening* might transfix the cruel oppressors among the dead.[46]

Those reading Equiano's biography from an Igbo point of view will perceive that Equiano harbored a peculiar sense of place that harkens back to his Igbo universe. He demonstrated this sense of place in his use of words, in his descriptions of the Igbo environment, in his relationship with his fellows, as well as in the ideas coming from his experiences. He expressed his Igboness through psychological identity and gave evidence of continued attachment to Igbo culture in a way that enabled him to make legitimate claims to an Igbo identity.

In "The Invisible Chi in Equiano's Interesting Narrative," Paul Edwards and Rosalind Shaw state: "At the centre of Equiano's expressions of faith is his *sense of a personal place* in a scheme of divine providence."[47] Edwards and Shaw recognized that Equiano's constant references to destiny, providence, and faith fit into the Igbo concept of *Chi* (a spiritual entity or personal god, often perceived as a person's double). As the determiner of destiny, a person's *chi* acts as the intersecting force that connects the mundane with the spiritual, wherein the core values of Igbo culture - "'individuality,' 'achievement,' a belief in 'destiny' - are linked to the supreme being and creator, *Chukwu* or *Chineke.*"[48] In addition to Edward's and Shaw's views, Igbo ethnography reveals that the *Chi* controls, protects, directs, and redirects an individual's life. In collaboration with one's *Chi*, a person's aspirations are realized. Individuals who fail to live up to cultural expectations are believed to have been abandoned by their *chi*. But in reality, the *chi* remains dormant, and can be activated at any time: *Onye kwe, Chi ya ekwe* (One has to agree with his *Chi*). Igbo identity appears as a direct consequence of the role of the *chi* in a person's life. Alienation of one's *Chi* means a disconnection from the Igbo symbolic place and subsequent loss of identity. Loss of face in the society negates a person's identity, leading to depreciating remarks from others such as, *iwu kwa nwa afo Igbo*? (Are you truly a uterine child of the Igbo?) In such circumstances, securing a place of honor in the world of the dead becomes an elusive dream. Adherence to core values increases one's sense of place and paves the way for a continued identity. The *chi* provides a sense of continuity from the literal Igbo place (life on earth) to the cosmological place—the world of the dead. An Igbo seeks to create a niche (or place) in the cosmological realm. Anthropologist Uchendu wrote: "For the Igbo, life on earth is a link in the chain of status hierarchy which culminates in the achievement of ancestral honor in the world of the dead."[49]

In *The Interesting Narrative*, Equiano laid claims to his Igbo identity by seeking foremost to realign himself with the cosmological realm in a manner that is truly Igbo. By regarding himself "as a particular favorite of Heaven," he is reiterating the Igbo belief that his affairs were controlled by cosmic forces. Statements such as "what faith had decreed no mortal on earth could prevent," "whatever fate had determined for me must come to pass . . . ," portray a style of discourse that is characteristically Igbo. In *Veiled Sentiments*, Abu Loghod[50] states that the particular ways in which individuals engage in self-presentation in discourse have their basis in "cultural ideals" and the revelation of one's "inner reality." Among the Igbo, cultural ideals that focus on the value system of society, that is, those that express commonly held ideas and beliefs that govern behavior, are encoded in everyday conversations. One's inner reality is also revealed in daily dialogues. According to Uchendu, Igbo people deem it "necessary for people to live transparent lives."[51] Hence, the preeminent theme in Igbo discourse is transparency. In keeping with his Igboness, Equiano sought to present himself as such. Through discourse, an Igbo engages in *Ituogu*, defined by Uchendu as affirmation of innocence. It is a conscious and oftentimes unconscious embodiment of the art of conversation.

Equiano relied on memories of his natural environment to identify the Igbo place. Equiano recalled an incident:

> I had observed that my father's house was towards the rising of the sun. I therefore determined to seize the first opportunity of making my escape. . . an unlucky event happened . . . One morning, while I was feeding some chickens, I happened to toss a small pebble at one of them, which hit it on the middle, and directly killed it... I ran into the bush thicket that was hard by and hid myself in the bushes . . . they searched . . . but, not finding me, they thought I had run away. . . . In that part of the country (as well as ours) the houses and villages were skirted with woods, or shrubberies, and the bushes were so thick, that a man could readily conceal himself in them, so as to elude the strictest search.[52]

A new vision of "country" emerges from this passage. "In that part of the country (as well as ours)" is indicative of an expansive whole. This whole encompasses the territorial unit in which his enslavement in Africa took place—the Bight of Biafra and its hinterland. He had developed a sense of the Eboe country (hinterland) as having similar geographic features that differ from the "many rivulets" characteristic of the coastal regions. By situating himself in the historical present of his memory, Equiano the adult was able to discern that although the Eboe-speaking hinterland differed in some ways and yet was similar to the cultures of the coastal regions, the two geographical enclaves combined to become one country; this was his own construction of space.

His use of "country" in this context differs from his other usages elsewhere in the narrative, including his use of "Eboe," in ways that may seem "ambiguous" in Alexander Byrd's terms. By naming the specific region of the kingdom of Benin from which he came "Eboe," Equiano was using

Eboe in a geopolitical sense. Yet, the combination of definable linguistic properties helped him to define the language group, Eboe (Igbo). When he passed through the various linguistic settlements, he derived a sense of place from the various settlements of the region. When he traveled in the Igbo region, he encountered dialectal differences in pronunciation and meaning unlike his own, and was able to discern phonological and morphological features of Igbo language that were similar to his Isseke dialect.[53] There were differences in the use of vowel accents and the use of morphemes. Thus, he was able to identify the domain in which Igbo was spoken, encompassing various clans and villages. In these instances, "Eboe" was used in linguistic terms in the narrative. If Equiano was "indecisive" and "seemingly confounded" by "Eboe" in Alexander Byrd's terms,[54] it was because his travels brought him into close contact with other Igbo groups that he may not otherwise have encountered in his life time. Those minor cultural differences among the Igbo might have been unsettling for Equiano, as he may have expected cultural and linguistic properties to be identical. Alexander Byrd went on to say that: "Vassa (Equiano) was so uncertain in his use of Eboe. His inelegance was evidence that the concept was a slippery one. And slippery it should have been. If Vassa was indeed born Equiano in Africa, it is quite likely that he grew up having never used the term to refer to himself personally or to his society more generally."[55]

This brings us to the issue of whether Equiano knew that he was Eboe before his capture, and at what point Igbo people identified themselves as Igbo. As far back as the origins of the Igbo can be traced, the concept of Igbo has always been present. The Europeans did not organize the Igbo to understand that they are Igbo, and neither did the Igbo consolidate themselves as a sovereign entity. Thus, an Owerri person knew that he was Igbo, but did not know the boundaries in which Igbo was spoken. "*Igbo kwenu!*" was the greeting throughout Igboland. The beginning of identity is as old as the language itself. Language identifies the Igbo and takes precedence over other cultural symbols and indicators. The symbolic referent of "Igbo" traverses the archetypical patterns of Igbo life to embrace the world of meaningful incidences[56] that are hidden in the subtleties of life, to show how the Igbo use symbolism to make sense of the world in a way that reveals their Igboness.

While explaining the initial experiences of slavery he had in his village of Isseke in Igboland, Equiano noted that he saw some stout, mahogany-colored men who were known to carry huge sacks in which slaves were put. Equiano referred to the stout, mahogany-colored men as "red" men. Similarly, when he got to the coast and saw the white slavers for the first time, he described them as also "red." Equiano, then, was speaking in ahistorical terms, because he was not comparing his views with those of the people he met in England in later years. He disengaged himself from other life experiences and went back to a particular spot in his memory to capture the racial distinctions he was able to make. He saw no distinction in skin color between the red men in Igboland and the white men he met on the slave ship. What is peculiar about the "red men" Equiano saw is that his people referred to them as "*Oye Eboe.*"[57] In terms of ascertaining identity, groups are always preoccupied with the "we" and "they." Despite the color differences between Isseke people and the red men, Equiano's people identified the red men as part of their linguistic and cultural group.

Another instance in which Equiano uses "Eboe" was when he replied to West Indian planters, who preferred the Eboe slaves who had a common language despite the various dialects. Those West Indian planters recognized the similarity in the various dialects of Igbo that served to identify the Igbo as a group.

Equiano also used the cultural similarities between the Jews and the Igbo to express his Igbo identity. Equiano states: "I was wonderfully surprised to see the laws and rules of my country written almost exactly here; a circumstance which I believe tended to impress our manners and customs more deeply on my memory."[58] Among the ancient Jews of Israel and Equiano's Igbo people, a patrilineal rule of descent based on a common ancestry was the norm. Both cultures practiced polygamy, including the levirate and sororate customs. Under the Mosaic Law, a menstruating woman was unclean for the duration of her menstrual flow and must remain in seclusion. Equiano indicated that he accompanied his menstruating mother to her seclusion hut. Both cultures believed in a Supreme Being or creator of all living things. Atonement for sins was highly recommended. Sexual fidelity, moral cleanness and modesty were expected of Jewish women. Equiano noted that the same moral principles applied to his Eboe women. He remembered that the women he met when he got to the sea coast were different from his Eboe women. He said: "Their women were not as modest as ours, for they ate, drank, and slept with their men."[59] Here, Equiano used "Eboe" in cultural terms and renders Eboe as a definite ethnic group.

The transposition of the Eboe place to the Jewish cultural place and vice-versa was an attempt by Equiano to construct a contiguous symbolic place in which the continuity of "Eboe" was reified and maintained. The commonality of experience between the Jews and the Eboe - enslavement - expresses their shared humanity. This is reminiscent of conditions where a history of displacement, dispersion, forced labor, and the denial of one's autonomy gave rise to a common feeling of belonging. It can be assumed that Equiano constructed a common "place" for the Eboe and the Jews based on psychological unity rather than on concrete reality. Explicit in the psychological domain of Igbo culture is the tendency to leave everything in the hands of *Chukwu*, the creator. Hence Equiano sought emotional support from the Bible for his socially constructed Igbo place.

Besides these usages of "Eboe," scholars have indicated that Equiano's usage of places and polities in Africa is confusing. The ambiguity in his use is that he applied the usage of "country" and "nation" in a context not used before and during his lifetime. In those days, a person's identity was with one's own clan, and the native word for clan was *"Obodo"* (country), *"Ala,"* (land), and *"Mba"* all of which mean "country" and "nation." In Igbo terminology, there are no separate words for "country" and "nation." A person's identity was reinforced by *allegiance to one's own clan*. A person's identity or sense of place was further reinforced by one's own action or behavior towards the clan: protection of the clan in warfare, participation in cultural rituals, preserving its culture, maintaining a cosmological balance, being at peace with the gods and the ancestors, and reinforcing kinship ties.

Another aspect of identity is the emphasis on "sentiments for clan." There was a tendency to recognize the differences of identity between one clan and another. To assert its own identity, one clan usually perceived itself in relation to other clans as symbolically opposed entities. For example, a clan may use a positive attribute of itself or a negative one for others as a means of self-congratulation or denigration of others. Since Equiano was writing about his African world, the "country" he wrote about was the clan. Certainly, Equiano saw the Igbo village or family as a microcosm of the Igbo nation. In this context, his use of "nation" refers to the Igbo linguistic and cultural group (ethnic), a definitional similarity found in the work of Njaka.[60] Despite minor cultural differences in marriage customs, food taboos, and ritual practices, Equiano saw certain unifying factors that could account for the designation of these clans as Eboe (Igbo): common territory; worship of the same deities and use of similar religious symbols; and such indices of identity in Igbo political structure and practices that include the *oha* political assembly, the *umunna* polity, and the council of elders whose judicial functions corresponded to those exercised by the Isseke council of judges.

In Kingston, Equiano observed that Africans assembled together on Sundays, noting that "each different nation of Africa meet and dance, after the manner of their own country. They still retain most of their native customs: they bury their dead, and put victuals, pipes, and tobacco, and other things in the grave with the corpse, in the same manner as in Africa."[61] By using "nation" in this particular instance, Equiano was referring to ethnicities, such as Igbo, Hausa, Swahili, Yoruba. The pattern of his writing in context, with regard to the juxtaposition and simultaneous use of "nation" and "country," indicates that "nation" refers to a particular geographic entity; in short, "nation" is the clan writ large: a profound linguistic and cultural group comprising the numerous clans in close proximity that together make up the Igbo nation. By "country" in this context, Equiano was not using European notions to refer to the smaller-entity clan that is kin-based. In this context, "country" encompasses the "clan" or "nation." The Swahili or the Zulu were viewed as hailing from a country that is different from that of the Igbo and the Yoruba. "Country" adopts its true meaning in European usage. It becomes a territory or region, distinguishable by features of topography that vary from one place to the other in the continent of Africa and elsewhere.

A non-Igbo scholar who perceives Equiano's use of "country" and "nation" may think he is talking about polities "presumably encompassing a number of settlements."[62] In Equiano's mind, rather, was the social structure of the African homeland, including settlement patterns, such as the clan, with definable physical boundaries. This is indicated in his description of one of the places he sojourned immediately after his kidnapping, a place where his language was spoken that featured building patterns similar to those of his Isseke home. Although he wrote of this place with much distinction, the evidence points to an alien Igbo clan with which he was not familiar. He wrote: "At length, after many days of traveling, during which I had often changed masters, I got into the hands of a chieftain in a very pleasant country."[63] His use of "country" here clearly refers to "clan." It is clear that Equiano recognized the difference between his clan and this other clan in question, hence the elaborate distinction. Alexander Byrd put it succinctly: "Clearly, language and culture were not the determining factors. Vassa understood that fundamental boundaries could and did exist among groups of people who spoke nearly identical languages and who shared many similar customs."[64]

What then is this distinction that exceeded similarity of language, culture, and geography of settlement? This distinction mirrored various cultural constituents that differed in form and practice from what obtained at Equiano's Igbo home, such as rites of passages, the *ichi* marks, dances, rituals, food taboos, songs, animal husbandry, art and folklore. For example, Catherine Acholonu's fieldwork at Isseke uncovered unique cultural practices that set Isseke apart from other Igbo areas. She states:

> Isseke people are very unique in their way of life, their culture
> and philosophy... Their proficiency and unrivalled aesthetic

> qualities in this area of the arts is not in question.... The homes
> of Isseke people were beautifully decorated in elaborate artistic
> designs which can still be seen today in the *obi* of Igwe Agbaka.
> These beautiful designs depict their attachment to their envi-
> ronment.[65]

Therefore, while there are general cultural patterns throughout Igboland, each Igbo group subscribes to its own internal cultural logic and symbols. This is why Equiano wrote about the blacksmith's place as a distinct place. Another reason for the distinction was that his Isseke people were not blacksmiths; his master, the chieftain, was a blacksmith. Although blacksmithing was prevalent in Igboland in those days, the craft was the prerogative of some Igbo communities such as Awka, and the near-by Agulu-Umana. Whether or not Equiano went to these particular smithing communities is not known. Whichever one he was taken to may have had ritual and secular activities similar to those found in other smithing communities. In addition to iron-working, some in the smithing communities specialized in woodcarving, including stool carving, panel carving, and masks (with much stylistic difference to what Equiano had seen), while the rest became specialists in divination, ritual medicine, and other kinds of economic activities. These factors buttressed the idea that although Equiano's Isseke and the blacksmith's place are Eboe speaking areas, they were symbolically opposed entities. This place was indeed another "country" (clan) that differed from Equiano's own place.

Equiano also struggled with the issues of language and culture elsewhere in the narrative. He wrote: "All the nations and people I had hitherto passed through resembled our own in their manners, customs and language: but I came at length to a country, the inhabitants of which differed from us in all those particulars."[66] By "nation," Equiano meant a clearly defined language/ethnic group, perhaps the Ijaw or the Ibibio. By "country," he recognized geographical features that differed from those of Isseke. He reiterated by saying, "From the time I left my own nation, I always found someone that understood me till I came to the coast . . . the languages of different nations did not totally differ nor were they so 'copious' as those of the Europeans, particularly the English."[67] When he said, "When I left my own nation," he meant his own Isseke clan and dialect. Since the languages he encountered did not totally differ, he recognized that they were Eboe (Igbo). His concept of ethnicity became fully entrenched in his psyche.

After his stay with his master, the blacksmith, he came to a town called Tinmah. The geographical landscape of Tinmah, which included coconuts and sugarcane, was one determining factor that surpassed language and culture, on one hand, and the realities of Equiano's Isseke home on the other. Equiano saw and tasted coconuts and sugarcane for the first time. Equiano understood that Tinmah was not part of his own Igboland; it represented another "nation," a different "country" (*obodo* or land or clan), encompassing a major, different language and culture, possibly Ijaw.

Indeed, my identification of the location of Equiano's Tinmah in the Niger Delta of Nigeria and Equiano's "Elese" are compelling pieces of evidence that lend credence to his claim of an African birth.[68] Nonetheless, contemporary challenges to Equiano's nativity, while anachronous to their historical antecedents, came into focus as a result of the Carolina birth certificate, but have to respond to the geographical evidence of Tinmah and Elese. Tinmah had peculiar characteristics; Equiano heard various languages spoken there. There were people who spoke his language, and the way they did things was identical to the norm around his father's house, which indicates that these people could have been Igbo slaves now settled there. Another possibility is that these were Igbo people now acculturated to Tinmah but retaining Igbo cultural patterns. The people of Tinmah had certain basic customs governing social relations, much like his Igbo people, such as the principle of respect for elders. For example, his owner's son would not eat until Equiano, who was older, had done so.

Tinmah was the final melting pot of all languages that he encountered in his itinerary. Equiano discovered many dialectal similarities of Igbo at Tinmah amid the deeper differences in some of the dialects, and noted languages that were not Igbo. He began to view the speakers from various Igbo clans as Eboe. Equiano also must have noticed some words from Kalabari or other Ijaw languages that had the same meanings in Igbo. When he encountered non-Igbo languages in the Biafran interior, he may have perceived that these languages belonged to what is considered today as the *kwa* family of languages, although the classification had not yet been made at that time. The linguistic differences between the "copious" English language and the *kwa* family of languages, such as the phonemes *kp, gh, ch, ~n, kw, ny, gw, gb, and nw*, stood out.

The economic features of Equiano's home included yam, the chief crop of the Igbo. Female crops including, cocoyams (*ede*), were planted in separate farms. There were fewer streams. When he left the Igbo-speaking territory, he saw lots of rivers rather than the yam plantations of his home. He felt a deep crisis of identity because his identity was tied to a particular environment. This was the beginning of his loss of identity, as his existence and humanity were linked to the land. Symbolically, this meant that the land that was the source of sustenance was divorced from his life. He was no longer surrounded by the familiar, which compromised his identity and challenged his concept of personhood and future roles. The order of geo-graphic and symbolic spaces of his Igbo world was responsible for seeing him through needed rites of passage to manhood. Equiano was aware that the new environment in which he found himself deprived him of certain rites of passage, such as the *ichi* mark he would have received in his Isseke home, that would have affirmed his identity. In essence, he had lost a major part of his male identity, status, and hierarchy.

Equiano's use of "country" transcends the commonly understood concept of village group[69] that has customarily been defined as indepen-dent polities of settlements bound together by "a mythical kinship unit with relationship becoming genealogically traceable within, and often between the kindreds that make up the villages;" they occupy a common territory with patrifocal compounds, "with villages scattered through the bush over a vast area," a place where the corporate identity of the person was developed, although he/she claims "descent from a mythical pair of ancestors."[70] Equiano's use of "country" referred to the "clan" that encom-passed several village settlements. For example, Mbaitoli is comprised of nine clans, with each clan consisting of several villages of common ances-try. Equiano's Isseke, fondly referred to by Equiano as Elese (*Ala Isse*), is, according to Acholonu, comprised of five (*Isse*) lineages that make up the clan Isseke.[71] In the narrative, Equiano laid greater emphasis on the clan as a whole - Essaka. His focus was not on the constituent parts. Alex-ander Byrd's initial assessments of the meaning of Equiano's "country" and "nation" corresponds to the concept of clan used in this work, which Equiano understood but did not articulate. Byrd wrote:

> In the *Interesting Narrative*, sometimes a nation or country was, quite simply, a town (a point that is significant for Measuring Vassa's probable connection to the Biafran interior.) ... So what exactly did Vassa mean by these particular usages of country and nation? They were different countries, in all likelihood, because they were *different towns.*[72] (Emphasis added).

Equiano's Essaka (Isseke) today is referred to as a town, as are other Igbo towns that were previously called clans. Irrespective of the definition of "town" as a heavily populated area with a fixed boundary that is larger than a village and smaller than a city, today's usage of "town," is the same as it was used historically— a non-kin grouping brought together by mod-ernization, trade and urbanization. Traditionally, the Igbo tendency is to conceive of their social organization in terms of descent groupings (clan) based on a common ancestry rather than on superficial classifications such as the village group.[73] Furthermore, the Igbo tendency towards the ancestral clan is evident in their use of the prefix *Umu* (children) in reference to village names. Upon his capture, Equiano's *umunna* identity was stripped and replaced with the identity of victim. The identity of victim was the mark of bonding for the slaves with whom Equiano was in captivity on the slave ship. They reminisced together about home, shared experiences and endured miseries together. His sense of place was kindled by these experiences. The fellow slaves became kin, mother, father, brother, friend and companion. A psychological Eboe "space" or place was constructed.

When Equiano asked the other slaves what was to be done to him, his age was younger and his personality weaker. His identity as a young Igbo boy influenced how he spoke to and acted towards the other Igbo slaves. The slave ship became a microcosm of the larger Igbo community he had left, thus reinforcing his sense of place. In reality, it was an alien environment, a slave ship with white slavers, but it had positive as well as negative effects on him. In his anguish, he could not jump into the water to drown himself; his only recourse was to accept the world fellow Igbo slaves had created on the slave ship. He had been severed from his home, and the ship was a symbol of his severed identity, disrupting his physical space, his position in the social landscape of the Igbo world, and his role in the cultural rituals. The slave ship deprived him of the future ability to have a homestead and of all other privileges accruing from manhood, such as inheritance rights, rights to land, a voice in the *Oha* (general assembly) and his autonomy in Igbo culture, all of which are particulars of identity in Igbo society. It also deprived him of power and authority and the future status of *ogaranya*, a coveted role in Igboland.

In the face of the paradox of the slave ship, Equiano was able to reconstruct the Igbo social landscape of his home. He recreated the Igbo community—the *umunna* and the *ikwu-na-ibe*. He turned to his *ikwu* for support. He took advantage of his age to find acceptance with older members of the slave ship. These were not blood relatives, and their identity changed with regard to Equiano. He recreated everyone's identity, all those he could identify as fellow Igbo; thereby creating new kinship ties. They became symbolic relatives. His new sense of place was symbolic—that was his Igbo world on the slave ship. He was home away from home among the Igbo slaves. His sense of place was validated among the Igbo slaves. He drew strength and consolation from the slave ship since there was no alternative to his new sense of place.

Equiano's identity tool box was immediately disrupted at the sight of white men. Prior to meeting them, his identity tool box contained the list of "countries" and "nations" in his itinerary. His meeting of white men marked the first time he designated all Africans as belonging to one country, a fact he articulated in later years.[74] A new meaning of "country" emerged that was different from his earlier version of clans and settlements. "Country" became the home of the white men that was far away. His concept of "nation" also changed, for these white men were English speakers.

Vincent Carretta stated that Equiano referred to white men whom he saw for the first time on the slave ship as "demons."[75] Indeed, Equiano thought they were demons, as would any Eboe who saw them for the first time. Equiano was merely capturing the world of spirits as understood in the Igbo world. Historical and anthropological literatures are replete with stories of first contact with white men by native peoples, all of whom thought they were gods. In Chinua Achebe's *Things Fall Apart*, the people of Umuofia, who heard stories of white men, believed that they were spirits.[76] In *The White Man Will Eat You*, William Wormsley noted that the Mbonggu of New Guinea thought that the white men were not human.[77] Thus, it was customary for native peoples to think of anything different as supernatural, and that is why Equiano thought that these white men were going to eat him.

Equiano was quick to assign a different identity to the strange-looking white men. His Igbo sense of place and cosmological balance were disrupted when he first saw the white men. Psychologically, Equiano was alone, without the Igbo gods that offered protection; he was like one without an identity. This psychological disruption was to be reversed when the other Igbo slaves informed him of the purpose of their enslavement, which was work. Equiano understood the organizational patterns of labor among the Igbo. Itinerant agricultural workers or cooperative work groups were formed who sometimes traveled to faraway places, to other villages to work, after which they returned to their respective villages. The hope of returning to his homeland held the promise of reclaiming his identity, an identity authenticated by his Igbo name, Olaude.[78] Equiano said: "I was born Olaudah, which, in our language signifies vicissitude, or fortunate also; one favoured, and having a loud voice and well spoken."[79] Equiano's identity is determined by, and encapsulated in, the meaning of his name - meaning that derived from "the social status" of his family (the circumstances of his birth) and his "destiny" (his future as supported by his *chi*). To be called "fortunate" is to absolve Equiano from its antithesis, the misfortunes of his life. "Fortunate" is pejorative when one takes into account the debilitating effects that preceded it. As an epiphenomenon, it brought into sharp focus the "vicissitudes" of his life as a reflection of the relationship between his name and identity. "Vicissitude" captures Equiano's life experiences: the changing phases of his life, alternated circumstances, and the ups and downs, including his enslavement. He was aware of this and it reflected in his sense of who he was.

From Equiano's narrative, we can conclude that Igbo identity is not monolithic nor is it intractable. It is multiparous and at once multipartite—it is constant, transitory, regressive and progressive. The constancy is seen in Equiano's inability to obliterate Igbo and Igbo realities from his psyche. The assimilated Equiano tried to acquire multiple identities, one British, and the other, French, through dress and hairstyle, only to return to his symbolic Eboe. His British identity was a camouflage of his attempts at emancipating Eboe and the rest of his "countrymen-Africans." One never fully, nor truly divorces oneself from one's essence—the core of one's existence.

Equiano's identity was transitory. He was an un-initiated son of an *ichi* bearer at Essaka. Outside of Isseke, his symbolic Eboe place was instrumental to the development of a *dimkpa* identity through hard work, and later, earned him an *ogaranya* (wealthy) status and identity among Eboe slaves. Equiano's foretold identity as a spokesperson was obstructed by enslavement and constituted a regression that prevented his entry into the ritual "space" of the *ichi*. His identity was restored in the fulfillment of "prophesy." It became progressive when he became a speaker for the abolition of slavery. Igbo identity is penetrative and is perpetuated through culture. A sense of *place* is its prime mover.

NOTES

1. Vincent Carretta, *Equiano, the African: Biography of a Self-Made Man* (Athens: University of Georgia Press, 2005). See also Paul Lovejoy, "Autobiography and Memory: Gustavus Vasa, Alias, Olaudah Equiano," *Slavery and Abolition* 27, no. 3 (December 2006): 317-347.

2. Paul Ricoeur, "The Model of the Text: Meaningful Action Considered as a Text," in *Hermeneutics and the Human Sciences: Essays on Language, Action and Interpretation*. ed. and translated by John B. Thompson (Cambridge: Cambridge University Press, 1981), 197-221.

3. Steven Feld and Keith Basso, eds., *Senses of Place*, (Santa Fe, New Mexico: School of American Research Advanced Seminar Series), 1996.

4. See *The Chronicle of Higher Education*, 23 September 2005. See also Jenifer Howard, "New Light on the Author of an Old Book," *Chronicle of Higher Education*, Volume L II, Number 9, 21 October 2005.

5. See also, Catherine Acholonu-Olumba, *The Igbo Roots of Olaudah Equiano. With a Reply to Vincent Carretta*, (Revised) (Abuja: AFA Publications, 2007), 289-290. See also Catherine Acholonu, "The Home of Olaudah Equiano: A

Linguistic and Anthropological Search," *Journal of Commonwealth Literature* XXIII, no. 1 (1987): 5-16.

6. Carretta, *Equiano*, 16.
7. Lovejoy, "Autobiography," 16.
8. Olaudah Equiano, *The Interesting Narrative of the Life of Olaudah Equiano, Gustavus Vassa the African, Written by Himself* (London, 1789), 5.
9. See Steven Ogude, "Facts into Fiction: Equiano's Narrative Reconsidered," *Research in African Literatures* 13, no.1, (Spring 1982): 31-7.
10. See Ike Anya, "Fireworks Fly at Equiano Conference," Nigeriaworld. March, 28, 2003. http://www.nigeriansinamerica.com/articles/261/1. (Accessed 10 April 2008). See also, Acholonu-Olumba, *The Igbo Roots*, 289-290.
11. L.O.I. Ogueze, "The Isseke Root of Olaudah Equiano," a paper presented at the International Conference on Africa and the Transatlantic Slave Trade: Revisiting the Olaudah Equiano Global Legacy, Imo State University, Owerri, Nigeria, 26-28 July 2007.
12. Dorothy C. Ukaegbu, "The Expression of Ndorondoro, Ituaka, and Igba-koaka among Contemporary Ogwa Igbo of Nigeria: An Interpretive Act," (Ph.D. Thesis, University of Massachusetts, Amherst, Massachusetts, 1995).
13. Equiano, *The Interesting Narrative*, 5.
14. See Jennifer Howard, "A Scholar Unravels an Ex-slave's Narrative," *The Chronicle of Higher Education* Volume LII, Number 3, 9 September, 2005. See also Carretta, *Equiano the African.*
15. Jennifer Howard, "Unravelling the Narrative," *The Chronicle of Higher Education,*" Volume LII, no. 3 (9 September 2005).
16. Anya, "Fireworks fly at Equiano Conference."
17. Carretta, *Equiano the African.* See note 15 on page 387.
18. On the validity of African oral tradition, see, Jan Vansina, *Living with Africa* (Madison: The University of Wisconsin Press, 1994) and Joseph Miller, ed, *The African Past Speaks: Essays on Oral tradition and History* (London: Dawson, 1980).
19. Emily A. Schultz and Robert H. Lavenda, *Cultural Anthropology: A Perspective on the Human Condition*, 3rd ed. (London: Mayfield Publishing, 1995), 32. See also Vansina, *Living with Africa.*
20. Howard, "New Light."
21. Carretta, *Equiano*, 139-140.
22. See Acholonu, *The Igbo Roots*, 33, 43.
23. Alexander X. Byrd, "Eboe, Country, Nation, and Gustavus Vassa's Interesting Narrative," *The William and Mary Quarterly* 63, 1 (2006), 2.
24. See also Abraham Rosman and Paula G. Rubel, *The Tapestry of Culture: An Introduction to Cultural Anthropology.* 8th eds. (New York: McGraw-Hill, 2004).

25. Maria G. Cattell, "Landscapes of People: Landscapes of Spirits: The Meaning of Place among the Abaluyia of Western Kenya," paper presented at a symposium on "International Perspectives on the Meaning of Place," Vancouver BC, Canada, July, 2001.

26. Conversation with Chima Korieh, 10 November 2007.

27. Belden C. Lane, *Landscapes of the Sacred: Geography and Narrative in American Spirituality* (Baltimore: The Johns Hopkins University Press, 2002), 6-8.

28. Feld and Basso, *Senses of Place*, 8.

29. Victor C. Uchendu, *The Igbo of Southeast Nigeria* (New York: Holt, Rinehart and Winston, Inc., 1965), 14.

30. Ibid., 11-12 (emphasis added).

31. E. N. Njaka, *Igbo Political Culture* (Evanston: Northwestern University Press, 1974), 155.

32. Cattell's, "Landscapes of People," 7.

33. Uchendu, *The Igbo*, 11.

34. F. Odun Balogun, "Self and Place in African and African-American Authobiographical Prose: Equiano and Achebe, Soyinka and Gates" in Paul Tiyambe Zeleza and Ezekiel Kalipeni, *Sacred Spaces and Public Quarrels: African Cultural and Economic Landscapes* (Trenton: Africa World Press, 1999), 206-211.

35. Balogun, "Self and Place," 206.

36. Mieko Nishida, *Slavery and Identity: Ethnicity, Gender, and Race in Salvador, Brazil, 1808-1888* (Bloomington: Indiana University Press, 2003), 74; See also Susan M. Marren, "Between Slavery and Freedom: the Transgressive Self in Olaudah Equiano's Autobiography," *PMLA* vol. 108, no.1. (Jan., 1993): 94-105.

37. In some correspondences, Equiano referred to himself as an Ethiopian, after signing his signature.

38. Byrd, "Eboe, Country, Nation," 2.

39. Byrd raised the issue of whether a collective Igbo identity existed among the slaves who came to the Americas. See Byrd, "Eboe, Country, Nation," 17.

40. Nishida, *Slavery and Identity*, 1.

41. Ibid., 137.

42. Karen Leonard, "Asian Landscapes Re-visioned in Rural California," in *Culture Power Place: Explorations in Critical Anthropology*, eds., Akhil Gupta and James Ferguson (Durham: Duke University Press, 1997), 118-136.

43. Leonard, "Asian Landscapes," 120.

44. Doris Francis, Leonie Kellaher and Georgina Neophytou, "The Cemetery: A Site for the Construction of Memory, Identity, and Ethnicity," in *Social Memory and History: Anthropological Perspectives*, eds. Jacob J. Climo and Maria G. Cattell (Walnut Creek, Calif.: AltaMira, 2002), 100.

45. Vincent Carretta, *Olaudah Equiano. The Interesting Narrative and Other Writings* (London: Penguin Books, 1998), 118.

46. Equiano, *Interesting Narrative*, 235-241 (my emphasis), cited in Edwards and Shaw, "The Invisible Chi," 151.

47. Paul Edwards and Rosalind Shaw, "The Invisible Chi in Equiano's Interesting Narrative," *Journal of Religion in Africa*, XIX, 2 (1989), 148.

48. Edwards and Shaw, "The Invisible Chi," 148.

49. Uchendu, *The Igbo*, 16.

50. Abu Loghod, *Veiled Sentiments: Honor and Poetry in a Bedouin Society* (Berkeley: University of California Press, 1999), 236, 257.

51. Uchendu, *The Igbo*, 17.

52. Carretta, *Olaudah Equiano*, 48-9.

53. For example, '*kele*' (Owerri dialect) and '*kene*' (Onitsha dialect), which means 'to greet.'

54. Byrd, "Eboe, Country, Nation," 2.

55. Ibid., 11.

56. Ray Grasse, *The WalkingDream: Unlocking the Symbolic Language of Our Lives* (Wheaton, IL: Quest Books, 1996).

57. See Carretta, *Olaudah Equiano*, 37.

58. Equiano, *Interesting Narrative* (1789), 172.

59. See Carretta, *Olaudah Equiano*, 54.

60. Njaka, *Igbo Political Culture*, 25.

61. Carretta, *Olaudah Equiano*, 172.

62. Byrd, "Eboe, Country, Nation," 4.

63. Carretta, *Olaudah Equiano*, 48.

64. Ibid., 5.

65. Acholonu, *The Igbo Roots*, 73-4.

66. Carretta, *Olaudah Equiano*, 53-4.

67. Ibid., 51.

68. See "A Question of Origin: A Scholar Examines the Authenticity of Slave Narratives," *Las Vegas Review Journal*, April 10, 2006; "Efforts To Establish Slaves Narrative Attracts Attention," *Las Vegas Review Journal*, December 18, 2006.

69. The concept of village-group, which laid less emphasis on the principle of descent, was first coined by colonial anthropologist, M. M. Green in, *Ibo Village Affairs* (London: Sidgwick and Jackson, 1947), 9, 11. Following Green, Adiele Afigbo adopts the same usage, in *Ropes of Sand*, (Nsukka: University Press Limited, 1981).

70. Ibid.

71. Acholonu identified the five (*isse*) roots.

72. Byrd, "Eboe, Country, Nation," 6-7.

73. The concept of a village-group is a misnomer.
74. In his 1788 letter to the British Senate in which he sought the end of slavery, Equiano referred to African slaves as "my country men." See Carretta, *Olaudah Equiano,* 339-340.
75. See *Chronicle of Higher Education,* 23 September 2005.
76. Chinua Achebe, *Things Fall Apart* (London: Heinemann, 1958).
77. William Wormsley, *The White Man Will Eat You: An Anthropologist among the Imbonggu of New Guinea* (Fort Worth: Harcourt Brace College Publishers, 1993).
78. H. A. Wieschhoff, "Social Significance of Names among the Ibo of Nigeria," *American Anthropologist* 43 (1941), 212; Uchendu, *The Igbo,* 60.
79. Carretta, *Olaudah Equiano,* 41.

Chapter 4

Status in Eighteenth-Century Igboland: Perspectives from Olaudah Equiano's Interesting Narrative

Dorothy C. Ukaegbu

Prior to the dawn of wide knowledge and scholarship on the African continent, much of the information on the continent came from European travelers and explorers, slave traders, and Christian missionaries. Most of these accounts, however, were stereotypes, containing exotic depictions of non-Western societies. As a result, some scholars relied on unverified information gleaned from early diaries of travelers, explorers, and slave traders, which formed the basis of their research and subsequent interpretations of Africans and their realities. In recognition of this problem, and in search of a means of rectifying it, the human sciences resorted to new frameworks of analysis that have challenged Western perceptions and representations of other societies. These new epistemological frameworks, including postmodernism, called for a re-assessment of the ways in which knowledge about a people under study is collected, interpreted, and constructed. Postmodernism, in particular, challenged positivism and its tendency towards nomothetic principles, by which data were used in formulating general theories and generalizations about the human condition.

Such general theories have also fallen short because they often neglected the voice and views of the subjects.[1] Paula Ebron noted that negative representations of Africa borne out of the West were instrumental to the colonization of Africa and proposed including local voices and initiatives in such discourses.[2] Other scholars have stressed the need to explore the possibilities of a postmodernist Africa that derive from an African perspective and channel issues away from Western provincial ideas.[3]

In this chapter, I revisit the issue of representation and interpretations of the "Other," given that it is a recurrent problem in the human sciences. The paper focuses on the work of Vincent Carretta on Olaudah Equiano, in which he uncritically uses information from early explorers' diaries and similar sources in his representation of the African society of Equiano's time. Carretta's use of such accounts in his earlier writings on Olaudah Equiano and also in his new book, *Equiano the African: Biography of a Self-Made Man*, gives a false rendition of Equiano's Igbo World. This paper challenges the dual concepts of '*gentleman*' and '*leisure*' as they are applied by Carretta to Equiano and proposes instead that the Igbo concepts of *ogaranya* (rich man) and *dimkpa* (strong man), symbols that lie at the heart of Igbo manhood, are more appropriate terms for Equiano's eighteenth-century Igbo World.

Olaudah Equiano was an eighteenth-century Igbo slave who, scholars argue, was born either in 1745 or 1747 at Isseke in the present-day Anambra State of Nigeria.[4] In his 1789 autobiography, *The Interesting Narrative of the Life of Olaudah Equiano, or Gustavas Vassa, the African Written by Himself,* Olaudah Equiano recorded the social and economic life of eighteenth-century Igbo society as well as his Middle Passage experience. His account of life in Africa, the Middle Passage and the system of slavery in the New World has served as a crucial source of information on eighteenth-century Igbo societies as well as the nature of slavery in the New World. As such, the book has been a source for anthropologists, historians and literary critics. Presently, it has become a threshold of literature, ripe for the analysis of literary genres from various intellectual traditions similar to those advanced by Harrow (1994) and Carretta (2005).[5]

THE PROBLEM OF INTERPRETATION

Prior to the publication of his book, *Equiano the African*, Carretta had published an article, "Defining a Gentleman: The Status of Olaudah Equiano or Gustavus Vassa," in which he used the Western concept of "gentleman" to describe Equiano's Igbo status, a pattern which defies analysis when used as a basis for understanding Equiano's eighteenth-century Igbo society. The significance of this case is that Carretta borrowed this concept from John Adams, whose memoir mentioned the *"Heebos"* and the *"Heebo* slaves" who had scarification marks ("breeches") on their foreheads. According to John Adams, the *"heebo"* slaves who had *"breeches"* were "gentlemen," beneath who were the lowly tasks assigned to slaves. In his *Sketches Taken During Ten Voyages to Africa, Between the Years 1786 and 1800,* John Adams writes:

> A class of *Heebos* [Igbos], called *Breeche,* and whom many have very erroneously considered to be a distinct nation, masters of slave ships have always had a strong aversion to purchase, because the impression made on their minds, by their degraded situation, was rendered more galling and permanent from the exalted rank which they occupied in their own country, and which was thought to have a very unfavourable influence on their shipmates and countrymen in misfortune. *Breeche,* in the *Heebo* language, signifies *gentleman,* or the eldest son of one, and *who is not allowed in his own country any menial office.* He inherits, at his father's death, all his slaves, and has the absolute control over the wives and children which he has left behind him. Before attaining the age of manhood, his forehead is scarified, and the skin brought down from the hair to the eyebrows, so as to form a line of indurated skin from one temple to the other. This peculiar mark is distinctive of his rank, the ordinary mark of the *Heebo* being formed by numerous perpendicular incisions on each temple, as if the operation of cupping had been often performed.[6]

I argue that John Adams did not render the true meanings of Igbo cultural concepts and thus misinterpreted the realities of the Igbo *ichi* bearer. Ichi (*breeche)* does not signify "gentleman" as John Adams portrayed. Following in his footsteps, Carretta misapplied the concept of the gentleman to Equiano's status. Carretta writes:

> In the cultures of both Equiano's native Ibo homeland and of Vassa's later British residence, a *gentleman* was ideally someone *who did not have to work for a living,* someone who *had the leisure* and disinterest required of a judge and legislator, and someone who lived by codes of honor, propriety and decorum[7] (Emphasis added).

The Western concept of *gentleman,* as defined in the preceding, was alien to Olaudah Equiano's eighteenth-century Igbo World. Explicating the concepts of *ogaranya* and *dimkpa* or *dike* uncovers the processes through which these concepts are rendered as the true delineations of high status, manhood, and ranking among the Igbo. It reveals the cultural meanings of these concepts, how they differ from Western notions of gentleman, and how seeming similarity in usage (all being forms of status) results in misrepresentations of Igbo realities. Whatever the *"breeches"* or scarification marks (*ichi*) could have meant to the Igbo were subsumed in their status indicators.

In his 1789 autobiography, Equiano identified his father as an *ichi* bearer, and described the *ichi* marking procedure:

> My father was one of those elders or chiefs I have spoken of, and was styled *Embrenche,* a term, as I remember, importing the highest distinction, and signifying in our language, a mark of grandeur. This mark is conferred on the person entitled to it, by cutting the skin across at the top of the forehead, and drawing it down to the eyebrows; and while it is in this situation applying a warm hand, and rubbing it until it shrinks up into a thick weal across the lower part of the forehead. Most of the judges and senators were thus marked; my father had long born it; I had seen it conferred to one of my brothers, and I was destined to receive it by my parents. Those *Embrenche,* or chief men, decided disputes and punished crimes, for which purpose they always assembled together.[8]

On the basis of Equiano's notion of *ichi* as a mark of grandeur, Carretta assumed that had Equiano not been sold into slavery and received his *ichi* marks, he would have led a life of leisure without manual labor in his Igbo environment. This brings us to the problem of the meaning of the Western concept of leisure and its applicability to the Igbo of the Eighteenth century. The issue will revolve around the interrelationship between leisure and the *ogaranya/dimkpa* symbols in terms of ideological valuations of gender status and the role leisure plays in the enhancement or devaluation of Igbo manhood.

INTERPRETING IGBO REALITIES: SYMBOLS OF MANHOOD

Resolving the interpretational/representational issues requires answers to the following questions: How were manhood and status measured among the Igbo and what were the criteria for ranking? Who was a *"dimkpa"* or a *"dike?"* Who was an *"ogaranya?"* How was the status of *dimkpa/dike* and *ogaranya* achieved? Was leisure part of the Igbo cultural value system, particularly in Equiano's eighteenth-century Igboland? Did 'slave' owners in Igboland live a life of leisure? Was leisure desired by the *ichi* bearer? What was the relationship between the ichi marks and the status of *ogaranya* and *dimkpa*? Does acquiring the status of *ogaranya*, *dimkpa*, and *ichi* marking warrant a life of leisure? Did the *embrenche* bearers work? What would be considered menial tasks for the *ichi* bearers, the thought of which led to those feelings of despondency in the *ichi*-bearing slaves about which John Adams wrote?

Answers to these questions require an analysis of the key symbols of Igbo manhood and how they operated in Igbo thought and action. The key symbols that define manhood in Igbo culture were the symbols of *dimkpa* and *ogaranya*. These two symbols embraced many basic orientations in Igbo culture, the medium through which Igbo people construct their manhood. Manhood was discovered, rediscovered, negotiated and attained through the symbols of *dimkpa* and *ogaranya*. They also provided the basic framework for illuminating life's experiences, cultural expectations, worldview, culturally approved goals, and strategies for success.

To better put this in perspective, anthropologist Sherry B. Ortner's pragmatic classification of symbols - namely, summarizing symbols and elaborating symbols - is useful in explicating the concepts of *dimkpa* and *ogaranya*. According to Ortner, summarizing symbols are those that condense meaning: e.g. the U.S. flag that represents "the American way," ideas, hard work, competition, democracy, freedom, and justice, among others.[9] An example of a condensing symbol in Igbo culture is the *ikenga* wooden symbol that, according to Njaka, was the object of "achievement," "prowess," "intelligence," and status in Igbo culture.[10] It signified the success of a man in confronting obstacles, such as in war, adversity, or any other achievement-oriented endeavor.

To be a man among the Igbo was to be an achiever or one who strived to achieve. The *Ikenga* was an instrument in the efforts made at maintaining the desired qualities and acquiring material and non-material objects that raised a man's status. *Ikenga* as a form of *arusi*, acted as the intermediary between a man and the great God—*Chukwu*. *Ikenga* was perceived as next to a person's *chi* (personal god) and was the target of disillusionment rather than the great God, *Chukwu*. In a sense, it was the embodiment of Igbo manhood and a powerful emblem upon which male authority and identity were constructed. In disappointment, a man relied on his *ikenga* to bail him out. As an emblem (symbol), the *ikenga* encoded key cultural messages and values that must be adhered to in order for a male to be perceived as a real man in Igboland. It was the covert, non-salient male voice—the hidden source of male authority. One who climbed the hierarchical ladder among the Igbo would have a respected voice, and aspire to leadership in his community.

Figure 5. 1. Kinds of Ikenga ©*A.B.C. Anyasodo.*

The pursuit of "*dimkpa*" status was a vehicle to successful social action, that is, those behaviors that inscribe manhood, whereby a person harnesses the value system of the culture - those indices that were culturally prescribed for manhood. An indispensable prerequisite for Igbo manhood was hard work. A *dimkpa* was one who had sound values, strength of character and a take-charge mentality; he was a *strong man* capable of hard work and who had the correct work ethic. One could not be a *dimkpa* if one sat back and let others do the work. A *dimkpa* was one aspiring to greatness rather than "the moderately prosperous," as Victor Uchendu stated.[11] *Dimkpa* was not necessarily associated with wealth. It had nothing to do with prosperity per se, as a person could be poor and still be a *dimkpa*. A poor person could be "*dimkpa*" if he was a problem solver and tackled difficult tasks. Another aspect of *dimkpa* was courage and fearlessness. Thus *dimkpa (dike), ogaranya* and *ikenga* were the three concepts that made up Igbo manhood.

Ogaranya, on the other hand, is associated with wealth. Uchendu referred to *ogaranya* as *nnukwu madu* (the rich)[12] while Acholonu described an *ogaranya* as "a man of large means."[13] *Dimkpa* was tied to achievement-oriented actions while *ogaranya* was tied to wealth and means—the end product of achievement. Even though the symbols of *dimkpa* and *ogaranya* were distinct, there were areas in which they converged. For example, a man who took a title, such as the coveted *Ozo*, had proved himself both a *dimkpa* and an *ogaranya*, and the more titles he took, the more he proved himself as both. The attainment of *dimkpa* status ordinarily preceded *ogaranya*. The hard work and spiritual strength of a *dimkpa* was the basis for achieving *ogaranya* status. Title-taking was among the practices that made a person an *ogaranya* and was a costly affair. It took the hard work of a *dimkpa* to produce the resources needed for the event. One could be an *ogaranya* and *dimkpa* at the same time if he worked hard in life. An *ogaranya* who continued to work hard was still a *dimkpa*. If he ceased to work hard by reason of sheer laziness or nonchalance, he ceased to be called a *dimkpa* by the people. While hard work and physical strength were the marks of a *dimkpa* and could be the basis for *ogaranya* status, *dimkpa* did not always translate into *ogaranya* status. A *dimkpa* could work hard without becoming an *ogaranya*, in which case he blamed the *ikenga* and his personal *chi*, but he did not lose respect. By definition, an *ogaranya* was a person of considerable wealth, *whether he worked for the wealth or inherited it*. In the case that the wealth was not acquired through hard work, such a person was an *ogaranya* but not a *dimkpa*.

The status of *ogaranya* drew an axis of variation in the productive systems of the Igbo. A gendered division of labor based on culturally- constructed gender roles was the paradigm for categorizing work and deciding which tasks were menial and unbefitting for an *ogaranya*. As a horticultural society that was also part-time hunter-gatherer, the Igbo male was in charge of the male crop (the yam), which was the source of male authority, and required manly attention. The females were in charge of the less ardous tasks involving the planting of the female crops—cocoyam, leafy greens, maize, beans, melon, pumpkins, peppers, and okra. Hunting in a dense Igbo forest involved "substantial life threatening risks,"[14] and was a source of male pride for those who took the risks. In contrast, the gathering of fruits, snails, and insects in the forest were the exclusive preserve of women and children and would be ludicrous for an ogaranya to participate in these activities. In addition to these economic activities, Amadiume noted that although men and women had access to the palm tree, women extracted palm-oil and kernels from its fruits. They made fuel from the chaff, medicinal soap, and used parts of the tree to produce light.[15] Women, along with children and young adults carried pots to the stream to fetch water. They fetched firewood, tended the chickens, swept the premises, and washed the garments of members of the household. They also processed cassava, pounded yam and cassava *foofoo*, dried the peppers from their gardens, washed the earthenware in which food was served, and they cooked. These domestic duties did not diminish the status of *ogaranya* women because they defined womanhood and placed women in the domestic arena—their ritual and symbolic place.

Male and female spaces were fully demarcated in traditional Igbo society. It would have been demeaning and horrifying for an *ichi* bearer to be relegated to the domestic arena where he would be symbolically stripped of his manhood and *ogaranya* status; hence, the "feeling of despondency" among the *breeche* slaves John Adams mentioned. Unknown to them, they were to perform similar agricultural tasks in the plantations in the New World. They may have been aware that some slaves were used as 'house slaves' who worked in the domestic arena and were at the beck and call of the master's wife and children.

One of the peculiarities of *ogaranya* was that a young person was not usually considered one. Thus, age was a qualifying factor for *ogaranya*. Young people, no matter how rich they were or how much they inherited at their parents' death, could not be *ogaranya* until they reached adulthood and proved themselves by displaying *dimkpa* qualities—tendencies toward hard work, participation in manly affairs, shunning feminine qualities, not crying in the face of adversity, adhering to correct values, et cetera. Thus, the *ogaranya* symbol was a condensing symbol that admitted only adulthood as an age referent.

In contrast, the symbol of *dimkpa* was an elaborating symbol that took in several referents, intersected with gender and age categories, and accommodated both male and female youngsters. Igbo children could be referred to as *dimkpa* if they showed extraordinary resourcefulness and strength. For example, a young person who encountered a ferocious wild animal and killed it became a *dimkpa*. A young person who protected the village from imminent danger, or a young person who performed an act that only an able-bodied male adult could do would be declared a *dimkpa*. A young boy who, after losing his father at a young age, was able to support his mother and siblings and engage in adult roles was a *dimkpa*. Again, his *dimkpa* status was based on good character and achievement.

Dimkpa and *ogaranya* intersect with gender. One might ask: could a woman be an *ogaranya* and *dimkpa* in Igboland? By all accounts, yes; although it was rarer to have the female *dimkpa* than the male. Females who surpassed the normal roles for women were *dimkpa*. Women of means could marry young women and let them be impregnated by available young men for the purpose of establishing families for the *ogaranya* women. This is what Amadiume referred to as the institution of the female husband.[16] The female husband was a *dimkpa* for undertaking the responsibilities of marrying women, the customary domain of males. In that case a woman was referred to as *dimkpa nwanyi* (a female *dimkpa*).

LEISURE AND THE IGBO WORK ETHIC

As the concept of work varied from culture to culture, so did the concept of "leisure." Leisure was a liability in Igboland. A life of leisure in Igboland would mean simply sitting back, not engaging in any laborious activity or running errands. Equiano would not necessarily have lived a life of leisure, especially in his early years and early manhood. He would have been at the beck and call of his older brothers or parents. This was the mark of a good child (*nwa nujuru mmiri ara afo*)—a child who is well nourished with its mother's breast milk. In symbolic terms, a child who was well-trained, disciplined, sensible, obedient, and respectful. He or she adhered to the dictates of the culture and was willing to perform small tasks. However, children's lives were not devoid of recreation. Equiano recalled that whenever adults in the neighbourhood were away, "the children assembled together in some of the neighbours' premises to play"[17] Anthropologist, Uchendu, noted that:

> Igbo children participate in two worlds—the world of children and the world of adults. Igbo children take an active part in their parents' social and economic activities. They are literally everywhere. They are taken to the market, to the family or village tribunal, to funerals, to a feast, to the farm, and to religious ceremonies. They help entertain their parent's guests. There are no children's parties which they are encouraged to dominate, nor are there parents' parties from which they are excluded. If there is a social or ritual ceremony going on in an Igbo village, everybody is welcome.[18]

Uchendu further observed that "Igbo children participate in the affairs of the adult world with childlike enthusiasm; in their own world they dramatize adult roles and spend *their leisure hours* doing "nursery" cooking, playing father and mother, holding "play" markets and mock fights"[19] (Emphasis added).

In his *Interesting Narrative,* Equiano recalled the occasional leisureliness that was tied into the artistic way of life of the Igbo. He wrote that his people loved life and spent their leisure hours in music-making, dancing, and other kinds of entertainment. He gave a detailed description of the artistic component embodied in dance:

> We are almost a nation of *dancers,* musicians and poets. Thus every great event, such as a triumphant return from battle, or

some other cause of public rejoicing, is celebrated in *public dances,* which are accompanied with songs and music suited to the occasion. The assembly is separated in four divisions, which *dance* either apart or in succession, and each with a character peculiar to itself. The first division contains the married men, who in their *dances* frequently exhibit feats of arms, and the representation of a battle. To these succeed the married women, who *dance* in the second division. The young men occupy the third; and the maidens the fourth. Each represents some interesting scene of real life, such as a great achievement, domestic employment, a pathetic story, or some rural sport; and as the subject is generally founded on some recent event, it is therefore ever new. This gives *our dances* a spirit and variety which I have scarcely seen elsewhere. We have many musical instruments, particularly drums of different kinds, a piece of music which resembles a guitar, and another much like a stickado. These last are chiefly used by betrothed virgins, who play on them on all grand festivals.[20]

The Isseke people, like other Igbo communities, engaged in occasional leisure. They worked hard in making artifacts intended for recreation, such as pottery and baskets.[21] As is art in small-scale societies, Isseke art was integrated into other aspects of culture. Music and dance played important roles in socio-cultural life; in pre-war and postwar activities; political affairs; ritual and ceremonial events such as marriages, funerals, births and naming ceremonies; and other rites of passage, including initiation. Music and dance constitute the hallmark of Igbo conviviality. They are imbued with cultural meanings and convey cultural messages, among which is leisure, or the need to celebrate life—life that has been sustained through hard work. Thus, the Igbo of the Eighteenth century would have engaged in some form of leisure, but not at the expense of their work ethic. As he grew up, Equiano would have started to work harder, to prove himself as a man and to cultivate the characteristics of a *dimkpa*. Brawn was the vehicle of status.

While other peoples cultivated their lands with the use of animals for labor, the Igbo relied on muscle power and never used animals. There were no beasts of burden in Igboland such as oxen or horses. A *dimkpa* had to work alongside the *ohu* or 'slave,' and this made him a *dimkpa*. The only exception was for the aged or sick whose lack of productivity was not intended for leisure, nor were they perceived as living a life of leisure, as leisure implied careless comfort. They did not retire; rather old people who were able still did what they could, such as assuming advisory roles.

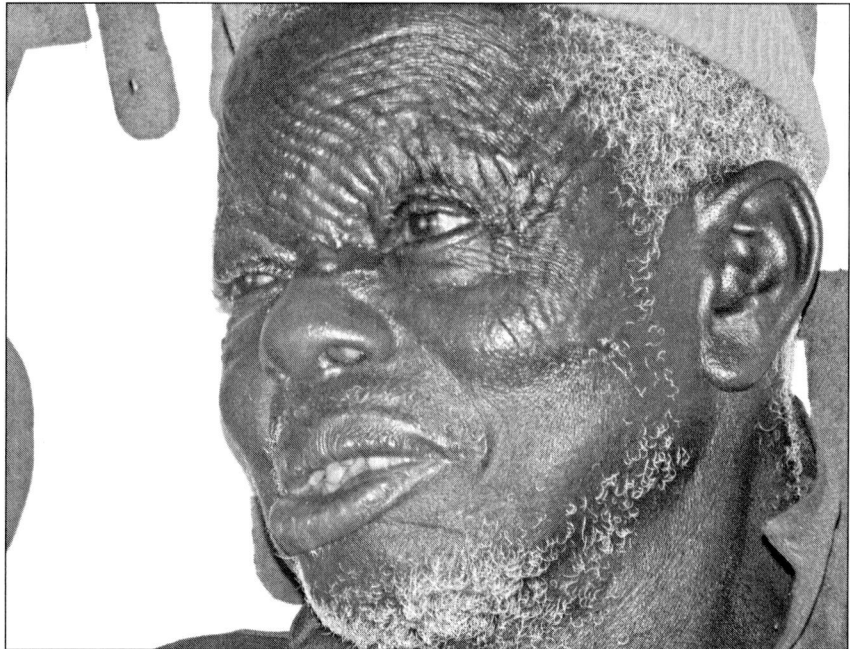

Figure 5. 2. An Isseke elder bearing the ichi mark described by Equiano. © *Chima J. Korieh*

A life of hard work was a paradox in Igboland, for even the richest did not sit idle. Like his elder brother, Equiano needed to have the character and hard work that accompanied *ichi* status. He would have been required to show that he was responsible and merited the *ichi* mark.

Carretta's misconception was based on Equiano's assertion that his father had a lot of 'slaves'(*ohu*); by implication, he assumed that Equiano's father lived a life of leisure and that his son would have as well. This assumption ignores the fact that slavery in Africa was different from slavery in the Americas, where slaves worked and slave owners lived a life of leisure. In contrast, Equiano's father and his elder brother, both of whom bore the *ichi* marks, and the rest of the family worked with his 'slaves' on the farm. On the day of Equiano's abduction, his parents, siblings and other members of the homestead "were gone far in the fields to labor."[22]

Equiano likely used the term 'slave' for the benefit of his Western audience and so did not render the differences between the Western and Igbo versions. The *concept* of 'slave' as understood in the West did not apply to the African world. Rather the 'slave' or *ohu* in Igboland was a member of the household who could even marry the master's daughter. In addition, he was not treated badly, and his *ohu* status was not permanent. The master did not delegate all work to the *ohu*. An Igbo man took pride in working his own land. He took pride in growing his own yams, the "king" of crops, that befitted (symbolized) his manhood.[23] It would be unbefitting for an Igbo man of Equiano's time to eat yam, which he did not take part in planting. In the Western world, the slaves did all the work while the master sat idle. Hence, Carretta wrote of the concept of leisure, which applied to Western society, where the master left all the work to the slaves and so had the freedom to live a life of *leisure*, all dressed up, riding his horses, taking a stroll, and carousing his harem of women. This was not the Igbo style, nor was it the Igbo attitude towards work. For example, in Achebe's *Things Fall Apart*, the protagonist's father Unoka was a vagabond who was not hard working. His son Okonkwo became the opposite, a workhorse who did not depend on *ohu* 'slaves.' Among the men of means in Okonkwo's high circles, i.e., the *ogaranya*, none depended on the *ohu* for his work and status, even though they had barns full of yams. These men of status were people who were able to work very hard.

The prevalent Igbo practice was to have guest workers during the planting season, whereby relatives and friends, members of the community, and people from other clans and villages assembled to work for the host - a gesture that was reciprocated in turn. The *ohu* system of servitude was not widespread in Igboland due to the Igbo dependency on communal cooperation. W.R.G. Horton confirmed that slave communities, such as those located in a northern Igbo village, were not prevalent elsewhere in Igboland.[24] Anthropologist Victor Uchendu described slave communities as "a very atypical structure for Igbo."[25] It is therefore dubious to imply that any man of high status in Igboland owned *ohu* 'slaves.' Ownership of *ohu* was not a requirement for high status, nor did the lack of *ohu* diminish one's status. Had Equiano been successful as an adult with the mark of *ichi*, he still would have worked. This work is the mark of a *dimkpa* and would be the basis for Equianos' *ogaranya* status since inheritance was not central to the acquisition of status. Igboland was not a society where one could survive by living a life of leisure. Carretta's concept of leisure was at odds with the context of Equiano's eighteenth-century Igbo society.

A closer look at Equiano's life at Isseke with regard to two main issues—his work life and the status of his father - provides new insights. According to Equiano, his *ichi*-bearing father had the role of judge and legislator. The *ichi* bearers settled cases and all kinds of disputes, and this work took them away from their homes. Did their role as judges qualify as work? Wallman defines work as an activity by which human beings wrest a living from nature and impose culture upon it.[26] The *American Heritage*

College Dictionary defines work as including mental effort directed towards the achievement of something. This qualifies the *ichi* bearer's activity as work, although it may not have been so conceived by the Igbo. In traditional Igboland, judges and legislators were responsible for the maintenance of social order. It was a duty owed to the gods, the ancestors and the people. Disputes were settled through the process of adjudication, wherein the third party, the judges of Isseke, had the power to impose a judgment on the offender. Equiano wrote that an adulterous woman was condemned to die by the judges but was spared when they learned she was with child. In 'mediation,' which is less formal, judges aided the disputants in restoring harmony through the negotiation process. Oftentimes, the atmosphere was highly charged, as emotions ran high and voices were raised. The judges had to tread carefully in the course of the deliberations and ensuing arguments, which was a very difficult task indeed since compromise, rather than the imposition of a judgment, was the goal.

Although in Wallman's terms, the judicial duties of the *ichi* bearers did not involve production and distribution of resources, they received compensation for work done well. In the course of their duties, they were fed well; goats and fowls were slaughtered to feed them and palm wine was provided. In addition, they took home large amounts of booty such as meat.

The Igbo enjoyed some form of leisure, but not at the expense of their work ethic. Leisure or recreation was compensation for hard work. It had its time and place in the daily life of the Igbo. According to Chinua Achebe, a person who made merry all the time was regarded as a good-for-nothing (*efulefu*), who did not adhere to the Igbo work ethic by working constantly on his farm.[27] Manhood or womanhood was thus devalued.

Equiano worked as a young boy. In his day, children, including the children of *ichi* bearers, often accompanied their fathers to work. This was a process of socialization. Every Igbo male had to be familiarized with the male crop, the yam, as it was a symbol of manhood. It would have been abnormal not to do this. Being an *ichi* bearing person or a family member of an *ichi* bearer did not warrant a life of leisure. *Ichi* bearers were *ogaranya* because they had achieved a high rank contingent on *dimkpa* status and proceeded to achieve a higher status in time.

EQUIANO'S STATUS

My discussion is centered on Equiano's status in Igboland had he not been sold into slavery. First, it must be understood that he was the son of a wealthy man and was in line to receive *ichi* marks. A common practice among Igbo men of high status was to bestow the *ichi* marks on all their sons, which constituted the first stages of male initiation rituals. According to Simon Ottenberg, a major part of ranking was the ability of fathers to bestow the necessary rites of passage on *first sons*.[28] This ceremony raised the status of the son while cementing his relationship with his father. One indicator of the *ogaranya* status of Equiano's father is that he was able to bestow the *ichi* marks not only on himself, but also on one of his sons, notably, his first son. In Equiano's case, he was not the first son and receiving the *ichi* marks meant a lot of expense and an extra financial burden. Acholonu described the bestowing of the *ichi* marks as a very expensive venture.[29] It took an *ogaranya* to garner the resources for the ceremony, which included goats slaughtered, yams cooked, and dozens of jars of palm wine for the crowd. In the case that Equiano's father did not have the means to confer the marks on Equiano, he would have had to work hard to garner the wealth necessary for the ceremony. Equiano's status, therefore, was not guaranteed, and he could either have ended up as a great man or as a vagabond. Furthermore, the chances of his success were not guaranteed since he was the youngest son and would not be the heir of his father's estate, a privilege left only to the eldest son by the rule of primogeniture. With the inherited resources, and the privilege of eldership, Equiano's eldest brother could outdo him in status, and this depended on the eldest brother's constant display of the good character and hard work that accompanied high status. Outdoing Equiano would involve 'varied accomplishments,' for the mark of status was not hereditary.

Acholonu identified some of these varied accomplishments, which, in my view, consisted of three structural categories or institutions besides the *ichi* bearing dimension. They were the *Nze Nzu*, *Ndi Ichie*, and *Igwe*. According to Acholonu, The *Nze Nzu*, are "the *ozo* titled-holders of Isseke" and "are also members of the cabinet of judges that Equiano spoke of, which was known as *Ndi Ichie*, who sit with the *okpala* or traditional head of the town (Eze) to decide cases and punish crimes."[30] She added that after the *ichi* scarification process, the man took the first level of the title of *ozo*, which was called *ozo ehi* (which involves slaughtering of a cow *(ehi)*. After *ozo ehi*, came the second level of *ozo*, called *ima nzu* (decoration with white chalk), which only married men, nobles, and the well-to-do could take. After the *ima nzu* title, a man became a member of the exalted council of *Nze Nzu*. White chalk was a symbol of purity and spirituality. The *Nze Nzu* were to be men of exemplary character; they were never to tell lies or indulge in any immoral, demeaning, or criminal acts throughout the duration of their lives. They were, thus, the custodians of order in the town. Membership in this exalted group qualified the *Nze Nzu* to become members of the *Ichie* (the cabinet of judges) and to become *Igwe*, the traditional head *(Eze)* of the town. Members of the *Nze Nzu* were, thus, the "senators" Equiano spoke of, while the *Ichie* were the "judges." Together, they constituted Equiano's "nobles" or *Embrenche*.[31]

Equiano's birth position as the youngest son, and the fact that he was destined to become a bearer of the *ichi* mark, provided no guarantee that he would have succeeded as a great man. In the case of his father's death, his father's eldest son would have become the custodian of his father's estate and given Equiano a portion due him according to tradition; his part of the inheritance would have served as his capital for building the wealth necessary for *igbu ichi*. Even so, he would have been required to display *dimkpa* qualities before he was deemed fit to receive the *ichi* marks.

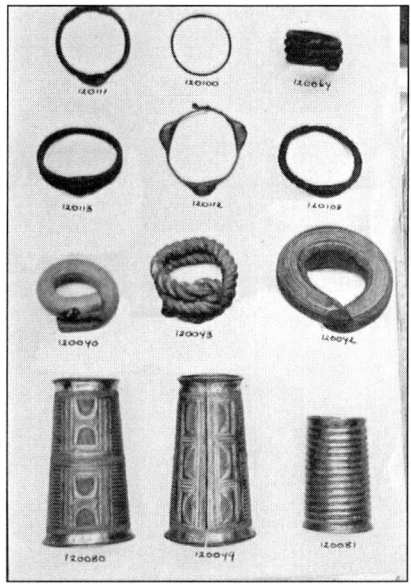

Figure 5.3. Anklets. The long ones are worn by titled males and the others by titled females. © *The Welcome Historical Medical Museum*

In my view, Equiano was already displaying *dimkpa* qualities in his childhood. Equiano's roles, along with those of other youngsters, were the marks of a *dimkpa*. He would climb trees to watch out for slave raiders, who appeared constantly at Isseke. If he saw one, he alerted the villagers. His role as protector of the village was the mark of a *dimkpa*. On the other hand, his inability to separate from his mother in his boyhood was not the mark of a *dimkpa*. According to him, he followed his mother to her place of seclusion during certain periods of the month - the menstrual cycle. This was considered unmanly, as Acholonu pointed out. Some degree of manliness was expected even of little boys as young as Equiano. Acholonu stated: "I believed at first that Equiano was sold because of his effeminate nature; his strong ties to his mother could have raised doubts in his father's mind or in any of his brothers or uncles who was in dire need of money. Hence he was sold off with his sister."[32] In her 2007 edition of "Igbo Roots," Acholonu corrected her views. She wrote: "But I believed also that Olaudah was singled out for sale because of his high prospects which might have inspired jealousy among his brothers who were in dire need of money and relevance."[33]

Simon Ottenberg, in his discussion of the Oedipus complex and its applicability to the Igbo, noted that Igbo boys were expected to separate from their mothers even before their pre-adolescent period: "to direct male sexual interests away from the mother, to other females, to end oedipal feelings aroused as an aspect of the growing sexual awareness of boys."[34] In describing the oedipal situation in general theoretical terms using the case of the Afikpo Igbo, he wrote:

> The close mother–boy tie during the nursing period followed by the entry of the father into the relationships at weaning creates a wish in the child to retain his intimate mother-tie, and hostility toward the father, who is partially replacing him…The father has ambivalent feelings towards the child, needing him for his own social advancement and yet having been sexually denied during the nursing period due to the boy's presence. The mother herself has conflicting concerns for husband and child. She may resent the enforced sexual taboo of the nursing period, while her husband is not restricted, and she may have difficulty in coping with her feelings of affection for both husband and child. . . . I believe that these Afikpo infancy conditions establish a strong Oedipus complex, one which Afikpo adults strive to resolve in order to produce warrior men… the physical movement of the boy from his mother's home aids in handling the Oedipal attachment of the boy to his mother and places him in a male milieu.[35]

On the basis of Ottenberg's analysis, Equiano's *dimkpa* potential was naught.

Was Equiano a gentleman or *ogaranya* and from whose point of view? Carretta declared Equiano a gentleman from the point of view of a Westerner. I agree with Carretta that Equiano was a gentleman in Britain. He rose from slavery to freedom and respectability. He possessed the qualities of an English gentleman, such as finesse, good manners, gentility and wealth. He was known to many and was a voice for abolition. Before he was stolen from Isseke into slavery, he was an aspiring *dimkpa,* but faltered on the way. He was not an *ogaranya* as a young boy in his homeland. Since he was a voice for abolition and the return of former slaves to Africa, he stood the opportunity of being deemed a *dimkpa* and *ogaranya* with accompanying *ichi* marks had he succeeded in returning to Isseke with his accomplishments in England, such as the status of writer, abolitionist and man of wealth.

Could Equiano be deemed a *dimkpa* anywhere? To be a *dimkpa* anywhere can be justified from only an Igbo point of view. Unfortunately, the Igbo people at home would have had no way of knowing about Equiano's achievements in Britain, and so, the only way they could have declared him a *dimkpa* was if he came back to Igboland. The Igbo slaves in Britain could have conferred new identities of *dimkpa* and *ogaranya* on Equiano—statuses that were legitimized by shared cultural understandings.

Among Equiano's people in today's Isseke, he has been honored and declared a *dimkpa* and an *ogaranya* because his life and works have been made known to the world through his autobiography.

THE POLITICS OF REPRESENTATION

Carretta's works is a form of the politics of representation and are peculiar in scope because they contradict the values and norms of ethnographic and historical praxis. They also neglect to address the asymmetrical power relations between the scholar and those being represented, as well as between Western epistemology and indigenous knowledge. Paul Lovejoy's article, "Autobiography and Memory: Gustavus Vassa, alias Olaudah Equiano," echoed the point made by Louise Rolingher that anthropologists and Igbo scholars and nationalists have shown less interest than other humanities scholars in Equiano's life and biography. In other words, Igbo people have not written much on Equiano. Although few, there are scholars of Igbo descent who have been, and are, engaged in research on Equiano, most recently in response to current challenges of his African birth. Yet the important issue remains that Carretta was unable to decipher the cultural meanings of the things Equiano described in the autobiography and, instead, glossed over the cultural particulars. Alexander X. Byrd admitted to experiencing difficulty in understanding Equiano's usages of English equivalents to render meaningful his Igbo culture.[36] This is evidence that scholarly work on Africa produced by non-Africans, often face the difficulty of rendering accurate cultural interpretations of Africa, interpretations that trained insiders would otherwise provide.

Indeed, sensitivity has been shown towards the contributions made by non-Western scholars, and the rewards gained from insider knowledge has provided a new perspective on non-Western societies since Edward Said's *Orientalism* (1978) brought attention to the unequal power of representation that tends to reflect the power inequality between the West and other societies. Yet, Lovejoy's comment calls to mind the issue of representation in anthropology, related social sciences and the humanities, which some have termed "the politics of representation."

While participation in scholarly research and writing is still polarized, some of the major issues of contention are methodological. Carretta undertook a comparison of Equiano's eighteenth-century Igbo culture and the culture of eighteenth-century Britain without consulting readings on Igbo culture. His "works" reveal a lack of knowledge of Igbo culture and the lack of any effort to comprehend it. This assertion is based on the fact that numerous works exist on the Igbo, including the ethnographic writings of British anthropologists at the beginning of the twentieth century; continued research and writings by colonial administrators and anthropologists; historical writings on pre-colonial, colonial and postcolonial Igbo society. Yet these sources were not consulted in his work. Not one was cited in his article "Defining a Gentleman: The Status of Olaudah Equiano."

Carretta's concept of "gentleman," while relevant in today's Igboland, did not apply to Equiano's Eighteenth-century Igboland. There are problems that characterize Carretta's work with regard to the Igbo. One is his "selectivity of data," and the second, the problems of "non-recognition" and "misrecognition."[37] In "selectivity of data," Carretta chose those writings he preferred to real accounts of the Igbo, ignoring myriad ethnographies on the Igbo. Anthropological ethnographies dealing with pre-colonial or traditional Igbo culture, close to what Equiano wrote about, were not included in the bibliography of his book. "Selectivity of data" raises issues of reliability and validity in terms of how these variables can be measured using a library-based pool of ethnographic data (as those used by Carretta) that are not obtained from his own direct observations or fieldwork among the Igbo.

For these reasons, I seek to capture in the following discourse, the history and features of this dialogue that deal directly with the problems identified with Carretta's work. In the 1970s, scholars such as Talal Asad began to deconstruct Western colonial writings, and called into question the ways the West portrays the other.[38] In his "Orientalist" discourse, Edward Said asserted that while the Orient is an integral part of Western material civilization and culture, Westerners wrote of the Orient as a different cultural ambient, which leaves an impression of Western superiority over the Orient by ignoring the role played by the Orient in the culture of Western civilization. This was Talal Asad's mindset in his later dialogues in the 1990s and beyond. Talal Asad, like many other scholars, dealt with similar issues of representation. In his view, the text is a forum for the orchestration of power as seen in the preferences we bring to discourse—preferences that spring from the sense of who we are. In his view, human beings are "already constituted" subjects "placed in networks of power," and it is this power that we reproduce when we read or write. This epistemological stance is evident, as in Carretta's neglect of Igbo data in his analysis of Igbo life. By such conduct, Carretta left himself open to possible questions about his motives and the basic intent of his work. Indeed, Asad pointed out that "insufficient attention" has been paid "to the problem of using and reading" ethnographies, "to the motives we bring to bear in our readings, as well as to *the seductions of text* and context that we all experience."[39] Asad goes on to explain how we, as represents of other people's realities engage in seductions of text. He states:

> In *reading* social texts (interpreting, explicating, and explaining) we inevitably reproduce aspects of ourselves, although this is not simply a matter of arbitrary preference or prejudice. We are all already-constituted subjects, placed in networks of power, and in reproducing ourselves it is also the latter we reproduce. To do otherwise is to risk confronting the powers that give us the sense of who we are, and to embark on the dangerous task of reconstructing ourselves along unfamiliar lines. It is, understandably, easier to use *our readings* to confirm those powers[40] (Emphasis added).

It is known that ethnographic modes of representation emerged in the crucible of understanding colonized peoples. This power has made itself felt through many kinds of writing. Yet this power does not presuppose Western perspectives on non-European peoples, since the problem of understanding is essentially representational. Carretta's problem is one that scholars, including Western writers, have recognized and have toiled to correct.

One area of discourse on the politics of representation/ethnographic writings has to do with the relationship between ethnographic representation and contextual imperatives with particular reference to Pierre Bourdieu's view, which, according to Jane Goodman, some works ignore when dealing with the issue of representation. Among these imperatives are the political and historical contexts that must be addressed before an issue can be understood and representation made fair. Goodman also notes that the aspect of Bordieu's work which finds salience is the concept of "misrecognition."[41]

Misrecognition occurs when the scholar is misled by ineffective informants, such that they stray on a wrong tangent, unaware of what the ethnographer wants. What is not recognized in the interaction between the ethnographer and the informants is that the informants did not understand the ethnographer's methodology and he/she did not explain it to them. There is a power imbalance between the informant and the scholar. This scenario is political because the informant is not sharing equally. The problem with Carretta's work is that he used no Igbo informants in his "gentleman" article—a form of misrecognition. John Adams, through his 1822 memoir, was his 'ineffective informant,' who spoke to him through his text; in hermeneutic terms,[42] Carretta disengaged himself from a dialogic encounter with the text—the memoir. Identifying the symbolic dimensions in the text, *heebo* and *breeche,* and situating them in their cultural context would have uncovered the Igbo realities.

In the *Interesting Narrative,* Equiano used the concept of "gentleman" to refer to status in the Igbo and the British societies which led to Carretta's analogy of both societies as sharing the same meaning. Equiano could not use the word *"ogaranya"* to refer to his British audience because of the differences in meaning. Thus, Carretta did not recognize Equiano's dilemma; neither did he place it in its historical context. Had he done so, he would have understood the Igbo world and its status symbols.

It is not surprising that Igbo scholars were perplexed when his version of Equiano's biography, *Equiano, The African,* was published. Dorothy L. Hogson has pointed out that the indigenous rights movements "link issues of representation, recognition, resources and rights," thus challenging and engaging "theories of culture, power, and difference."[43] The only indigenous rights movement that has arisen to date to protect the authenticity of a slave narrative of Equiano's time is the Isseke movement of Equiano's home.[44] The Isseke response is a way of engaging transnational discourses.

In the article, "Ethnographies as Texts, Ethnographers as Griots," Paul Stoller calls to mind efforts of anthropologists to reexamine the ethnographic methods of data collection and interpretation.[45] According to Stoller, these attempts at critical self- reflection encouraged by Clifford Geertz in the 1970s gave rise to a new discourse that split into two parts. The first part, the philosophical critique, was concerned with "the politics of anthropological representation and the politics of interpretation." They were disenchanted with ethnographic realism, especially the construction of societies as whole entities. They questioned the fundamental principles of ethnographic authority, the muted voices of the people under study, and the kinds of interpretation given.

In Jean M. Langford's "Cultural Encounters," the problem of representation is touched on by reference to the condition of those who are misrepresented.[46] Langford has noted Talal Asad's recognition of World

War II as the starting point of Western anxiety about the "Other," arising as a result of dislocations of the social and psychological identity of the "West" in this period. In Langsford's view "othering" can be articulated as a means of stabilizing an otherwise fragmented identity. Carretta's role in representation is a throwback to the heyday of this predicament, using contradiction and exaggeration to dismiss his detractors. Hence, a problem of identity, which may be understood from his contemporary sense of identity in the world, is a world of crisis for the Westerner. In the context of this discourse, it is understood that the West controls a world whose societies are difficult to handle in this present age. As the West evolves, the societies of the "Other" continue to evolve as well, and it becomes difficult to handle their essence. The West continues to be removed from "the other." Carretta's selectivity of data is part of the anxiety of some Westerners who did not expend maximum effort in those activities that help to fully understand the "Other." That which is not understood – Igbo ideas, concepts, symbols, and ethnographic data - is ignored.

In the 2005 colloquy with the *Chronicle of Higher Education*, over the controversy surrounding Equiano's nativity, Carretta indicated that the Igbos were displeased with him over the issue of Equiano's baptismal records and the ship's muster roll that point to a South Carolina birth rather than an African one. The response of both Igbo and non-Igbo scholars alike had much to do with the legitimacy of Carretta's evidence. Indeed, the major problem faced by many scholars remains the inappropriate ways cultures are often represented by outsiders. Scholars should take into consideration the epistemological issues that have often persisted when writing about other cultures, taking a cue from the 'humanism' advanced by the discipline of anthropology.

CONCLUSION

I have attempted to present an "insider's" view of the socio-cultural realities of the Igbo. The critical perspectives of Westerners have been beneficial for evaluating what we now know about ancient and modern societies of Africa. Nonetheless, recognizing the native's point of view is beneficial in methodological terms; by having direct access to cultural facts elusive to the outsider; thereby unmasking the salient features of the hidden cultural patterns. In the British culture in which Equiano lived, the status of gentleman was a prerequisite for a life of leisure, whereas an inherent dichotomy between status and leisure persisted in traditional Igbo culture. The complementary opposition between them lies in the idea that a life of leisure was inimical to the survival of the group. On the other hand, occasional leisure enhanced the status of the *ogaranya*—the anthropological "Big Man"—who demonstrated his generosity and wealth by throwing a feast.[47] In return, his *dimkpa/ogaranya* status was acknowledged by the people.

ACKNOWLEDGEMENTS

I acknowledge the late Dr. Ambrose Ekwueme Ogbonna for his contributions to this work, particularly in the explication of the concept of *dimkpa*. I thank my Department chair and co-author, Dr. Kevin Rafferty, and the College of Southern Nevada for supporting my trip to the 2006 conference of the Trans-Atlantic Research Group (TARG), held at Owerri, Imo State, Nigeria, for the presentation of this paper. I thank Dr. Chima Korieh for critical insights on this chapter.

NOTES

1. Abraham Rosman and Paula Rubel, *The Tapestry of Culture: An Introduction to Cultural Anthropology*, 8th Edition (New York: McGraw-Hill, 2004), 21-3.
2. Paula Ebron, *Performing Africa* (Princeton, N.J.: Princeton University Press, 2002).
3. Zine Magubane, *Post Modernism, Postcoloniality and African and African Studies* (Trenton: Africa World Press, 2005).
4. Catherine Acholonu, *The Igbo Roots of Olaudah Equiano: A Linguistic and Anthropological Search* (Owerri: AFA Publication, 2007).
5. Kenneth Harrow, *Thresholds of Change in African Literature: The Emergence of a Tradition*, Studies in African Literature (Portsmouth N.H.: Heinemann, 1994) and Vincent Carretta, *Equiano, the African: Biography of a Self-Made Man* (Athens: University of Georgia Press, 2005.
6. John Adams, *Sketches Taken During Ten Voyages to Africa, Between the Years1786 and 1800* (London, 1822), 41-42.
7. Vincent Carretta, "Defining A Gentleman: The Status of Olaudah Equiano," *Language Sciences* 22, (2000), 391.
8. See Vincent Carretta, *Olaudah Equiano: The Interesting Narrative and Other Writings* (New York: Penguin Books, 2003), 32-33.
9. Sherry B. Ortner, "On Key Symbols," *American Anthropologist* vol. 75 no. 5 (1973): 1338-46.
10. E. N. Njaka, *Igbo Political Culture* (Evanston: Northwestern University Press, 1974), 45.

11. Victor Uchendu, *The Igbo of Southeast Nigeria* (New York: Holt, Rhinehart, and Winston, 1965), 92.

12. Ibid., 92.

13. Acholonu, *The Igbo Roots*, 17.

14. Nancy Bonvillain, *Women and Men: Cultural Constructs of Gender* (Upper Settle River, NJ: Pearson Prentice Hall, 2007).

15. Ifi Amadiume, *Male Daughters, Female Husbands: Gender and Sex in an African Society* (London: Zed Books, 1987), 37.

16. Ibid.

17. Carretta, *Olaudah Equiano*, 46-47.

18. Uchendu, *The Igbo*, 61.

19. Ibid.

20. Carretta, *Olaudah Equiano*, 34.

21. See Acholonu, *The Igbo Roots*, 74.

22. Carretta, *Olaudah Equiano*, 46.

23. Chima J. Korieh, "Yam Is King! But Cassava is the Mother of All Crops: Farming, Culture, and Identity in Igbo Agrarian Economy," *Dialectical Anthropology* 31, nos. 1-3 (2007): 221-32.

24. W.R.G. Horton, "The Ohu System of Slavery in a Northern Ibo Village-Group," *Africa: Journal of the International African Institute* 24, no. 4, (Oct., 1954): 311-36.

25. Uchendu, *The Igbo*, 84.

26. Sandra Wallman, *Social Anthropology of Work* (London: Academic Press, 1979), 3-4.

27. Chinua Achebe, *Things Fall Apart* (London: Heinemann, 1958).

28. Simon Ottenberg, *Boyhood Rituals in an African Society: An Interpretation* (Seatle & London: University of Washington Press, 1989).

29. Acholonu, *The Igbo Roots*, 17.

30. Ibid., 48.

31. Ibid., 49.

32. Ibid., 16.

33. Acholonu, *The Igbo Roots*, 38.

34. Ottenberg, *Boyhood Rituals*, 199.

35. Simon Ottenberg, "Oedipus, Gender and Social Solidarity; A Case Study of Male Childhood and Initiation," *Ethos* 16, no.3. (September, 1988): 335-38.

36. Alexander X. Byrd, "Eboe, Country, Nation, in Gustavus Vassa'a Interesting Narrative," *William & Mary Quarterly* 63, 1(2006): 123-48.

37. See Jane E. Goodman, "The Proverbial Bourdieu: Habitus and the Politics of Representation in the Ethnography of Kabylia," *American Anthropologist* 105, no. 4 (2003), 782.

38. Talal Asad, *Anthropology and the Colonial Encounter* (London: Ithaca Press, 1973).

39. _____, "Ethnography, Literature and Politics: Some Readings and Uses of Salman Rushdies the Satanic Verses," *Cultural Anthropology* 5, no. 3 (Aug., 1990): 239-69.

40. Asad, "Ethnography," 240.

41. Jane E. Goodman, "The Proverbial Bourdieu: Habitus and the Politics of Representation in the Ethnography of Kabylia," *American Anthropologist* 105, 4 (2003), 782.

42. Paul Ricouer, *Hermeneutics and the Human Sciences: Essays on Language, Action and Interpretation* (Cambridge: Cambridge University Press, 1981).

43. Dorothy L. Hodgson, "Introduction: Comparative Perspectives on the Indigenous Rights Movement in Africa and the Americas," "In Focus: Indigenous Rights Movements," *American Anthropologist* 104, no. 4 (2002), 1037.

44. L.O.I. Ogueze, "The Isseke Roots of Olaudah Equiano," a paper presented at the International Conference on Africa and the Trans-Atlantic Slave Trade: Revisiting the Olaudah Equiano Global Legacy, Imo State University, Owerri, Nigeria, 26-27 July 2007.

45. Paul Stoller, "Ethnographies as Text/Ethnographers as Griots," *American Anthropologist* 21, no. 2 (May 1994): 353-66.

46. Jean M. Langford, Review, *Cultural Encounters: Representing 'Otherness*, edited by Elizabeth Hallam and Brian V. Street (New York: Routledge, 2002), *American Anthropologist* 105, no. 2 (2003), 92.

47. Raymond Scupin, *Cultural Anthropology: A Global Persective*, 6th edition (Upper Settle River, NJ: Prentice Hall, 2007).

CHAPTER 5

OLAUDAH EQUIANO AND THE QUESTION OF AFRICAN IDENTITY

OGBO UGWUANYI

INTRODUCTION

This chapter examines the various dimensions of the crisis of African identity and the efforts to address them in African scholarship. It begins by identifying the source of the crisis with the argument that the entrance of Africans into the intellectual map of Europe in the status of slaves constitutes an underlying source of contempt for the Africans' humanity and identity. Yet one of the earliest rebuttals of this encounter, through the work of the Igbo slave Olaudah Equiano who wrote and campaigned against slavery, and whose autobiography presents an account of a noble African identity, was a viable attempt to restore the dignity of Africans.

The paper argues that Equiano made a difference for people who were ready to engage in a dialogue with Africans about their common humanity with Europeans despite the fact that the very assumption of racism upon which this encounter was based, abhorred such a dialogue. It further argues that since institutional racism with its ethnocentrism often looks inward rather than outward, the "common humanity/African identity" framework upon which a dialogue with the "other" depended is often ruled out. Almost like religion, racism induces constructed beliefs and attitudes re-enforced by myth; the recognition of the need for an African identity defined and borne out of "racism" becomes a concrete phenomenon. Hence, a philosophical analysis of "African identity" calls for an examination of the "epistemology of racism," that will illuminate their interconnectedness. By highlighting the fault with racism, this paper argues that the problem of African identity no longer lies with Equiano or the African, but with racism itself. The paper further argues that, by extension, Equiano who, in his most undignified status as a slave, addressed the problem, stands as the most "credible voice" for Africans in matters of identity and dignity. His voice embodied experiences and incidences that reveal the complexities of racism, but also drew from his African background as a source for comparison.

ISSUES IN AFRICAN IDENTITY AND THE AFRICAN RESPONSE

A major issue in African identity is how to provide a reliable and productive definition of the African person and institutions in such a manner that it can generate a worthy and positive belief in African humanity. It is the issue of how to achieve a positive idea of the African character in such a way that it does not stand to imply the deficiencies of the entire human history – an implication by which negative vices, failures and deficiencies of mankind, when they are found in Africa, and even when they do not find their origin in Africa, are unilaterally declared and devised to be known and defined as African. The effort to articulate, define and defend the African identity runs through several scholarly works in the humanities in contemporary Africa; thus one can validly claim that this has been the major theme in African scholarship in the post-colonial era. The question of African identity has remained a persistent issue in literature, history, politics, or philosophy; Africa's pre-occupation with the theme of identity is, however, understandable. The European-educated African, placed as it were between traditionalism and modernity, remains, in the words of D. U. Opata, "an intellectual hybrid in dire need of constant critical self reflection about both his identity and status in the world." Thus, the concern with issues of identity necessarily stems from a desire "to rediscover himself and conceptualize in what respects he can be authentically characterized."[1]

To resolve this crisis and be authentically characterized are important desires for the African. In the first place, the history that preceded this wrong characterization is so influential that it would arguably need almost the period it took to damage the African humanity to undo the damage. Apart from the racial philosophy of Fredrick Hegel, who in his "hateful attitude towards Africa"[2] provides strong rational grounds to institute a world ruled by racism, and who denied Africans a place in "world history," "the entrance of Africans into European history, which came in the status of slavery, presaging an era of merchandise in human misery,"[3] constitutes a vital source of wrong identity for Africans.

Other factors include "the darkness of human geography" (the position that argues that the north wind produces different effects on men). This theory, advanced by the Franciscan friar Bartholomew the Englishman, holds that "while the North wind makes men of the north tall and fair in body, the hot moist wind of the South makes men of the South not so bold nor so wrathful as those of the North."[4] There is also the biblical factor, which saw Africans as divinely ordained slaves to humankind.[5] This position, well articulated by Edward Blyden, infers from the Ethiopian factor in the Bible that Africans were destined to be humble servants to other races of humankind.

The consequence of these claims is that centuries after the heinous crimes of slavery, imperialism and colonialism, Africans are beleaguered with how to achieve a new identity as an effective anti-thesis to the wrong characterization of Africa. As what was founded on some ill-conceived intellectual presupposition, it would take no less than a well-conceived intellectual proposition to undo the damage and recreate the African identity. As Abiola Irele puts it,

> The intellectual presuppositions of colonialism represented a formulation in negative terms of African identity; its racism was a large statement about the nature of the African which called for a refutation. In the intellectual confrontation with imperialism, it was necessary to enforce this refutation by elaborating a new set of valuations which reversed the terms of the colonial ideology.[6]

Africa's effort to address the question of her identity is historically traceable to the dramatic upsurge of black consciousness in the United States of America between the two world wars in what is popularly referred to today as the Harlem Renaissance. During this period, "Africa became a strong valourized symbol and the obsessive centre of a quest for identity,"[7] as proud sons of Africa glorified all things black as a positive way of uplifting the identity of the Blackman. Thus, they elevated all things and branded them in the ideology of blackness: "black power," "black color," "black Africa," and "the Napoleonic power of black man." In the same vein, the apostle of black pride, W. E. B Du Bois, initiated Pan-Africanism in Paris around this period. Through this organization, he contributed to the cause of African identity and the evolution of black race, and this, according to Russel L. Adams, "was manifest by his stated belief that black people were, through racial superiority and integrity, destined to humanize the civilized world."[8] It is in line with the new aspiration that Dr. Aggrey once said, "He who is not proud of his colour is not fit to live." This is against the backdrop of the fact that color had become the basis for racism, dignity and identity in the world and that Africans needed to advertise a belief in their color to be relevant enough in the world.

The ideological origin of Africa's quest for identity is of immense historical significance; that it was anchored on a form of what Sedar Senghor in his theory of negritude, called "anti-racist racism," deserves to be recalled. Europe's wrong notion of African humanity had found a racial ideological support in the hands of well-respected sons and thinkers of the enlightenment, including Immanuel Kant and David Hume. In his *Von den Verschiedenen Rassen der Mendchen* (1775), Kant, for instance, held that the black race emerged as a result of humid heat beating on the skin of origin species that, according to him, were the white species. In his review of Johann Goltfried Von Herder's *Ideen Zur philosophie der Geschichte der Menschheit* of 1785, Kant held that it is possible to demonstrate that the (indigenous) Americans and blacks are a spiritually decadent race among other members of human race.[9] With ideological support from prominent intellectual philosophers of the enlightenment like Kant and Hume, the effort to institute a wrong notion of Africa was eminently conceived. How elaborate and eminent the effort to address the assumptions on which these efforts were anchored is what this essay will establish.

The Harlem Renaissance addressed many issues relating to African identity: racial segregation, political disenfranchisement, economic labor, exploitation, and cultural discrimination.[10] In addition, it also laid a solid ideological groundwork for further efforts to address the question of African identity. Such gallant efforts as those of Pro-African intellectuals like Edward Blyden and Leopold Sedar Senghor were arguably inspired by this movement given the similarities in their vision and mission. It is also important to note here that this is where we trace the historical origin of the expression "African" or "black" personality, which has become a prominent ideology on the question of African identity. In the historical expression of Langston Hughes, which he wrote on June 23, 1926, the distinguished Black American poet said: "We, the creators of the new black generation, want to express our black personality without shame or fear. If this will please the whites, much the better, if not, it does not matter."[11]

The Harlem Renaissance or the era of blackism was followed by the emergence of nationalism in Africa. Nationalism in Africa took several forms: namely, cultural nationalism, plaintive nationalism, radical nationalism, pan-African nationalism and ideological and integral nationalism.[12] Cultural nationalism saw Europe's invasion of Africa, "in terms of cultural inferiority of the Africans or the non-existence of African culture.... Thus, nationalism from this point of view is an attempt to define oneself as a cultural people. It was nothing more than the colonized's plea for acceptance by the colonizer as a cultural man rather than a cultureless beast."[13]

Plaintive nationalism on the other hand was a quest for cultural rights of the African. Under this form of nationalism, Africans had managed to put across the message that they were cultural people and wished to be organized into the colonizer's pattern of social order. The essence of plaintive nationalism "was a request for assimilation into the colonizer's society in the colonies."[14] Radical nationalism, on the other hand, was revolutionary in form and content. It was a demand for the termination of colonialism; hence, it gave rise to Pan–African nationalism and ideological nationalism, which were committed to fashioning blueprints for the emergent, independent African nation-states.

If the crusade to address the question of African identity was gathering momentum in the political life of the African, it was not left out in African arts and humanities. Here, a new consciousness emerged as African thinkers put their creative talents toward promoting the cause of African identity. The first congress of Negro writers took place in Paris in 1956 and was closely followed by a second congress held in Rome in 1959.[15] In these forums, African writers discussed strategies for the re-creation of African identity; the need for the rehabilitation of African culture and for its proper integration into world culture. They resolved to institute an African Cultural Research Centre and to translate the works of Negro writers into autochthonous language. They also recognized the place of philosophy in the elaboration of culture, and through its commission on philosophy, raised important issues that reveal the relevance of concepts that emanate from the African world.[16]

These congresses thus announced the emergence of African literature as a strong vehicle for the expression of African humanity; and did this before the emergence of African history and African philosophy as a distinctive mode of enquiry on the problem of identity in Africa. African literature had done remarkable work to foreground issues in this regard. But African literature was multi-cultural in its desire to satisfy various national demands. The question that has arisen from this is whether we can talk of African identity or African identities. In South Africa, the main emphasis has been the evils of racism. In French-speaking Africa, this literature has dwelt on asserting the African identity and rejecting assimilation. In English-speaking Africa, the writers' concern has been to portray the tension that arose out of the conflict between western and traditional values and the after-effect of the cultural clash between the European and the African values.[17]

Among the Anglophone writers, the over-bearing influence of this conflict is evident in several literary works whose themes justify this claim. In Ferdinand Oyono's *Houseboy* and Alex La Guma's *A Walk in the Night*, the theme of colonial injustice dominates the works. In Chinua Achebe's *Things Fall Apart*, Elechi Amadi's *Concubine* and John Munonye's *The Only Son*, we see the original traditional African discussed as an anti-thesis to the illusion that Africans were a "cultureless" people. In Chinua Achebe's *No Longer at Ease* and Mongo Beti's *Mission to Kala*, the illusion of progress that characterized modern Africa constitutes the theme. In *Wealth for Udomo* and *One Man One Matchet*, Peter Abrahams and T. M. Aluko discuss the theme of nationalism. In Wole Soyinka's *The Interpreters* and Chinua Achebe's *A Man of the People*, we see the African writers' disenchantment with the inability of their politicians to control the affairs of their new states. In Ayi Kwei Armah's *The Beautyful Ones Are Not Yet Born* and Duosu's *The Gab Boys*, we read the theme of freedom, which in modern African states soon turned into a nightmare. In Ngugi wa Thiogo's *A Grain of Wheat* and Sembene Ousmane's *God's Bits of Wood*, the writers confront the theme of commitment.

Among the Francophone writers, the themes, however, center on the need to realize the individual through the expression of freedom. The example of Cameroonian literature demonstrates this. Richard Bjornson, in *The African Quest for Freedom and Identity: Cameroonian Writing and the National Experience* (1991), puts it that ". . . in Cameroon that communal discussion revolves around two crucial issues: the desire for freedom from various forms of oppression and the need to forge a valuable sense of individual and creative identity."[18] Summarily, therefore, we can argue that African literature revolves around such great themes as freedom, injustice, culture, corruption, communalism, et cetera, all of which border on the conflict of values in precolonial and post-colonial Africa and on the challenge of recreating African identity by way of ensuring that the transitional phase of African life does not erode all the noble cultural values that define the African people, or institute a fresh world where transition becomes an institution. How temporary and transitional is that African phase at the moment? These issues can only be addressed by a literature that tells the story of an enduring African spirit that perseveres in the current historical and cultural trauma.

If we turn to African history to examine its contribution to the quest for African identity, we shall discover that African history has also addressed issues and themes that rotate around the theme of African identity. In his search for African identity, the African historian has, as S. S. Nyang puts it, "found it necessary to analyze and to understand better the historical forces affecting Africa in the human drama."[19] To do this, he has engaged in the dual function of determining the nature of these forces and how they determine the independence of African historical knowledge. He has tried to capture the African past in its glories and glamour as a sure way of giving it its desired identity.

Perhaps it is this ambition of African history that has made it stand out as a subject of contempt among European scholars, who, in the footsteps of Hegel, argue that Africa has no past, and if it has any, it is an unhistorical past. Hugh Trevor Roper, the Regius Professor of History, for instance, has had this to say: "Perhaps, in the future, there will be some African history . . . but at present there is none: There is only the history of Europeans in Africa. The rest is darkness . . . and darkness is not a subject of history."[20] To repudiate claims such as this, African historians have directed their skills and scholarship to demonstrating what should constitute the subject of African history. Kenneth Dike, an African historian of repute, argues that Africa is a historical phenomenon and that unwritten evidence (oral and artificial) is there to justify the claim to African history.[21] Similarly, Ade Ajayi, another pioneer historian, lays emphasis on what he considers to be "a peculiar characteristic of African historical thought, that is, the idea of the continuity of the past in the present, the unbroken nature of time in African historical thought[,]"[22] as a way to validate his claim that there is African history. On another note, Cheik Anta Diop, the Senegalese historian, goes back to Egypt to establish the history of Africa. Diop examines Egyptian civilization and discusses the monumental achievement of this civilization as reliable evidence of African history. He makes use of available evidence - biological, linguistic, sociological, et cetera - to establish the originality of Egyptian civilization. As one commentator has it on him,

> Diop developed a chemical process for testing the level of melanin in the skin of Egyptian mummies he studied in the Museum of man in order to establish their black African ancestry. His close examination of primary sources and his knowledge of metallurgy enabled him also to establish that the iron artifacts found in the ancient Egyptian empire were not intrusions from a higher stratum nor the accidental by-product of another process . . . but very strong evidence of the invention of iron-melting by the Egyptians long before the Hittites and Assyrians.[23]

With the assistance of the Congolese Egyptologist and linguist Theophile Obenga, Diop made a penetrating study of Egyptian languages, and in 1974, added a new insight into African history with the opinion that the Egyptian language is African and generally related to a family of African languages that include his own native Wolof.[24]

Perhaps it is in Walter Rodney that African history records its greatest achievement in the effort to address the question of African identity. Rodney, in his monumental work, *How Europe Underdeveloped Africa* (1972), goes into the heart of the matter and tries to present a detailed historical treatise on an *independent Africa* that was cut short by Europe's intrusion into Africa. He traces the economic history of black Africa, the skills of the continent, as well as the evolutive stage of the African society before the rape and conquest of Africa by Europe. He borrows the Marxian thesis to argue that, like the European society that passed from communalism to slavery, to feudalism, then to capitalism, and was heading to socialism, the African societies were undergoing this developmental process before their development was hijacked by Europe.

In it all, African history has furthered the cause of African identity creditably. The success in this regard is that, today, the subject of African history is studied among non-African nations. Moreover, the history of Africa is not the history of Europe in Africa, but the history of an independent Africa that had contact with Europe, which, in the important, prophetic desire of pioneer African leader Kwame Nkrumah, is being narrated by the African himself.

African philosophers would have, more than the scholars of other disciplines already discussed, provided a lasting answer to Africa's quest for identity given the critical, deconstructive and reconstructive potentials of philosophy. African philosophy as a subject of study began in the "sixties" as a debate on whether or not there was African philosophy, a debate that disabled evolution of viable philosophical growth. To ask whether there is or can be African philosophy is largely a mark of pessimism, which cannot promote the growth of African philosophy. Ironically, before this debate, African philosophy had recorded important and enduring achievements. Apart from ancient thinkers such as Zera Yacub of Ethiopia, who could be regarded as an African equivalent of Socrates, Africa had also had important thinkers such as St. Augustine in 350 A. D. and William Amo in 1770 A. D. The contemporary debate and doubt regarding African philosophy dates back to the publication of an important work entitled *Bantu Philosophy* in 1956 by Placid Tempels, a Belgian priest. This treatise, which was an attempt to interpret the worldview of the Baluba people of Congo, was published as a philosophical justification of the difference between the worldview of the Baluba people of Congo and those of the Western World, and as an effort to account for this difference within the realm of philosophy. Thus, the publication questioned, or better put, rebelled against, the ideals of the colonial administrative policy in Congo that portrayed the African as "an empty vessel, requiring education in the spheres of religion and civilization in order to be rendered truly human."[25] The provocative and revolutionary nature of his work did not go down well with the colonial powers in Congo; hence he was banished from Congo by the Colonial administration and the Catholic Church due to their notion of Tempels as posing a threat to their policies and practices.[26] The intellectual offence, or so it was conceived, of Tempels, is that: "If the African was recognized as having a "philosophy," the African could, by implication, be said to have civilization. This notion presented a threat to the superiority of the European, as justified by enlightenment philosophy, as well as to the economics of the colonial mission."[27] Thus, despite the fact that Tempels wrote primarily to guide the Europeans on how to accomplish their mission in Congo, the fact that he designated the Bantus as a philosophical people, people who had reason and justification for the way they thought and lived, did not portray him in a positive light to other Europeans.

Another relevant level at which philosophy has attempted to address the problem of identity in Africa is the level of ideology in what has been branded the nationalist-ideological school of thought in African philosophy. At the level of ideology, the effort to address the problem of African identity came through ideologies such as the *negritude* theory of Sedar Senghor and Kwame Nkrumah's theory of *consciencism*. Negritude, in particular, attracted wider attention because it accounted for the African difference at the level of reason. Its central logic was that emotion is African, while reason is European. In particular, it was a formalization of the crisis since it came to speak for Africa but did so with a wrong, defensive notion of Africa. Hence, it has been qualified as "considerably notorious"[28] and has had the negative effect of heightening the crisis. It has, perhaps for this reason, been called "romantic primitivism."[29] We must, however, note that negritude was not the invention of Sedar Senghor himself. The word negritude was originally used by Aime Cesaire, the Martinique poet. In the poem that bears the theme "Return to My Native Land," originally published in the *Parisian Review* of 1939, Cesaire had said:

> Hooray for those who never invented anything: for those who never explored anything, for those who never conquered anything,
> Hooray for joy,

Hooray for love,
Hooray for the pain of incarnate cheers;
My negritude is not tower and no cathedral; it dives into the red
flash of the soil.[30]

In Cesaire's original version, negritude is more of celebrity, a joyous
appraisal of the past that can be likened to Ayi Kwei Armah's message in
his novel *Two Thousand Seasons* (1973).

It is in Senghor, however, that negritude became an ideology, as he tries
to give it a functional relevance. He defines it as "The whole complex of
civilized values—cultural, economic, social, and political, which characterizes black people, or more precisely, the Negro-African World."[31] Senghor's
quest for difference, which he saw as the underlying measure of African
identity, led him to "celebrate the fact that our traditional mind is of a non-
analytical bent,"[32] and to conclude that emotion is African while reason is
European. But this position is more or less a celebration of a non-rational
identity that devalues the quality of African humanity. Identity without
reason could at best be described as sub-human, and this has largely become
the interpretation of Senghor's theory of the African identity. Apart from
the denigrating impact of this position, Senghor's theory undermines the
need for rational depth on the question of Africa identity.

In any case, Senghor saw his view as beyond romanticism and primitivism. In an important response to Ezekiel Mphalele, one of the ardent
critics of negritude, he had argued that "Negritude is nothing more or less
than what some English speaking Africans call personality."[33] But this,
on a critical look, may be a mere exaggeration, for while "the concept of
African personality, is assertive, the concept of negritude is revivalist [.]"
Indeed the concept of African personality as championed by Nkrumah
has a broader character and is considered more pragmatic than negritude.
Hence, his theory is considered a more viable alternative to negritude. This
theory is branded consciencism. For Nkrumah, consciencism is

> The map in intellectual terms of the disposition of forces which
> will enable African society to digest the Western and the Islamic
> and Euro-Christian elements in Africa, and develop them in
> such a way that they fit into the African personality . . . the
> philosophical standpoint which, taking its start from the present
> content of the African conscience, indicates the way in which
> progress is forged out of the conflict in that conscience.[34]

Consciencism is a pragmatic theory directed towards "the redemption of the African society" through a rational mediation of the tensions from Euro-Christian and Arab-Islamic forces that define and characterize the new Africa.[35]

Edward Blyden's well-researched treatise, *Christianity, Islam and the Negro Race* (1967), stands as a monumental achievement of an African anthropologist on the issues relating to African identity. Blyden comes out with a bold defense of the black race. He asks: "Did slavery not prevail in every country in Europe?"[36] He criticizes very biased minds like Samuel Baker and all other anti-black writers by emphasizing the positive potential of the Negro. For Blyden,

> The mistake which Europeans often make in considering questions of Negro improvement and the future of Africa, is in supposing that the Negro is the European in embryo – in the undeveloped stage – and that when, by and by, he shall enjoy the advantages of civilization and culture, he will become like European; in other words, that the Negro is on the same line of progress, in the same groove, with the European, but infinitely in the rear.[37]

For Blyden, the Negro race is a distinct race with a distinct role to play in the human race, or to borrow the words of Sedar Senghor in the "civilization of universal,"[38]

> It is not a question between the two races of inferiority or superiority. There is no absolute or essential superiority on the one side, nor absolute or essential inferiority on the other side. It is a question of difference of endowment and difference of destiny. No amount of training or culture will make the Negro European; on the other hand, no lack of training or deficiency of culture will make the European a Negro. The two races are not moving in the same groove, with an immeasurable distance between them, but on parallel lines. They will never meet in the place of their activities so as to concede in capacity or performance. They are not identical, as some think, but unequal; they are distinct but equal.[39]

Blyden's attempt thus reveals a bold anthropological endeavor to articulate the theory of African identity. This notwithstanding, the discourse on African identity appears, to have suffered a neglected dimension. There seems to be a gap in the entire discourse on African identity. This arises from its inability to account for the answers to the question of African identity as provided by African slaves whose servitude stood at the birth of the crisis. What was the reaction of African slaves to the new identity conferred on them both by slavery and the new culture obtained under this? Did they accept their new identity? What was their reaction to their identity in the New World during their first formal contact with alien identity represented by the "master"? We will address these issues through the life and works of the Igbo slave Olauda Equiano who was an eloquent spokesperson of African slaves and who, through his writings and actions provides a clue to the reaction of other slaves on the issue of African identity.

AFRICAN IDENTITY: THE RESPONSE OF OLAUDAH EQUIANO

A reliable response to the crisis of African identity came through an important Igbo slave, Olaudah Equiano, who was there at the birth of the crisis. Thus, if "the entrance of Africans into the intellectual history in the status of slaves"[40] was fundamental and foundational to the crisis of African identity, the re-entrance of Africans into the intellectual history of Europe as masters of their destiny through the life and work of Olaudah Equiano, which is an almost quick rebuttal of this wrong intellectual foundation, is a strong and reliable response to this problem. Equiano's thoughts and works are well documented in his famous autobiography, *The Interesting Narrative of the Life of Olaudah Equiano or Gustavus Vassa: The African*. A review of the entire work is not the focus of this section of our work; rather, our concern is to highlight important landmarks in the life of Olaudah Equiano as narrated by him, for which his life served as an anti-thesis to all that the denigration, defamation and destruction of African identity represents. Olaudah Equiano was typically an African who represented the cultural potentials of the black world. Equiano defied cultural and racial hegemony and insisted on his African identity and uniqueness by functioning under the status of a slave, the very institution that was employed to subjugate his humanity, to assert the African will and autonomy. Hence, he defied the inhuman circumstance of his slave status to achieve a quality of life marked by outstanding creativity, a deep sense of duty and commitment to the ideals of justice that stand as worthy efforts to "Africanize" the world.[41]

I shall seek to establish these claims by discussing the significant qualities of Olaudah Equiano: namely, (i) Equiano's dynamism and adventurous spirit, (ii) Equiano's campaign against slavery and (iii) Equiano's creative ingenuity and egalitarian individualism.

At various stages of his life, Equiano was a gun-powder carrier, or "powder-monkey" as they were called; a guager; a hair dresser; a steward; a project co-ordinator in the Caribbean; a preacher; a civil servant and resettlement officer (involved in resettling slaves in Sierra Leone); a writer; a lecturer; and a campaigner against slavery. While some of these duties were imposed on Equiano by his slave status and circumstance, some of them were what he chose for himself. To have functioned in these different capacities demonstrates clear evidence of mental strength and vigor and an ability to negotiate life to one's favor, which is the defining sign of creative intelligence. Olaudah Equiano, in this instance, would simply be saying that human intelligence is an asset that can function optimally in any space where the viable conditions that promote and fertilize it are available.

Equiano exploited the ethics of labor that define life in his culture to function in the two cultures that defined his new world. He had written of his life in the Igbo village of Nigeria before his captivity: "we are all habituated from our earliest years. Everyone contributes something to the common stock and as we are unacquainted with idleness we have no beggars."[42] However, the kind of labor he was forced to learn in the new world was considerably and significantly different from what obtained in the African village of his origin. How he functioned under his new circumstances to live a profound life of labor and duty should, then, be a subject of interest.

Olaudah Equiano functioned as a creative Igbo/African personality within an alien culture. No sooner had he found himself in an alien world than he began to use the cultural resource of his African background to recreate himself, adapt to his slave status and acquire the necessary skills he needed to survive in the new world. The breath of his humanity was high and wide, as he refused to be limited within the confines of one race and color. He participated in British wars and, by so doing, confirmed his readiness to contribute to the new nation in which he found himself. He was an explorer who was involved in the attempt to achieve Britain's imperial claim on India; and if this expedition has any positive claim to human history, it would be unfair to exclude Olaudah Equiano's contribution.

Thus, when Kwame Appiah seeks to theorize on the notion of race that will dissolve the pervading theory that difference defines racism, it sounds reasonable to argue that Olaudah Equiano had lived this in the eighteenth century by exhibiting an appetite for dynamism and cultural growth.[43] It is, therefore, plausible to argue that Olaudah Equiano had reconfigured the theory of race by his unusual dynamism in order to capitulate racism, especially in its negative and destructive dimension. To have functioned as an African slave in several ways that define him as an European, and to have lived according to the dictates of modernity in more than one way that deserve to be remembered, as an explorer, a civil servant, a merchant, a humanitarian involved in re-settling of slaves in Sierra-Leone, provide enough evidence for a claim that Olaudah Equiano advanced the cause of being human and reconfigured the theory of race. Indeed, it is quite doubtful if any European adventurer in pre-colonial and colonial Africa exhibited such quality of vitality and dynamism as Olaudah Equiano. Evidence of a European adventurer in Africa who absorbed and adapted to African culture in such a way as Olaudah Equiano absorbed European culture is yet to be discovered. Thus, he demonstrated the unusual capacity of the African to accept and absorb change, part of which has been the charge against that capacity in issues relating to identity. In this way, Olaudah Equiano is a fresh thesis who deserves study in issues relating to doubts and contempt of African identity and personality.

It is important to note that the qualities Olaudah Equiano exhibited are qualities that define life in the Igbo world of Equiano's origin. In an essay entitled "Authentic Existence in Igbo Understanding,"[44] I had argued that the drive for achievement is a prominent aspect of Igbo worldview, that it serves as a yardstick to demonstrate the idea of authentic existence. The man who could be characterized as living in an authentic manner in the Igbo world is a man of outstanding achievements: a man of honor, of wealth, of greatness: a man that wins many titles. Hence the Igbo attach a high value to human achievement and are well known as a cultural unit in black Africa that holds to a strong concept of progress and success. Because of this, the late Igbo economist Pius Okigbo described them as a restless and active people "dedicated to improve their lot by self-effort rather than by charity."[45] For this reason, a man in the Igbo world is judged and must work hard to carve a niche for himself even when he is considered to be born with a silver spoon in his mouth.

The British Vice-consul on what was then known as the Oil River Protectorate once described the Igbo as "exceedingly industrious."[46] The late Igbo poet and thinker D. I. Nwoga also provides a complimentary view in this regard with the view that, for the Igbos, "No work was too hard to be tempted, no job too menial to be used in the struggle with the world of achievement."[47] For a people who have such important values as these, it is very wrong to invent a fresh identity of failures and weakness and vest them with such as obtains with the modern categorization of the African identity. For if duty and commitment are the hallmark of the values and virtues that define nobility and greatness in the modern instance, we can reliably argue that Africans of Igbo extraction had such values and lived by them. The achievement drive that defines modernization is an inherent part of the Igbo world-view, and one would need to exorcise the Igbo race from the African world to hold any doubt about the strength and quality of African worth and identity in this regard.

Perhaps, the last basis on which to validate the claim that the various dimensions of identity find adequate answers in the life of Olaudah Equiano is his autobiography, published in 1780. Equiano's autobiography is an interesting document of life and truth. Ordinarily, autobiography is a mere story about oneself written by oneself. But the creativity in Olaudah Equiano comes out in the success that defined his book. Equiano's book had six editions in twenty-two years. It was translated into Dutch in 1790, into German in 1792, into Russian in 1794, republished in the United States in 1791 and in Ireland in 1792, amongst other publications. His choice of words and pattern of documentation makes his work exceptional; because of this, it stands as evidence of African ingenuity in arts. Equiano provides an effective translation of Igbo words to account for his life in a pre-literate Igbo world. Indeed, as Catherine Acholonu, an important researcher on Olaudah Equiano, has observed, "Equiano wrote his story at a time when West African languages had not yet been put into recogniz-able writing."[48] But he was able to express Igbo ideas and words through an English form of expression. This explains why the world *Isseke* is written *Essaka*, and Equiano writes *Eboe* rather than *Ibo*. It also explains why we read *Embrenche* instead of *Mgburichi*, which, as revealed by Acholonu, is the more commonly accepted concept within the Isseke community that we can associate with Equiano, and which denotes the sacrificial mask prevalent in Isseke town of his time.[49]

To have documented a life that began in a pre-literate and a pre-alpha-betical linguistic group in the inhuman era of the slave trade, when memory and self-pride suffered a most miserable harm, and to have preserved it for memory, was an extra-ordinary achievement. For this, Olaudah Equiano is an enduring subject of discourse more than two hundred years after his death. He is strong evidence of that creative intelligence that, in the words of Nigeria's President Nnamdi Azikiwe, is "the soul of scholarship[.]"[50] We cannot desire more cogent evidence to demonstrate that Olaudah Equiano has the intellect that can equal or equate that of any creative genius in any age, nation or race of the world. For this reason, any attempt to "inferior-ize" the African intellect and provoke a diversionary thesis against African humanity through a crisis of identity is weak and ineffective.

While it may, however, be wrong to hold any particular group as being particularly responsible for recreating the African crisis, it may again be right to hold that both the creator and victim of the crisis need proper intellectual repositioning by reading about Olaudah Equiano and how his life and work addresses some of the doubts that define the crisis. Identity itself is subject to our desire and expectation and is often valued according to how it meets these qualities. Should the apparent failure of resilience and adaptation to modernity at the moment influence us, for which we are more prepared to define Africa in terms of a weak and negative identity, it is important to remind ourselves of the legendary resilience of Olaudah Equiano at the worst period of the slave trade.

That is not the final issue on Olaudah Equiano. His quality of intellect empowered him to go on lecture tours with his published work, which took him to England, Scotland, Wales, and Ireland. Equiano turns his autobiography into a document on slavery, one that goes further to provide theories on morality, sociology and politics. He reminds his captors, whom he referred to as the haughty Europeans, "to recollect that his ancestors were once like the Africans, uncivilized and even barbarous" and argues that the presumed African difference is unfounded; for as he witnessed, "the Spanniads, who inhabited America, under the Torrid Zone, become as dark coloured as native Indian of Virginia."[51]

Equiano narrates how his trip to the West Indies exposed him to the worst cases of slavery, which as he put it, "might serve for a history of the whole" and which represents, typically, how the slave masters had exploitted their human resources by doing evil.[52] The slave dealers, he holds, would only have had to reverse their passion for enslaving others to become humanists of the first order. He provides a deep insight into human nature with the argument that "the totality of mistaken avarice corrupts the milk of human kindness and turns into gall."[53] If his masters were not slave masters, they might have been generous, as tender-hearted and just as they were "unfeeling, rapacious and cruel."[54] Thus, for Olaudah Equiano, human differences converge at negative points, such as evil, which have no race or color, and which express their weight and worth in social constructions and values through human choice. Under this circumstance, they seek justification through a fresh category of difference to justify their misapplication of social constructions and values. These categories are often constructed out of prejudice and lead to a racist view of "the other." Thus, while it may be wrong to enslave "the other," it may be considered tolerable when slavery, even on a massive scale, is applied to a people with a category of difference. Differences become a kind of religion to be worshipped and divinized as they assume the moral basis or force to subjugate others by denying them basic freedoms. If differences serve to define and justify slavery, why not hold onto and justify it and deepen the difference? This is how racism promotes slavery and vice versa. Thus, it is in a wrong notion of difference that we must seek to understand the basis for the distortion of African identity; for while slavery has been abolished, the theory of difference that promoted its monumental damage to African humanity persists in the mind.

At the root of it all is the denial of difference as an expression of freedom: the freedom to be different. By this, I mean the denial of difference as an important value for "the other." The man who denies or ascribes certain identities to Africans, especially those that impair the quality of their freedom to be different, ironically wants to be given the freedom to hold this opinion. He wants to differ from a contrary opinion on the Africans even as he would not want the Africans to differ from his view. Hence, it is a cause for wonder that the freedom that advanced modernity is the very ideal that is denied others through a deliberate and wrong categorization of "the other." If freedom is the ideal of modernity, then even the choice to be black or stupid must be respected.

This turns our mind to racism, the bastion of human claims to difference, at a rather dangerous level. What is a race? Where or when does the notion of human race end, and how should it be conceived in the midst of a persisting racial divide among a presumably singular human race? Are the human differences on which we construct the idea of race merely sociological or fundamentally biological in origin? Put simply, is belonging to any race an item in the blood or an invention or even an intent made by time and circumstance? Do we in any way have differences in intelligence among the different races of humanity or are we rather the inventors of these differences?

These questions deserve attention because race and racism have been deepened to function and produce deep psychological consequences, breathing injustice, inequality, hatred and contempt among a presumably human race, undermining the roots of humanity and the basis of a human (common/one) race. No theory harbors such a dangerous basis for human differences as racism, yet no theory may have been more impotent in the attempt to promote human welfare, especially in the global cum capitalist world of today - a world where wealth and status dictate and define social interaction worldwide. Thus, notwithstanding the important discovery published in *The Crisis*, an important journal of the American National Assembly for the Advancement of Colored People in 1911, that "the civilization of a . . . race at any particular moment of time offers no index to its innate or inherited capacities,"[55] racism has continued to speak and sustain the opposite by advancing a wrong idea of the other, and this has remained sharper and deeper when color is applied to strengthen the logic of difference. But this again suggests that racism can only be as weak and faulty as color can be, for even color is remade by mixing it with another color. By this, I mean I mean that racism is an irrational judgment that is not grounded on reason and logic but seeks to apply reason and logic to validate its position.

Recently, James Dewey Watson has provoked an idea that suggests that racism is an enduring cultural belief. Watson has, in plain language, come out with a claim that "black people are inherently less intelligent than whites."[55] Coming from Watson, a Nobel prize winner, this position is nothing short of what Edward Pilkington has rightly called "racism hiding behind the cloak of scientific jargon,"[56] a sickening re-statement of the 1994 racial intelligence theory of Richard Herostein and Charles Murray in their book, *The Bell Curve.*

I do not consider myself an expert on the biological sciences or a "eugenicist" capable of contributing to this controversy, but it would not be out of place to point out that intelligence must be qualified to retain its meaning. There are different types of intelligence, and any authority that wants to enlarge human imagination by providing a theory of intelligence must be specific in stating which type of intelligence he or she is talking about, before he or she deserves a worthy response. But if Watson can make this claim despite the overwhelming evidence of the growing relevance of the black man in knowledge and creativity, there is need to examine further the roots of the racism that animates this view. His position urges us to go deeper, to question the thinking that generates and re-generates the belief in racism.

EPISTEMOLOGY OF RACISM

What pattern of thinking leads to a racial idea of the other? What manner of thinking misleads the mind to see truth and reality in terms of a group or collectivity and seeks to institute a difference in these terms even as we know the "particular" or the "individual" affords more avenues to truth than the collective? I call this the epistemology of racism, the pattern of knowing or the category of knowing the other that emanates from racism and entrenches racism.

Du Bois, the well-known theorist of race, identified eight races in the world - Slavs, Teutons, English, Negroes, the Romance, Semites, Hindus and Mongolians - and provides the provocative statement that the deeper differences among these races are spiritual and psychological.[57] I shall not dwell on a critique of this position. I consider Kwame Appiah, from whom this view is lifted, to have a relevant response to this claim.[58] It is, however, my view that human differences, to a large extent, come within acquired and learned beliefs, habits, attitudes, all of which pre-dispose human beings to think in one way or the other, especially in relation to another. I seek to support this with a claim: we can enjoy "love" or "kindness" from a person but retain an idea or a view of him or her that limits the quality of his or her kindness. In the same vein, the value or regard we assign to ideas and concepts about a people depends to a large extent on our idea about the people. An idea may be good, but an attitude to the source of the idea may limit the impact it makes in our lives. The regard we assign to an idea may sometimes emanate from our view about the person who holds or originates the idea.

By epistemology of racism, then, I imply a pattern of knowing that functions with a predisposition to difference as the root or foundation of truth. It seeks to translate difference into a principle and determines truth and value in terms of its potential to reinforce a predetermined difference. It is a cognitive process that translates human differences into a principle and infuses them into spiritual, sociological and psychological relations. This pattern of knowing and determining truths functions in contrast to important theories of knowledge such as phenomenology or the theory of detachment. Edmund Hurssel, the father of phenomenology, once recommended that thought should attempt to grasp the thing in the human process of knowing by which the true essences of things disclose themselves to the mind. By this, I mean that for Hursel the thing should be allowed to reveal itself to consciousness. Reality should be allowed to reveal or manifest itself so that consciousness would be consciousness of something. This kind of epistemology is reversed in an epistemology of racism. Here, attitudes or beliefs displace reason and determine truth. In a reverse way and by an alternative formula, it holds that accidents such as attitudes, belief, biases and prejudices should institute or define the substance.

This pattern of knowing would, for instance, be articulated as, "*He is black therefore He is irrational,*" with no underlying premise of reason to establish whether there is any relationship between color and reason. As a result, this pattern of knowing exploits all items that influence or attempt to displace uniformity, sameness or common categories in order to institute a difference and re-enforce it through a logic of negation. It attempts to provide fresh conditions of knowledge that stand outside the canons of proper conceptualization such that only selective conclusions that re-enforce differences are sustained and validated. For this reason, it produces truth, views and values that create and recreate conflicts, and by "resolving" these conflicts in its favor, it sustains its worth and meaning. This epistemology functions in other human constructions with bi-polar characteristics such as ethnicity, chauvinism, xenophobia, feminism, et cetera. Even within a believably common race, it obtains as a method of creating and sustaining the ideology of difference. I shall demonstrate this with the *osu* caste system, a common belief in several areas of the Igbo culture of Nigeria.

In several Igbo part of Nigeria, a curious caste system obtains where a clan, village, or community is categorized as *osu* (outcast). The said people are denied certain rights and privileges such as honor, title taking or inter-marriage on the ground that either (i) their progenitors committed a taboo against the land by going against a social custom in the past or (ii) their progenitors belong to the gods, and hence they are considered sacred and social interaction with them is prohibited by the gods. This phenomenon is well portrayed in Chinua Achebe's novel entitled *No Longer at Ease*, where it served as the basis for a cultural clash against a marital desire.

Now the interesting thing about the *osu* caste system is not that it advertises and institutionalizes a wrong basis for difference, but that it translates constructed differences into human biology, by which children born to *osu* parents inherit the *osu* and the sanctions associated with it. We are then led to think that at the heart of this wrong theory of difference is an attempt to construct a permanent image of the other that is inferior enough to promote a superior notion of the self. Because of this, there is an attempt to create and recreate differences as a way of attempting to meet the tension that defines the encounter with the other. There is already a categorization of the other that needs to be preserved to retain a posi-tive view of the self, and this becomes a basic tool to meet this encounter. Thus, historicizing differences becomes a solution to the problem. Since the "de-othering" afforded by a theory of differences instituted by history and culture is readily available and authoritative enough, it is adopted as a response to the problem. By relying on history, therefore, differences are constructed to function in favor of racism.

But this theory of difference, however, shows that racism and its claim to difference and the effort to justify it arises from the same human quest for difference, identity and individuation. The principle through which the mind attempts to reduce or "de-other" the other is the same principle through which it seeks to assert an identity. At the heart of it all is the desire to assert one's identity by destroying or disfiguring the identity of the other. This pattern of "de-othering" is what is at work in the phenom-enon of racism.

CONCLUSION

This chapter has attempted to provide a survey of the various dimen-sions of the crisis of African identity and attempted an answer to the crisis by looking at the life of an important Igbo slave, Olaudah Equiano, who functioned in the era of slavery. The focus on Equiano in this matter is meant to underscore the historical origin of the crisis and the place of creative intelligence and originality in re-asserting the African identity. The position of the paper is that Olaudah Equiano had much of these virtues and by so doing, provided an exemplary response to the crisis by his resilience and strong will during the era of the slave trade. Thus, if the African slave could function as remarkably as he did at such trying times, then a positive idea of Africa should have been long re-established. The paper believes that the Afro-pessimism of the moment should not obtain and should not be a conclusive thesis on African identity. The crisis of African modernity at the moment is in no way comparable to the slave period when an African slave demonstrated the quality of his humanity and re-asserted an African identity.

The chapter has also examined the basis of racism, which is often used to promote a wrong idea of Africa. It has examined the epistemological roots of racism to deduce why racism prefers to reduce or "de-other" the other in order to be able to categorize or accept him or her. It located this in a conscious quest by the agent or "de-otherer" for a superior identity; and it observed that since the desire for identity is a re-current demand on the human person, racism is an attempt to provide a permanent answer to the problem by placing the other in a wrong order. By permanently instituting a notion of difference through racism, man seeks to provide a ready-made answer to the desire and demand for difference.

The chapter provides a deeper basis for self-reflection to any mind that prefers to see the other with a wrong category of difference, a mind that, for this reason, may advance strong reasons in favor of racism in order to satisfy the desire or right to be different that he denies the other through such wrong categorization. And how contrary it is, or should be, to try to claim for oneself what one is not ready to give to another: the right to be different. This is one position from which the chapter views its relevance.

NOTES

1. D. U. Opata, "On What is African?", a seminar paper presented at the William Amo Centre for the Study of African Philosophy, University of Nigeria Nsukka, 6 February 1992.

2. Innocent Onyewuenyi, *The African Origin of Greek Philosophy* (Nsukka: University of Nigeria Press, 1993), 100.

3. Luke Nnamdi Mbefo, *The Reshaping of African Traditions* (Enugu: Snaap Press, 1988), 21.

4. Ibid., 23.
5. See D.C.M. Mutiso and S. W. Robio, eds., *Readings in African Political Thought* (London: Heinemann, 1975).
6. A. Irele, *The African Experience in Literature and Ideology* (Ibadan: Heinemann, 1981), 17-18.
7. Ibid., 102.
8. Russel L. Adams, *Africa* no. 79 (March 1978), 38. Cited in C. M. Ezekwugo, "Cultural Revival: The Role of Black Intellectual Elites," *The Philosopher's Digest*, (1991), 12.
9. D. A. Masolo, *African Philosophy in Search of Identity* (Indiana: Indiana University Press, 1994), 3-4.
10. Ibid., 10.
11. Ibid., 3.
12. Mutiso and Rohio, *Reading*, "Introduction."
13. Ibid.
14. Ibid., 321.
15. S. A. Gakwandi, *The Novel and Contemporary Experience in Africa* (London: Heinemann, 1977), 3.
16. Mutiso and Rohio, *Readings*, 321.
17. Gakwandi, *The Novel*, 7.
18. C. Dunton and C. Richard Bjornson, "The African Quest for Freedom and Identity: Cameroonian Writing and the National Experience," *West Africa Magazine*, (9-15 August 1993), 417.
19. For details see *ODU: Journal of West African Studies*, no. 14 (1983).
20. Hugh Trevor Roper, *The Rise of Christian Europe* (London, 1963) in *Listiner*, 28 November 1963), 871.
21. A. E. Afigbo, "Of Men and War, Women and History," valedictory lecture delivered at the University of Nigeria, Nuskka, 1992.
22. Ibid.
23. C. Anta Diop, "Death Shall Not Find Us Thinking That We Die," in *African–American Humanism: An Anthology*, ed. Norm R. Allen (New York: Promotheses Books, 1991), 137.
24. Ibid.
25. Moya Deacon, "The Status of Father Tempels and Ethno-Philosophy in the Discourse in African Philosophy," in *Philosophy from Africa*, second edition, eds., P. H. Coetzee and A.P.J. Roux (Cape Town: Oxford University Press of Southern Africa, 2002), 103.
26. Ibid.
27. Ibid.
28. I. Okpewho, "Myth and Rationality in Africa," *Ibadan Journal of Humanistic Studies* no.1, (April 1981), 28.

29. Ali A. Mazrui, "Political Nostalgia," *Ibadan Journal of Humanistic Studies,* no. 2, (1981), 7.
30. Ibid.
31. L. S. Senghor, "What is Negritude"? Excepts from a speech at Oxford University in October 1961. See Mutiso and Rohio, *Readings,* 83.
32. K. Wiredu, *Philosophy and an African Culture* (Cambridge: Cambridge: University Press, 1980), xi.
33. Mazrui, "Political Nostalgia, 7.
34. Kwame Nkrumah, *Consiencism: Philosophy and Ideology for Decolonization with Particular Reference to the African Revolution* (London, 1970) cited in Mutiso and Rohio, *Readings,* 644.
35. Ibid.
36. Edward W. Blyden, *Christianity, Islam and the Negro Race* (Edinburgh: Edinburgh University Press, 1967), 111-29, cited in Mutiso and Rohio, eds., *Reading,* 13.
37. Ibid.
38. Senghor, "What is Negritude," 83.
39. Blyden, *Christianity,* 16.
40. L. N. Mbefo, *The Reshaping of African Traditions* (Enugu: Snaap Press, 1988), 21.
41. What I imply by the term Africanize here is the attempt to promote a positive idea of Africa by exhibiting the cultural values that molded Olaudah Equiano at the early development of his life in the Igbo-African village from where he was abducted.
42.   Olaudah Equiano, *The Interesting Narrative of Olaudah Equiano, Written by Himself* ed., Robert J. Allison (Boston: Bedford/St. Martin's, 1995), 39.
43. Kwame A. Appiah, *In My Father's House: Africa in the Philosophy of Culture* (Oxford: Oxford University Press, 1992), 6.
44. L. O. Ugwuanyi, "Authentic Existence in the African Understanding," (M.A. Dissertation submitted to the University of Nigeria, Nsukka, 1993).
45. Cited in J. O. Oguejiofor, *The Influence of Igbo Traditional Religion on the Socio-Political Character of the Igbo* (Nsukka: Fulladu Publishing Company, 1996), 22.
46. Oguejiofor, *The Influence,* 18.
47. Ibid.
48. Catherine Acholonu-Olumba, *The Igbo Roots of Olaudah Equiano: An Anthropological Research* (With a reply to Vincent Carretta) (Revised edition) (Abuja: Afa Publications, 2007), 27.
49. Ibid.
50. Cited in "Emeagweali: All Rise for the Computer Whiz-Kid," a citation of Philip Emeagwali for the Award of an Honorary Degree of the Doctor of

Science Honoris Causa of the University of Abuja, *UNIBUJA News Journal* 12, no.3, (Jan-June, 2005), 46.

51. Equiano, *The Interesting*, 2.
52. Ibid., 5.
53. Ibid., 62.
54. Ibid.
55. See Appiah, *In My Father's House*, 34.
56. Watson's claim was widely published in several web sites worldwide as well as newspapers. See for example, "How can DNA genius James Watson believe Black people are less intelligent than White," *Daily Trust*, (October 24, 2007), 9.
57. See *West Africa*, "The Intelligence Race," 27 March 1995.
58. See Appiah, *In My Father's House*, 28.
59. Ibid., 29.

CHAPTER 6

BETWEEN LITERATURE, FACTS, AND FICTION: PERSPECTIVES ON OLAUDAH EQUIANO'S *THE INTERESTING NARRATIVE*

ELIZABETH ODACHI ONOGWU

Olaudah Equiano's *The Interesting Narrative of* the *Life of Olaudah Equiano, or Gustavus Vassa, the African¹* offers a very unique perspective on slave writings and set the precedent for most slave literatures. It is in Equiano's autobiography that we first see a vivid description of the African Igbo child-Equaino before he was captured into slavery. The question though is, how much of his vivid description is the fact, how much of it is fiction and of course how much of literature does it have? This chapter argues that, like most autobiographical works, Equiano's *Interesting Narrative* contains elements of fiction, while at the same time representing the fact, even the truth of his life and times.² It is a double edged analysis which viewed the autobiographical genre from more than one angle—a closer reading. After reviewing the existing arguments, the paper argues that *The Interesting Narrative of the Life of Olaudah Equiano, or Gustavus Vassa, the African* is a product of literature, fact, and fiction.

The term autobiography has come to assume different meanings over time. Different scholars have diverse definitions of the term but most of these definition share Georg Misch's idea of autobiography. To him, autobiography "can be defined only by summarising what the term 'auto-biography' implies – the description (graphia) of an individual human life (bios) by the individual himself (auto)."[3] James Olney, a leading scholar in autobiographical literature has this perceptive definition of autobiography as "the sifting of memories and the recreation of events to see how they relate, where they connect, what pattern they establish."[4] In a book published seven years later, Olney defines autobiography as a "study of the way experience is transformed into literature, a study of the creative process, a humanistic study of the ways of men and the forms taken by human consciousness."[5]

All these definitions quite agree with the step-by-step definition by Misch. Beyond the seeming individuality of the genre, autobiography still makes room for things around it as it is basically the life of an individual in relation to his surroundings. This perhaps is what Kolawole Ogungbesan had in mind when he said "Autobiography portrays human life as actually lived by the individual, and the social and historical world in which he lived."[6] This goes to prove the point that "all autobiographies contain to some degree a description of their times."[7] For it is within the autobiographical genre that one has the privileged access to the particular experience of a group of people. The slave narrative, for instance, which is the general term for account of the lives by former slaves mostly written by them, gives information as to the experience and nature of slavery. The same can be said of the Black experience which can all be deduced from particular autobiographies. It is in autobiographies more than historical texts that the histories of Blacks were preserved for under the pretence of writing about their own lives, former slaves wrote about the experience of slavery and of their times.

According to Olney, the first autobiography was written by W. P. Scargill in 1934 with the title, *The Autobiography of a Dissenting Minister.* First in the sense that Scargill is the first to call his book by the name of auto-biography as people like Jean-Jacques Rousseau, Michel de Montaigne, St. Augustine, and Plato wrote well before Scargill, but they called theirs "confessions" or "essays" which are actually autobiographies in every sense of the word. Autobiographies have since moved to be known and identified by different forms and names. For instance, an autobiography does not have to come in form of a prose before it is an autobiography as Paul Valery and Olney have been able to prove with *La Jeune Parque* and T. S. Eliot's *Four Quartets* respectively.

Autobiography can be broadly divided into informal and formal. The informal autobiography consists of memories and reminiscences which usually emphasise what are remembered rather than who is remembering it. The formal autobiography is a sort of biographical truth[8]. This type of autobiography involves the consciousness recollection and reshaping of one's life story. This is the type of autobiography we are most acquainted with and it is under this category that Olaudah Equiano's *The Interesting Narrative* falls.

THE INTERESTING NARRATIVE – SYNOPSIS

Born around 1745, Equiano was the son of an Igbo Chief of Essaka (Isseke) in what is present day Nigeria. Equiano was kidnapped along with his sister while playing and was sold into slavery. In slavery he was later sold to English slave traders, who transported him to Barbados in the West Indies. After two weeks Equiano was again taken to Virginia and sold to a local planter who later resold him to Captain Henry Pascal, a British naval officer. It was Pascal who renamed him Gustavus Vassa a name he rejected but he was thoroughly beaten until he answered to the name. Under Captain Pascal, he was exposed to military actions during the Seven Years War between the British and the French, but at the end of the war, Pascal reneges on his promise of freeing Equiano and instead sold him without warning to Captain James Doran. His new owner takes him to the West Indies and sells him to a merchant called Robert King. Equiano, clever as he was, saved enough money to buy his freedom in 1766.

As a freeman, Equiano went back to London and thence commence on a series of voyages of commerce and adventure to the West-Indies, the North Pole, and North America. He returned to London and becomes thoroughly concerned with his spiritual well-being. He converted to Methodism and worked closely with Granville Sharp to fight for the abolition of slavery, a major cause which *The Interesting Narrative* was meant to advance. *The Interesting Narrative* was published in 1789, three years after his autobiography; he got married to an English woman.

CLOSER READING

The Interesting Narrative when studied superficially is an autobiography. After all, George Misch defines that genre of truth telling as "the description (graphia) of an individual human life (bios) by himself (auto)."[9] All these elements exist in Equiano's book. Equiano begins his narrative in the most honest and truthful manner thus:

I believe it is difficult for those who publish their own memoirs to escape the imputation of vanity; nor is this the only disadvantage under which they labour: it is also their misfortune, that whatever is uncommon is rarely, if ever, believed; and what is obvious we are apt to turn from with disgust and to charge the writer with impertinence. People generally think those memoirs only worthy to be read or remembered which abound in great or striking events; those, in short, which in a high degree excite either admiration or pity: all others they consign to contempt and oblivion. It is, therefore; I confess, not a little hazardous, in a private and obscure individual, and a stranger too, thus to solicit the indulgent attention of the public; especially when I own I offer here the history of neither a saint, a hero, nor tyrant.[10]

This humble yet ardent and convincing manner is the way *The Interesting Narrative* begins. He impresses the sincerity of his autobiography to us by a preamble to the description of his life. This research aims at questioning the authenticity of his recollection. It questions the truthfulness of the description of his life. The study does not go about this questioning on the hard ground of fundamental truth especially pertaining to the author's birth place and origin like Vincent Carretta does in his book. This is because this researcher has seen core evidences that proves his Igbo Isseke origin and cannot prove the author otherwise. The questioning however will come as a result of the genre which *The Interesting Narrative* assumes – that of an autobiography. This research will demonstrate that while most of what Equiano has written is true, a percentage of it is doctored truth. Roy Pascal puts it succinctly when he says that "the autobiographer half discovers, half creates a deeper design and truth than adherence to historical and factual truth covered ever claim to."[11] It also proves that another percentage of it is literature which means that it is at the same time fictional and political as Ngugi Wa Thiongo notes that literature from such oppressed societies must take sides.

The primary concern of this chapter is not to verify the truth of the narrative but to see how far it delves into literature and politics by ascertaining how much of it is fiction and how much of it is politics both of which are embodiments of literature.

THE INTERESTING NARRATIVE AS FICTION (NOVEL)

Inasmuch as James Olney echoing Stephen Dedalus argues that autobiographies lacks the whole of "wholeness, harmony, and radiance," which all fictions must have, further stating that, an autobiography can achieve harmony and radiance but certainly not wholeness as by "its very nature, the self is (like the autobiography that creates it) open-ended and incomplete: It is always in process or, more precisely, is itself a process" (25), *The Interesting Narrative* can still be screened with a literary eye as most autobiographies, and indeed *The Interesting Narrative* mirrors not just the life of the narrator but the times, the Igbo-African society, and the black experience as a whole. For under the guise of writing his life story, Equiano narrates in detail the experience of slavery and the barbaric behavior of white slave owners and traders. Thus the genre can be analyzed using the necessary conventions used for any fictional novel.

Point of view:

In the analysis of fiction, point of view according to R. F. Dietrich and Roger H. Sundell refers to "the position from which the narrator views the action – detached or involved, inside or outside, far or near, or any stage between."[12] Point of view is broadly classified into first person and third person and by position into omniscient and limited.

Most autobiographies are written in the first person participant narrator since the narrator is the major actor in the book around whom the story of the book revolves. *The Interesting Narrative* however is not content with this single point of view rather, due to the double vision of Equiano as someone with double identity, the author glides freely from the first person participant narrator to the third person omniscient and oftentimes editorial narrator. Sometimes, the author comes in to comment directly on the evils of slavery. Vincent Carretta submits that "Equiano addresses his audience from two positions at once. On a narrative level, he speaks of the past events from the perspective of the time in which he is recalling them," (xix). The implication is that the autobiography becomes highly fictionalized. A good example in his narration is his description of the middle passage.

> The first object which saluted my eyes when I arrived on the coast was the sea, and a slave-ship, which was then riding at anchors, and waiting for its cargo. These filled me with astonishment, which was soon converted into terror, which I am yet at a loss to describe, nor the feelings of my mind. When I was carried on board I was immediately handled, and tossed up, to see if I were sound, by some of the crew; and I was now persuaded that I had gotten into a world of bad spirit, and that they were going to

kill me. . . . Indeed, such were the horrors of my views and fears
at the moment, that, if ten thousand worlds had been my own,
I would have freely parted with them all to have exchanged my
condition to that of the meanest slave in my own country.[13]

Here the author speaks as a first person narrator who actively par-
ticipates in the happenings. In fact, at this point he is a central character
through whose eyes we get to know most of the experience of the author
and other slaves. In another instance, Equiano narrates from the point
of view of the third person. He takes it a little further by coming in to
comment and sometimes passes negative or positive judgment on an issue.
At this time he speaks from the point of view of the third person omniscient narrator. Here again, an instance will suffice.

The treatment of the slaves was nearly the same: So nearly
indeed, that the history of an island, or even a plantation, with
a few such exceptions… might serve for a history of the whole.
Such a tendency has the slave-trade to debauch men's minds,
and harden them to every feeling of humanity! . . . It is the
fatality of this mistaken avarice, that it corrupts the milk of
human kindness, and turns it into gall. And, had the pursuits
of those men been different, they might have been as generous,
as tender-hearted, and just, as they are unfeeling, and rapacious,
and cruel. Surely this traffic cannot be good, which spreads like
a pestilence, and taints what it touches! Which violates that first
natural right of mankind, equality and independency, and gives
one man a dominion over his fellows which God could never
intend! For it raises the owner to a state as far above man as it
depresses the slave below it; and, with all the presumption of
human pride, sets a distinction between them, immeasurable in
extent, and endless in duration.[14]

Here the author intrudes to comment objectively and directly on the
characters involved in slave trading i.e. the white slave traders and owners
on the one hand and the black slaves on the other. He detaches himself
from either party so as to feel free to comment. He views the situation
from all angles and even observes that "had the pursuits of those men been
different, they might have been generous, as tender-hearted; and as just,
as they are unfeeling, and rapacious and cruel."[15] Thus the author from his
omniscient position is able not only to observe but to weigh the effect of
slavery on both the slave owners and the slaves themselves.

Language

According to Georges Gusdorf,

> Autobiography... is unquestionably a document about a life, and the historian has a perfect right to check out its testimony and verify its accuracy. But it is also a work of art, and the literary devotee, for his part, will be aware of its stylistic harmony and the beauty of its images.[16]

The stylistic harmony and the beauty of its images which Gusdorf talks about abound in their numbers in Equiano's *The Interesting Narrative*. Equiano, like a fiction writer deploys a range of stylistic techniques and a rich use of imagery in his book. In the *Interesting Narrative*, we come across carefully selected words which enjoy deeper meanings than the literal meaning we are acquainted with. A good instance is the image of painting human beings, slaves, in the form of cargoes or goods that are made for sale and subsequent consumption. This clearly is fiction in the sense that, if the autobiographer remembers events and put them down carefully, he certainly does not remember the words used. His selection of words, the images cast and the effect intended are all fictional. Once again, we will return to the scene of the middle passage to draw out glaring examples: "The first object which *saluted* my eyes when I arrived on the coast was the sea, and a slave-ship, which was then riding at anchor, and waiting for its *cargo*... when I was carried on board I was immediately *handled, and tossed up*, to see if I were sound."[17]

In this extract, we see the careful use of language. The sea for instance is personified as we're told it "saluted" the author's eyes. But more than that, the author invokes the image of slaves on the slave-ship as "cargos" who like cargos are "handled, and tossed up to" ascertain their soundness. We are told of how the ship is loaded with all her "cargos"[18] and discharges her "cargos."[19] The author submits that "I used frequently to have different cargos of new Negroes in my care for sale."[20] This paints the image of human beings as goods, a choice of word deliberately selected by the author to create a strong effect on the reader. Closely related to the image of human beings as cargos is that of parcels. On arrival in Barbados, the author said the slave traders put them in "separate parcels."[21] Also, on a given signal, the author said "the buyers rush at once into the yard where the slaves are confined and make choice of that *"parcel they like best."*[22] All these examples go to show how slave trading has the tendency to reduce individuals (the slaves) to nothing but mere objects or property which is owned by an individual who therefore has license to use and abuse them [it] as he wishes. The author was clearly able to bring out this effect by the use of carefully selected words.

Selection of Events

Northrop Frye in his *Anatomy of Criticism* sees autobiography as nothing but fiction since the two are the product of the same impulse. To him, "we may call this very important form of prose fiction the confession form."[23] Barret J. Mandel quoting Patricia Meyer Spacks' analysis of William Cowper's *Memoir* says of the autobiographer as always:

> Selecting, repressing, interpreting his experience, according himself importance as unique personality, he exercises his fantasy by making himself. . . . Reading his work may provide the same imaginative complexities as experiencing a novel; the presumed difference in authorial intent between fiction and factual records makes little necessary difference in effect, though it poses philosophic and literary questions.[24]

This observation is truer of Equiano's *The Interesting Narrative* than it can ever be of Cowper's *Memoirs*. For in *The Interesting Narrative*, we find the conscious sifting of events which Equiano engages in. Here, the author only takes time to narrate favorable events of his life and leaves out unpleasant tales just like he left out unfavorable reviews of the first edition from the list of reviews that appeared at the blurb of the novel. At other times, the author selects events so as to not bore the readers with continual narration of the obvious barbarity of slave traders. Whatever the intent is, the implication is that, autobiography is factual and true to life, when you consciously sift events, chronologically arrange them to give the narration a sort of unity, you are no longer writing facts but fiction. A good instance of the selection of events is found in this excerpt:

> I saw many cruel punishments inflicted on the slaves in the short time I stayed here. In particular I was present when a poor fellow was tied up and kept hanging by the wrists at some distance from the ground, and then some half hundred weights were fixed to his ancles. In which posture he was flogged most unmercifully. There were also, as I heard, two different masters noted for cruelty on the island, who had staked up two negroes naked, in two hours. The vermin stung them to death, I heard

a gentleman, I well knew; tell my captain that he passed sentence on a Negro man to be burnt alive for attempting to poison an overseer. *I pass over numerous instances, in order to relieve the reader by a milder scene of roguery* (My emphasis).[25]

Closely related to this passage is another incident:

> One day. . . two of my wearied countrymen who were chained together . . . preferring death to such a life of misery, somehow made through the nettings, and jumped into the sea; immediately another dejected fellow . . . followed their example . . . two of the wretches were drowned, but they got the other, and afterwards flogged him unmercifully, for thus attempting to prefer death to slavery. In this manner we continued to undergo more hardships *than I can ever relate;* hardship which are inseparable from the accused trade.[26]

The author says "My life and fortune have been extremely chequered, and my adventures various. Even those I have related are considerably abridged...."[27] The author himself confirms that he selects the events to relate and the ones to leave out. This implies that *The Interesting Narrative* is an edited version of the author's life. It also implies that fictional elements like the cutting and joining of events to give the narrative chronology and a perfect – whole as well as to make it interesting were introduced.

THE INTERESTING NARRATIVE AS LITERATURE (POLITICS)

In 1981, Ngugi Wa Thiongo in his *Writers in Politics* asserts that:

> Literature as a creative process and also as an end is conditioned by historical social forces and pressures: It cannot elect to stand above or to transcend economics, politics, class, race, or what Achebe calls 'the burning issues of the day because those very burning issues with which it deals take place within an economic, political, class and race context. Again *because of its social involvements, because of its thoroughly social character, literature is partisan: Literature takes sides, and more so in a class society* (My emphasis).[28]

Ngugi's observation is very true of the bulk of African literature whether autobiography, fiction, drama or poetry. Ngugi's observation is even truer of *The Interesting Narrative* as Equiano's autobiography is conditioned by historical and social forces and pressures. *The Interesting Narrative* addresses "the burning issues" of its time—the era of slavery. Since literature is a means to an end, and because literature is socially involved, it is partisan. And because literature is partisan, it "takes sides and more so in a class society." The type of literature that will emanate from an oppressed group and a former slave, must necessarily take sides no matter how spiritual the author gets. By solely deciding to be a writer, one has made a choice to become partisan, and in effect, political. Ngugi opines that "every writer is a writer in politics."[29] Equiano in writing *The Interesting Narrative* is political and his literature whether it is autobiographical or fictional is partisan. This therefore implies that, in arguing that Equiano's *The Interesting Narrative* is the product of literature, facts and fiction, the researcher is invariably saying that the narrative is at once political and fictional and is based on facts. On several occasions, the author abandons facts and fiction and gets political. In this regard when literature becomes politically inclined, it is used as a tool. Literature as a tool works to show the world the barbarity and cruelty of that "accursed trade" and all other forms of oppression. The author makes a case for the slaves, condemning the brutality of the slave owners as in the following excerpt:

> Are slaves more useful by being thus humbled to the condition of brutes, than they would enjoy the privileges of men? The freedom which diffuses health and prosperity throughout Britain answers you – No when you make men slaves, you deprive them of half their virtue, you set them, in your own conduct, an example of fraud, rapine, and cruelty, and compel them to live with you in a state of war; and yet you complain that they are not honest or faithful. You must stupefy them with stripes, and think it necessary to keep them in a state of ignorance; and yet you assert that they are incapable of learning; that their minds are such a barren soil or moor, that culture would be lost on them; and that they came from a climate, where nature (though prodigal of her bounties in a degree unknown to yourselves) has left man alone scant and unfinished, and incapable of enjoying the treasures she has poured out for him! An assertion at once impious and absurd. Why do you use those instruments of torture? Are they fit to be applied by one rational being to another?[30]

This rather lengthy quotation lays bare the political undertone in *The Interesting Narrative*. Equiano records his resentment for the dehumanizing system of slave trade, and then mobilises people against slave trade, racism and oppression. He resents the "impious" and "absurd" assertion that puts on record the half humanness of the black race. This has always been the excuse of the slave traders and colonisers for subjecting the black race to all manner of ills. Writing in his *Letter to the Treasurer of the Society Instituted for the Purpose of Effecting the Abolition of the Slave Trade*, the Revd. Robert Boucher Nikkols opines, "I never heard of poems by a monkey or of Latin odes by an oranoutang."[31] Equiano's narrative has been able to once again debunk the myth of African primitivism. Equiano in this passage dispenses with every spiritual and pious tone to really make a sound argument against the "accursed trade." Equiano needs to assume this tone because "all art aims to evoke; to awaken in the observer, listener or reader emotions and impulses to action or oppression" to echo Ngugi.[32] If *The Interesting Narrative* was ever aimed as a tool of the abolition of slavery, then its tone necessarily has to get acerbic to effectively serve the role it was meant to perform. This accounts for the overtly aggressive language with which Equiano conveys his anger. The emotional tone all adds to the poignancy with which he totally rejects the trade in humans. In chapter twelve of Equiano's narrative, the author argues vehemently against slave trade once again bringing to light its inhumanity of the trade and then submitting in particular that the slave trade makes no sound economic sense.

> Tortures, murder, and every other imaginable barbarity and iniquity are practised upon the poor slaves with impunity. I hope the slave trade will be abolished. I pray it may be an event at hand. The great body of manufacturers, uniting in the cause, will considerably facilitate and expedite it; and as I have already stated, it is most substantially their interest and advantage, and as such the nation's at large, (except those persons concerned in the manufacturing neck-yokes, collars, chains, hand-cuffs, leg-bolts, drags, thumb screws, iron-muzzles, and coffins; cats, scourges, and other instruments of torture used in the slave trade). In a short time one sentiment alone will prevail, from motives of interest as well as justice and humanity. Europe contains one hundred and twenty millions of inhabitants. Query: How many millions doth Africa contain? Supposing the Africans, collectively and individually, to expend £5 a head in raiment and furniture yearly when civilized, &c., an immensity beyond the reach of imagination.[33]

Here, the author makes a strong political case against the slave trade. He advances reasons why slave trade should be abolished because, as he argues, it makes no economic sense to trade in humans. To him, if Europe substitute machines for human labor as they later do, their manufactured goods will be well marketed in Africa provided Africans are not depopulated. Consequently, the body of manufacturers will be the better for it, except those involved in the manufacture of various instruments of torture. Again, the author carefully intersperses his narrative with poetic verses, some of which he titles "miscellaneous verses." In them, the author takes time to reflect upon his life, review his narration so far and in some other cases convince us of his beliefs. Some of these verses are strong political verses. For instance, he paints the picture of what life would look like without the reality of slavery. We find another poem which gets sorrowful and emotional as all hopes for slaves seem lost, and a strongly worded poem appears to educate slave owners on the need to treat their slaves with respect.[34] The author in addition uses these verses to intimate us of his spiritual conviction thus we find the author talking about Jesus Christ as the pilot and compass. This perhaps convinced Carretta to see Equiano's narrative as belonging to the genre of spiritual autobiography, arguing that Equiano's narrative is obviously influenced by John Bunyan's *Grace Abounding to the Chief of Sinners* and Daniel Dafoe's fictional *Robinson Crusoe*. The work is however richer than the spiritual autobiography can offer.

The poetic verses much like the interludes in Ezekiel Mphahele's *Down Second Avenue* are "deep critical thought [which] . . . serve as a suitable artistic avenue for channeling of [Equiano's] protest against [slavery] are also literary devices."[35] The introduction of the verse serves to make the structure of *The Interesting Narrative* complex, and less digestible than a straight forward autobiography.

CONCLUSION

The Interesting Narrative is a complex piece which is fictional, political and truthful at the same time. In addition to combining all these, the structure of Equiano's narrative is complex. It is made complex due to the many genres the work contains as well as the dense use of imagery, the poetic language, the grandiloquence and most often, the politics. The author in addition to combining the genre of autobiography and fiction also introduces copiously, the poetic genre. He does this by interspersing his narrative with poetry which is at once political and spiritual. At other times, he borrows from other fictional, poetic and dramatic sources. For instance, he relies heavily on John Milton's *Paradise Lost* and Shakespeare's

Othello; Carretta has been able to prove that: Equiano also relies heavily on John Bunyan's *Grace Abounding to the Chief of Sinners*[36] and Daniel Dafoe's *Robinson Crusoe.* He also quotes from the law (p. 109) and from the Holy Bible on countless instances. All these come in to make the structure and technique of *The Interesting Narrative* complex. At a point, the work assumes the epistolary technique of writing as it just becomes letters and correspondences.

With so many external sources, with more than one point of view and more than one genre, with the beautiful use of language and dense imagery, as well as the complex structure found all in *The Interesting Narrative,* (while not agreeing with Vincent Carretta that the book belongs to the genre known as spiritual autobiography) one is tempted to agree with him that Equiano's *The Interesting Narrative* has some doctored truths, some manipulations, and some aspects of an autobiography. At best, *The Interesting Narrative* is literature, fiction, and facts.

This conclusion not withstanding, *The Interesting Narrative* bears so much truth especially in Equiano's account of his Igbo origin. This is because so much of the life events and cultural practices described in the book bear a lot of resemblance to the culture, practice and way of life of the Isseke Igbo. The facial marks described in the early parts of the book as well as their cultural life are still in practice in this part of the country where he originated.

NOTES

1. Olaudah Equiano, *The Interesting Narrative and Other Writings,* ed with Introduction by Vincent Carretta (New York: Penguin Books, 1995).
2. For a recent challenge to the authenticity of Olaudah Equiano's African birth, see Vincent Carretta, *Equiano, the African: Biography of a Self-Made Man* (Athens: University of Georgia Press, 2005).
3. Georg Misch, *A History of Autobiography in Ambiguity Vol. 1.* (London: Routledge and Kegan Paul, 1960), 5.
4. James Olney, *Tell Me Africa: An Approach to African Literature* (New Jersey: Princeton University Press, 1973).
5. _____, ed., *Autobiography: Essays Theoretical and Critical* (New Jersey: Princeton University Press, 1980), 271.
6. Kolawole Ogungbesan, "Autobiographies in Africa" in *Literature and Society in Africa: Selected Critical Essays of Kolawole Ogungbesan* comp. & ed. David Ker (Ibadan: Spectrum Books Ltd., 2004), 47.
7. Ibid., 47.
8. *Microsoft Encarta Encyclopedia,* 2005.

9. Misch, *A History of Autobiography*, 5.
10. Equiano, *The Interesting Narrative*, 31.
11. Roy Pascal, *Design and Truth in Autobiography* (Cambridge: Harvard University Press, 1960), 37.
12. R. F. Dietrich and Roger H. Sundell, *The Art of Fiction* (New York: Holt, Rinehart and Winston Inc., 1967), 111.
13. Equiano, *The Interesting Narrative*, 55.
14. Ibid., 111.
15. Ibid., 111.
16. Georges Gusdorf, "Conditions and Limits of Autobiography," in *Autobiography: Essays Theoretical and Critical*, ed., James Olney (Princeton, NJ: Princeton University Press, 1980), 43.
17. Equiano, *The Interesting Narrative*, 55.
18. Ibid., 58.
19. Ibid., 99.
20. Ibid., 104.
21. Ibid., 60.
22. Ibid., 61.
23. Northrop Frye, *Anatomy of Criticism*, 307.
24. Barret J. Mandel, "Full of Life Now," in Olney, ed., *Autobiography: Essays Theoretical* 47.
25. Equiano, *The Interesting Narrative*, 172.
26. Ibid., 59.
27. Ibid., 236.
28. Ngugi Thiongo Wa, *Writers in Politics* (Ibadan: Heinemann, 1981), 6.
29. Ibid.
30. Equiano, *The Interesting Narrative*, 111-2.
31. Cited in Carreta, *Equiano, the African*, xi.
32. Thiongo Wa, *Writers in Politics*, 6.
33. Equiano, *The Interesting Narrative*, 234.
34. See Ibid., 97-8 and 112.
35. Tyodzuah Akosu explores the relationship between autobiography and apartheid in South Africa in his book *The Writing of Ezekiel Mphahlele, South African Writer: Literature, Culture and Politics* (New York: Mellen University Press, 1995).
36. John Bunyan, *Grace Abounding to the Chief of Sinners* (New York: Penguin Classics, 1987).

ENCOUNTERS WITH EUROPE

Chapter 7

Neoliberal Tradition in Pre-Colonial Igbo Societies

Raphael Chijioke Njoku

B ut one thing is certain; the Ibo does not think very much of us. Dis-
sociated from our inventions, the gramophones, the cars, the riffles,
the thermos flask and the riches he imagines we all possess, he sees little in
us. When he strives to copy us, it is not because of the courage or wisdom,
the virtues or the talents he may see in us, but simply because we represent
to him success. In ourselves we do not interest him except in so far as we
contribute to his own interests—*Sylvia Leith-Ross, 1937.*[1]

INTRODUCTION

The above quotation from British colonial officer and scholar, Sylvia
Leith-Ross, aptly sums up her country's frustrations with the Igbo people
of southeastern Nigeria and a belated admission of failure in attempts by
the colonialists to negate the local culture to an inferior position. This paper
accentuates the significance of Igbo pre-colonial institutions in light of the
emergent neoliberal political and economic values as first articulated in the
"Washington Consensus" of 1989 and defended by the advanced democra-
cies of Western Europe, United States, Australia, Canada and Japan. The
argument is made that the pre-colonial Igbo sociopolitical institutions

compare favorably to the sum of values considered as neoliberal today and therefore capitalism liberalization is not necessarily European or American or Asian or African; it is an amalgam of values drawn from different regions of the world.

Since neoliberalism is a loaded concept, it is important to start off by clarifying its usage here as a movement espousing economic deregulation and political decentralization. The exponents of the Washington Consensus (including the International Monetary Fund, World Bank, and the Paris Club) projected these values as crucial for sustaining development in the western world as well as securing the elusive socioeconomic and political development in the Third World. Neoliberalism, a refurbished idea from the classical liberal traditions of the seventeenth and eighteenth centuries, seeks to shift economic control from government to private sector. Its opponents, especially those from Latin America and Africa, argue that the neoliberal charter is hypocritical in conception and imperialistic in practice. This is because the set of policies it offers, tend to privilege big businesses and stifles both small-scale enterprises as well as local industries.[2] Hence, Alfredo Saad-Filho advances an alternative path, to the Washington Consensus, which will focus on social programs designed to meet the basic needs of the masses. These include the equitable distribution of income, wealth and power, and the preservation of macroeconomic stability. Saad-Filho has labeled his thoughts "pro-poor macroeconomic policies."[3] The relevance of the neoliberal concept for this paper resides with its cardinal ideals of political decentralization and economic deregulation, rather than its malcontents and imperialistic applications.

"PRIMITIVE" AFRICANS vs. "MODERN" EUROPEANS

For the benefit of those unfamiliar with this group, the Igbo people have inhabited their present southeastern Nigerian homeland for at least more than 4,000 years. It is therefore no surprise that they have virtually lost any coherent external tradition of origins. The Igbo, who never established a centralized kingdom like some of their neighbors, were organized in small independent villages, which was also the highest unit of political organization. In 1900, there were over a thousand villages and the average population of a village could be anything between 2,000 and 20, 000 people. Writing in 1947, colonial scholar, Margaret M. Green, estimated the population density of the Igbo country at between 450 and 1,000 people per square mile.[4] In 1906, Major A. G. Leonard estimated the entire Igbo population at between five and six million people.[5]

As the Igbo did not establish a centralized kingdom, the early British colonial administrators and scholars that arrived in the Igbo country in the late nineteenth century spared no words in describing the indigenous institutions and cultural practices as "primitive" and "barbaric." Sir Frederick Lugard, the architect of the indirect rule system and first Lieutenant Governor-General of Nigeria, for instance, depicted the Igbo people as being in a "stage of primitive savagery."[6] Margery Perham, a prominent colonial officer and writer, perceived the Igbo sociopolitical organization of the Igbo as "unorganized," and "particularly barbarous and intractable."[7] Such perceptions represent a pervasive ideology widely shared by the Europeans in attempts to justify their "civilizing" missions in Africa. Adiele Afigbo correctly notes that the various colonial critics of the Igbo system approached their assessment of African indigenous cultures from a position that equaled political centralization to "civilization" while decentralized forms of administrative and political systems (as common, for instance, among the Igbo, Idoma, and Efik/Ibibio groups of Nigeria) were portrayed by the aliens as "a deeper descent into savagery and lack of identity."[8] Attempts to refute this colonial ignorance in scholarly fashion was pioneered by Kenneth Dike's 1956 *Afrikanistiks* (nationalistic) historiography which asserts that "beneath the apparent fragmentation of authority [in Igbo politics] lay deep fundamental unities not only in the religious and cultural sphere but also . . . in matters of politics and economics."[9]

Since the rise of African nationalist historiography in the 1950s, further objective assessment of the so-called "primitive" Igbo indigenous institutions and practices have shown that the social systems favorably compare with those propelling the recent transformations on the global stage. One could, therefore, argue that there is no so-much distance between the "primitive," the "modern," and the "postmodern." Igbo indigenous institutions, in many ways, reflect a miniature version of the evolving global quest for capitalism liberalization and political decentralization, which gained momentum with the fall of the Eastern Bloc in 1989/90. As a marker of the new world order, non-stateside actors like civil society networks, gender and human rights activists, and so on, have since the 1990s, assumed more leadership roles in the quest for liberty, minority rights protection, consolidation of free market economies, regionalisms and free movement of peoples and labor in a multinational cooperative framework.

In the contemporary global system that has seen the western world exasperate other cultures with its claims to liberalism as solely ensuing from western civilization, it is fascinating to observe that the pre-colonial Igbo had indigenous institutions with attributes of democratic values, flourishing civil society networks, and absence of totalitarian leaders. The indigenous culture also upheld individualism, women's rights, and human rights. The Igbo culture in particular, and most indigenous African societies in general, could also boast of a religious tradition that not only allowed the adherents freedom of worship but also predated the "protestant ethic," which emerged in Europe with the rise of the Calvinists and the Puritans of seventeenth century England.[10] Revisiting the characteristics of the Igbo indigenous ways is important because the recent gravitation towards universal democracy, freedom and empowerment for all citizens, and so on, represent an assemblage of values from world cultures rather than a set of values unique to the Europeans as some have claimed.[11]

IGBO TRADITION OF REPUBLICANISM

From the political standpoint, the contemporary neoliberal reforms demand upon authoritarian leaders in all regions of the world to transform state institutions into democratic systems. This goes along with civil society empowerment, respect for human rights, protection of minority rights and rights of women, and other categories of previously marginalized and silenced citizens.[12] Democracy in this context means respecting the people's rights to choose their leaders in a free and fair election. It also means that every citizen should enjoy the right to aspire for elective positions irrespective of one's inherited status. Ironically, while democratic stability has proved a daunting challenge for the African postcolonial state, the Igbo lineage/village square (*amamgbakọ*), like the *demos* of the ancient Greek, inculcated democratic values—thus revealing that popular forms of government was also indigenous in Africa.

The Igbo village assembly was the largest unit of political organization in the indigenous society. The assembly comprised those communities which have co-opted individual families in the defence of their territories, venerated the same major deity Earth Goddess (or *Ala* shrine), and reconciled their land using rights. Often, these communities have acknowledged the right of the same village group head (*Onye ishi ala*) to supervise land use and the rituals connected with the observance of common laws.[13] Given the absence of individuals assigned with enormous political authority in the Igbo village system, the early Europeans quickly saw the Igbo as people without kings (*Igbo ewéghị eze*)—suggesting a lawless people lacking in culture, civilization and discipline."[14] Absence of a central authority did not, however, suppose absence of leadership or even suggest lawlessness. Such ideas existed only in the imaginations of outsiders obviously ignorant of the local culture. While he pre-colonial Igbo society was well organized, the people expressed their pride in saying there was no kings or centralization of power in the hands of individuals as well as their culture of freedom from a certain forms of servility often associated with those who lived under feudal monarchies.[15] In her study titled "Patterns of Authority in West Africa," Paula Brown identified four systems of political organizations indigenous to the Africans. These include: (1) kinship-based authority system; (2) kinship and associations-based authority system; (3) kingship, associations, and centralized authority state systems; and (4) consolidated centralized state authority systems.[16] Similarly, M. Fortes and E. E. Evans-Pritchard recognized two major categories of African political organizations. In the "A" group are the centralized systems and in the "B" group are the decentralized groups or what the authors labeled "stateless societies."[17] Identified in the later category are the Igbo, Angas, Birom, Idoma and Ibibio/Efik of modern Nigeria, Tallensi of Ghana, Tonga of Zambia, Langi of Uganda, the western Dinka and the Nuer of Sudan, and the pre-nineteenth century Nguni of South Africa. A more nuanced division, however, would be one that transcends the temptation of categorizing cultures into the "stateless" and "centralized" or "primitive" and the "modern." None of these acronyms accurately represents the Igbo indigenous democratic institutions. Igbo government at all levels of the sub-lineage, lineage, and the village depended on direct democracy, while at the level of the village-group it depended on representative democracy.[18]

In broad terms, the Igbo operated two varieties of political systems— the monarchical and village republic. The monarchical system as found in Onitsha, Oguta, and Aro, for instance, developed as a result of their age-long contacts with non-Igbo neighbors with centralized state systems like the Benin to the west, Efik to the east, and Igala to the north.[19] Hence, Alagoa explains that, such monarchical institutions as found in Umueri, Aguleri, Nri and Oreri "were chiefly institutions uncharacteristic of the Igbo country."[20] In both the presidential monarchy and the village republic, the distribution of power, authority, and the processes of local administration are the same. The elders ruled by representation, participation and negotiation. The notion of difference is found primarily in the king's ceremonial objects and titles.[21]

In the Igbo practice of direct democracy, heads of the various households discussed the affairs of the units at the sub-lineage and the lineage levels. In the village assembly, all the adult members of the group participated in decision-making. The village assembly had an inner council made up of the lineage heads (the *Amaala*) that deliberated on village affairs.[22] The sub-lineage, the lineage, and the village assembly were levels of direct democracy where every adult male, or female in some cases, was directly involved in the affairs of the group. The village-group assembly, a clear example of representative democracy, was made up of the representatives of the member-villages.[23]

A VIBRANT CIVIL SOCIETY IN COLLECTIVE GOVERNANCE

With no standing army or police, civil society actors formed part and parcel of the strength and resilience of the indigenous political system. In the past two decades, scholars have stressed upon the imperative of civil society networks in both political and economic development. William Galston has identified ways civil associations—labor unions, networks of dissident intellectuals, and churches—could enhance liberal democracy. (a) They serve as an effective source of resistance to oppressive governments. (b) The representation of previously unheard voices addressing issues of transnational significance such as the environment, population, the status of women, human rights, and even disarmament. (c) A basis for criticizing the excesses of both the state and the market and, (d) a response to the increasing anxiety that the traditional agents of socialization, solidarity and active citizenship were breaking down.[24] In light of this, civil associations create favorable conditions for political associations. Elaborating upon this, Galston argues that,

> The more individuals get used to the idea of coming together for economic, social, or moral purposes, the more they enhance their capacity to pursue 'great undertakings in common.' On the other hand, political associations pave the way for civil associations. A free political system creates strong incentives for extensive political associations.[25]

Afigbo explains that in Igbo indigenous society, the idea of a political community is more than just association of fellow citizens bound by common interests. Igbo politics was a sort of spiritual commonwealth; conceived for regulating normal life among "brothers," defined broadly to absorb strangers.[26] As an arm of government, civil associations formed an indispensable part of the Igbo indigenous sociopolitical system. While the village assembly took decisions on common matters affecting the people by popular vote, the kinship system, age grades, secret societies, women's and men's associations and other forms of civil society groups helped in enforcing the decisions of the assembly.[27] These non-stateside actors (social clubs, the age grades, secret societies) in addition with the village government prepared the youth for public leadership by initiating them into the associations as they came of age. Through these avenues the Igbo youth who was expected by his society to ascribe memberships in these association, imbibed the cultural belief in the preeminence of institutional authority over that of the individual (*Ohadike*). In pre-colonial Igbo society, a man might have a domineering authority within his family, in public power resides with the people.[28]

The point here is that liberal democracy, as advocated by the rich western nations today, may be lacking in modern Africa, but it is crucial to locate the problem in its historical context. In the early twentieth century, the European colonial rulers found Igbo political culture bewildering because life in average European societies were organized in nation states, or in such tribal communities as Scotland, Basque, Flanders, and the various city states of Italy and Germany. The Igbo resisted centralized statehood either by subtle design or incorporation by conquest. The Igbo strength of character resided in their indigenous political culture.[29] Indeed, political culture as defined by Arend Lijphart then is "the pattern of cognitive, evaluative, and effective orientations toward political objects."[30]

The Igbo democratic political culture was more advanced than the various brands of inchoate democratic institutions just mushrooming in western societies after the eighteenth century. For instance, while France, Britain, and the Netherlands had managed to reform their state systems from monarchical control to semblances of democracy between 1789 and 1900, Germany, Italy, Portugal and Spain were still struggling under the burden of the most dangerous dictatorships as late as 1945. Dictatorship regimes in Spain only subsided after the death of Francisco Franco in 1970. As Olaudah Equiano's memoir published in 1789 informs all, democratic republicanism was so entrenched in the pre-colonial Igbo politics that aspirants to public positions do not necessarily have to project themselves for political appointment. It was rather the group to which the aspiring leader belongs that freely recognized those individuals with leadership skills.[31]

Igbo indigenous leaders often accepted the people's admonitions whenever they deviated from the dictates of culture.[32] Since Igbo pre-colonial society was predominantly agriculture-based, those successful farmers who had publicly displayed their success and wealth through title-taking shared with the lineage heads the primary responsibility for ordering society. The elders and family heads had the required skills for conflict resolution and diplomatic relations. Their successes also enabled them to build up political clients who were maintained with the surpluses created by large households. The indigenous political elite "were also respected by their less successful neighbors who needed their patronage and protection or simply admired them and sought, or hoped to be like them."[33] Overall, "many were the foci of authority and so complex the checks and balances that the [Igbo chief] was barely a little more than a titular official except in a [few border] communities."[34]

CULTURE, HUMAN RIGHTS AND WOMEN'S RIGHTS

The turbulent nature of the postcolonial African states plagued by socioeconomic and political issues has brought into debate the imperative of freedom as a prerequisite for human development and societal progress. As African leaders are increasingly indicted on human and group rights violations, they are equally putting up defenses in attempts to justify their actions. At the center of the argument is the contention whether western notions of human rights should be accepted as a yardstick of judgment on human rights violations in Africa. In their different studies, Jack Donnelly and Rhoda Howard have argued that traditional African societies did not have a concept of rights, since fundamental human rights are universal in scope and application, as inherent in one's humanity, not community. At best, the authors contend that these indigenous societies had notions of human dignity but not rights.[35] The position taken by Donnelly and Howard represents not only some of the well-known challenges to the position of ethical relativism but more importantly the familiar arrogation of liberal values to European cultural heritage. At best, Donnelly grudgingly admits that there are other trajectories for human rights within the liberal tradition, but which being outside of the conception of the individual are therefore "atomistic and alienated from society and the state."[36]

Okey Martin Ejidike and others, who are in opposition to the Donnelly and Howard's view, contend that pre-colonial Africa had clear concepts of human rights and that Africans enjoyed specific rights.[37] Although in most instances the right of the individual came second to that of the community, individuals had clearly demarcated rights to life, economic pursuits, association, expression, marriage, and so on. These rights contrast sharply from the regime of rights the British colonialists introduced in eastern Nigeria from 1900. One important point of reference is the contrast between Igbo pre-colonial human rights regime and the colonial regime. To make this more intelligible, it is imperative to provide a brief highlight of the underlying concepts of the state, authority, power, and the spiritual and cultural symbols of death penalty in Igbo indigenous society.

The indigenous Igbo society regime on human rights and death penalty was a juror-political construct based on the idea of the individual to the culture in general, as well as the cultural articulation of "proper" behavior.

In the indigenous system, hardly were individuals subjected to the supreme penalty because of either their opposing political views or religious beliefs. Most offences that attracted the death penalty in the indigenous Igbo system, such as the birth of twins and offences considered taboos were not directly connected with any political derivatives.[38] The offences considered most serious were prosecuted in connection with certain religious laws associated with the Earth Goddess (*Ala*). A breech of these laws was believed to disrupt the cosmic harmony, hence it was considered as grievous (*nsọ ala*).

Meanwhile, such offences as murder and treason, for which death penalty is still applicable in the United States for instance, rarely attracted the death penalty in the indigenous Igbo penal code. Certain cases of manslaughter were even honored and rewarded with titles when it was executed in order to preempt a common threat to the entire society. Otherwise, adjudications in murder or homicide cases were approached through negotiations involving those surviving the victim and the suspect's relatives and the community at large. In this sense, the Igbo socio-cultural derivative and views of capital punishment was more pragmatic than the outsider would admit.

Another issue of concern in the contemporary neoliberal order is about women's rights and women's empowerment. Feminist anthropologists endorse the view that context is critical in our understanding and exploitation of any given situation. Radhika Coomarswamy argues that in the contemporary world, "Women's struggle for human rights often positions them in opposition to the family and social networks where their roles and rights have been defined."[39] In consideration of the sanctity of the family network, however, women, especially mothers, often choose not to seek empowerment and freedom in order to avoid conflicts with their kin. While women's rights have become an issue for development across the world today, pre-colonial Igbo women had enjoyed culturally sanctioned rights. Politically Igbo women exclusively managed their own affairs as well as participated, in matters affecting the entire kinship or village group. Writing about the Igbo decision-making process in 1789, Equiano explains that it was "separated into four divisions" comprising "the married men, the married women, the young men and the maidens."[40] While this division allowed women the right to 'self-determination,' married women occupied a special position in the social fabric of the culture and customs. Infringements on these rights by the colonial state of course explain the main reason Igbo women took on the colonial authorities in series of riots that dogged the colonial period including the famous Aba Women's Riot of 1929/1930.[41]

In matters related to religion, women who performed ritual functions enjoyed more freedom and privileges than most men. Above all, Ifi Amadiume underscores the flexibility of gender relations in the Igbo country. Citing the Nnobi people of old Anambra state, for instance, Amadiume noted that this fluidity resulted in both role and status ambiguity. The culture allowed for the incorporation of "certain categories of women into the male category, giving them positions of authority in the power structure. Daughters were, for example, regarded as males in relation to wives."[42] Economically, Igbo women were independent of men. The economy was structured in gender specific terms, which reflects gender sensitivities. There were certain crops like cassava, pumpkin leaves, and so on regarded as women's crops.[43] Also the processing of palm oil and palm kernel were exclusively left for women even though men harvested and cut the palm fruits.

FREE MARKET ECONOMY AND INDIVIDUAL ENTERPRISE

The contemporary western-led neoliberal reforms beckons on Third World governments to embrace the "virtually universal spread of free-market capitalism."[44] To this regard, the creditor western nations have pressured African leaders to eschew state control of the economy as practiced through import restrictions, price control, intervention in foreign currency exchange and regulation. While these common "vices" indulged by African postcolonial leaders have endured, the Igbo pre-colonial political elite had no control over trade and marketing and there was virtually nothing like a state-run economy as obtained in the contemporary world. The village markets usually located between one and two mile radius were not within the Igbo chiefly control. The result of studies by Gloria Chuku and others have attested to the fact that women, rather than men, dominated the local markets.[45] Among the Igbo, market prices are a function of a "rigorous system of bargaining," and often women performed better than men.[46]

While men dominated the regional or long distance markets until 1900, the Igbo chief could hardly abandon his daily religious functions in pursuit of commercial benefits.[47] Amongst his Achi people of Mbieri, Pa Golden Bennett Opara, a retired, postal officer, recalls that the chief priest of the community "used to be a very wealthy man until he succeeded his father as chief priest." Since then, "his wealth never expanded" because the indigenous tradition dictated what the leader could eat, and where he could spend the night.[48] This made it difficult for the traditional Igbo chief to travel often and on what conditions he could be away from his duties. This and other limitations associated with chiefly authority made it unlikely that the leader could engage in long distance or international commerce effectively enough to build up resources with which to push for a larger and more visible political role than what tradition ordinarily prescribed.

The case of Eze Aro could further serve as another example of the limitations of Igbo leaders' power over trade. While the Aro became a regional force through their commercial exploits, the influence, which this brought them, augmented not so much the power and status of the Eze Aro (Aro monarch).[49] Rather, the Aro "Long Juju" (*Ibini-Ukpabia*), associated with immense religious and judicial powers, became the instrument of Aro commercial dominance in the Igbo country and beyond.[50] Aro middlemen controlled the hinterland trade in slaves and local produce. Similarly, in Umunoha community, "what was powerful, influential and dreaded beyond Umunoha was the *Igwe-ka-ala* oracle rather than the village chief."[51] Without any privileged access to material resources of his community, the archetypical Igbo indigenous chief was simply a figurehead, a first among equals. Even though the people of Oguta community regarded their monarch (*Obi*) as the "highest king" (*Eze Igwe*) and accorded him the exclusive prerogative in cases of homicide, the monarch had no other power for unilateral political action. Writing in 1880, Bishop Ajayi Crowder of the CMS confirmed this by reporting in his journal that "one common advantage which characterized the Ibo country is want of a king who is a supreme head of the nation."[52]

An important feature of the new global economic order is the emergence of transnational or regional economic blocks like the European Union (EU), North American Free Trade Agreement (NAFTA), Economic Community of West African States (ECOWAS), and so on. The idea behind the formation of these regional co-operations is to promote unity and peace among member states through removal trade barriers, regulation of import/ export duties, and free movement of peoples. Before the era of the Atlantic slave trade, which reached the Igbo interior in the seventeenth century, the local people had established both internal and external trading contacts with their non-Igbo neighbors. As Afigbo stated, "Trade and marketing in Igbo culture arose out of the tradition of reciprocal gift exchanges by which individuals and groups at first got rid of what they had in excess and obtained what they lacked."[53] In both the internal and external trades, market forces determined the prices of various products. Organized guilds of smiths at Awka, Nkwere, and Abiriba had their ironwork businesses extending beyond Igboland.[54] The Akwette specialized in textile materials which had reputation for durability. Some markets such as Nkwo Ibagwa, and Afo in Obollo, for instance, became famous as centers for the reputable

Akwette woven clothes.[55] Akwaete clothes found their ways outside Igbo-land to Ijo in the Niger Delta, Igala and Idoma in the north and so on—in exchange for fish, crayfish, iron bars and other items of interest. According to P. A. Talbot, the "export trade in (local) cloth flourished until the third quarter of the nineteenth century, whence it gradually declined owing to great expansion in the import of Manchester goods."[56]

The relationship, which built up between the Igbo and their non-Igbo neighbors, were important. The "people were innocent of the kinds of "global" stereotypes and prejudices which today make it "rational," "just" and even "politically advisable" to attack other ethnic elements in various societies.[57] The Aro trading system, which connected hundreds of satellite communities across the length and breath of the Igbo country, was a highly organized concern. Meanwhile, the Nri constituted themselves into a priestly aristocracy that dominated traditional medicine and priest-craft in most of Igbo land.[58] The Nri also claimed to have had ritual functions performed in the coronation of the kings (*Obas*) of Benin. This at least would indicate early contact with, or awareness of the existence of Benin.[59] Igbo goods like ivory and slaves, were exchanged for goods coming probably from as a far away as Venice and India. The external trade exchanges introduced goods such as swords and guns some of which became status symbols. Through this commercial exchange, the competitive feature of Igbo social life was reinforced.

Like the contemporary regional economic co-operations between member states in Africa, Europe, North America, and Asia, certain rules guided the safe conduct of long distance trade in the precolonial Igbo country. Besides the priests and diviners of Nri who enjoyed the privilege to travel unmolested throughout Igbo land because of their priestly functions during important rituals and social ceremonies, the pre-colonial Igbo travelers and businessmen were required to observe certain rules for the same reasons we have travel regulations biding all international travelers today. Observance of these rules distinguished genuine businessmen from troublemakers and bandits. Some of the common observances included traveling in groups or in caravans with armed escorts, the payment for protection from local patrons known for their wide ranging influence and contacts, familiarity with the passwords of the secret societies which operated along one's routes, and payment of tolls which went into the maintenance of the young men who cleared the routes and patrolled them, among others.[60]

The movement of people and goods fostered on this mutual understanding and co-operation ensured the distribution of goods and articles of culture across all parts of the Igbo country. This helps to explain the striking uniformity in culture and language, which existed in Igbo land in spite of the fact that the people never came under the umbrella of one state. However, this cultural homogeneity does not imply the absence of minute differences among the various villages. The most important point is to stress that Igbo society and culture did not evolve in isolation from neighboring societies. While the Igbo lent some of their traditions to their neighbors, some elements of internal developments found among the Igbo were in return, either stimulated or supplemented by impulses radiated by neighboring non-Igbo groups. The dynamics of lending and borrowings is common trend in our world of globalizing cultures today.

Similar to the present global order dominated by United States of America, the Aro of southeastern Nigeria dominated their southeastern Nigerian neighbors. As the US today control the world with superior technology and military muscle, the Aro employed the use of their all-powerful oracle known the *Ibiniukpabi* (Long Juju) and their military alliance with the Ohafia, Abam and Edda as instruments of fear and domination. The Aro-Ohafia-Abam-Edda military alliance like the US-led North Atlantic Treaty Organization (NATO), accorded the Aro the military muscle to threaten and often raid other communities who were opposed to their commercial and religious interests. This advantage allowed them to maintain a complex network of client-patron relationships across southeastern Nigeria, with the metropolis Arochukwu.[61]

The Aro preeminent position was to change with the proclamation of British Protectorate of Southern Nigeria in 1900, which brought Arochukwu district within the Old Calabar Administrative Province. For the British to gain effective control of the Igbo hinterland, the Aro influence in the area had to be uprooted. According to Colonel Moorhouse, "It was inevitable, in my opinion, that in the extension of the [British] Administration, there should be a conflict between the Government and the Aros in the conditions that existed at the time. It was in order to break down the trade monopoly of the Aros far more than any missionary influence that the decision to open up the country was made.[62] The end of Aro hegemony in eastern Nigeria commenced with their defeat in the 1901-1902 British expedition that culminated in the destruction of the *Ibinukpabi*.[63] The fall of the oracular power paved the way for the gradual introduction of Christianity and western education into Aro society and beyond.[64]

The Igbo and their neighbors got what they wanted through this regional trade. Basic needs like salt, iron, fish, game, and clay for ceramics, and fibers for weaving, were easily obtained.[65] But this was just one out of other forms of regional co-operations among Igbo villages and their non-Igbo neighbors.

INTER-STATE RELATIONS

Although the Igbo village group was the largest unit of political organization, it did not function altogether as an island among a comity of other villages. As the Igbo proverb goes, "It is only proper that the left palms should wash each other so that both might be clean." Victor Uchendu interprets this idiom as underlying the understanding that "social life demands 'beneficial reciprocity.'"[66] The entire territory harboring Igbo-speakers could be described as an informal commonwealth connected by economic, matrimonial and other social linkages. In view of the degree of political independence enjoyed by each of these villages, it is important to explain also the functions of certain pan-Igbo institutions, which helped to regulate inter-village relationships. Among such institutions were the title lodges, the secret societies, and professional associations like the guild of diviners, hunters, smiths, and oracular agents. Through the understanding that existed among members of these associations, the cross-fertilization of ideas was facilitated. More importantly, the agents of the famous Igbo oracles like *Ibinukpabia* of Aro, Chukwu, *Agbala* of Awka, and *Igwe-ka-ala* of Umunneoha, regulated conflicts involving individuals and groups.

There was also the Igbo institution known as *Iggandu* or *Igbandu*. This was a system by which two or more villages or village-groups, which have no formal ties of blood relationship artificially, contracted one for themselves by performing certain rituals. The usual practice was for the leaders of the villages in question to meet at their traditional boundary. There the elders could perform some rituals involving an animal holocaust and mix this up with some blood drawn from the veins of all present and they all partook in the cooking and eating of the holocaust. A memorial tree would be planted to mark the occasion, which now binds members of the villages concerned together as "brothers." As obtains in pacts and alliances involving modern states, the villages involved in the *Igbandu* institution are bound by common interests and are encouraged to resolve their future conflicts amicably and never to resort to violence as a means of settling disputes involving members of the alliance. Pa Abiazieje, the chief priest *Eze-Ala Akuuba* (*Arunsi*) of Achi-Mbieri community explains that in some cases, such as that involving Achi and Eziome villages of Mbieri, the contractual relations strictly forbid citizens from "the two groups to inter-marry because 'sisters' and 'brothers' from one family are not supposed to marry."[67]

Among the pre-colonial Igbo, "war was not a very specialized business, at least not to the extent it came to be in European society or even some African societies like the Yoruba, Hausa, Mandinka, and Soninke. Thus, there were no professional soldiers even though the Igbo border villages faced constant military threats from their Edo, Ijo and Igala neighbors.[68] Instead every able-bodied adult would normally be called up to fight in defense of his community.

INDIVIDUAL AND GROUP RIVALRIES

Competition and rivalry were common features of the Igbo socioeconomic and political life. As Afigbo puts it, "Individual rivaled individual, social segment rivaled social segment and gods rivaled gods."[69] This culture placed a premium on achievement and ensured that those who were born with social disadvantages could, with hard work, overcome their disadvantages by accumulating wealth and using this to buy titles and membership in other privileged associations.[70] Healthy competition provided the motivation for achievement and honor in a free and liberal society.

The *Ikenga* institution helped to entrench and emphasize the peculiarity of individualism and free enterprise with the understanding that success and failure is a function of individual efforts and divine blessings. In other words, *Ikenga* helped to generate that healthy competition for which the pre-colonial Igbo were widely known.[71] The *Ikenga* cult helped to underlined in the Igbo culture that individuals were the architects of their own destinies and that they should not attribute too much fate or the support of their families and lineages. According to Dele Jegede, *Ikenga* in Igbo tradition means a testimony of a person's right hand, a symbol of hard work and success. It embodies the tool or instrument with which the Igbo man or woman clears the way in his or her aspiration for success and dominance in social, political, economic, and personal ventures. In the African moral universe in which success is often attributed to a life of morality, the *Ikenga* also symbolizes moral probity and physical and material success. An individual or a community could own an *Ikenga* object, often carved in wood. An individual's *Ikenga* is consecrated and placed in a personal space where it is fed regularly with items such as kola nuts, palm oil, or the sacrificial blood of animals. In essence, the *Ikenga* is regarded as a spiritual alter, self-image or personality, and not necessarily an art.[72]

Like the bourgeoisie culture in Western Europe, the "Igbo saw failure in this world as a terrible calamity which implied damnation and so did everything possible to avoid it. It is this fear of failure, this drive to succeed here and attain the status of an *ogaranya* (rich man), which helped to account for the economic drive of the Igbo man as for the high score and prestige set on hard work, resourcefulness, foresight and rugged individualism.[73] However, an aspect of traditional Igbo-religious ethic which tends to act as a drag on individual economic development was the kind of lifestyle expected of the successful man. The wealthy in Igbo culture was expected to be generous and to entertain lavishly and extensively. Otherwise, his wealth would soon provoke widespread envy and hatred. Consequently, members of his age-grade or village would not readily respond to calls for labor from him. It was also believed that the gods would soon get angry with him, while "children would not come to him."[74]

Besides, a successful man was expected to advertise his success in ways established by custom. He had to take titles, buy membership in the leading secret societies and lodges like the *Ozo*, *Ekpe*, and *Ogwo* society, and also feast members of his age grade periodically.[75] Each of these involved the floating of large and expensive feasts in which much of the material rewards of a man's years of enterprise, foresight and thrift could be swallowed up in unbroken festivities lasting on occasions for eight days. If a man wanted ascribe to the *Eze ji* ("yam king") title, for instance, he would first consider the cost of a lavish feast for his village and all members of this title-group from his and neighboring communities for several days. As the case may be, yams from his own farm will be used for this feasting. "Among the Ohozara of the North Eastern Igbo, for instance, the aspirant to *Eze ji* was in addition required to kill a horse for the title society."[76]

CONCLUSION

This paper focused on indigenous Igbo socio-cultural and political institutions and practices with a view to show that the values embodied by the neoliberal movement (among other things political decentralization and economic deregulation) have been part of Igbo pre-colonial ways of life. Igbo indigenous institutions were characterized by democratic decision-making processes, non-stateside or civil society empowerment, individualism, gender empowerment, human rights protection, free market economy, regional economic and political co-operations, and free movement of people and labor. These attributes made the Igbo world a neoliberal world in microcosm. Contrary to the malice and ignorance of the early European colonial scholars and politicians who qualified the Igbo customs and culture as "barbaric" and "primitive," the indigenous political structures did not breed anarchy. Though the Igbo system was complex, it also served efficiently the needs of the pre-colonial society.

NOTES

1.   Silvia Leith Ross, *African Women: A Study of the Ibo of Nigeria with foreword by Lord Lugard* (1937; reprint New York: F. A. Praeger, 1965), 356.

2.   A good case of opposition is embodied in the world system theory popu-larized by the separate studies if Immanuel Wallerstein and Gunder Frank. See Immanuel Wallerstein, *World System Analysis: An Introduction* (Durham: Duke University Press, 2004); *The Capitalist World System: Essays* (Cambridge and New York: Cambridge University Press, 1979); and Gunder Frank, *Capitalism and Development in Latin America* (New York: Penguin Books, 1971).

3.   Alfredo Saad-Filho, "Life Beyond the Washington Consensus: An Intro-duction to Pro-Poor Macroeconomic Policies," *Review of Political Economy* 19, no. 4 (Oct. 2007): 513.

4.   Margaret M. Green, *Igbo Village Affairs* (1947; reprint New York: Frederick A. Praeger, 1964), 34, footnote.

5.   Major A. G. Leonard, *The Lower Niger and its Tribes* (1906; reprint London: Frank Cass, 1968), 31.

6.   See Public Records Office National Archives Kew (hereafter PRO), CO 879/88/12. Administration of Tropical Colonies: Memorandum by Sir Frederick Lugard and Related Papers, July 1905.

7.   See A. H. M. Kirk-Greene, *Lugard and the Amalgamation of Nigeria: A Docu-mentary Record compiled and introduced by A. H. M. Kirk-Greene* (1937; reprint London: Frank Cass, 1968), 56; Margery Perham, *Native Administration in Nigeria* (1937; London: Frank Cass, 1968), 21.

8.   See Adiele E. Afigbo, "The Idea of Igbo Nationality and its Enemies" in Toyin Falola ed., *Igbo History and Society: The Essays of Adiele Afigbo* (Trenton, NJ: African World Press, 2005), 425-28.

9.   Kenneth O. Dike, *Trade and Politics in the Niger Delta 1450-1830* (Oxford: Clarendon Press, 1956), 44.

10. For an authoritative insight on the emergence of the Calvinists and Puritans in England and the rest of Europe see Max Weber, *The Protestant Ethic and the Spirit of Capitalism* trans. by Talcott Parsons (1902; reprint New York: Scribner, 1930).

11. For a heated debate on this, see for instance Robert Marks, *The Origins of the Modern World* (Lanham: Rowan and Littlefield, 2005).

12. At least the western donor nations and institutions streamlined these demands as preconditions for loans and debt relief for debtor nations. See Thomas L. Friedman, *The Lexus and the Olive Tree: Understanding Globaliza-tion* (New York: Farrar, Straus, Giroux, 1999), 167.

13. National Archives Enugu (hereafter NAE), AFDIST 13/1/6. Report on the Cult of *Arunsi* Edda, 1934.

14. Adiele E. Afigbo, *Igbo Enwe Eze: Beyond Onwumechili and Onwuejeogwu* (Okigwe, Nigeria: Whytem Publishers, 2002), 1; Cyril Agodi Onwumechili, "Igbo Enwe Eze?' (The Igbo have no King?)," 2000 Ahiajoku Lecture (Owerri, Nigeria: Ministry of Information and Culture, 2000), 18.

15. Afigbo, *Beyond Onwumechili*, 1.

16. Paula Brown, "Patterns of Authority in West Africa," *Africa* 21, no. 4 (Oct. 1951): 261-78.

17. M. Fortes and E. E. Evans-Pritchard (eds), *African Political Systems* (London: Oxford University Press, 1940), 5-6.

18. Adiele E. Afigbo, "The Indigenous Political Systems of the Igbo," *Tarikh* 4, no. 2 (1973): 15 [12-23].

19. NAE, ARODIV 3/1/55. Anthropological Report on the Aro Confederation by Matthews and Shankland, 1945.

20. See E. J. Alagoa, "The Niger-Delta States and their Neighbors 1600-1800," in Ade Ajayi and Michael Crowder (eds), *History of West Africa* (Ibadan: Longman, 1971), 300.

21. NAE, ONPROF 8/1/4702. Anthropological Report on Onitsha Province by Meek C. K., 1931. See also Ikenna Nzimiro, *Studies in Igbo Political Systems: Chieftaincy and Politics in Four Niger States* (London: Frank Cass, 1972), 41-64, 65-93.

22. NAE, CSE 1/85/4596A. Anthropological Research by on Onitsha Province by Jeffreys, M. D. W. 1931.

23. See M. M. Green, *Ibo Village Affairs* (New York: Frederick A. Praeger, 1947).

24. William A. Galston, "Civil Society and the "Art of Association," *Journal of Democracy* 11, no. 1 (2000): 64-5.

25. Galston, "Art of Association," 68-9. Although dictatorship regimes affect the flourishing of civil associations as individuals become isolated, privatized, and demoralized, Galston argues that autocrats are mistaken if they believe that they can divert political energies into private civil endeavors.

26. Afigbo, "Indigenous Political System," 5-6; 10.

27. For an elaborate anthropological and ethnographical study on this, see NAE, AWDIST 2/1/314. Memorandum on Age (Class) Grade, 1927.

28. Elechukwu N. Njaka, *Political Culture* (Evanston: Northwestern University Press, 1974), 59.

29. Adiele E. Afigbo, "Towards a History of the Igbo-Speaking Peoples of Nigeria" in F. C. Ogbalu and E. N. Emenanjo eds., *Igbo Language and Culture* (Ibadan: Oxford University Press, 1975), 4.

30. Arend Lijphart, "The Structure of Inference," in Gabriel A. Almond and Sidney Verba (eds), *The Civic Culture Revisited* (London: Sage Publications, 1989), 38.

31. See Olaudah Equiano, *Interesting Narrative of the Life of Olaudah Equiano or Gustavus Vassa the African Written by Himself* vol. 1 (New York: W. Durrell, 1789), 36.

32. Njaka, *Political Culture*, 63.

33. Adiele E. Afigbo, "Among the Igbo of Nigeria," *Nigeria Magazine* 146 (1983): 5-6.

34. Afigbo, *Beyond Onwumechili*, 13

35. See Jack Donnelly, *Universal Human Rights in Theory and Practice* (Ithaca: Cornell University Press, 1989), 46-47; 71; and Rhoda J. Howard, "Women's Rights in English Speaking Sub-Saharan Africa," in Claude E. Welch Jr. and Ronald I. Meltzer (eds), *Human Rights and Development in Africa* (Albany: State University of New York Press, 1984).

36. Donnelly, *Universal Human Rights*, 46; 71.

37. Okey Martin Ejidike, "Human Rights in the Cultural Traditions and Social Practice of the Igbo of Southeastern Nigeria," *Journal of African Law* 43 (1999): 71-98.

38. For a report on the taboo against twins, see NAE EP 10460, CSE 1/85/5172. Human sacrifice and destruction of twin children in Nsukka District, 1938.

39. Radhika Coomarswamy, "To Bellow like a Cow: Women, Ethnicity and the Discourse of Rights," in *Human Rights of Women: National and International Perspectives* (Philadelphia: University of Pennsylvania Press, 1994), 52-3.

40. Olaudah Equiano, *Interesting Narrative of the Life of Olaudah Equiano or Gustavus Vassa the African Written by Himself* vol. 1 (New York: W. Durrell, 1789), 36.

41. NAE ABADIST 13/13/26. In Aba Division (1929-1930); NAE B 1544 CSE 3/17/15. Women Dancers Propaganda - anti government development in, 1925; OKIDIST 1/1/2. Tax disturbances, 1930.

42. Ifi Amadiume, *Male Daughters, Female Husbands: Gender and Sex in an African Society* (London and New Jersey: Zed Books, 1987), 51.

43. NAE, RIVPROF 8/15/390 memo "Cultivation and consumption of crops in Owerri province," from D. O. Bende to R. O. P., 21 June, 1928.

44. Friedman, *Lexus and Olive Tree*, 167.

45. Gloria Chuku, *Igbo Women and Economic Transformation in Southeastern Nigeria 1900-1960* (New York: Routledge, 2005).

46. See Uchendu, *The Igbo*, 16.

47. For an interesting and dramatic expose on this, see Chinua Achebe's *Arrow of God* (London: Heinemann, 1963).

48. Golden Bennett Opara, 95, Interview at Umuokoro, Achi Mbier, June, 18, 2007.

49. NAE, ARODIV 20/1/15. Being the various accounts of Intelligence Reports on the Aro Clan, Arochukwu District, Calabar, 1927.

50. NAE, ABADIST 20/1/3. Long Juju of Aro Report on, 1909-1923.

51. Adiele E. Afigbo, *Igbo Political Leadership: Past, Present and Future* (Okigwe, Nigeria: Whytem Publishers, 1999), 6-7.

52. Church Missionary Society (CMS) Archives, London: CA3/04(a), Charge at Onitsha, 13 October 1874; also CMS G3/A3/0, Crowther's Report of the Niger Mission, 1880. See also "Memorandum submitted by the Oguta Town Council."

53. Adiele E. Afigbo, "Prolegomena to the study of the Culture History of the Igbo-Speaking Peoples," 35. In Falola, ed., *Igbo History and Society*, 82.

54. See Afigbo, "Towards," 5.

55. NAE, ABADIST 9/1/1303. Akwete cloth weaving, Aba Division," D. O. Aba to the Resident, Owerri Province, Umuahia, 18 June, 1947; NAE OP. 1760 Vol. I, Local Industries Ondist 12/1/1224; and NAE Memo No. NS. 810/16 of May 31 1938 from D. O. Nsukka to Senior Resident Onitsha Province.

56. Percy Amaury Talbot, *The Peoples of Southern Nigeria: A Sketch of their History, Ethnology and Languages with an Abstract of the 1921 Census* Vol. 3 (1926; reprint London: Frank Cass, 1969), 941.

57. Adiele Afigbo, *The Age of Innocence: The Igbo and their Neighbours in Precolonial Times* (Owerri: Ministry of Information, 1981), 13-15.

58. NAE, OP 196, ONPROF 7/18/99. Anthropological report on the taking of the titles of Eze of Aguku (Nri), and Ozo in the Awka Division (1931). See also Afigbo, "Towards," 5.

59. Adiele Afigbo, "Igboland Before 1800," in Obaro Ikime, ed., *Groundwork of Nigerian History* (Ibadan: Heinemann, 1980), 410-28.

60. Afigbo, *Age of Innocence*, 17-18. See also David Northrup, *Trade without Rulers* (London: Clarendon Press, 1978).

61. NAE, ARODIV 20/1/15, 7; ARODIV 3/1/55, 8, being the various accounts of Intelligent Reports on the Aro Clan, Arochukwu District, Calabar.

62. See Nigerian National Archives Kaduna (hereafter NNAK) Minute dated 28/9/1920 attached to letter No. 2532 of 17/12/21 in the file Conf. No. 80/1920.

63. NAE, ARODIV, 20/1/15, 13; ARODIV, 31/1/55, 15.

64. See ARODIV, 20/1/15, 13; ARODIV, 31/1/55, 15.

65. A. E. Afigbo, "Precolonial Trade Links between Southern Nigeria and the Benue Valley," *Journal of African Studies* 4, no. 2 (1977): 119-39.

66. Victor C. Uchendu, *The Igbo of Southeastern Nigeria* (New York: Holt, Rinehart and Winston, 1965), 14.

67. Pa Abiazieije, 99, interview, Umuleleke, Achi, Mbieri, June 18, 2007.

68. Adiele Afigbo, Towards a Study of Weaponry in Precolonial Igboland (1984), 11.

69. Adiele, Afigbo, "Indigenous Political System," 12.

70. NAE, CSE 1/85/9938. Igbo People - Title Taking Among, 1932-1933; OP 237, ONDIST 12/1/136. Ndichie and Ozo titles, 1942.

71. Mr. Ikemerem Anochiri, 92, Interview, Umuagwuruachi, Achi, Mbieri, June 20, 2007.
72. Dele Jegede, "African Art" in Toyin Falola, ed., *Africa: The End of Colonial Rule and Decolonization* (North Carolina: Carolina Academic Press, 2002), 280-1; Adiele E. Afigbo, *Ikenga: The State of our Knowledge* (Owerri: RADA Publishing Company, 1986), 8.
73. Adiele E. Afigbo, "Religion and Economic Enterprise in Traditional Igbo Society," in Toyin Falola, ed., *Igbo History and Society*, 297-305.
74. Adiele "Religion and Economic Enterprise," 303.
75. NAE, CALPROF B1680/15-3/7/10. Secret Societies in Southern Provinces, 1915.
76. Afigbo, "Religion and Economic Enterprise," 303.

CHAPTER 8

GATHERING FIGS FROM THISTLES: HINTERLAND SLAVE TRADE AND THE CHRISTIANIZATION OF IGBOLAND, 1900-1950

OGBU U. KALU

THE PROBLEM

Scholars have drawn attention to the antiquity and persistence of slavery in Africa into the early twentieth century. Therefore, there is an interest in the role of slavery in the political, economic, and social transformation of African communities.[1] Less attention has been paid to the relationship between the slavery structure and the spread of the gospel. An aspect of the neglect is ideological. Slavery is morally dehumanising, reprehensible and a spiritual bondage. Indeed, it has been perceived as one socio-economic institution that thwarted the development path of Africa and as the instrument with which Europe underdeveloped Africa. Slavery has been imagined at polarities with core Christian values. It is as if the gospel were fig and slavery thistle; and one cannot reap figs from thistles.

Yet, the missionary enterprise among the Igbo of Southeastern Nigeria blossomed in the years when the British moved into the Igbo hinterland and essayed to abolish slave trade, establish legitimate trade and install new administrative structure. The histories of slavery and the gospel became intricately interwoven even when moral mapping imaged them otherwise. Lamin Sanneh paints the motif in a continental canvass:

> The era of abolition, 1780-1890 is also the era of Christian missions in Africa and the two shared chronology for better than fortuitous reasons. The campaign to abolish the slave trade, finally won in 1807, was the engine that moved the modern history on the back of the missionary movement. A straight historical line can be traced from the anti-slavery campaigns of emancipated slaves like Olaudah Equiano, Ottoban Cugoano, Paul Cuffee and David George to patriotic and nationalistic champions like Samuel Adjai Crowther, James Holy Johnson and Herbert Macaulay. These so-called recaptured Africans, westernized and Christianized, would form the crucial buffer between an ascendant, exploitative western colonialism and a weakened African continent, more brokers and mediators than collaborators.[2]

Thus, while the moralist may view the relationship as a futile effort to gather figs from thistles, Sanneh pictures abolitionism as the engine that moved the modern missionary enterprise. This chapter narrows the focus onto Igboland, 1900-1950, when the encounter between Christianity and slavery was at the cutting edge and produced much complexity and ambiguities. It will use cameos woven from personal biographies and select encounters to explore the relationship through the eight sub-cultural theatres of Igboland.[3] The sub-cultural areas enjoy identifiable cultural configurations and ecological features. The presumption is that the dominant cultural forms affect the pattern of both the vertical and horizontal expansion of Christianity. Yet this paper will not pursue the elaborate implications of the concept. Rather, the cultural theatres will be used as geographical pegs to show the provenance of each pattern of relationship in time and space. The core of the paper is a certain irony in the relationship, wherein the slave traders and the slave routes became the instruments and routes for spreading the gospel.

Much of Igboland constitutes what scholars would call the hinterland of the trans-Atlantic slave trade, conducted by a number of middlemen but dominated by Aro and Ubani (Delta) middlemen. This chapter, therefore, revisits certain aspects of Aro historiography. The story is located in the aftermath of the British march into the interior, a comical war prosecuted against the Aro that soon turned into the "pacification" of Igboland. It was a period characterized by the lack of clear policies in some areas and obstacles to implementation in others. Thus, abolition did not mean the end of either the slave trade or slavery. A. E. Afigbo argued that the middlemen in the hinterland were unaware of the new policies on the transatlantic phase and that this resulted in a glut of the slave commodity. Ohadike added that there was a dramatic drop in the price of slaves on the Lower Niger after 1840.[4] The complexity of the situation, therefore, was created by the internal adjustment dynamics of the key players—the government, the missionaries, the Aro middlemen and the indigenous communities. It is essential, therefore, to focus on periodization in both narrative discourse and analysis.

MISSIONARIES AND THE SLAVERY QUESTION

Beyond the theological expressions of moral antipathy, there is little evidence that missionaries had built any internal capacity for dealing with the slavery-ridden conditions in the mission fields. Indeed, missionary practice did not always follow the biblical tradition. Richard Gray has provided fresh data from the Vatican Archives on the situation in the Kongo and Soyo kingdoms. He illustrated the ideological milieu from which missionaries dealt with the slave question. Quite telling were the petitions of Lourenco da Silva, the response of the Capuchins, and the career of the Girolamo Merolla da Sorrento. The Capuchins covered their unkerygmatic theology with casuistry, for instance, essaying to determine whether a slave was sourced from just or unjust capture. The Vatican itself had an ineffective structure for useful intervention. The *padroado* system ensured that no nuncio could apply a Christ-like ethic. Rome was too far away to be really disturbed by the evils of the slave trade. The Capuchins, therefore, merely worried about the sale of slaves to the heretical Dutch.[5]

This attitude could be further illustrated with the career of chaplains in the many forts on the coast of the Atlantic and Indian Oceans. There were at least twenty-one forts on the Atlantic coast by the end of the eighteenth century. Some had chaplains at various points in time. Whether white or black, chaplains were often compensated by payments in trade goods. They forayed into the interior and participated in slave trading just as the other traders. Some careers ended when some chaplains abandoned their clerical pretences and became fulltime traders. Thus, the evangelization process before the resurgence of missionary enterprise in the nineteenth century collapsed on the touchstone and allure of slavery and the resistance from indigenous religions.[6]

The evidence for the early part of the nineteenth century indicates that missionaries purchased slaves for various reasons, sometimes for domestic use and labour in the mission village. At other times, they purchased slaves in diaconic service, rescue and as a means of gathering converts. On the eastern coast of Africa, the British government deliberately delivered freed slaves to plantations run by missionaries. Such was the huge coffee plantation run by the Holy Ghost Fathers in Bagamoyo, whose grand pretence of evangelizing slaves failed to recognize the suffering of slaves and did nothing to ameliorate it. The tragedy was that instead of converting and training these unfortunate young people, the mission turned them into permanent labourers. Some escaped.[7]

In Igboland, the missionary response to slaves touched off the debate of whether the early patrons of Christianity were primarily for the *ohu* (slave) social class. Missionaries created sanctuaries for escaped slaves. On the east African coast, the *watoro* factor in Christianization has been a source of scholarly discussion. Missionary attitude on the slave issue may have stemmed from two sources: racism, which suffused the ideological milieu of the home bases of the enterprises, and missionary theology, which (a) drew a distinction between slavery (domestic) and the slave trade and (b) did not object to the use of slaves in domestic and agro-industrial production. Indeed, slavery dove-tailed neatly into the labour source for a cash crop economy and legitimate trade. The harsh treatment of slaves and domestic servants by the early CMS missionaries in Onitsha became an aspect of the internal conflict among the Saro missionaries who distinguished themselves by their raucous quarrels.

Our concern here is not to repeat the accounts of the episodes that were churned out during the messy debacle about Adjai Crowther's regime but to draw attention to the irony that slaves, slave routes and ex-slaves contributed immensely to the process of Christianizing various cultural theatres of Igboland either by hindering or by assisting the process. The focus is to explain why each pattern occurred in each context.

The first knot that tied the slave trade to the missionary enterprise is that re-captured slaves played key roles in the evangelization of Igboland. Abolitionism was equally the engine that moved the missionary enterprise in Igboland. The Igbo re-captives in Sierra Leone, concentrated in Regent (one of the settlements for recaptured slaves), formed an Igbo Association under the leadership of the irrepressible William Pratt and lobbied for a mission to Igboland. Ethnic identity and rivalry was so strong among the recaptives that it produced the Gobolo War in 1830 between the Igbo and the Yoruba. Thus, when the mission to Yorubaland succeeded in 1842, the Igbo lobby became more strident, lobbying Vidal, Schon and Salisbury Square.

They showed off Simon Jones and John Christopher Taylor as capable Igbo missionaries. Simon had been on the 1841 expedition. When nothing seemed to be happening, the Igbo Association funded a team of four to the Niger—comprising Edward Jones, Principal of the Fourah Bay Institute; John Smart, the headman of Regent; and two others. It failed. When the sky brightened with the success of Baikies's expedition of 1854 and Mcgregor Laird's licence to initiate a new expedition in 1857, the Igbo took this as their answer. They expected their son, J. C. Taylor, to lead it and were disappointed that Venn should involve Crowther. In 1859, the Association thanked Salisbury for establishing "a mission in the banks of the great Niger[,]" adding that "Whilst we could not but, as Christians, glory in the success which has attended the labours of your society in the Yoruba country, yet our hearts have been still more cheered from the fact that Christianity has begun to dawn on our native land." They remitted the grand sum of fifty-four pounds, six shillings and two pence to assist the society, with a promise to give more financial aid in the future. Saved from slavery and Christianized, these Igbo sought to bring the gospel to their own people.[8]

A certain darkness started to envelop the scene on the Niger coast soon after. Both the CMS and RCM (who joined the affray in 1885) were forced by the exigencies of the mission field into a strategy based on slaves and compromise. Firstly, the location of the mission field—far from the Atlantic coast—put the missionaries more greatly at the mercy of traders than necessary. Secondly, court-alliance strategy bred a deliberate courting of the patronage of traditional rulers and entanglement and controversy with the guardians of indigenous cultures. Traditional rulers encouraged slavery. Indeed, there was no sensitivity about the immorality of slavery. Much to the contrary, the Igbo differentiated between *ohu* (ordinary slaves) and *osu* (slaves dedicated to shrines and deities). The stigma of *osu* was indelible. Thirdly, the Christian village strategy was as disastrous in Onitsha as the *sixa* proved to be in Mong Beti's *The Poor Christ of Bomba*. It betrayed the missionary's image of Igboland and was characterized by racism and class differentiation. Though missionaries purchased slaves as a form of rescue or liberation, they used them for menial labour. Soon, a scandal emerged in the Protestant camp because of the brutality of missionaries toward domestic slaves. In a celebrated case, a slave girl died. Strangely, the missionaries were black Sierra Leonians, and it took a band of evangelical white missionaries (Brooke, Dobinson and Robinson) to denounce the segregation and abuses. However, this triggered the Niger crisis of the 1890s.

In conclusion, the profile of missionary response to slavery had certain bold features: first, Buxton Fowell's remedy to the African slave trade that linked the missionary, the commissar and the merchant tended to create a pattern that compromised the missionary's message, especially on such matters as the slave question. Second, the use of charitable institutions and the purchase of slaves created as many problems as they solved. Missionaries soon realized that they must build the church on firmer social props. The surge into the hinterland, in the wake of the Aro expedition, soon obviated the dependence on the marginalized slave population. Third, in spite of any criticisms of Saro agents in the early period, their pioneering role as blacks in the evangelization of Africa cannot be ignored. The first set of educated blacks, coming from this category, fed into the larger repertoire of African-American ideologies such as *back to Africa, ebony kinship, saving Africa through religion and black manifest destiny*.[9] It has been argued that the role of the Saro constitutes the "preface to modern Nigeria." Admittedly, it was not a halcyon period for the Igbo or for their Saro kindred. The turbulent career of John Christopher encapsulates the pain. As he himself predicted in anguish when leaving Onitsha, the system would collapse on Adjai Crowther and his sons. It did. At the root was the fact that missionary enterprise in this period failed to bring a spiritual critique to the system of slavery in the African society. Secular forces and the exigencies of the mission field compromised missionary ideology.

EVANGELIZING THE HINTERLAND: ARO EXPEDITION AND ITS AFTERMATH

The Background

Just as the ripples from the Crowther disaster were reshaping the religious landscape of the Niger Delta, a momentous event occurred that changed the history of Igboland. The decision to invade the Aro who lived in the Igbo hinterland in 1900/1901 has been subjected to economic and political analysis. Economically, the establishment of legitimate trade would not be possible unless the middlemen were wiped out. A coterie of governors found it difficult to implement the new dispensation built on the tripod of legitimate trade, native courts and new administrative structure. They blamed the failure on the Aro and exaggerated the nature, size, and tensile strength of an "Aro empire." There is no doubt that the Aro had an impact on the trade politics of the Cross-River and thwarted Ralph Moor's plan to open the hinterland for white trading companies. However, there were other key players: the Efik traders were opposed to Moor's plans because they would be sidelined. The Umon resented Efik incursion and policed their section of the river and market. The Akunakuna kept everyone at bay from the lower Cross River. The Ezza and Ejagham joined the affray. [10]

The location of Arochukwu is important. It stands on the confluence of the Enyong Creek and Cross River in Eastern Igboland. An invasion from the Niger River or the Calabar must traverse much of the Igbo hinterland. Thus, the three-pronged attack in 1901/2 virtually triggered the conquest of Igboland. Pacification teams continued to hold off local resistance until the outbreak of the First World War. Analyses of the various forms of primary resistance constituted the staple diet of African historiography in the early 1960s and bear little repetition.

From a military perspective, there is a consensus that the expedition was disappointing. The Aro villagers ran away and two villages were burnt. The important factors here are the nature of the trade pattern and the entrepreneurial dynamics in the aftermath. The size of the expedition fed on the exaggerated diet such as has been recaptured in an article by G. I. Jones, "Who are the Aro?" (1945). They were numerically few and were, politically, a weak assemblage of three disparate ethnic groups—Igbo, Akpa and Ibom. Their rich traditional culture blended a host of Cross River cultural forms. As adept traders, they indulged in little agriculture. Each section of Arochukwu appeared to have specialized in building a trade network in specific cultural areas of Igboland and founded immigrant settlements. Thus, Aro settlements spread through much of Igboland, providing a network that facilitated cultural exchanges as well as supplied European goods in exchange for slaves and other indigenous products. Thus, one could expect the trading oligarchies built around family, kin and village to respond to the British intrusion by adapting to legitimate trade. The expedition was an attempt to force the pace of economic transformation. Initially, the Aro responded with subterfuge, thinking that they could outwit the force of change; after all, their motto was *"Ako bu Ije"* (cunning is the art of survival).

The expedition was important for missionary enterprise as an arm of the colonization enterprise. However, the encounter between the Aro and the missionaries proved to be complex, replete with ambivalence and the pains of adjustment to the new dispensation. As Archdeacon Crowther (1903) enthused, "The barriers which prevented Europeans from penetrating the hinterlands have been removed. A new era is opening for the immense Ibo race."

In all slaving societies, the process of adjustment creates internal turmoil. The intensification of chieftaincy disputes and social disharmony among the Efiks provide a comparative picture. There, the effects were ameliorated by an early avowal to cooperate with the new forces. Both King

Eyo Honesty II and King Eyamba V made strenuous efforts to diversify their economies. Surplus slaves would be put into agro-industrial projects while Christianity and schools would be used to Europeanize their communities. Obviously, the Governor, John Beecroft, nudged them towards these modern notions.

THE BLOCKING TACTICS BY ARO SLAVE TRADERS

Unlike the case of the Efiks, the immediate aftermath of the Expedition shows the Aro struggling to keep the regional slave trade going and determined to hinder missionary activities. In 1906, some of those who ran away from Arochukwu returned home. The British chose an enterprising man, Kanu Okoro, and installed him as the chief or *Eze Aro* even though he did not come from the ruling family. His incredible longevity on the throne, lasting through eighty years, stabilized the adjustment process.

Indeed, early reports would lead one to expect that missionaries came into a very discomfitured Aro oligarchy. Recent historiography has, however, drawn a more balanced picture of a community undergoing vast reorganization with a great deal of pluck and adaptability. Some of the Aro endeavoured to continue the old system under subterfuges and cloaks. For many years, they continued to manipulate the northeastern Igbo with the Ibini Ukpabi Oracle. The Resident for Owerri, Frank Hives, tacitly acknowledged that "From the information received during the last fifteen years, I think the Long Juju has been in existence ever since it was supposed to have been broken by the Aro expedition in 1901."[11] In 1925, a new Resident came to the same conclusion: "the Chukwu, however, is still thought of with awe by many, especially by the Nenwe (from Agwu Division) who come down in hundreds at the end of the year to labour in Aro farms."[12]

The evidence points to a certain direction. Those Aro villages that specialized in trading among the lower Cross River ethnic groups borrowed the Ejagham word for God, *Ibin Ukpabi*, and established an oracle in the ravines of Arochukwu. *Ibini Ukpabi* means *Chukwu*, God in the Igbo language. The Aro mystified and manipulated the concept among the northeastern Igbo—primarily the Abakiliki, Ezza, Ikwo, Ezzikwo, Nenwe, and Awgu. These groups share an identical ecology and economic structure. Indeed, when a fourth raid was made on the oracle in 1925/6, most of the rescued votaries came from this area. This does not diminish the fact that, at a certain point in time, votaries came from as far as northwestern Igboland. However, the influence of the oracle gradually waned, retreating to the contiguous areas where it originated. The oracle was used to obtain slaves rather than to settle disputes among Aro traders. As Felicia Ekejiuba has demonstrated, the oracle was not an aspect of primal Aro religion.[13] A saying confirms that an Aro son did not tell another that *Ibin Ukpabi* sent greetings or asked about his well-being precisely because every Aro person knew that the oracle was a slaving mechanism.

The force of resistance in the immediate aftermath explains the slow pace of missionary enterprise into the Aro enclave after the first ululations that followed the attack on the Aro. [14] For instance, the Calabar Mission (Presbyterians), who were on the outskirts of Arochukwu and had made little progress since 1846, did not start work there until 1907. Mary Slessor fumed in 1903 and threatened to start work on her own to forestall the Anglicans and Catholics. The fact was that only the Obikinta and Amanagwu villages, which had been burnt down during the raid, acquiesced easily.[15]

Rather, the new dispensation was fraught with economic and social hardship, an enormous degree of vagrancy as liberated slaves lost contact with former homes, high prices of local and imported foodstuffs and the vagaries of changing values of the manilla. This trend worsened as Europe gradually went to war.

Moreover, defeat scrambled the Aro social order and gave those of slave status the opportunity to rewrite the histories of the various villages and to seek for better status. The confusion became the dominant factor in Aro history and the peg on which missionary activity was hung. In 1944, for instance, when there was an attempt to institute the Native Authority structure, the conflicting claims filled a bulky "Aro File" in the District Officer's Office. At Obinkita, for instance, the chief during the expedition was Nna Nwa Ojim of Ndi Akwete Compound. The government arrested him on behalf of Obinkita. His brother, Okara Onyekwere, assumed his role. By the time he died, new power groups had emerged: a certain Ekpo Onyerisara from Ndi Okoro captured the chieftaincy, followed by Nwankwo Okoro from Ndi Otu and Okereke Abah from Ndi Chioka. In a matter of forty-five years, a new succession tradition had emerged. The traditional head of Obinkinta was no longer selected automatically from a particular family in Ndi Akwete. The power shifts resonated in the various forms that Aro resistance took. These shall be demonstrated with examples from different cultural theatres.

TRADE BOYCOTT

In general, the Aro maintained trade routes that carried a variety of goods, including slaves. From the Delta and Atlantic seaboard, they brought European goods; from northern Igboland, horses; and from the many palm belts of the Southeast, palm oil. Aro settlements located in Isu, Ikwuano,

Oboro, Umunna, and Okigwe and in various locations in the lower Cross River developed palm oil plantations. As internal demand remained high, the markets in Arochukwu, Bende, Uzuakoli, Afikpo and Uburu continued to be slave markets. It was common knowledge that if the Aro patronized a particular market, the reputation and size of that market would escalate. For instance, when the District Officer settled in Bende, the reputation of its market was threatened. When the Bende allowed William Christie of the Primitive Methodist Mission to open a mission base in 1909, the fate of the market was doomed. The Bende people offered bribes to the Aro, who rejected the bribes and headed for Ozuitem and Uzoakoli. The Bende people did their very best to convince the Aro that the Methodist presence was an unwelcome imposition and that they refused to patronize the mission. Even the ebullient Fred Dodds (1913) acknowledged that "Bende itself is a most troublesome problem. So far, mission effort seems to have been utterly wasted. But this, I am persuaded, is not so, for if tangible result are nearly nil, I am conscious of an ever increasing friendly atmosphere." Norcross (1923) put it more graphically:

> Bende was a hard nut to crack in those days... the most you can do is to try and influence a handful of boys or, day after day. Take out a Bible picture roll and watch a compound family dwindle away to nothing before you are through your story. And there an old chief passes away and the men of Bende mark with a prolonged drunken orgy.[16]

SUBVERSIVE MASKING TRADITION AND THE *EKPE* SECRET SOCIETY

Another strategy of resistance was the use of the *Ekpe* secret society. For instance, on a Bende market day, the Aro would influence Ameke Abam folks to start an *Ekpe* dance early in the morning. No woman would be allowed outside. Non-initiates could not move past the *Ekpe* and so the Igwu River on the south entrance into Bende would be blocked off. The Aro tended to serve as diplomatic advisors to many communities, and their hostile whispers of resistance would recur throughout the period and determine the fate of much missionary ardour. The *Ekpe* factor is an important ingredient because it served as a means of circulating secret information. Yet *Ekpe* was not of Igbo origin but was borrowed. Known as Nyampke, it originated among the Ejagham (Ekoi) as a Leopard Society. It developed a rich secret language known as *nsibidi*. This could be written, mimed or expressed with sign language made with the head, hand, leg and so on. This enabled the *Ekpe* initiates to communicate privately in the presence of non-initiates. Trade secrets could be shared and business tricks devised. Training for higher echelons equipped one with greater business acumen. As *Ekpe* spread by Aro influence through the Cross River basin, it created a homogenous group that percolated Aro influence. *Ekpe* arbitrated trade disputes, oiled the mechanism of the trade routes and posed a formidable enemy to missionary enterprise.

There is another important factor: namely, that unlike the Aro political system, *Ekpe* was woven into the fabric of governance in certain communities of the basin. From Uzuakoli through Umuahia to Mbawsi and Ngwa in Southern Igboland, *Okonko* ruled the communities. This differed from the situation existent from Abam through Ohafia, Ihechiowa, Ututu to Arochukwu, where *Ekpe* served only as a club for wealthy males. It was never a part of the indigenous administrative structure but existed as a power node, with much influence at the informal level. In those areas where *Ekpe* ruled the community, it dovetailed into primal religiosity as a bulwark of resistance to Christianity. This factor suffuses the story of communities in Southern and Eastern Igboland who opposed Christianity. The argument here is that the slow pace of the horizontal (rather than vertical) expansion of Christianity was often determined by socio-political factors, and the role of *Ekpe* loomed large. For instance, the entry of Catholicism into villages of Old Umuahia was because an enterprising missionary regaled the populace with the similarities between *Ekpe* ideology and the Christian values of thrift and co-operative sharing. He averred that *Ekpe* was a mutual aid society. The people welcomed him.

The obstructionist tendency of *Ekpe/Okonko* society was because missionary attitude was confrontational to secret societies and oracles. The government had not evolved her own cultural policy and was caught unprepared to take sides. On the one hand, colonial government utilized *Ekpe/Okonko* notables to run the new courts, mobilize labour and preserve order; on the other hand, she was fearful of the competition and power of these men over the populace. In the lurch, government urged the two parties—missionaries and *Ekpe*—to live peacefully. The weak stance favoured the *Ekpe/Okonko* groups.[17]

The most notable Christian counter force to *Ekpe* in the 1900's was the charismatic ministry of the Garrick Braide movement. At it spread like a wave from the rivers of the Delta into Igboland, 1910-1939, oracles, shrines and cultic symbols of traditional religion were consigned to bonfires as votaries abandoned the gods of their fathers for the healing miracles of the holy water. The strategy was characterized by power-encounter.[18]

INFORMAL PROCUREMENT STRATEGY

Kidnapping

Perhaps the strongest force of Aro resistance was by destabilising the social order through kidnapping. A band of people called "Ndi Ogaga" (Wandering Strangers) roamed villages, kidnapping young boys and girls, or an incautious person on lonely journeys, or labourers on an isolated farm. Many villages posted vigilante age grades to counteract these. But the dread was so strong that it got into children's folk tales and determined the habitat structures. A troublesome child would be threatened with the prospects of being kidnapped or even sold to "Ndi Ogaga."

Duping by "Consul Men."

In the same vein, Aro agents would pose as consul men to deceive vulnerable and illiterate rural dwellers. These were the Aro agents. Fair-complexioned Aro people would dress up as government agents, carrying, perhaps, a pocket dictionary and pen and would visit markets as "consul men," ordering whatever wares pleased their fancy. This kept communities insecure. The same Aro would offer their services to draft petitions to the authorities. In the case of the Ovim-Isiukwuato axis, the plague of "consul men" backfired because the people pleaded with Methodist missionaries for protection and accepted their school and church in return. This coincided with the shift of Methodist bases to the railroad junctions as the new Eastern railway line opened. A booming period started for the mission. Thus, through trade boycott, manipulation of oracle, use of *Ekpe* Secret Societies, *nsibidi* (kidnapping), brazen duping by "consul men," secretarial and diplomatic services, and the spread of European goods and culture, the Aro blocked the path of Christianity. It was as if the gospel seed fell among thistles.

FIGS FROM THISTLES?: THE ARO AS MISSIONARY AGENTS

From the end of the First World War, the situation changed dramatically. Many communities wanted education and "white power." Missions expanded. Ironically, missionary expansion increased the demand for teachers, while missionary personnel remained small. The increased demand in Eastern Igboland was met with Aro personnel. This was because, in the midst of the resistance, some Aro saw cooperation with the new dispensation as the reasonable option. This intensified the elements of ambivalence that persisted until the end of our period. Was it a mere instrumentalist response? The career of Mazi Nwafor Ogwuma would suggest otherwise.

The backdrop to his career started in 1904 when the Niger Delta Pastorate sent a delegation led by J. A. Praff and consisting of Alexander Hart, Hezekiah Pepple, Mathew Waribo, Strongface and Jacob Epelle to evangelize Arochukwu. They won six converts before a partitioning of mission fields delimited the area to the Presbyterians. Rev. Rankin and later, J. A. T. Beattie utilized the services of the six Aro men to build a Presbyterian presence from 1907. One of the men, Mazi Nwafor Ogwuma became the pillar of the new Church. His surviving son claims that this early convert was born in Ibom Village about 1858. He was a successful slave dealer and polygamist. Soon after the expedition, he was picked to serve in the native Courts. As a District Officer commented,

> The chiefs of Aro, who have been always shown a higher degree of intelligence than the neighbouring tribes, have taken a keen interest in the development of the District, and in their capacity as native judges, they maintained a very fair standard of justice.[19]

Ogwuma was one of those who assisted Archdeacon Dennis in the translation of the Igbo Union Bible, a feat of vernacularisation that has determined the fate of Christianity in Igboland and the Igbo language for better or worse .

In the phenomenal growth of Presbyterianism between 1907 and 1920 in Cross River Igboland, Aro agents such as Ogwuma, John Ijeoma, Okafor Uro of Amankalu, and a host of others bore the pioneering brunt as teachers and evangelists. A summary of Presbyterian statistics produced between 1902 and 1920 indicates that the Church added 175 extra outstations within the period and showed a better performance than the period between 1846 and 1902. But when Presbyterian influence moved into the salt brines of Uburu and Okposi, the Aro traders tried unsuccessfully to block their entry. The semi-savannah plain with heavy clay soil is suitable for yam, rice, and millet. The clay encouraged pottery and the salt brine supplied Igboland and made Uburu's market famous in the period. The wealth of the zone attracted the Aro. Moreover, as the Eastern railroad (built 1913-1916) was designed to pass through Uzuakoli, the Aro shifted the slave market to Uburu. While this was in progress, a reconnaissance team of Presbyterian missionaries led by Dr. J. W. Hitchcock arrived in 1912. As he reported to the Mission Council,

The reception at Uburu town was not very hearty, and there was some difficulty in obtaining a place to stay. The attitude of the Chiefs was certainly affected by the return to Uburu, two days before the arrival of the committee, of the old deposed Chief who had been imprisoned for two years for resistance. He was highly excited and somewhat intoxicated, and the present chief, Ago Nwa Abasi was at first far from gracious.[20]

After the proposal, something strange happened. A woman who had returned from Calabar mobilized some young men to intervene, insistent that the missionaries should be welcomed. They argued that it was rumoured that the government in Calabar would raid Arochukwu that year and that a "house of book" was not a court but a school. As Hitchcock miffed, "The distinction between government and mission was therefore explained, it is doubtful if the distinction was fully understood."[21] Meanwhile, Hitchcock outplayed the Aro by dispensing free drugs. Excitement grew and the community even offered to erect the quarters and school.

With missionary influence spreading further up the Cross River, the Aro put up a last ditch block among the Abakiliki, Ikwo and Ezza of Northeastern Igboland with much success. Cultural factors aided them. Even the British respected this warlike group of clans for their farming industry. They rejected colonialism. An expedition in 1905 failed to convince them. When the Presbyterians attempted to open a mission at Okpoto, the Ezza raided and utterly wiped it out, slaughtering the intruders. In 1922, the Primitive Methodists treaded where the Presbyterians feared to and met a similar fate. The Presbyterians blamed their failure on the Aro, who convinced the Ezza that Presbyterianism was Efik trading influence writ large. In the rivalry that dominated trade politics, the whisper carried immense implications. A perceptive missionary reported:

> It has been the experience of the missionaries that the Aro have the power of opening and closing doors in every Ibo district. In Okigwe, the Methodist sphere, doors are open. In Abakiliki, they are at present closed. In Okigwe the Aro influence is friendly and the towns are under the influence of that section of Arochukwu. In Abakiliki the Aro influence is hostile and the towns are under the influence of that section of Arochukwu which has, as yet, held aloof from the mission. In these towns, the influence of Chukwu is powerful and antagonistic of Christian mission.[22]

The resistance held until 1937 and, thereafter, a combined force of Catholics, Presbyterians, and Methodists wore down the resistance. Tangible results only appeared around 1967. The decline of the Aro oligarchy and the government's development projects forced the door open. However, the labours of intrepid native agents cannot be overlooked.

BASKETFUL OF FIGS: THE ARO AND PRIMITIVE METHODIST EVANGELIZATION OF CENTRAL IGBOLAND, 1910-1950

Between 1910 and 1927, the Primitive Methodists achieved significant success in the evangelization of central Igboland and moved into the northern sector. The slavery factor was crucial in the feat. Admittedly, other factors contributed: firstly, there was a change of leadership in the Primitive Methodist camp, which gave the energetic William Fred Dodds an opportunity to prove his mettle. Secondly, colonialism had been consolidated, thereby inducing a changed attitude to Christianity, and education prospered. Thirdly, African Christian initiative intensified. Much of this was by those who, through trade, encountered Christianity and saw the handwriting on the wall of the future. All these could be illustrated with the volte-face among the Aro. For instance, at Okigwe, there was an interesting trader who had two names: Mathew Freeman for white men and Udoka Ukeje for natives. Even though he was a Presbyterian, he organised a group of Christians in his village and, through contacts in Calabar, invited Fred Dodds to take over the group. He represents a class of slave traders who changed their stripes and became the best instruments of propagating the new dispensation. He informed Dodds that,

> I don tell the Chiefs, I say de gospel be only ting can save dis country. And dey say dat s'pose he be true for so, I must look dem som man for come teach dem. So dis time I say, 'Alright I go Calabar, I find good man for come.[23]

Freeman-types led the spread of the gospel and Christian alliance in communities such as Ihube, Amuda, Eziama, Ibunta, Uturu and Isiagu. Eziama was evangelized by a man named Kokai, "an erstwhile Presbyterian," who invited the Methodist, Norcross, from Amuda. This latter place had a frightening reputation for head shrinking until it was evangelized by a certain Izuegbu, described as "another ex-Presbyterian, an entirely illiterate man. But in spite of the handicap has assembled a large body of Christians and built a church."[24] A nearby Aro Settlement, Ndimoko, had a worshipping group of eighty persons in a church "founded by a man who had been operated for some temporary form of blindness by CMS medical missionary and cured."[25]

Ibunta, another Aro settlement, had been evangelized by a young man who trained at Jamestown, a Presbyterian enclave 200 miles away. As a trading community, many spoke Efik and could sing choruses in Efik language. The most enduring aspect of this community is that it produced a corp of brilliant indigenous evangelists and writers. Chima Nwana occupied an important place in the history of Methodism in Igboland. His cousin, Peter Nwana, wrote a classic historical novel, *Omenuko*, that describes the pattern of the Aro slave trade. It was written in Igbo language and was used in teaching Igbo literature and language until lately. Albert Nwosu, an Igbo, pioneered Methodist enterprise in Agbani and Igumake (Middle-Belt, Nigeria). John Okereke and Issac Egbunuonu both have rich biographies that depict the nature of the contribution of Christianity by an erstwhile slaving community. The story of the evangelization of Arondizogu, Akokwa, Isuochi, Obodo and other communities of Central Igboland run along the same groove. Those who travelled widely acquired new ideas and, as a process of adjustment, propagated the new Christian ideology in their cultural theatre. These data would support Horton's intellectualist explanation of conversion: namely, that religious change occurred through enlargement of the social scale.

Two other cameos illustrate the connection between slavery and Christianity from other perspectives. The story of Methodism in Item is an intriguing human story of how a slave boy turned into an intrepid missionary. A young man, Ucheya Aju Ucheya, was born in Okoko Item and was later pawned in lieu of debt to an Arochukwu trader by his brother, Mazi Anyangwo, a palm oil trader. The Aro trader, in turn, sold him to a Niger or Ubani man, Albert Hart. This is an indication of how a trading method devised by whites for securing debts in the trans-Atlantic trade was introduced into the commercial techniques of the hinterland by the Aro. In normal circumstances, the Igbo secure debts with blood covenants (*igba ndu*), oaths sworn on shrines or graves, collateral with land, and collateral with moveable goods and articles of clothing. Pawning with a human being would be unusual because of the sanctity of life. But the Aro brought the adaptation into the interior as a part of legitimate trade. Just as Europeans may sell an unredeemed pawn into slavery, the Aro sold pawns.

Ucheya was renamed Emmanuel Hart by the new owner. He acquired some education salted with Christianity and prospered to such an extent that he gained the leadership of his master's house. But he still pined for home. One day, while on a business trip to Azumini in southern Igboland, he met an Item trader who confirmed the survival of his brother and family. He was so emotionally overpowered by the zeal to redeem his native land through religion that he gave up his powerful position as the leader of Abbey Hart house and returned to Item. His vigorous and impressive evangelical career soon touched off a spiritual revival in the area, characterized by a new song and dance, revivalist and itinerant mission, and iconoclasm directed against primal religion.

The guardians of the sacred calabash struck back and burnt his church. The government's security forces responded, at first without success, as the Ameke Item people chased out an Assistant District Officer in 1915. When reinforcement arrived, the place was "utterly deserted or apparently so. The little party had been seen approaching, and everyone fled in some cases leaving pots still boiling on the fires."[26] A monetary fine and punitive quartering of soldiers calmed the situation, but the prospects of peace came with Emmanuel Hart's alliance with the Primitive Methodists. As H. G. Brewer put the matter, "No one will ever know the trials he endured. He and his followers were flogged and robbed, their women were outraged, their church was burnt down." Emmanuel Hart returned from slavery at the age of twenty and died by the time he was twenty-six years of age, but his impact in those few years established Christianity in Item, Alayi, Aba, and Mbawsi. According to F. O. Ikwuka's *Nmalite Methodist Church N'ala Aba* (The Origins of the Methodist Church in Aba), a classic account of the growth of Methodism in the Igbo language, Ogbonnaya Ojukwu, who founded Primitive Methodism in Aba (now a sprawling commercial township), was a prominent disciple of Hart; so were the earliest patrons from Hart's home town.

Hart's story introduces another element: namely, that the path of Christianization followed the slave trade routes maintained by Ubani traders. The story of the Christianization of the Ngwa, Akwete, Azumini, Ndoki and the rest of southern Igboland is dominated by this factor. Firstly, the Garrick Braide movement came into the region through the Azumini/ Akwete axis and quickened the pace of vertical expansion throughout southern Igboland as far as Bende. In this region, the excitement with the gospel produced widespread iconoclasm: the hot embers of the gospel formed the bases for new missionary insurgence in the post-World War II era by Roman Catholics, Qua Iboe Mission, Seventh Day Adventists and the Niger Delta Pastorate. They all benefitted from the achievements of the Garrick Braide Movement, which collapsed after the late 1930s because of poor funding and a weak institutional base.

Early Sabbatharianism in Igboland benefited from the shifts within the former slave trade routes. Delta traders who settled on the Aba Waterfront witnessed to their trading partners and made them observe the Sabbath instead of trading on holy days. The Epelle family, in particular, combined trading with robust evangelism. Other Delta traders came through the River Niger to Ossomari and down the Urashi River to Owerrinta. They, too, evangelized along the old slave trade routes that had become the palm oil trade routes. The Qua Iboe missionary, W. L. Wheatley, has left a fascinating account of this area in his memoir, *Sunrise in Nigeria* (1977). Their missionary influence ranged from Oguta through to Ife in Mbaise.

Perhaps the most compelling data on this is from northeastern Igboland. Horton (1954-1956) showed how the *ohu* (slave) factor was a core aspect of the social structure of the communities in the Nkanu and Nike axis. The axis was the nodal point for north-south trade in Igboland. The northern trade route came through Iddah and Ogrugu (near Adani) and provided contact with Hausa/Fulani horse traders. Dane guns and slaves were the other commodities. The southern route ran through Awka and passed the Nike axis to Bende. The Aro sold slaves, while Awka blacksmiths practised carving, metal work and divination. An eastern route passed here from Nkalagu to riverine communities such as Ezza, Izzi, and Ikwo, who were pushing on the Ukelle dwellers of the river's littoral for more land.

Another interesting feature is the proliferation of slave-inhabited villages. Several explanations are given: for security reasons, the *amadi* (freeborns) founded slave-villages on the border to buffer themselves. Thus, the slave-villages could be traced to the patron communities: Iji village established Akpuoga, Nchatancha, Onugba, and Obinagu. Ibagwa village founded Ugwogwo, Eko, Agbogazi and Ogbake. Amoji village founded Ugu Ohu and Nkubo. Two slave villages, Nneke Uno and Onyoho, could not be easily traced to a founding patron. But the other ten are located on a crescent-shaped boundary of the *amadi* group of villages. It has been surmised that during the abolition process, the slaves who had grown richer than their masters founded their own villages. Two obvious facts were that in spite of legal constraints, the slave population outgrew the *amadi* population, and the slave villages became wealthier as they adapted to legitimate trade. A Methodist missionary, Richardson (1923) observed that,

> Quite a number of the natives take their fruits from palm trees and prepare oil therefrom. This being of excellent quality finds a ready sale. A few of the more wealthy natives breed cattle . . . . Given enough food, money and goods sufficient to meet the demands of their animistic religion, also enough to warrant them having a gay time during the oft-recurring feasts, what more do they want. Their ideals are low, thus their demands are small.[27]

He was chagrined by their low interest in the gospel. In hostility, the people had burnt the house of Nwosu-Igbo, the Arondizuogu evangelist. Then, something happened in 1922 that catalyzed a state of civil war that lasted through the next decade. The discrepancy in wealth between the ex-slaves and masters led to a demand by the former for an increased political voice. Government policies remained ambiguous but tended to support the *amadi* villages against the claims of the slave villages. The missionaries intervened, urging the ideal of freedom and enabled the *ohu* (slaves) to consolidate by adopting Christianity as an instrument of emancipation. It paid dividends, as missionaries guffawed in their house magazines. To date, the progenies of the *ohu* villages are litigating in Enugu courts.

To buttress the interpretation further, there is evidence that among the Udi in northern Igboland, for instance, in Amokwe village, the Aro settlers were very prominent in patronising Christianity. This dovetailed into a new programme best prosecuted by Chief Onyeama of Eke. This enlightened despot saw that the shift of the Provincial capital from Calabar to Enugu in 1906 constituted a threat to his sovereignty. But he avoided confrontation and mobilized the Igbaja clan, served as the president of the Native Court, supplied labour to the colonial government and posed as a friend to modernity. He sought the education of his people in the English language and culture. Since the Anglicans had a policy of teaching in the vernacular, the chief fended them off from his kingdom, claiming that his people knew enough of the vernacular and needed a different type of educational diet.[28] Thus, from 1910 to 1950, Christianity grew in the cultural areas where the slave traders had dominated. The Aro slaving oligarchy gave their support.

CONCLUSIONS: GATHERING FIGS FROM THISTLES?

There is little doubt that the fortunes of slavery and Christianity were interwoven for better or for worse. From the Sierra Leone roots, recaptives played key pioneering roles. At the initial insertion of Christianity into the hinterland, the slaving oligarchy used a variety of means to hinder both the vertical and horizontal spread of Christianity. But the tensile strength of the external change agents forced adjustments. From the end of the First World War, the new dispensation opened up the slave trade routes to the service of Christianity in the southeast, east central, north and northeast of Igboland. Indeed, data abound for other cultural theatres and this paper has avoided the wider impact of the World Wars on Igbo communities. Equally crucial is the pattern of the collapse of opposition in various cultural areas. It occurred faster in some than in others, but soon turned into an avalanche in all places by the early 1940s. The Aro spread European goods and culture into the hinterland and thereby created the base for the acceptance of Christianity. Some Aro patronized Christianity both out of conviction and as an instrument of adjustment. Ex-slaves and traders brought the new ideology home as a form of development.

But the Aro continued to be ambivalent. Some tried to outwit change or kick against the prick—sometimes succeeding, as in the northeast, and at other times failing. By the 1930s, colonialism and Christianity consolidated and eroded Aro influence and resistance. Indeed, by 1949, missionaries had staked out large areas of operation and consolidated some. Communities were literally begging for schools and teachers. They would send delegations to far-away mission centres with twelve pounds sterling as the deposit for the teacher's salary and a promise to build the infrastructure, carry the loads for the teacher and perform other demands. Igbo entrepreneurs pioneered secondary education by the 1940s.

By all accounts, the proliferation of "bush" schools was seen as the index of the triumph of both the missions and civilization. The missionary and the commissar could pat themselves on the back for having gathered figs from thistles. Then, something happened in 1949 that was like a bolt from the clear sky. In that year, at Afara Umuahia, an exuberant Faith Tabernacle pastor encouraged ex-members of the *Ekpe* Society to reveal the secrets of the Leopard cult during Sunday school classes. The information seeped out and the cult lashed out in violent revenge. They first passed notices to all the cult centres in southeastern Igboland. On an arranged day, mayhem broke out: they burnt schools and churches until 1950. The colonial officers were shaken up as the poor security apparatus was exposed.

Was Christianity sitting lightly? Or, was it that the new change-agent needed to negotiate the boundaries, which may lead to routinization? Obviously, rapid vertical expansion did not mean depth of domestication or horizontal growth. Christian values rankled, and primal culture was not overawed by the implosion of the gospel. Individuals were still trying to work out adequate responses to the new force in the 1950s.

A last concern here is whether the flare could be seen as an aspect of persistent Aro influence—a matter that has come under the historiographical anvil. The picture of an Aro Empire painted by colonial officers contradicted the facts. M. A. Onwujeogwu turned the [29]searchlight away from the Aro onto the Nri, unearthing an ancient civilization that he declared to be the heart of Igbo civilization. Thurstan Shaw's archaeological findings aided this. A. E. Afigbo riposted that there was never an Nri hegemony over Igboland; rather, the Nri served as ritual agents who itinerated just like the Awka or Abiriba or the Nkwerre, each performing certain salutary roles in the development of the Igbo civilization. Thus, the missionaries may have had the last laugh as the products of mission schools dismantled the pedestal of Aro reputation.

NOTES

1. Paul Lovejoy, *Transformation of Slavery: A History of Slavery in Africa* (Cambridge: Cambridge University Press, 1983).
2. Lamin Sanneh, Review of Adrian Hasting's, *The Church in Africa* (Oxford, 1994) in *Missiology* 26, (1996), 540.
3. Culture Areas of Igboland: North: Nsukka—Udi axis or Enugu State; Northeast: Abakiliki, Nike, Awgu, Ohaozara (Afikpo, Uburu etc.) Or Ebonyi State; North-West: Oji River to Onitsha or Anambra State; West: Asaba and Igbo sections of Delta State; South: Ngwa, Umuahia, sections of Abia State, Mbaise (Imo State); East: Cross River Basin: Bende through Ohafia to Arochukwu (Abia State); Central: Okigwe to Owerri: Nkwerre, Mbano (Imo State); South-West: Oguta, Ohaji, Egbema, Ikwerre-Igbo (Imo+ Port Harcourt).
4. Adiele E. Afigbo, *The Abolition of the Slave Trade in Southeastern Nigeria, 1885-1950* (Rochester: University of Rochester Press, 2006); D. Ohadike, "The Decline of Slavery among the Igbo people," in *The End of Slavery in Africa*, eds., S. Miers and R. Roberts (Madison: University of Wisconsin Press, 1988), 437-461.
5. R. Gray, *Black Christians and White Missionaries* (New Haven, Yale University Press, 1991).
6. See David Kpobi, "African Chaplains in Seventeenth Century West Africa," in *African Christianity: An African Story* ed, Ogbu U Kalu (Pretoria: University of Pretoria, 2005), 140-69; D.N.A. Kpobi, *Missions in Chains: The Life, Theology and Ministry of Jacobus E.J.Capitein, 1717-1747* (Boekecentrum, 1993); W. H. Mobley, *The Ghanaian's Image of the Missionary* (Leiden: E.J. Brill, 1972). The force primal religiosity has been paid attention by many scholars. See for instance, Robin Law, "Religion, Trade, and Politics on the Slave Coast," *Journal of Religion in Africa* 21, 1 (1991): 42-77. The argument here is, therefore, not a monocausal explanation which hinges on slavery.
7. Paul V. Kollman, *The Evangelization of Slaves and Catholic Origins in Eastern Africa* (Maryknoll, NY: Orbis, 2005).
8. Ogbu U. Kalu, *The Embattled Gods: Christianization of Igboland, 1841-1991* (Lagos/London: Minaj Publishers, 1996), 70; idem. "Beyond Nationalist Historiography: White Indigenizers of the Igbo Church, 1876-1892" in *A Tapestry of the African Past*, eds., Ogbu Kalu et al (Lagos: Vista Books, 1993);

Felix K. Ekechi, *Missionary Enterprise and Rivalry in Igboland, 1857-1914* (London: Frank Cass, 1972).

9. Ogbu U Kalu, "Ethiopianism and the Roots of Modern African Christianity," in *The Cambridge History of Christianity: World Christianities, c1815-c1914*, eds., Sheridan Gilley and Brian Stanley (Cambridge: Cambridge University Press, 2006), 576-92.

10. F. I. Ekejiuba, "The Aro Trade System in the 19th Century, *Ikenga, Jnl. of the Inst. of African Studies* 1, 1 (1972):10-21; Adiele E. Afigbo, "The Nineteenth Century Crisis of the Aro Slaving Oligarchy of South-Eastern Nigeria," *Nigeria Magazine*, 110/112 (1974): 66ff; Walter I. Ofonagoro, "The Aro and Delta Middlemen of South-Eastern Nigeria and the Challenge of the Colonial Economy," *Journal of African Studies* 3, 2 (1976): 143-164; Kenneth O. Dike and Felicia I. Ekejiuba, "Change and Persistence in Aro Oral History," *Journal of African Studies* 3, 3 (Fall,1976):143-64.

11. National archives, Enugu (NAE), Frank Hives Report, C/40/21; Calprof 4/10/31.

12. I read Archdeacon Crowther's letter when it was in the former CMS Archives, London; G8/A/0, Crowther to Baylis, 5/10/1903; NAE, C/40/21 Calprof 4/10/31; and Calprof 5/16/46, Frank Hives Report.

13. F. I. Ekejiuba, "Aro Traditional Religion," *West African Religion*, 8 (1971).

14. Ogbu U. Kalu, "Battle of the Gods: Christianization of Cross River Igboland, 1903-1950," *Journal of the Historical Society of Nigeria*, 10, 1 (1977): 1-18.

15. Ogbu U. Kalu, ed. *A Century and Half of Presbyterian Witness in Nigeria,1846-1996* (Enugu: Presbyterian Church in Nigeria, 1996), Chapter 3.

16. The Primitive Methodist material is treated more fully in Ogbu U. Kalu, "Early Primitive Methodists on the Railroad Junctions of Igboland, 1910-1931," *Journal of Religion in Africa* 16, 1 (1986):44-66.

17. Ogbu U. Kalu, "*Nsibidi*: Pictographic Communication in Pre-Colonial Cross River Basin Societies," *Cahiers D'etudes des Religions Africaines* XII, 23/4 (Jan/Juill,1978): 97-116; idem., "The Irony of Colonialism: Formulation of Cultural Policy in Colonial Nigeria," in *Tradition and Modern Culture* ed, Edith Ihekweazu, (Enugu: Fourth Dimension Publishers,1985), 125-138; idem., "Missionaries, Colonial Government and Secret Societies in South-eastern Igboland," *Journal of the Historical Society of Nigeria* 9, 1 (December, 1977): 75-90.

18. Ogbu U. Kalu, "Waves from the Rivers: The Spread of Garrick Braide Movement in Igboland, 1914-1934," *Journal of the Historical Society of Nigeria* 8, 4 (June, 1977): 95-110.

19. NAE, Presbynig, 1/1/6 items 39 of 4/10/1911 and item 900 of 23/2/1922.

20. NAE, Presbynig, 1/1/6 item 98 of 1/10/12. See, E. N. Eze, "The Presbyterian Missionary Enterprise in Ohaozara, Cross River Igboland, 1906-1966," (MA dissertation, Religion, University of Nigeria, Nsukka, 1989).

21. NAE, Presbynig 1/1/6 item 98 of 1/10/12.

22. G. Johnston, *Of Maxim and Guns: Presbyterianism in Nigeria, 1846-1966* (Ottawa: Wilfrid Laurier University Press, 1988), 28; A. E. Afigbo, "Trade and Politics on the Cross River, 1895-1905," *Transactions of the Historical Society of Ghana* 13, 1 (June, 1972): 21-49.

23. SOAS, London, Primitive Methodist Society papers (hereafter PMS papers): Dodds Correspondence, 1913 Microfiche Box, 1164 (2); Ogbu U. Kalu, *Embattled Gods: Christianization of Igboland, 1841-1991* (Trenton NJ: Africa World Press, 2003), 180.

24. Ibid.

25. Ibid.

26. SOAS, London, PMS papers, "Ibo Opening" 1925 by William Dodds. Microfiche Box, 1164 (3).

27. Carolyn Brown, "Testing the Boundaries of Marginality: Twentieth Century Slavery and Emancipation Struggles in Nkanu, Northern Igboland, 1920-1929," *Journal of African History* 37 (1996): 51-80.

28. His great grandson, Dillibe Onyeama wrote his biography, *Onyeama of Eke* (Enugu: Delta Press, 1983).

29. M. A. Onwujeogwu, "Evolutionary Trends in the History of the Development of Igbo Civilization in the Culture Theatre of Igboland in Southern Nigeria," *Ahiajoku Lecture, 1987*. For a failed attempt to repair the Aro myth, see, J. O. Ijoma, "The Aro and their Neighbours," *Nigerian Heritage* 4, (1994): 36-49.

CHAPTER 9

GENDER AND CLASS TRANSFORMATION RESULTING FROM THE ATLANTIC SLAVE TRADE AND COLONIALISM

J. AKUMA-KALU NJOKU

This chapter explores the social and cultural transformations of Igbo traditional social statuses and gender roles resulting from the Atlantic slave trade and colonialism in the Bight of Biafra. This chapter draws attention to how the Atlantic trade and colonialism significantly changed social statuses, marriage, gender, and the class system in Igboland. The central argument of this chapter is that social and cultural transformation is so complex a phenomenon that it should be seen from more than one perspective, including the imposed rigid assimilation model, the creative ethnicity perspective (the African model), the new identity formation model, and the resistant perspective, in order to explain how cultural transformations are enacted, resisted or negotiated, and to see the emergent quality of social and cultural transformation.

The issue of social and cultural transformation has engaged the attention of scholars for a long time. Scholars have offered a wide frame of reference within which to examine the dynamics of social contacts and cultural transformation across cultures. For some, the shared experiences and collective memories of social groups shape the direction of social changes and cultural transformations. Indeed, the realities of identity formation and cultural transformation focus on the involvement of various social categories of identity formation—sexuality and gender, race, age, class, and ethnic groupings.[1] The idea that societies have the capacity to shape the direction of change in their culture offers analysts the opportunity to look at social and cultural transformations not only from the imposed one-sided context, but also as a condition of creative ethnicity. From 1500 to 1700, there was a rapid social and cultural change in Kongo. Rapid expansion of the slave trade led to increased militarization of the society and the presence of two classes of slaves: those who were considered exportable and those who could not be sold.

Essays on *Africa's Later Past*, a book edited by Graham Connah, are important reminders of the dynamic character of Africa's later past. Instead of seeing Africa from the hegemonic position of "a continent woken from a timeless sleep by the intrusion of European colonialism,"[2] contributors to this volume provide useful insights into many dimensions of transformation in the face continuing traditions. For example, they demonstrate the cultural capacity of Africans to adaptively respond to the "profound impact of cattle pastoralism, the development of cultural complexity, the growth of pre-colonial African urbanism, the fundamental role of climatic change, the appearance of iron-working technology, the proliferation of trading networks, the increasing level of interaction with the outside world and the impact of European expansion"[3] and other examples of the many transformations that took place during the later prehistoric and early historical period in Africa. As we shall see from this paper, the Igbo people have directly retained some aspects of their community's traditions regardless of changing economic conditions, colonialism, and British acculturation. As years go by, every society undergoes some transformations in its social institutions due to historical changes, especially as a result of contact and interactions with people from other regions of the nation or the world.

In a collection of essays edited by Linda Heywood, *Central Africans and Cultural Transformations in the American Diaspora*,[4] the contributing scholars give us insights into how African peoples re-shaped their cultural institutions in Central Africa, where they interacted with the Portuguese under repressive conditions until 1800. Scholars who see transformation only from a hegemonic and disruptive perspective often ignore this dimension of transformation. Seen from these models of transformation, namely, the creative ethnicity perspective (the African model), rigid assimilation model, the identity formation model, and the imposition and resistant model, it becomes analytically useful to examine "how transformations are enacted, complicated, or resisted" and negotiated to see the emergent quality of transformation. With a particular reference to Africa, many scholars have discussed the complexities of social transformations.[5]

I use Adam Ferguson's characterizations of societies outside of Europe in the eighteenth century and Michael Echeruo's thought on the state of Igbo society in the nineteenth century as points of departure. Another point of departure is John Oriji's historical analysis of transformations in the Ngwa clan, which I will extend with the case study of Ohafia. In the end, I present a model of neo-Igbo traditionalism as a desirable approach to shaping the direction of social and cultural change in the twenty-first century, as globalization is completing what started with European mercantilism in the colonial period.

But before we begin a close examination of the contributions of the Atlantic slave trade and colonialism to social formation and transformation in Igboland, it is important to consider how Europeans viewed pre-Atlantic world societies. According to Adam Ferguson, for instance, eighteenth-century Europeans apparently saw African societies in two broad viewpoints: First, as some of the other nations outside of Europe "who dwell in the less cultivated parts of the earth," where "they entrust their subsistence chiefly to hunting, fishing, or the natural produce of the soil."[6] Nations in this category had little attention to property and scarcely any beginnings of rigid social subordination or distant governance. Second, as nations depending for their provision on pasture, they knew what it was to be poor and rich. They knew the relations of patron and client, of servant and master, and suffered themselves to be classed according to their measures of wealth. They had to make such a distinction in order to create a material difference of character, and maybe furnish two separate heads, under which to consider the history of mankind in their crudest state: that of the savage, who is not yet acquainted with property; and that of the barbarian, to whom it is, although not ascertained by laws, a principal object of care and desire.[7] As we shall see in this paper, the Igbo nation would have fit better in the former than in the latter category. In either case, the Europeans saw African societies as their burden and their principal object of care, if I understand Ferguson correctly.

Reflecting on the Igbo society during this period, Professor Michael Echeruo, in his inaugural *Ahajioku* lecture, writes that, "Igbo society, at least in the nineteenth century, was a harsh and even brutal one to live in. Traditionally hard-working, the Igbo man found the chaos of the changing world around him both seductive and disorienting." He continues,

> A man was a man only if he could both cater for his family and defend that family. In the changing environment gener-

ated by the slave, trade, a man could also boast openly of his own individual prowess, not now in the farm, but in the oil or the slave trade. Arising directly from this, each man (and each community) assumed sole responsibility for his own (or its own) defense. Violence was inevitably involved in this expression of power and provision of defense.[8]

In the article "Transformations in Traditional Ngwa Society," John N. Oriji reviewed many early twentieth century synchronic and diachronic theories of social transformation. Oriji questioned the legitimacy of some of the earlier models couched on the now outdated evolutionary theory. Oriji concluded that social change and structural transformation "is stimulated by internal and external factors."[9]

Few, if any, will argue against the fact that Ferguson's eighteenth-century characterization of certain societies as places where people entrusted their subsistence to farming, hunting, fishing, or forest industry is reflective of Igboland. In that same vein, few will argue against the claim that the eighteenth-century Igbo were a people without a central form of politically-mediated government. And there is a preponderance evidence to support Echeruo's idea that Igbo society in the nineteenth century was a harsh and difficult.[10] Grim as the fact of the Atlantic slave trade was, many, especially the Aro traders and other perpetrators and their Ohafia warrior cohorts, were enthused and excited by this tragic event in human history.

Colonialism would eventually complicate these issues as far as the impacts of European encounters with African societies were concerned. For purposes of effective European mercantile and colonial administration in Africa, African societies had to undergo some kinds of acculturative social transformations. There is no doubt that the eager acceptance of the introduction of the trade in palm oil and palm kernels and, later, mission schools and European cultural ideals, were seductive and disorienting to most Igbo. Since that much is true, the challenge of this paper is to demonstrate and analytically examine the specific kinds of transformations that have taken place as a result of the Atlantic slave trade and colonialism in Igboland.

PRE-ATLANTIC TRADE BASES OF SOCIAL STATUS

Before the period of the Atlantic slave trade there were three bases for determining social status: namely, (1) landownership, (2) extraordinary service to Igboland (Igbo; *Igbo Mkpa*) or to community safety (killing a tiger, for example), and (3) yam wealth. A man from a landholding family or lineage was honorifically referred to as *Amadi* (*Ama di*): "there is land."

Men who by their contributions to their villages, village groups or clan became famous in Igboland earned the appellation (*Odenigbo*).

Table 9.1. Igbo Appellation of the Famous

Categories of Celebrity/Fame	Details
Di Nta	Distinguished Hunter
Di Mgba	Distinguished Wrestler
Di Ogu	Great Warrior
Di Bia (Dibia)	A diviner/augur/herbalist/healer on beck and call
Di Ochi	Famous palm wine taper
Di Ike	Someone of great strength
Ochiri Ozuo	One famous for taking in and bringing up or training so many people
Ome Ji (elege ndi ikom)	Reserved for a lady who equals men in yam production
Ogbu ji	Great Yam Farmer

In some places, such as Edda, Abam, and Ohafia, warriors, especially successful headhunters (*Ufiem)*, who upon their return from war presented heads to the village *Ikoro* (drum),[11] were ranked higher than those who returned without heads, and way above the *Ujo*—those who, due to fear, avoided going to war.

By far, the most significant determinant of social status was yam—the principal product of the land. The wealthiest men were the successful farmers. A man of mean order could rise to prominence if he became successful in yam production. Okonkwo of Umuofia in Achebe's *Things Fall Apart* is a good example. If Okonkwo were from Ohafia, he would have been known as *Ogbu Ji* or "Yam Lord."

Table 9.2. Social Classes in Akanu Ohafia

Utu Afa Ohafia (Appellations of fame)	Areas of Remarkable Accomplishments
Di Ji/Ogbu Ji	An accomplished farmer
Ome Ji	One whose yam harvest is greater than normal
Osu (Osu Ofia)	Famous as a bush slasher

Di Bia (Dibia)	A diviner/augur/herbalist/healer on beck and call
Di Mgba	Distinguished Wrestler
Di Ogu	Great Warrior
Ome Okwu	Master mound maker
Di Ike	Someone of great strength
Di Nta	Distinguished Hunter
Ochiri Ozuo	One famous for taking in and bringing up or training so many people
Okpa Aku	A wealthy person
Udo Ogu	Famous warrior
Udo Nsi	Famous Dibia

But behind every successful yam lord were his wife or wives and children. Women played and still play major roles in reproduction and production at the family, community, and regional levels. In some places, a wife who had ten children was highly rewarded by her husband with a goat and became a celebrity. Women bore the children who provided most of the labor force who produced the yam wealth upon which men's social statuses depended. Women were also the main producers of the other farm products and staples of the forest industry upon which the general populace depended for subsistence.

That was the case throughout Igboland when farming was the most important means of livelihood. That was the time when people in Akanu Ohafia could proudly say, according one of their folk songs,

Gi buru iri ga a-mba nde oduo,
agu anighi ekwe gi mee iri;
o'u gi buru iri bia Akanu,
Akanu ekedua ji oba.

Take your music to other places
and hunger will hinder your performance,
But take your music to Akanu;
you will find barns filled with yam.

That was when service to the community was a virtue and yam was king—the mainstay of rural economy—and social status centered on yam in Akanu Ohafia. In fact, up until the early twentieth century, a man's status or dignity depended upon the performance of four yam-related rituals

208

namely: (1) *Ike Oba* (Barn Raising), (2) *Igwa Oba* (Barn Sanctification), during which ritual the *Ifejuoku Nfujuoku* or *Njuoku ji* (*Njoku Ji*) shrine was constructed, and the chief celebrant placed the biggest yam from his harvest on the *Njoku Ji shrine;*[12] (3) *Igwa Nnu* or consecration of the first 400 yams (*aka oba*), and (4) *Ime Okere Nkwa* (Drumming celebration of Achievement and Dignity of Labor). For a man to host this festival, he had to have more than 2,800 yams (*aka oba ji asaa*). During the celebration, the chief celebrant placed 2,800 yams at measured distances from his barn to his hamlet arena.

Social statuses based on yam involved a descending order of importance, including *ime nkwa* (sponsoring a special instrumental music and dance ceremony), *igwa nnu* (the consecration of 400 yams), *igwa oba* (consecration of the barn), and *ike oba* (barn raising). After performing the *ime nkwa*, the chief celebrant became a member of the *Obimba* (Heartland). He would have earned the appellation of *Ogbu Ji* and become a famous Igbo celebrity (*Odenigbo*).

Things began to change during the Atlantic trade, not only in terms of social status, but also in the transformation of gender roles, class and demographic shifts. The formation of new Igbo communities grew extensively in Southeastern Nigeria. The population clusters of Igbo-speaking peoples in the Delta and the greater Slave Coast region, including Fanando Po, can trace their origins to the Atlantic trade in slaves, and later, fish, salt, palm oil and kernel.[13]

This development dealt a severe blow to farming and radically transformed the criteria for judging social status in Ohafia. When the first graduates of mission schools became clerical staff, typists and stenographers for the colonial administration; teachers for schools; and religious personnel for churches, the dynamics of class system became very complicated, leading to rapid social differentiations and stratifications in Ohafia - as was the case in other places in Igboland.

Perhaps there is no better example anywhere else in Igboland than in Akanu Ohafia to illustrate what Echeruo had in mind when he wrote, "In the changing environment generated by the slave, trade, a man could also boast openly of his own individual prowess, not now in the farm, but in the oil or the slave trade."[14] From the primary occupation of the Ohafia people in farming, emphasis shifted to warmongering and slave-recruiting during the period of the Atlantic slave trade, and, as a result of colonialism, drifted further away to other areas of professionalism at the expense of farming.

Table 9.3. Appellations Resulting from the Atlantic Slave Trade

Appellation	Explanation
Ibibio na Ngwa	Named after the age grades that fought wars at Ibibio and Ngwa lands
Mba Idima	Named after the age grade that fought the Idima war
Mba Achara	Named after the age grade that fought the Achara war
Mba Isiagu	Named after the age grade that fought the Isiagu war
Mba Asaga	Named after the age grade that fought the Asaga war
Amasiri	Named after the age grade that fought the Amasiri war
Akanu Ukwa	Named after the age grade that fought the Ukwa war
Ndi Eni	Named after the age grade that fought for the Eni of Aro
Bianko	Named after the age grade that fought for the Bianko of Aro

While all these were going on, that is before and after the Atlantic slave trade and the colonial period that quickly followed, and, in fact, up to the present, adult females played, and continue to play, important roles in reproduction and production at the family, community and regional levels. Women continued to bear children, and through them, Igbo society regenerated itself. Together with the children they bore, women continued to provide the labor that produced the wealth, yam, and other staples upon which social status depended. Nevertheless, women did not escape the effects of the transformation that was taking place. It used to be the convention that certain roles were distinctly reserved for women and others for men. There have always been some essential differences and overlapping similarities in the gender roles. Variations in gender roles should not be overlooked in discussing culture, which itself is infinitely emergent and changing.

There were significant gender transformations as well. During the Atlantic slave trade, women, together with their children, began to bear most of the brunt of the hard manual labor it took to produce the yam and other staples upon which social status depended. This was especially the case when more and more men were required as slave raiders, escorts, and porters. Women bore the brunt of food production to replenish the decreasing number of men in the labor force and meet the demands for food to feed the communities and sustain the regional slave trade. Most able-bodied young men were constantly gone; older men and big farmers began to marry more and more wives, including the young Enugwu wives (probably slave girls) whose children became *umu-afo* (free born) and enlarged their farm labor force. Men also began to get additional labor by owning slaves who were eventually incorporated into the community as free men. Many started getting house servants or attendants (*umu-mbina*) and paid laborers (*ndi ozi-ego*) to perform all kinds of farming-related duties. Some even started to use cult servants (*ndi osu*) for duties other than the sacred. Trusted slaves, especially *the ndi oku* (*oku azu, dinta,* etc.), were allowed to remain on the compound and helped in the reproduction process. Some of the strong and hardworking among them married the daughters of the Enugwu wives and become free citizens of their respective villages.

Some villages began to get additional labor by owning slaves (*ohu*), using cult servants (*ndi osu*), getting house servants or attendants (*umumbina*), and bonded or indentured servants or paid laborers (*ndi ozi-ego*). As time went on, when it became evident that many slaves were escaping, men resorted to marrying more and more wives in order to get their own children. The names Ohuabunwa and Nwagbaoso, Nwaka (as in *Nwa ka aku,* (a child is greater than wealth) implying that *ohu bu aku*) (a slave is wealth) can only make sense in that context. Buying female slaves became a way to have *nwa afo* (free born or citizen). Incidentally, the status of slave women changed when they became wives and bore children. The importance of such women in the sections of Igboland that are matrilineal, especially in Ohafia, became generally elevated. They became not only wives but also daughters and members of the matrilineal kinsfolk of their husbands or the person who initially brought them to the village. Such wives and kindred became more valued than the women who became wives through endogamous marriage.

At the same time, it became the habit among men of wealth, particularly those in Aro compounds, to have as many indentured servants and pawned maids as possible. Later, those who could not fulfill the conditions of their indenture or pawn agreement became slaves or married into the household of large slaveholders or were sold into slavery. Many Aro slaveholding families preferred to marry their slave girls to their sons or relatives in their farm villages. According to one of the descendants of the famous Okoro Oji of Ujari in the Arochukwu (*Aro Ulo*) homeland, "our great grandfather used to send his children on errands to populate his farm villages"[15] in the Ito or the greater Ujari or Aro Diaspora communities in Igboland. More than is generally realized, many communities, including Amankwu in Abia State and Amuro in Imo State, owe their origins to the farm villages (*ulo ubi*) the Aro established as centers of food production to support the regional slave trade. The first effective settlers of these villages were usually the sons of the slave holders, but by and large, the populations of the villages were disproportionately female. Once a female slave married, her slave status was nullified. The off-spring of such marriages became freeborn citizens. Even without the formality of marriage, if a slave girl got pregnant in the compound of her owner, her status changed, regardless of whether the man who was biologically responsible for the pregnancy was himself a slave. Polygamy became the order of the day in the farm villages.

At the end of the overseas slave trade, Europeans introduced trading in other goods, especially palm oil and, later, kernels. Many former slave dealers and traders became the agents of European trading companies and began to trade in cash crops meant for overseas markets. Being an agent of European traders became a sign of high status. Some farm villages became cash-crop plantations or centers for processing palm oil and kernels for the new, lucrative palm-produce business. Many village farmers began to resort to gathering palm fruits. And between planting and harvesting periods, many men and women travelled to farm villages to earn wages from processing palm oil and crack kernels for plantation owners or for their agents.

One of the fundamental cultural changes of the shift from farming to palm oil and kernel production was that the traditional Ohafia social stigma of *Onye hapuu ubi ga igbu akwu wu onye nko (onye umengwu)* (lazy person) lost its effect. Prior to this time, it used to be that the Ohafia looked down upon any person who depended on anything else than yam production as a means of livelihood. The agents of the big trading companies such United African Company (UAC) and John Holt became so very prosperous that they could join the *obimba* (movers and shakers) group. Even some of those who were celebrated farmers sold their yams and became successful buyers and sellers of palm kernels. No longer was a farmer the villager who was higher in social status than the trader (*ono n'ulo ka ndi afia/ahia*). Traders who peddled their wares to distant places, especially to the urban centers, became the preferred husbands. *Ozu afia* (trader) became a prestigious appellation. The most successful traders and the agents of the trading companies dealing with palm products became the new generation of *obimba*.

COLONIALISM AND SOCIOECONOMIC TRANSFORMATION

Colonialism has always been viewed as a powerful political, social, and cultural system of economic exploitation. But many recent studies show how cultural groups responded to colonialism. Stanley Brandes sees Mexicans' adaptive use of their *Días de los Muertos* in the context of Roman

Catholicism's All Saints' Day as a creative response to colonialism, allowing them to maintain their traditional spirituality and custom of honoring their dead.[16] Masco makes a similar point when he argues that *Kwakwaka'wakw* ceremonies can only be understood within the context of and as a response to the British colonization of Vancouver Island in 1849.[17] And the Bribris use folk narratives to represent their memories of the power relationships between themselves and their Spanish colonizers. While it is important to study the folklore of the colonized, Julien's study draws attention to the significance of the dissenting voices to both the colonized and the colonizers.[18] Meanwhile, Gloria Raheja shows that colonial powers selectively appropriated native oral narratives in order to foster the illusion of the colonized's consent during the period from 1870 to 1920.[19]

We can also find similar examples from many African peoples. In some cases, the desire and mandate for transformation of African societies during the colonial period was deliberate. F. Grevisse, writing as both historian and civil servant, makes this clear when he examines the Belgian policy, which introduced a body politic of delineation and established a center for the domestication of Africans: "This newly circumscribed social 'body' was composed of Africans who were supposed to incarnate an absolute beginning of history."[20] And the center "became the exclusive locus for a radical reconstruction . . . The reconstruction or transformation" was oriented according to a series of demands associated with the purpose of the colonial school, a new hierarchical administration and toward the promotion of a new system of values at three fundamental levels: (1) Christian marriage and patrilineal succession was imposed de facto as one model of and project obedient to Christian norms and integration within the colonial order; (2) French language and later Swahili was imposed through education; and (3) the professionalization of the inhabitants—(a) clerks and nurses, etc. (b) merchants, and (c) sub-clerical standard grades.[21]

For V. Y. Mudimbe, the Christian reconstruction of the African mind and the civilization of Africans was the ground upon which the colonial authorities could promote the development of a new memory, or upon which they could foster rifts within the human environment if their role and authority became threatened. . . . The physical space of the center, divided among the linguistic sub-cultural groups was the site of a sociological competition. Like his Congo counterpart the Igbo student caught between the boundaries of two memories, attempted to prove that in his thoughts, life, and work he had succeeded in repressing the traditional African memory. He would then unconsciously assimilate the new modes of thought and action through forced acculturation. Mudumbe, in characterizing the Congo student of that time, puts it this way:

His history, as well as his individual consciousness, was supposed to begin with the colonial system. In concrete terms, a
series of procedures and tests for selection was permanently in
place, forcing the evaluant to submit to this transformation. The
schools and churches constantly evaluated intellectual capacities, facilitating a careful screening of potential candidates from
early childhood for integration into the new professional hierarchy.[22]

In the case of Nigeria, Christianity and colonial administration led to
rapid social differentiations and stratifications that changed the Igbo society.
For many places in Africa during the colonial period, opening of mission
schools by Christian denominations for training clerical staff for colonial
administration, teachers for schools, and religious personnel for the churches
further transformed the dynamics of marriage, gender, and the class system.

Two of the most enduring aspects of colonialism in Africa are the
dresses and dress codes and the *lingua franca* found in most African countries. From the period of Portuguese involvement in the slave trade in
West Africa, European forms of dress started to replace - in Nigeria, for
instance - the Igbo clothing made from local materials. Pre-colonial forms
of dress included *ogodo, aji*, and *okara* for adult males; *nwa-iba* for boys;
and *udo* or *olokpo* for girls. Prior to the Portuguese involvement in the lives
of the people, local textiles were used for indigenous dress. Beginning with
the Portuguese in the 1600s and throughout the colonial period (1885 to
1960s), European types of clothing became the norm. The colonial masters
used schools and churches to impose European dress codes on the colonized. Among those in the greater society who did not go to school and/or
were not converted to Christianity, it was not uncommon for boys and
girls eight years and under to walk about naked during the colonial period.
Today, Igbo chiefs and some kings, like European monarchs, wear crowns
and red caps adorned with colorful glassy beads.

Consider, for instance, what Columbus said of the red caps and beads
he gave to the American Indians: "I gave to some among them some red
caps and some glass beads, which they hung round their necks, and many
other things of little value. At this they were greatly pleased and became so
entirely our friends that it was a wonder to see."[23]

The reflection of the linguistic effect of colonialism in African folklife
is obvious when one looks at the *lingua franca* of many African countries
and the languages of instruction, administration, command, and operation in most postcolonial nations and institutions. Contemporary verbal
expression or verbal folklore provides the best examples of the encoding of

the metaphors, images, and themes of colonialism. In the village of Akanu Ohafia in Nigeria, some people remember the arrival of the Europeans by when they were asked to stop wearing *olokpo* around their waists. One individual recalled this song:

Ee Bekee, ee	Oh Europeans, Oh
Ee Bekee, ee	Oh Europeans, Oh
Ee, Bekee,	Oh Europeans,
Wo si anyi gbekwa olokpo eje	They asked us to stop wearing *olokpo*.
Bekee,	Europeans
Eye Bekee, agbahile	The European era has arrived.

Some songs make telling comments on the social conditions of the laborers during the colonial period. A good example is a song that alludes to the men who constructed the railroad that runs from Port Harcourt in the south to Gombe in the north. The laborers were paid three pence a day. Many left their villages to do the hard labor of digging up and carrying stones for the north-south railroad. Some died of fatigue. If a laborer escaped and returned home, the colonial masters sought his arrest. Court messengers were sent to deliver such orders to the heads of the escapee's home village. Thus, such messengers had a bad reputation for the kind of job they did. Besides, messengers were among the lowest paid civil servants. They were lower in status than the laborers. The following set of songs and chants can only make sense when considered against the background of that specific colonial experience:

Mgbe anyi gara igwu okwute	When we went to excavate stones,
Onye nwulu, o zulu ike	The dead went to rest.
Gbam gbam n'olu oyibo!	Dig, dig in European's work.
Onye nwulu, o zulu ike.	The dead went to rest.
Onye muru nwoke gbere aro	Rejoice not if you have a male child.
Mgbe anyi gara n'ugwu Awusa	When we went to Hausaland
Ehee, eheee	Oh no, no, no
Mgbe anyi gara n'ugwu Awusa.	When we went to Hausaland.
Laborer, toro toro, e dey	The laborer was paid three pence a day;
Onyenwe ya nai nai, e dey.	His owner/contractor nine pence a day
Nwa kotima otule ntu	Poor court messenger,
Onye lebera ka gi mma.	The laborer is better than you.

CONCLUSIONS

The complexity of social change and cultural transformations are compounded when we add issues such as the intersection of changes with continuities, ethnocentrism, and forced acculturation. Emerging from this complex social dynamic is the arrangement of people into a five-part hierarchical order in Igboland: namely, (1) stratification based on kinship system, (2) stratification based on landownership, (3) stratification based on agricultural economy, (4) differentiation based on Igbo religion, and (5) stratification and class system based on the Atlantic slave trade and the post-abolition trade in palm produce, and colonialism. Undoubtedly, scholars can gain insight into a group's response to colonialism by examining relevant expressive items and forms of their folklore. Customs and ceremonies, songs, names and naming, as well as cultural tools and decorative objects, express ideas, narrate experiences and articulate thoughts about colonialism. They thus inform not only anthropological studies, but also a wide array of scholarly fields, from history and political science to literature. Based upon new evidence, we should endeavor to be more selective in our appropriation of Western ways of life. We should incarnate our repressed tradition; that is, we should embark on a kind of neo-traditionalism or a carefully structured transition or regeneration that brings together our experiences. In doing so, we must continue the standard Igbo habit of selective appropriation. Innovation is an inherent part of Igbo aesthetics. We can never come to a time when the Igbo will discontinue their habit of selectively appropriating. We will continue to pick and choose diverse elements from our neighboring Nigerian ethnic groups and from peoples of other world cultures. In doing so, we remain committed to service (*Igbo mkpa*). Our moral assignment in a world culture that is increasingly global is to get from the world everything we need to be of service to Igboland in the spirit of *igbo mkpa*.

NOTES

1. See for example, the work of the research group at the University of Wollongong (UOW) http://www.uow.edu.au/arts/research/ict/ [Accessed 29 June 2006].
2. Connah Graham, *Transformations in Africa: Essays on Africa's Later Past* (London: Leicester University Press, 1997). See http://arts.anu.edu.au/arcworld/aboutus/connah.htm. [Accessed 29 June 2006].
3. Ibid.
4. Linda Heywood, *Central Africans and Cultural Transformations in the American Diaspora* (Cambridge: Cambridge University Press, 2001).

5. These are summarized in John Thornton, *Africa and Africans in the Making of the Atlantic World, 1400-1800* (Cambridge: Cambridge University Press, 1998), 72-3. See also John Thornton "Demographic Effect of the Slave Trade," *The Journal of African History* 30, no. 3 (1989): 365-94; Patrick Manning, "Local versus Regional Impact of the Export Trade," in *African Population and Capitalism: Historical Perspectives*, eds. Dennis D. Cordell and Joel W. Gregory (Madison: University of Wisconsin Press, 1994), 35.

6. Adam Ferguson, *An Essay on the History of Civil Society* Part 1 (1809 reprinted 2007) in *Of the History of Rude Nations.*

7. Ibid.

8. See Michael Echeruo, "A Matter of Identity –Ahamefula." 1979, Ahiajoku Lecture (Owerri: Ministry of Information and Culture, 1979).

9. See John N. Oriji, "Transformations in Traditional Ngwa Society," *Ikenga: Jouranl of African Studies*, 4, no. 2 (July 1980): 23-39.

10. Echeruo, "A Matter of Identity."

11. See Ngwobia Uka, "A Note on the Abam Warriors of Igboland," *Ikenga* 1, no. 2 (1971): 78-79.

12. These would be edible or yams not seed yams meant for planting.

13. See http://www.bartleby.com/67/885.html [Accessed June 29, 2006].

14. Echeruo, "A Matter of Identity."

15. Interview with Okoro Orji, Amanagwu, November 2005.

16. *Stanley Brandes* Días de los Muertos *in* Writing Culture/Selling Oaxcca (1998) http://ethnographic.wordpress.com/2007/10/29/death-and-life-here-and-there/ [Accessed March 22, 2008].

17. Joseph Masco, "Competitive Displays: Negotiating Genealogical Rights" From http://www.jstor.org/sici?sici=0002. http://muse.jhu.edu/journals/callaloo/v022/22.3julien02.html. [Accessed 22 March 2008].

18. Catherine Julien, *Reading Inca History* (Iowa City: University of Iowa Press, 2000).

19. See Gloria Raheja, "Caste, Colonialism, and the Speech of the Colonized," *American Ethnologist* 23, 33 (1996): 494-513.

20. F. Grevisse and Albert Gille, "The Social and Scientific Role of C.E.P.S.I.," *African Affairs* 49, no. 195 (April 1950): 151-57.

21. See V. Y. Mudimbe, *The Idea of Africa* (Bloomington and Indianapolis: Indiana University Press, 1994), 130-33.

22. Ibid., 133.

23. Wilcomb E. Washburn, *The Indian and the White Man* (Garden City, NY: Anchor Books, 1964).

Chapter 10

Episodes of Igbo Resistance to European Imperialism, 1860-1960

Felix K. Ekechi

This essay focuses on Igbo encounters with the Europeans between 1860 and 1960. Essentially, it is a story of aggression and response, which involved British consuls, traders, missionaries, and colonial officials, who together created the conditions for resistance. This chapter, therefore, critically examines and analyzes how European imposition of alien ways of life, and particularly British colonial rule, sparked Igbo resistance, which lasted up to Nigeria's independence in 1960. The essay largely argues that early European intrusions into the people's way of life, British conquest and the imposition of colonial rule and political domination, made possible by British violence, violated the Igbo principle of "live and let live" and thus catalyzed widespread resistance.

Resistance, as discussed in this essay, encompasses both violent and non-violent responses to unacceptable cultural, social, economic, and political interference and innovations. Non-violent responses included songs, words of protest (language), demonstrations, dancing, and so forth, directed against the intruders and invaders. Violent resistance, on the other hand, refers mainly to military confrontations. Altogether, resistance against British imperial presence, in whatever form, was aimed at the preservation and/or maintenance of traditional Igbo way of life (culture), political autonomy, and sovereignty.

Studies of European-Igbo encounters from about the mid-nineteenth century to 1960 abound.[1] Therefore, I need not dwell in detail on all the aspects of pre-colonial and colonial encounters/confrontations. Rather, my interest here is essentially to highlight *selected episodes* and *patterns* of Igbo resistance, which involved both male and female groups, each responding to perceived, or actual, threats to cultural/traditional values, and the general wellbeing of the people. The analysis hereunder is multi-layered, reflecting gender-specific cases.

Let me begin with this caveat: First, the Igbo, who today live on both sides of the River Niger in southern Nigeria and adjoining areas, as well as on the eastern Benue River, are a very republican and democratic people. In the words of the eminent Igbo nationalist, Mazi Mbonu Ojike, "We, the I[g]bo are the most decentralized and least bureaucratic in our political organization. . . . The political system is so highly democratized that no one feels that one's freedom is stifled."[2] Secondly, the Igbo share in common a social-religious ideology, which upholds the sacredness of personal/group autonomy and identity, encapsulated in the concept of "every man a king." As Richard Henderson put it, without this deep-seated belief in freedom and liberty in Igbo social ethos, "the Igbo man might not know what it was to be fully a man."[3] In short, the Igbo reject the high-handedness of rulers, often associated with kings, and hence the anti-king sentiment that is often found in most Igbo societies. To many, in fact, a king per se is an enemy—"Ezebuilo," to borrow an expression from Chinua Achebe. In essence, the concept of king, symbolizing dominance and oppression is clearly antithetical to Igbo social and political philosophy. Simply stated, resistance to oppression and domination constitutes an ever-present characteristic feature of Igbo social and political life.

Even the Igbo in the Diaspora, and particularly in America, did not lose this ingrained conviction of personal freedom; on the contrary, they asserted their rights of manhood by resisting denials of freedom and liberty, domination, dehumanization and exploitation stemming from slavery. They did so loudly through either migration (flight) or by committing suicide. Thus the love of freedom embedded in Igbo/African culture fostered or engendered the urge among slaves to "fly, fly, and fly away" from the white man's oppressive regime in American society.[4] Elsewhere, Igbo aversion to all forms of domination and exploitation were often manifested in voluntary migration (flight from places of actual or perceived oppression and domination), open revolt via military confrontation, and other forms of protest and/or civil disobedience. The recurring wars between the Igbo and the Benin Kingdom in pre-colonial times, for example, exemplify recourse to military strategy to escape political domination and economic exploitation, on the one hand, while Owerri oral traditions provide another illustration of civil disobedience and migration to a new settlement.[5] Even in contemporary Nigeria, the Igbo have continually protested against social, economic and political domination and marginalization.

ACCOMMODATION-AMBIVALENT RELATIONSHIP: PATTERNS OF IGBO-EUROPEAN RELATIONS IN PRE-COLONIAL TIMES

A careful examination of archival documents reveals that early European-Igbo encounters were far from being hostile. On the contrary, the evidence clearly shows that the Igbo (*nde* Igbo) were (and still are) a very hospitable people. Hence, Igbo people accorded their guests a warm welcome when they first arrived. After all, being themselves "prodigiously itinerant" traders and fortune hunters, the Igbo certainly appreciated the value of being made welcome wherever they went. Thus, nde Igbo take acts of hospitality very seriously, at least as demonstrated in the offering of kola nuts to guests, as the symbol of welcome, love, and cordiality. In essence, the offering of kola nuts to guests symbolized or signified social acceptance—an admirable Igbo socio-cultural life that was duly acknowledged by the early European traders, and particularly the missionaries. Reporting of visits to the Igbo villages in 1905, for example, Archdeacon Tom Dennis of the CMS intimated his mother thus: "We were greeted with 'nnoa' or welcome; the king and elders gave us fowls, yam, kola-nuts, etc." as a symbol of hospitality.[6]

Similarly, in the era of palm oil trade (c.1830-1880), amicable guest-host relationships prevailed. Studies show that the Igbo *did not* initially (and still do not) hate the white man. On the contrary, early attitudes toward the "visitors," who purportedly came as "friends...to open the country in the interior to Commerce and Civilization," appeared markedly hospitable. Reporting of his encounter with the Igbo people of Elele ("Lelele") in present Rivers State, in 1892, Consul Campbell acknowledged that the people appeared genuinely "friendly," especially when they learned that "my mission" was to make treaties "of friendship and commerce" with them and their chiefs. He went on to say that, perhaps because "No white man had ever visited this town . . . the excitement of the populace was [consequently] considerable."[7]

Even Sir Ralph Moor, Commissioner and Consul General of the Niger Coast Protectorate, known derisively among the Igbo as the *Otikpo*

Obodo (Destroyer of towns), equally acknowledged that the Igbo towns "we visited" in the Ngwa and Obohia areas, in the late 1890s, were generally well-disposed "towards us." It was therefore his opinion that the Igbo *"are peaceful and by no means a fighting people"*[8] (my emphasis). This assessment though not wholly an accurate picture per se, coming directly from an avowed militaristic British imperialist, is indeed significant. It bolsters my argument of Igbo hospitality and accommodation. Whatever the case, the message was clear enough: early Igbo-European encounters appeared markedly friendly.

Yet, as Campbell and Moor later discovered, the Igbo people were no fools. On the contrary, savvy and "uncanny in business and diplomacy," as the missionary John Taylor once observed, the Igbo could easily "read" the minds/intentions of their guests. Specifically, despite their professions of "friendship and comity," the Igbo were able to discern quickly the permanent interests of the imperialists, In other words, distrust of the British strangers crept in as soon as their true intentions became apparent. Captain Campbell was thus perceptive enough to observe this, and hence reported to his superiors that the Igbo had surprisingly grown *"suspicious of our [real] intentions"* (my emphasis). In time, therefore, hostility and conflict replaced hospitality, cordiality, and accommodation, essentially because British imperial motives had become patently clear. Simply stated, British imperial policy of control and domination, as reflected in the instructions from the Foreign Office to Consul Claude MacDonald, was unmistakable. The instructions stated as follows:

> The system [of trade,] hitherto in force under which the coast chiefs have exacted comey [tax] from traders must be finally abolished. [And further,] the chiefs must be made to understand that their claims to levy imposts and regulate commercial intercourse must be surrendered to the Protecting Power. . . . You will undertake under your immediate control the inter-tribal and foreign relations of the native chiefs. The question of raising revenue to cover the expenses of administration requires your immediate attention.[9]

The implications of these declarations were both obvious and ominous. First, they were designed to undermine the political power of indigenous rulers. Second, they were framed to undercut the rulers' economic prerogatives. Thus faced with threats of loss of political power and economic control, the rulers braced themselves for the looming, and inevitable conflict. In response, they called British bluff by declaring the "declarations" null and void. In their further expression of resistance, the rulers decreed: (a) That, the concept/ principle of "free trade" was inadmissible; and (b) That the collection of tolls on the roads and markets must be enforced as of old. Simply stated, they reaffirmed their political authority to *regulate* commercial transactions. And when the consuls and the traders predictably objected, the rulers, as elsewhere, closed the roads and markets so as to protect their economic interests.[10] Equally striking were the decrees that prohibited trade with the "intruders," again as resistance to the changing terms of trade in favor of the expatiates. The significance of these measures were not lost on Capt. Campbell himself, who correctly perceived these antagonistic laws "against us" as signifying the changing political tide. The rulers, he ruefully reported, have "suddenly [become] most inhospitable . . . towards us."[11] From now onwards, not surprisingly, British stereotypes and images of the Igbo changed dramatically, ranging from the Igbo being "troublesome," "truculent," and "hard to deal with" to a primitive people, who refuse to accept the "civilizing mission" of Western capitalism, etc. The result was the series of military encounters that characterized late nineteenth and twentieth-century Igbo history. For purposes of analysis, we shall divide the Igbo-British military confrontations into two major phases: engagements in the Western and Eastern fronts.

ANGLO-IGBO CONFLICT IN THE WESTERN FRONT

Years before the establishment of British direct rule in Igboland (1900-1910), resistance against the missionaries and the Royal Niger Company had been on stage west of the Niger from about 1888-1904. Briefly, resistance by the Ika Igbos (now Anioma) and their neighbors represented the first phase of conflict. The activities of the missionaries, and the British Royal Niger Company, perceived by the Anioma Igbos as the slow but steady perversion of Igbo sense of values and morality, triggered the stiff resistance against the missionaries and the RNC, which in modern historical literature has become legendary. To the elders, missionary propaganda, with all its implications and consequences (introduction of alien or "new ways of life"), and the exploitative policies of the Company, details of which are discussed later, had become intolerable interference. Hence, both agents of radical change were regarded as "subversive and dangerous innovators," who had perverted traditional norms.

Let us take a brief look at the cause and effect scenarios. First, the cheating and monopolistic activities of the British Royal Niger Company (RNC) rankled, meaning that the Company's operation caused intense anger and frustration among the Niger Delta city-states. A missionary's eyewitness account reveals the terror that was perpetrated by the Niger Company, and hence the widespread hatred of the Company and its agents. Wrote the missionary, "The hatred of the Company is widespread all along the River."[12] Specifically, the local people complained bitterly about the under-payment for their palm oil and palm kernel products by company agents, as well as the land-grabbing proclivities of the RNC. Worse still were the periodic bombardments of towns and villages, which have been documented in historical accounts. Altogether, the commercial and political misdeeds of the company rankled, and as discussed below, provoked armed resistance.

Secondly, missionary evangelism (propaganda) added fuel to the already smoldering cauldron. Apparently alienated from the traditional society, converts, who metaphorically "no longer [spoke] the language of our fathers," violated native laws and customs with reckless abandon. Perhaps even more irritating were the misguided attacks and desecration of religious shrines and temples—the traditional places of ritual and worship—by the over-zealous neophytes. For the elders and others to have thus, simply looked on, while the old society appeared in imminent danger of collapsing under the weight/impact of missionary Christianity, seemed tantamount to self-imposed destruction—certainly unthinkable. Thus, predictably, steps were taken to combat the missionary-induced assaults to native laws and customs—*Omenala/omenani*.[13]

Furthermore, the Royal Niger Company's persistent meddling in the domestic slavery issue and other commercial matters added salt to the festering wound. Although the Atlantic slave trade had been abolished in 1807, slavery nevertheless persisted. Thus, in 1891, the British Foreign Office issued specific "Instructions" to Consul MacDonald regarding domestic slavery. It stated, among other things:

> Your object should be, by developing legitimate trade, by promoting civilization, by inducing the natives to relinquish inhuman and barbarous customs, and by gradually *abolishing slavery, to pave the way for placing the territories . . . directly under British rule.*"(My emphasis)[14]

The RNC enforcement of the abolition decree sparked spirited resistance in Asaba, essentially because, in Asaba, as Elizabeth Isichei has shown, slaves were acquired "primarily for burial ceremonies and for services such as manual labour on their farms for the production of palm oil and other needs." Slavery in Asaba, in other words, seemed to have been an essential part of the domestic economy.[15] Thus, while the British and the RNC explained their motives for the abolition in moral and humanitarian terms, the Asaba people, on the other hand, saw it as a threat to their social and economic interests; and hence the attacks on RNC factories and other establishments. Unfortunately, Asaba resistance led to a most disastrous outcome: brutal bombardment by the RNC that left the town in ruins.[16]

The bombardment of Asaba in 1888 was a prologue to punitive actions against the Anioma people. Royal Niger Company imperial activities (land seizures etc.) and violations of commercial norms, coupled with missionary assaults on Igbo traditional religion, created conditions for rebellion. The Ekumeku Society, a secret and nocturnal organization, assumed the mantle of rebellion/resistance against the two imperial agents, the RNC and the Roman Catholic missionaries of the Society of African Missions (SMA), both with headquarters in Asaba. In large measure, the Ekumeku rebellion was in response to the missionaries' cultural intrusiveness as well as the Royal Niger Company's assertions of political and commercial dominance. Indeed by the 1890s, the entire Anioma region and beyond was engulfed in wars of liberation. As the historian Don Ohadike has chronicled, the Ekumeku fiercely attacked both the company's and the missionaries' stations in Asaba. The rebellion spread to other Anioma towns and villages. This guerrilla war of 1898 against the combined RNC/British forces was particularly ferocious at the strategic town of Ubulu-Ukwu where, according to Ohadike, the "Ekumeku riflemen occupied the natural and artificial trenches they had dug on the eastern approaches of [the town]." Not only did the Ekumeku warriors temporarily keep the enemy at bay, but they also harassed the combined RNC/British forces for a long period of time through the effective use of guerilla war strategy. Elsewhere, wars of resistance also raged.[17] In a sense, Igbo military response to British imperialism had thus begun.

In the end, however, British superior firepower led to the defeat of the Ekumeku movement by 1904. The aftermath was predictable: British occupation and consolidation of power over the entire Anioma and other western non-Igbo communities.[18] Don Ohadike has catalogued some of the pernicious impacts of British colonial rule in the Anioma territory as follows:

> After their military conquest the British continued their brute force philosophy. . . . [Consequently,] severe political strife and social insecurity marked the ensuing colonial period. The imposition of indirect rule, based on the native courts and warrant chiefs, undermined the democratic principles of the people. . . . Elders and lineage heads, as well as the age-grades

and secret societies, who had participated in clan governments, were elbowed into a state of insignificance. . . . [I]ndirect rule proved itself a useful administrative expediency, even if it was also faulty, disruptive, and burdensome.[19]

However, resistance to British imperialism was not confined to the Anioma country; rather, it was widespread, but the outcome was unfortunately ominous—British conquest and colonization. A brief examination of the dynamics of sociopolitical change might be useful, beginning with a discussion of Onitsha-Royal Niger Company-missionary relations. By 1860, both the British traders and the Protestant missionaries had established stations at Onitsha, a strategic river port. While palm oil trade and missionary propaganda flourished, alien cultural and commercial innovations, as might be expected, inexorably began to alter the texture of society. Difficulties with the RNC and the expatriate missionaries escalated to a point of conflict and violence. First, missionaries' arrogant preaching of the superiority of Christianity to Igbo Traditional Religion attracted hostile reception. For example, when the so-called "messengers of liberation" sought to convert the elders, the response was unequivocally, no; "We are already set in our traditional ways." The missionaries were therefore asked to go and preach to the children. But then, the conversion of the young ones resulted to unanticipated consequences—the violation of *Omenala*, and/or behaviors unbecoming of a well-socialized son/daughter of the soil. Presumably alienated from the traditional society, as a direct result of missionary influences, the converts grew wild, and smashed the sacred religious shrines (temples) "with all temerity"—similar to the misguided iconoclasm of the so-called "born again Christians" of our time! Worse still, the converts became overtly disobedient to the elders, whom they treated with disdain, noting that they (elders) no longer deserved respect, because they were "heathens" and/or "pagans."

Bewildered, the elders thereupon declared Christianity unacceptable, inasmuch as "this new religion" had become too intrusive and had also turned the converts into "madmen." The corrupting influences of the foreign traders (Europeans and Africans),[20] equally created tensions as well as conditions for prompt and corrective action against the forces of change. In effect, the elders were poised to prevent the society from being turned upside down. To this end women, the dibias (native doctors), and the elders (polygamists), resolved to confront the "cultural polluters" and the "dangerous innovators." We shall at this juncture first examine the women's "anti-pollution" movement in the Onitsha District, discussed below as the female militant protest.

FEMALE MILITANCY

It should be appreciated that, when confronted with problems, Nigerian women have traditionally organized themselves into a formidable social force. Such organization(s) may be for religious, social, and political causes.[21] In the Onitsha case under review, the untoward events that accompanied missionary enterprise in Onitsha had invariably caused concern and uneasiness and thus compelled women to resort to spiritual forces or mediums for the restoration of traditional patterns of Igbo way of life. Operating under the inspiration of the spirit force known as Odesoruelu—"Restorer of Traditional Way of Life"—the women from around Onitsha, namely Obosi, Nkwere, Nsugbe, Ogbunike and Ogidi mobilized themselves in a war-like fashion. They marched from place to place singing traditional songs that articulated rejection of the radical changes in society. They swept the compounds and pathways and warned that all roads and compounds that had seemingly been polluted since the advent of the foreigners must be kept clean again as in the ancient days. They further warned the populace against warfare, which had apparently intensified since the advent of the traders and the missionaries. Additionally, the women decried the violations of native laws and custom as well as the disruptions of the social/religious order by the over-zealous Christian converts. They bemoaned the passing away of the "good old days" and particularly agonized over the sharp rise in the prices of foodstuffs and other trade goods. Of grave concern too was the high cost of living, which had forced the poorer classes "to steal" and/or to pawn their children to the rich.

Additionally, the women decried the high incidence of death brought about by the smallpox pandemic, allegedly through the agency of the expatriate missionaries and traders. Altogether, the social disruptions catalyzed the women's collective movement, aimed at the restoration of the social and moral code. Simply put, women had become public defenders of tradition and morality and thus sounded the clarion call for the purification of society, which, as they said, had been "spoiled" by the Europeans.[22]

The local authorities, on the other hand, equally took steps to combat the clear and present danger, which the missionary "intruders" and the converts' outlandish behaviors posed. Again, the message was clear: the threat toward disintegration and destabilization of society must be arrested. Hence, it was that the traditional rulers passed laws prohibiting missionary evangelization. Furthermore, to rekindle cultural consciousness among the youth/converts, they banned the wearing of imported clothes and decreed a return to traditional cultural patterns of life. In essence, the old elite thereupon served as the precursors of the dress protest movement of the 1940s, ardently championed by the cultural nationalist Mazi Mbonu Ojike—the "Boycott King" of the Nigerian cultural nationalist movement. His dogma: "Boycott all Boycottables," included European "food, drink, fashion, marriage system and all imported luxury."[23]

Missionaries' reaction to the changed situation was quite predictable: they regarded restrictions on Christian missionary proselytization and the wearing of foreign clothes as tantamount to persecution. It was indeed against this backdrop that the Rev. John Taylor lamented: "Our lives are in imminent danger and we cannot tell what may yet befall us." As to the prohibition against alien life styles, he ruefully acknowledged its immediate impact: "This cultural protest against the introduction of an alien life-style has caused church attendance not only to slacken, but members of the congregation have also discarded Western clothes."[24] Interestingly, the missionaries had premonitions of trouble looming in the background because of their savage attacks on traditional religion and the people's way of life. Said Rev. Henry Dobinson of the CMS: "I could not help feeling sure that Christianity would provoke much opposition in the [country]... . I could [also] see the people react impatiently as we spoke of the folly of idols, and of juju worship."[25] But it was not Christianity per se that triggered resistance but rather missionary insensitivity to African traditions and way of life, coupled of course with the indiscretions of the converts, as already discussed above.

Nevertheless, the missionary iconoclast Rev. J. A. Robinson of the Church Missionary Society (CMS) minced no words in advocating a social revolution: uprooting of the very foundations of African/Igbo culture—religion, religious beliefs, social customs and practices. In his view, the "lopping off of a few branches of a corrupt tree" is insufficient; rather, "the whole tree must be torn up from the roots." In practical terms, traditional religion and all its paraphernalia must be attacked, and destroyed.[26] In utter amazement and dismay, Igbo elders saw their world under attack, and therefore cursed the missionaries and their accomplices, who "have come to destroy rather than to uphold the traditional ways of life." This was the basis for labeling the missionaries as "dangerous innovators."

Of course, cultural accommodation was not part of the missionary's raison d'etre. Rather, as T. O. Beidelman correctly notes, "The raison d'etre of mission work is the undermining of a traditional way of life." Thus, "The missionary, at least in the past, was unashamedly ethnocentric, [and] he saw the struggle to impose his values as loving and altruistic." In plain terms, the missionaries' aim in Africa generally was to wage "active aggression upon Heathenism, wherever and whenever it can be reached."[27]

At any rate, as in the Onitsha case, protests by women against "violations" of *omenala* occurred in places like the Ngwa, Bende, Ohaoffia and Cross River zones. Women's resistance revolved around the question of infanticide, or the killing of twins. Seen from the moral and humanistic point of view, the missionaries' intent was to save twin babies, and hence the injunction that, "if twins were born in the towns" at all the mission stations, both the mother and the twins were to be brought to the mission for safety. But to women, this appeared as an intrusion into traditional social customs and practices. Thus, once again, women opposed foreign intervention and innovation, which they considered inimical to traditional life and culture—reaction that totally amazed the missionaries. While "the principal men [in town] could be depended on to aid our design" to end the immolation of twins, remarked the Rev. H. M. Waddell of the Presbyterian Mission, it was the women, who offered the "greatest opposition" to the proposition of saving twins. They "murmured and contradicted us [openly] and repudiated the doctrine of twins as [not being] monstrous and abominable, and [thus] spat out in disgust at the mention of such a thing."[28] Clearly, the attempt to protect twin babies and their mothers was not popular among women, and hence the resistance to reform.

Similarly, in the Owerri area, twin births were abhorred, simply because multiple births by humans were considered as unnatural. Twin babies, therefore, were often put in pots and exposed to the mercy of the elements—weather and the carnivorous beasts. Even mothers of twins were at times banished. But, as elsewhere, missionaries' concerns and humanitarian intervention saved many twins and their mothers, via the establishment of missionary hospices and Babies Homes. Yet, despite missionary attacks and prohibitions against twin immolation, it was British colonial injunctions *backed by the gun* (force) that ultimately brought the practice of infanticide to an end.[29]

In retrospect, it might indeed be tempting to construe women's opposition in this matter of infanticide as the reaction of "blind romantics," or indeed, as evidence of unenlightened reactionary elements. But this would be a mistake. For, once again, women's opposition was directed against foreign interventions and innovations perceived as threats to *omenala*. In that case, women might even be seen as playing the role of catalysts of nationalist consciousness, and not as obscurantists, or, as the imperialists viewed them, elements opposed to the advance of civilization. At any rate, this topic of infanticide "is not easily discussed in a dispassionate manner; nor necessarily should it be."[30] Thus, seen from the nationalist perspective, it could be argued that women were the champions of a nationalist cause—the preservation of tradition—even though, in the long, women seem to have been the great beneficiaries of the externally-induced socio-cultural change. On the other hand, it should be appreciated that, in certain situations, women historically served as the fervent advocates of "progress and development" exemplified in their passionate embrace of modernity: missionary education.[31]

THE DIBIAS AND POLYGAMISTS: CULTURAL PROTAGONISTS

Extant historical literature is replete with accounts of resistance against missionary propaganda by the traditional elite, namely native priests (dibias) and polygamists on grounds of missionary attacks on native life and culture. First, it should be noted that the dibias/native doctors traditionally performed multiple functions: as priests, diviners, healers, etc. As the custodians of traditional religion and messengers of the gods, they offered sacrifices to the gods and ancestors; they healed the sick; they also made medicines for a variety of purposes. Prior to the advent of Western medicine, for instance, "These doctors use[d] herbs, roots, faith, surgery, and hypnotism to cure numerous diseases" Additionally, "In times of social crises . . . [the Igbos] generally consulted oracles and/or the diviners (dibias) to discover the source or cause of their problem(s)."[32] Is it any wonder, therefore, that the dibias would be predictably incensed when the missionaries decreed that their followers should renounce the traditional religion, abstain from the use of native medicines, and further, that Christians should abjure traditional religious practices? Add to these the mindless destruction of religious shrines and "objects of worship" by over-zealous converts. Under these circumstances, missionary propaganda was deemed to have posed a clear and present danger to the dibias' craft and/or functions. After all, their religious and social profession was as well a very lucrative enterprise.

Consequently, just as the missionaries had their eyes set on the fundamental transformation/restructuring of traditional African society, so also were the Igbo traditionalists firmly determined to maintain the traditions and customs bequeathed to them by their ancestors. When therefore the dibias and the polygamists saw their religious and social positions and interests threatened by the so-called "messengers of liberation," they not surprisingly felt constrained to fight back. Among other things, they passed laws prohibiting missionary proselytization; they imposed fines on converts for desecrating religious temples etc. In sum, missionary attacks on traditional life and culture, coupled with the outrageous behavior of the over-zealousness of converts, led to persecution. However, in Onitsha, it was the timely intervention of the king (Obi Akanzua) that provided the converts and the missionaries some respite:

> Let no one of you my subjects, nor my under-chiefs, molest the Christians. Whoever shakes off the traditions of moa [spirit] worship, leave him or her alone, for he or she knows how they feel.[33]

Overwhelmed with joy at the turn of events, Rev. Taylor reported to his superiors in London: "The late persecution [against] the converts is now waning away." Yet, salivating over the converts' violations of religious prohibitions, such as the destruction of shrines and tampering with sacrificial offerings, Taylor boasted that the dibias' wings had finally been clipped. "Already the dibeas are ashamed . . . and could not [again] boldly show their nose . . . as their craft is now in danger of being exposed before the pure light of Christianity."[34]

Yet, as the defenders of tradition, the dibias arguably remained the missionaries' most inveterate antagonists. Indeed, despite missionaries' brutal attacks and injunctions against the use of native medicines and traditional healing processes, the influence of the dibias persisted. Even to this day, both the traditionalists and the seemingly "good" Christians continue to consult the dibias, clearly illustrating the persistence and resilience of traditional religion *and* the dibias' medical practices.[35]

Polygamists too joined in the chorus of resistance against the missionaries' intrusiveness into traditional or institutional structures. Particularly of concern were the attacks on polygamy and the attempts to replace it with monogamy on the grounds that polygamy was incompatible with the Christian principle that monogamy was the ideal family life (marriage). In reply, however, polygamists countered by declaring monogamy "contrary to God's Law," and therefore, "not good for a man." After all, they argued, polygamy confers social-cum sexual, political, economic and diplomatic advantages to the man and hence its acceptance as the ideal African marriage/family life.[35a] Thus, in opposition to missionary attacks and prescriptions, the polygamists, who also happened to be the political leaders, attempted to nip the missionary movement in the bud. Laws were issued prohibiting missionary activity. In extreme cases, the missionaries themselves were expelled and the converts chased away from the towns and villages or fined for obtrusive behavior. Thus, the monogamy-polygamy question pitted the polygamists against missionaries for much of the missionary era.

The European missionaries largely viewed polygamy (polygyny) as "evil" and "sinful," and therefore destined for destruction, and/or abolition. The African polygamists, on the other hand, hailed polygamy as their ancestral legacy, which must be preserved. The confrontation led the church authorities to decree that Christians should embrace monogamy as the ideal Christian marriage, and that polygamists were not to be admitted to the church on the grounds that admitting them would affirm the legitimacy of the institution of polygamy. Bishop Crowther stoutly defended the prohibition on polygamists, and explained his objection to their non-admission to the church as follows:

> The heathens will affirm that the life of polygamy as practised by their forefathers was more suitable to them than that introduced by the new religion, and needs no change.... The converts, who had renounced polygamy before they were received into the Church, will be shaken in their faith. [Besides] The heathen young men would take advantage of the admission of their fathers into the Church, and wait till they had married many wives, and then apply to be received; if their fathers would be received as such, why should not they [themselves].[36]

Admission of polygamists to the church implied dismissing extra wives but one and thus "breaking up normal home life, and surrendering much of one's social standing [as well as] denying oneself many of the joys of public life."[37] Yet ironically, some polygamists became Christian converts but paid dearly for their apostasy. Among other things, they were subjected to extraordinary adverse life experiences, such as social isolation, loss of status, and equally deprivation of property etc.

Quite predictably, the monogamy-polygamy question brought a rift within the Christian Church itself and particularly within the Protestant churches. To some Christians, traditional marriage (polygamy) was preferable to monogamy, and hence, to the dismay of the missionaries, many opted for traditional marriages. In short, many Christians resorted to multiple marriages. Equally significant is the fact that, in recent years, Protestant churches have adopted a new policy toward polygamy and polygamists. For example, they now allow the admission of polygamists as bona fide members of the church, without requiring that they first abandon other wives except one in order to become Christians. Today, in Nigeria, we see especially the *rich* polygamists, who give substantial donations to the church, being not only admitted to the church but are even blessed by pastors as they are conferred chieftaincy titles. In effect, the ultra-conservatism of the missionary pioneers, with regard to the non-admission of polygamists as bona fide members of the church, has been replaced by the modernizing liberalism of their successors. Finally, it should be emphasized that neither the missionaries nor the British colonial administration could possibly "wish away" polygamy as an African marriage institution, for, as a matter of fact, polygamy remains an enduring African family life, even though its practitioners are now limited.

COLONIAL RESISTANCE IN THE EASTERN FRONT: THE AROCHUKWU EXPEDITION

British penetration into the Igbo-hinterland east of the Niger began with the celebrated Arochukwu Expedition of 1901-1902. For all intents and purposes, this era and beyond marked the period of storm and stress, representing the fateful period of British military conquest, characterized by violence, and the establishment of colonial rule in Igboland. The British argument for the military onslaught was cast in humanitarian terms: to stop the slave trade, human sacrifice, and to destroy the Arochukwu oracle (the Long-Juju), which had been an "obstacle to civilization" and missionary penetration. But as historical studies have amply shown, the principal objective was *economic*—the British desire to take control of "the country of the producers." In essence, the imperialists were desperate to take over and exploit the oil-rich eastern Nigeria territory, using the so-called "Long-Juju" as the rationalization or excuse. As the British policymakers declared, "it is absolutely necessary to break up the Aros," who had for long resisted British penetration and exploitation of the Igbo territory.[38] Essentially then, British penetration of the rich palm oil region was an act of aggression and violence.

In preparation for the war, the British mobilized an extraordinary military force, made up of the West African Frontier Force comprising soldiers from the Gold Coast (now Ghana), Northern Nigeria, etc. These were divided into four columns: the Akwete, Oguta, Elele and the Owerri columns, all placed under Col. Montanaro, designated as the Commander of the Aro Field Force. Additionally, Roman Catholic and Protestant missionaries were recruited to serve as military and medical chaplains. Altogether, the "Aro Field Force" consisted of 1,550 soldiers, 75 military officers, several European NCOs, 7 medical officers, and 5 political officers. The Arochukwu Expedition (war) thus began on 1 December 1901 and lasted up to 24 March 1902.

Though less well armed than the colonial forces, the Igbos and their immediate neighbors nonetheless fought brilliantly in defense of their independence and sovereignty. In the Owerri sector, for example, the elders challenged the colonial forces to a duel: "If you want war, come; we are ready."[39] In retrospect, the elders seemed to have underestimated the power and determination of the British, who were out to conquer and rule. So, they came in hordes, and the outcome, as discussed below, was both catastrophic and far-reaching.

LET THE DRUMS ROLL

In anticipation for war, the Big Drum generally rolled. In practical terms, the talking drum summoned warriors to arms. In addition, special strategies were developed, which included the construction of trenches and pits (filled with spikes), and recourse to spirit mediums. As to the latter, the elders generally invited medicine men (dibias) to make war-medicine (*ogwu agha*), which included charms worn around the neck or armbands with magical powers and/or concoctions, which were anointed on the body of warriors that purportedly immunized them against the "flying bullets of the enemy."[40] Emboldened by the supposedly powerful war-medicines, the warriors thereupon engaged the enemy *without any shred of fear*. In other words, they fiercely and courageously stood toe to toe with the enemy, confident that the war medicines would protect them against enemy guns.

Prior to going to war, the Igbos also consulted oracles such as the Ibiniokpabi (alias: Chukwu/Arochukwu Oracle), *Igwekala, Ogbunorie, Amdioha Ozuzu, Agbala*, and others. The motivations were many: (a) to secure medicines that would thwart the evil designs of the enemy; (b) to obtain the support of the oracle so as to be able to "drive out the white man from the land;" (c) to swear an oath of unity and solidarity. In the case of the *Ogbunorie* Oracle at Nsu, the priests supplied the water from the sacred lake (Mmiri Ihiafor) that surrounded the oracle. Assurances of support, and medicines acquired, therefore provided psychological anchor (comfort) and conveyed a sense of invincibility. Thus spiritual or religious symbols played critical roles in the social mobilization and resistance to external aggression, as was the case during the British colonial conquest and consolidation of colonial rule in the late nineteenth and early twentieth centuries.

Armed with an assortment of guns and rifles, especially the ubiquitous Dane guns, and emboldened by oracular and/or dibias' medications, the warriors confronted the colonial forces with courage and determination. In other words, they offered spirited resistance. As an Igbo elder recalled the experience: *ike nibe ya ezuru*, meaning that force was met with force. But, unfortunately, the colonial forces seemed equally determined and ready to

Figure 10. 1. An Igbo warrior dressed for war dance. National Archives London. INF 10/254

Figure 10. 2. War Dance. National Archives London. INF 10/254.

demonstrate "who is the master." An Owerri elder described the experience thus:

> They [British soldiers] came in hordes, shooting and seizing animals. They burned farms and houses. [Above all,] Cannon thundered [everywhere], smoke filled the horizon, and fear and panic seized every man and woman...leading ultimately to desertion from the villages to escape the disastrous war of the white man.[41]

The British commander in the Owerri sector, Major Trenchard, nevertheless acknowledged the determined resistance of the local forces. "The enemy, who occupied strategic positions in the bush and in the trenches, attacked [fiercely and] furiously from all sides," resulting, as he admitted, in "heavy casualties." Trenchard further conceded that, "There is not a single town here that has not fired at us." However, as often happened during these military confrontations with the British colonial soldiers armed with superior firepower, the outcomes were generally deadly and disastrous: the African warriors were mowed down from afar with Maxim and Gatling guns. Besides, disaster and terrorism pervaded the landscape, as the soldiers "burnt down whole villages, wantonly destroyed farms and other property, seized goats and cattle, took hostages, and demanded heavy ransom."[42] Overall, as the foregoing clearly indicates, the British were brutal. They were indeed the precursors of the likes of Brigadier Benjamin Adekunle of the Nigerian army, who, in 1968, swore to crush Biafra by all means including starvation:

> I want to prevent even one Ibo having even one piece [of bread] to eat before their capitulation. *We shoot at everything that moves, and when our forces march into the centre of Ibo territory, we shoot at everything, even at things that do not move.* (My emphasis) [43]

Severe punishments characterized British colonial conquest and consolidation of colonial rule. As per British colonial policy, for example, resistors were to be *severely* punished, including military occupation, which in itself implied near-total disaster and devastation. "Where a town refuses to submit to Government control, or supervision, it is our policy . . . to occupy it . . . until the chiefs and [their] people have been made thoroughly to understand that Government laws must be obeyed."[44]

These dreadful episodes of violence and destruction clearly convinced the Igbos that the British, after all, "did not come to this country as friends, but as enemies." In the final analysis, the British triumphed. The powerful Arochukwu Oracle, known to the Europeans as the "Long-Juju," was destroyed. What followed thereafter was the consolidation of British colonial rule, still characterized by extraordinary violence against the Igbo and their neighbors, euphemistically described in colonial literature as "pacification" (making peace). In reality, however, this meant the era of violence and brutality: "Very destructive of African law and order, this violent process was largely completed during the 1920s," but it brought profound and irreversible changes.[45]

Resistance movements against the imposition of colonial rule and colonial exploitation remained intense and widespread. In other words, colonial resistance movements raged over forced labor and taxation, to which we now turn.

FORCED LABOR AND TAXATION

Essential components of the imperial burden included the imposition of forced labor and taxation. These were indeed concrete symbols of over-lordship and/or domination. Forced labor was particularly resented because it degraded and dehumanized the victims. It also entailed the loss of freedom, and equally embodied personal disrespect and abuse. Is it any surprise, therefore, that anti-British sentiments reigned supreme everywhere? As the District Commissioner H. M. Douglas, at Owerri, ruefully acknowledged: "With the exception of a few towns all the country . . . is decidedly hostile to the Government."[46] More specifically, revolts/ resistance greeted the imposition of the Forced Labor Ordinance/Law. By this Ordinance, Africans were impressed into unremunerated labor. As the Rev. M. D. Opara, MP reminded the British imperialists, "the Easterner's mind is repugnant to anything forcibly pressed [upon him]."[47] Therefore, resistance to forced labor and taxation—the two cardinal innovations that characterized the consolidation of British colonial rule, was widespread, and reflected *rejection* of British authority and assumptions of supremacy.

Under the compulsory labor law, Nigerians were forced to make roads, clear waterways, carry loads, including even carrying colonial officials on hammocks, and of course work on the railways. An Igbo elder recalled the experience of the carrier system this way: "The loads were heavy. And we traveled for many, many miles [through unfamiliar places] without food, water, or rest. . . . [Worse still,] the harassment from the soldiers, or the DC, or the overseers [was extreme].... This is why we often dropped the loads, escaped into the bush and returned home. But [alas,] if you were caught, that was the end of your life."[48] Indeed, forced labor was onerous. It often resulted in the premature death of the victims, either through over-exaction or perhaps more glaringly because of the brutality from the labor overseers. Accounts of the horrors of forced labor appear in virtually every anti-colonial historical study.[49] In Owerri, for instance, H. M. Douglas, the District Commissioner (1902-1906), had the reputation of being "a great road builder." In the eyes of his colonial superiors, he was an exemplary imperial officer: "There is no district in the Protectorate that can even compare with Douglas' as for the roadwork that has been done." He was equally praised for his contributions towards the conquest of the

Aros: "Mr. H. M. Douglas was very useful to me at the time of the Obegu raid [wrote Montanaro, Commander of the Aro Field Force] and [he] acted with energy on several occasions during the [Arochukwu] operations."[50] But Nigerians, on the other hand, perceived Douglas as "a bad English man"—Beke Ojoo—precisely because he was a hard taskmaster and a brutal man as well. In fact, Douglas had a pathological addiction to cruelty and violence. His extraordinary harshness and violence rendered him persona non grata in Nigerian. Even his European counterparts chastized him for his cruelty towards the colonized. The Anglican bishop, Herbert Tugwell, wrote him as follows:

> From what I heard from people as I passed through your District . . . your system of administration appears to be well nigh unbearable. The people complained bitterly of your harsh treatment of them. . . . [My advice to you therefore is this:] Adopt a kindlier and more generous attitude towards a subject people.[51]

As already noted, coercion characterized the Labor Ordinance. Defiance of Government authority to make roads or to work on the railway or even to carry loads often resulted in the imposition of fines, public flogging, imprisonment, or all of the above. Imprisonment itself was an unusually harsh experience, inasmuch as most of the inmates died in captivity. To many, imprisonment was thus almost tantamount to being sentenced to death. Hence, forced labor was intensely hated. That it rankled can be illustrated in the occasional murder of those who enforced it— chiefs, court messengers, district officers, etc. The murders of District Commission S. O. Crew Read, and Dr. Stewart are two classic examples of extreme cases of reactions against colonial over rule. In the Crew Read case (1906), the Colonial Office in London sympathized with his aggrieved Africans, whose vengeance was described as "heroic and noble," simply because of the unusually onerous and imperious exploitation involved. The message was therefore clear: violence begets resistance and violence. As for Dr. Stewart, who was killed in 1905, not necessarily because of his enforcement of the labor law per se but because of a mistaken identity. He was believed to be Douglas, and hence the retaliatory violence meted to him. The British administration rather predictably, launched a punitive war against the perpetrators, which thus heralded the celebrated Ahiara Expedition (1905-16), already treated exhaustively elsewhere.[52]

TAXATION AND ITS AFTERMATH

Direct taxation was introduced in Eastern Nigeria in 1928, after years of equivocation, even though it had been introduced in both the Northern and Western Regions since 1914. The imposition of taxation on eastern Nigerians was justified on two grounds, namely, that it was a necessary means of raising revenue, and secondly, that taxation was an instrument of imperial control. "To pay tax is to admit the over-lordship of the person to whom it is paid." Besides, taxation was directly related to forced labor: "Taxation is the only possible method of compelling the [Africans] to... seek work," the British governor of Kenya arrogantly quipped. [53] Taxation, therefore, became an inescapable burden of colonialism, which Africans and particularly Nigerians in general, intensely resented. In the Eastern Nigerian case, it meant that people were now faced with questions of authority and control. Thus, almost everywhere in Southern Nigeria, the introduction of direct taxation ignited widespread resentment and revolts, as illustrated in the anti-tax rebellions of 1916 and 1918 among the Yoruba and the anti-tax riots in the Warri Province in 1917-28. [54]

The best celebrated, and certainly most far-reaching anti-tax rebellion in Nigeria, was the Women's War of 1929, in Eastern Nigeria, otherwise called the Aba riots in "official" accounts. The literature on this is abundant and easily available; therefore, I need not dwell on it extensively here, except to emphasize its *impact and/or legacy*. Politically, the Women's War or tax rebellion resulted in the fundamental restructuring of the British system of colonial administration in Eastern Nigeria. First, the war marked the demise of the Indirect Rule System, which brought with it political destabilization (through the creation of warrant chiefs) and widespread corruption. The Women's War, therefore, was a violent response to British imperialism, whose impact was quite far-reaching. For example, "After almost thirty years of administrative bungling and insensitivity to indigenous political systems, the [colonial] government [after the rebellion] was forced to admit that the warrant chief system was a failure."[55] Thus, in the modernizing era of 1930's Nigeria, the end of the indirect rule system heralded the era of (or return to) popular democracy, consistent with Igbo indigenous, democratic system of government. Political governance thereafter rested on political participation of the villagers, implying government of the people, by the people, and for the people. Put differently, it was now government from the grassroots and no longer from the top down. Thirdly, and perhaps most fundamentally, the end of the Lugardian system of government brought with it the deconstruction and/or de-gendering of local politics—a milestone in contemporary Nigerian political history. This meant that the long-standing "edging out of the female" from politics and administration had come to an end. Henceforth, women became a critical factor in governance. For instance, not only were women members of the *reformed* native courts and councils, but they also exercised considerable influence over the selection of new chiefs and councilors. [56]

Allied to the above women's militancy was that of Northern Igbo women painstakingly documented by Nwando Achebe. As she documents, women in the Nsukka zone "joined together and made war" against the chiefs and titled men—collaborators in colonial oppression and exploitation. "They burned down entire compounds in some cases, destroyed home medicines, and set all livestock free." In addition, the women declared war against labor and war recruiters during the Second World War: "Nsukka women were enraged at the forced conscription of able-bodied men for the railway construction...and to serve in the British colonial army during World War II." And they also vented their anger and frustration at the warrant chiefs and the sanitary inspectors, whose extortion and corruption reached unacceptable proportions. On the whole, Nsukka women, as was true elsewhere with their counterparts, clearly played a major role in the expressions of resistance to British colonial over-rule through mundane dancing and satirical songs, etc.[57]

In sum, Igbo resistance to Western Imperialism was widespread and involved various segments of the population. As already demonstrated several strategies were used—military and non-military measures to maintain political independence and sovereignty. These struggles culminated in the nationalist "fight" for independence in 1960, of which the Igbo educated elite were in the vanguard. Even in contemporary Nigeria, cries of oppression and marginalization still reflect the culture of resistance against policies of domination and exclusion and hence the demands for rectification.

NOTES

1. See Elizabeth Isichei, *The Ibo People and the Europeans: The Genesis of a Relationship, to 1906* (New York: St. Martin's Press, 1973); Felix K. Ekechi, *Missionary Enterprise and Rivalry in Igboland, 1857-1914* (London: Frank Cass, 1972): 14-23; A. E. Afigbo, "Patterns of Igbo Resistance to British Conquest," *Tarik* 4, no. 3 (1973); S. N. Nwabara, *Iboland: A Century of Contact with Britain 1860-1960* (Atlantic Highlands: NJ: Humanities Press, 1978).
2. Monu Ojike, *My Africa* (New York: Barnes & Noble, 1946), 232.

3. Cf. Richard N. Henderson, *The King in Every Man: Evolutionary Trends in Onitsha Ibo Society and Culture* (New Haven and London: Yale University Press, 1972), 528.
4. Cf. Toni Morrison, *Song of Solomon* (New York: Plum Books, 1987).
5. See Don Ohadike, "Igbo Benin Wars," and Felix K. Ekechi, "War, Migration and Settlement in Owerri Oral Traditions," in *Warfare and Diplomacy in Precolonial Nigeria*, eds. Toyin Falola and Robin Law (Madison: African Studies Program, 1992), 166-75 & 208-17.
6. CMS Archives: ACC/89/F1, *Archdeacon Dennis Letters*, 1905:
7. Foreign Office, London: FO84/2194, Kenneth Campbell, Report of Entry into Igboland, 22 February 1892.
8. FO 2/101, Moor to Foreign Office #37, 6 May 1896.
9. FO 84/2110, FO to MacDonald, 18 April 1891.
10. Cf. Walter Ofonagoro; Toyin Falola and Akanmu Adebayo, *Culture, Politics & Money Among the Yoruba* (New Brusnwick, NJ: Transcation Publishers, 2000).
11. Campbell, Report 1892.
12. CMS: ACC/89/F1, Dennis Journal, 7 March 1895.
13. Ekechi, *Missionary Enterprise*; Ohadike, *Anioma*, 133.
14. FO84/2110, FO to MacDonald #2, 18 April 1891.
15. Elizabeth Isichei, "Historical Change in Ibo Polity: Asaba to 1885," *The Journal of African History* X, no. 3 (1969), 424.
16. Felix K. Ekechi, "Merchants, Missionaries and the Bombardment of Onitsha, 1879-89: Aspects of Anglo-Igbo Encounter," *The Conch* 5, ½ (1973): 61-81.
17. Don C. Ohadike, *The Ekumeku Movement: Western Igbo Resistance to British Conquest of Nigeria, 1883-1914* (Athens: Ohio University Press, 1991), 121-2.
18. See Philip Igbafe, "Western Igbo Society and its Resistance to British Rule: The Ekumeku Movement, 1898-1911," *Journal of African History* 12, no. 3 (1971): 441-59.
19. Don C. Ohadike, *Anioma: A Social History of the Western Igbo People* (Athens: Ohio University Press, 1994), 225-26.
20. CMS: G3/A3/O, Taylor's Report on Onitsha 1864; Bishop Crowther, Report of the Niger Mission, 1880.
21. Nina Mba, *Nigerian Women Mobilized: Women's Political Activity in Southern Nigeria, 1900-1965* (Berkeley, Calf.: Institute of International Studies, 1982).
22. For an eyewitness account of the Odesoruelu phenomenon see CMS: CA3/037, John Taylor, Journal entry 25-29 Feb. 1864. Also, see Ekechi, *Missionary Enterprise and Rivalry*, 23. For similar purity campaigns see: Misty L. Bastian, "Dancing Women and Colonial Men: The Nwaobiala of 1925," in *"Wicked" Women and the Reconfiguration of Gender in Africa*, eds. Dorothy L.

Hodgson and S. A. McCurdy (Portsmouth, NH: Heinemann, 2001), 109-29.

23. See *West African Pilot*, 3 June 1947; P. O. Esedebe, *Pan-Africanism: The Idea and Movement, 1776-1963* (Washington, DC: Howard University Press, 1982), 180.

24. Taylor, *Journal*.

25. CMS: G3/A3/O, "Notes of a Journey into Ibo Land, Jan. 5-10, 1891," 21.

26. Ibid., Robinson to Lang, 5 Aug. 1890.

27. T. O. Beidelman, *Colonial Evangelism: A Socio-Historical Study of an East African Mission at the Grassroots* (Bloomington: Indiana University Press, 1982), 29.

28. H. M. Waddell, *Twenty-Nine Years in the West Indies and Central Africa* (London: Frank Cass, 1970), 483-4.

29. Ekechi, *Tradition and Transformation*, 66-7.

30. Steven C. Dinero, review of *Female Infanticide in India: A Feminist Cultural History*, in *Journal of Third World Studies* XXIII, no. 2 (2006), 221.

31. Ekechi, *Tradition and Transformation*, 77.

32. Mbonu Ojike, *My Africa* (New York: Barnes & Noble, 1946), 154; Felix K. Ekechi, "The Medical Factor in Christian Conversion in Africa: Observations from Southeastern Nigeria," *Missiology: An International Review* XXI, no.3 (July 1993), 294.

33. CMS: CA3/O37, Taylor's *Journal*, entry for 14 January 1863.

34. Quoted in Ekechi, *Missionary Enterprise and Rivalry*, 18 & 17.

35. Cf. Christopher I. Ejizu, "Down but not Out: Contemporary Forms of Igbo Indigenous Religion," *Proceedings of the International Symposium on Religion in a World of Change* (Owerri: Bishop Whelan Research Institute, 8-12 Oct. 2002), 2.

35a. See F. K. Ekechi, "African Polygamy and Western Christian Ethnocentrism," *Journal of African Studies* 3, no. 3 (Fall 1976): 329-49.

36. CMS: G3/A3/O, "Notes on the Life of Polygamy in West Africa, Jan. 1887."

37. Ekechi, *Missiology*, 293. Also Ekechi, "African Polygamy"; Elizabeth Isichei, *Entirely for God: The Life of Michael Iwenne Tansi* (London: Macmillan, 1980), 4-7: on the ordeal of Chief Idigo of Aguleri.

38. For a fuller account of the Aro Expedition see Ekechi, *Missionary Enterprise*, chapter VI: "The Pacification of Igboland, 1900-1910."

39. Ibid., 126.

40. G. T. Basden, *Among the Ibos of Nigeria* (London: Frank Cass, 1966), 288.

41. Ekechi, *Tradition and Transformation*, 13.

42. Isaac M. Okonjo, *British Administration in Nigeria, 1900-1950: A Nigerian View* (New York: Nok Publishers, 1974), 57.

43. Herbert Ekwe-Ekwe, *Biafra Revisited* (Bershire, England: African Renaissance, 2006), 6.

44. PRO: CO52O/82, Egerton to Colonial Secretary (Crew), 8 Oct. 1909.

45. Basil Davidson, *Modern Africa: A Social and Political History*. 3rd edition (London: Longman, 1994), 12.

46. NNAE: CO520/31, Douglas: Report on the Owerri District, 30 June 1905.

47. Nigeria National Archives, Enugu: Rev. M. D. Opara, *Parliamentary Debates of the Eastern House of Assembly*, 1955.

48. Ekechi, *Tradition and Transformation*, 39-40.

49. See Allen Isaacman & Barbara Isaacman, *Mozambique: From Colonialism to Revolution, 1900-1982* (Boulder, CO: Westview Press, 1983)

50. Ekechi, *Tradition and Transformation*, 19, 37.

51. CMS: G3/A3/O, Tugwell to Douglas, 18 Dec. 1905. It is ironic that the major street in Owerri Township is named after Douglas!

52. Felix K. Ekechi, "Igbo Response to British Imperialism: The Episode of Dr. Stewart and the Ahiara Expedition, 1905-1916," *Journal of African Studies* (1974): 145-67.

53. Ekechi, *Tradition and Transformation*, 165; B. A. Ogot and W. R. Ochien, *Decolonization & Independence in Kenya, 1940-93*, 7.

54. See for instance Toyin Falola, *Colonialism and Violence in Nigeria* (Forthcoming); Oboro Ikime, "The Anti-Tax Riots in Warri Province, 1927-28," *Journal of the Historical Society of Nigeria* 3, no. 3 (Dec. 1966): 559-73.

55. Ekechi, *Tradition and Transformation*, 169.

56. Cf. Felix K. Ekechi, "African Women and Politics: A Case Study of Chief (Mrs.) Margaret Ekpo of Nigeria," in *Current Discourse on Education in Developing Nations: Essays in Honor of Robert Tabachnick and Robert Koehl* eds. Michael O. Afolayan et al (New York: Nova Science Publications, 2006), 97-121.

57. Nwando Achebe, *Farmers, Traders, Warriors, and Kings: Female Power and Authority in Northern Igboland, 1900-1960* (Portsmouth, NH: Heinemann, 2005), 180-86.

Chapter 11

Revolution and Reaction in Eastern Nigeria, 1900-1929: The Background to the Women's Riot of 1929

Adiele E. Afigbo

It "has to be remembered," wrote Dr. James Crawford Maxwell, Commissioner for Owerri Province, in 1916, "that there are certain minds to whom . . . a change in the settled order of things can only be for the worse-'the past is a rose whose faded petals are forever sweet.'"[1] This dictum applies with almost equal force to all conservative elements in any society at any time in history. It is thus not surprising that with a consummate disregard of the strains and stresses which must have existed in their traditional societies, as is the case in any other society, conservative Igbo and Ibibio elders today give the impression that until the coming of European rule the Igbo and Ibibio lived in a world of perfect harmony which gave all and sundry the opportunity to attain the good life by following traditions and customs which embodied the accumulated wisdom and experience of the ancestors. Without much over-simplification it can be said that for these elders the pre-colonial period of their history was one during which their gods looked upon their world and saw that it was good. In the light of this conviction, these elders see the advent of British rule as making a sudden and regrettable break with a glorious past as a result of which things began to fall apart.[2] It is hardly necessary to point out that nostalgic views of the past such as this one tend to lead to romanticism in and falsification of history. None the less a historian cannot hope to understand the true origin of the reaction of the conservative section of any Africa society to colonial rule unless he is prepared to follow these bewildered men and women into the deepest recesses of their thoughts and, as much as possible, see the innovations of the colonial years in the same perspective as they did. Thus in this article it is argued that European rule inaugurated a many-sided revolution which was in no way congenial to the temperament of the conservatives among the Igbo and Ibibio peoples of eastern Nigeria; and that the Women's Riot of 1929 must be seen as one, if not the most violent, of the people's reactions to this revolution.

In the first place, the new regime was imposed with high-handedness and a reckless disregard of the people's cultural achievements and religious susceptibilities, which those affected, saw as unparalleled in their history. Villages, which offered any resistance to the advance of the British, were, when captured, burnt to the ground. Village heads, who were usually the ritual heads of their communities and who in consequence occupied quasi-sacred status, when invited to peace parleys were 'perfidiously' seized and subjected to humiliating treatment. They were released only after either their ransom was made by the payment of a cash fine or by the supply of food to the military, or by the making of new roads often through a stretch of bush, the entering or traversing of which tradition clearly forbade. Shrines were taken and destroyed as though they were not the habitations of gods whose presence in the indigenous community the people regarded as a *sine qua non* for the existence of a balanced society. This type of wanton 'sacrilege' touched its zenith during the Aro Expedition of 1901-1902 when Colonel Montanaro captured Arochukwu and proceeded to blow up with modern explosives the famous Aro Long Juju or *Ibini Ukpabi* which for centuries had occupied a place of central importance in the religious and judicial life of the people living on the stretch of land lying roughly between the Benin and Cross Rivers. Among the people in this area the news was received first with sneering incredulity and then with utter bewilderment. To them, as to Western Europeans after the sack of Rome by the barbarians, it seemed that the foundations of civilization had given way. Where *Ibini Ukpabi* "fled" before the triumphant advance of the British, it was believed lesser oracles like *Igwe-ka-ala* at Umunoha or *Agbala* at Awka could not hold their own.[3]

While the people were still dazed by this blow, the British proceeded to introduce the Warrant Chief System, an institution that until its collapse in 1929 dominated the people's life in a way no other single measure in this period did. Under the false impression that Eastern Nigerian communities, as some other communities elsewhere in Africa, were ruled by "kings and chiefs," the British appointed a "chief" or sometimes several "chiefs" for each village or group of villages as the case might be. These "chiefs" were given "warrants" or "certificates of recognition" which made them the sole executive heads of their communities and entitled them to be called from time to time to participate in the trial of cases in the "Native Courts" which were established under the system. In a number of places, the men who were appointed Warrant Chiefs were the traditional ritual heads of their villages, but in the overwhelming majority of cases, they were either scoundrels or just ordinary young men of no special standing in indigenous society who had been pushed forward for the specific purpose of parleying with the white men.

The institution of the Warrant Chief System was seen as the rape of the indigenous political constitution of the people. Everywhere the popular assembly, which hitherto had been the sovereign body of each autonomous unit, was superseded by the Native Court and the pretentious Warrant Chiefs. To the people the Native Court was "native" only in name. Its procedure was patterned on that of the British courts. The territorial extent of its jurisdiction was unparalleled in the people's political experience. In the pre-colonial era, the largest effective and functioning political unit was generally the village group while the clan made up of villages tracing descent to a common ancestor was generally the largest unit with any sort of informal political organization. But the Native Courts established by the British generally comprehended groups of "clans" and often "sub-tribes" irrespective of what hitherto had been the relationship amongst the units brought under one court. The Owerri Native Court, for instance, served villages from the Isu and Oratta sub-tribes -two ethnic groups which were not the best of friends.[4]

Also since the proceedings of the Court were guided by detailed regulations drawn by the law officers of the Government and since the court was required to administer, from time to time, laws made by the Central Government, the Court Clerk, often a half-educated man, was generally the only person in the court who could read these complicated legal drafts with any semblance of understanding. Flaunting his 'superior' education and often a more sophisticated dress, as well as the ink-pots, pens, pencils, books and the numerous forms which he needed for his work, but which the illiterate regarded with awe, the clerk was able to establish an ascendancy over the "chiefs" and their people which was so absolute that the 'chiefs' whose servant he was supposed to be, came to address him as "master."[5] Though in theory the Native Court was supposed to administer "native law and custom," in practice the law administered was law modified to suit British conscience, that is a *corpus juris,* which, from the point of view of the people, was far from traditional and customary. There was thus hardly any feature of the Native Court by which the people could identify it as indigenous.

Lacking both the tradition and the goodwill of the people to support them, the Warrant Chiefs resorted to all sorts of measures to build up petty autocracies for themselves. They had in each ward of the village their agents, the so-called *headmen* or *"minor chiefs"* some of whom the Government recognized through the conferment of caps. Through these subalterns, the Warrant Chiefs made their wills and those of the Government known to the people. These headmen, from the nature of the job that they had to do, for instance catching men to work on the roads or to be engaged for head porterage, were generally young men. In spite of this fact, like their masters the Warrant Chiefs, they treated the elders and titled aristocracies, in whose hands power and authority had lain in the pre-colonial era, with scant ceremony.[6] No force, which the people could muster, neither public opinion nor brute force, was effective against this untraditional coterie since only the government could depose them. In the village, the Warrant Chief usurped the traditional position of the popular assembly, settled cases on his own authority, prosecuted those who attempted to seek justice through the traditional methods and acquired the power to commandeer the age-grades to do his own private biddings. The extent to which real power left the hands of the elders, title lodges and secret societies for the hands of the "new men" associated with the Court is illustrated by the fact that many who earned the money with which they would otherwise have bought admission into one or more of the ancient privileged associations, used it in lobbying Warrant Chiefs, Clerks, Court Messengers and Interpreters to help make them headmen or, better still, Warrants Chiefs. The constitutional revolution wrought by the Warrant Chief System was as far-reaching as it was unsettling.[7]

Unfortunately for the British Administration, this "supercession" of the old political institutions by the Warrant Chief System was not accompanied by a disposition on the part of the Warrant Chiefs, Court Clerks, Court Messengers and headmen to promote justice and mitigate the burdens, which the new regime imposed on the people. After complaints against the Warrant Chief System based on its untraditionality, the next loudest complaint of the people was against corruption and deliberate perversion of justice under the system. The Warrant Chiefs saw themselves as the employees of the Administration rather than as the representatives of the people. They did not see themselves as performing the old traditional functions but as dispensing a "new type of justice." In this frame of mind, they were emancipated from those tight traditional controls, which in pre-colonial times helped to promote justice within the village. Therefore, they felt that their new positions should pay. In consequence, litigation in the Native Court became another name for competitive bidding.[8]

Going pari *passu* with the widespread perversion of justice in the Native Courts was the more astonishing fact that the Native Court system of law administration exposed society to many hazards from which, it was believed by the people, it had been adequately protected in the pre-colonial era. In the first place, the scale of punishment provided for offences under the Native Court system often erred on the side of leniency and thus exposed society to the evil-minded. There was, for instance, the case of larceny of livestock and farm produce, which amongst various Eastern Nigerian people was treated with justifiable severity since the economy was mainly agricultural. This particular crime could on occasions bring the death penalty on the offender, especially if caught in the act. In some cases, the thief was adorned with broken vessels and empty snail shells, paraded round the local market and subjected to withering ridicule. Unrepentant thieves were often sold into slavery. But under the Warrant Chief System, the highest punishment prescribed for this crime was imprisonment. It was not only that the terms of imprisonment were never sufficiently heavy from the point of view of the people, but also that when compared to traditionally accepted forms of punishment, imprisonment appeared like child play. An Abakaliki Warrant Chief disgusted with the futility of imprisonment as a deterrent for crime told the Lieutenant Governor of the Southern Provinces in 1924 that a prison was "a feeding house to which people repair to get fat and fit." The inadequacy of punishment for thieving, noted an Administrative Officer in 1930, "has become one of the standing grievances of the people."[9]

But even a worse consequence of the warrant chief system of justice from the point of view of the people, was the fact that it exposed society to the anger of the gods. In traditional law, offences were divided into two broad groups—those against individual human beings, which involved no offence to any supernatural agency, and those against society, which involved offence against the gods and the ancestors. The settlement of the latter under traditional law generally started with the punishment of the offender but also included a ritual propitiation of the deity who was believed to have been offended through the crime in question. But in the Native Court, the satisfaction of an outraged community in proved criminal cases was supposed to be achieved with the imprisonment of the criminal or some such punishment. This involved a civil conception of 'community' and law-administration which was psychologically and emotionally alien to the people, and which above all 'placed' them under the threat of the dreadful consequences of divine wrath.[10]

The untraditionality of the Warrant Chief System or rather the open conflict between the established ways of the people and the new modes of the alien regime was not the sole cause of the hostility with which Eastern Nigerians regarded the colonial government. There was also the fact that British rule, especially as expressed through the Warrant Chief System, which touched most people was oppressive to many. The use of forced labor for road-making and for building Government stations and quarters, the use of conscripted carriers as the main means of transportation for more than two and a half decades, the depredations of the licentious court messengers, and the use of the Court itself as a means of oppressing the weak, were the things which helped to create that widespread feeling of oppression which predisposed people to rise.

In 1903 the Protectorate Government had made a law under which the 'chiefs' could be called upon any time to supply labor for either the construction of roads or the maintenance of those already made. This labor was both forced and unpaid. Going along with this was a practice by which 'chiefs' could be (and were) called upon for the supply of carriers who were used to transport the loads of officers going on transfer or of soldiers on duty away from barracks. Though carriers were paid at the then liberal rate of one shilling a day, head carrying was as much hated as labor on the roads. Under both systems, people were compelled to work against their will. Also in the early years of the British regime, the recruitment of men for either duty was a bitter experience for the people. The general method was to send teams of Court Messengers into the villages to conscript young men. This was never accomplished without an exhausting chase since people would usually take to the bush as soon as the alarm was raised that Court Messengers were about. Those who gave the Court Messengers much trouble before being caught were treated with a brutality that would have shocked even men acquainted with the worst excesses of the slave hunt. Those caught were chained together like a slave gang and led to the scene of the work. Though by the end of the first decade of the century this inhuman method had been abandoned for the method of allowing 'chiefs' to do the recruitment through their headmen, the brutality of the earlier method left a deep impression on the people. This change did not make either roadwork or head loading any less detested. Both those working on the roads and those transporting goods were supervised by Court Messengers who are said to have behaved with the inhumanity of those supervising slave labor. There was the extra inconvenience that people who had made their own plans were forced without notice to abandon them to work for the government or face prosecution in the Native Court.[11]

The Court Messengers, both in and out of the court, exploited the ignorance of the masses. A man who took out a summons against his adversary was forced, after paying the correct fee for the summons, to give the Court Messenger who was to serve the process an extra two shillings or a cock and provide him with free food for as long as he was in the village or the summons would not be served. People on whom civil summonses were to be served were often arrested on the ground that what were issued against them were warrants of arrest, but were promptly released if they were able to pay considerable sums of money to Court Messengers. Since Court Messengers were widely known to be the agents of the Government they got away with most of what they did as it was generally believed that they were acting on instructions. Thus, they could visit village market, buy their needs at their own prices and force anybody to carry these purchases home for them.[12]

Over and above this political revolution and misrule was the undermining of many accepted practices and institutions, an ever-increasing conflict between the old and the new in which the latter steadily gained the upper hand. One of the first tasks, which the British set themselves to accomplish in Nigeria, as elsewhere in Africa, was the stamping out of the so-called barbarous practices, which still formed part of the social and religious life of the people. Among the earliest and most far-reaching of these reforms was the prohibition of the use of ordeals and oracles in the settlement of difficult cases. The very existence of the Native and British courts, which were given exclusive powers in the trial of cases, was by itself a campaign against these practices. For much of this period the British prosecuted those who were caught resorting to these tried and time-honored ways of enforcing conformity to accepted practices.[13] There was also a campaign against such harmless and socially useful practices as title taking. In 1902, for instance, the Government prohibited the taking of a number of titles at Obosi (Onitsha) because the Government claimed the desire to buy these titles accounted for the rampancy of theft.[14] The District Commissioner, James Watt, in 1907 prohibited the taking of *Igwe* title among the Nsugbe because, he claimed, those who took the title thought it conferred on them an unrestricted right to other people's wives.[15] Another of the ancient practices against which the Government campaigned was the killing of twin children and the expulsion of twin mothers from the community of their fellow human beings. In 1907, for instance, the Native Court of Ikot Obong, Ikot Ekpene, instituted proceedings "for desertion and non-support" against husbands who had driven away their wives who gave birth to twins. In consequence, the men agreed to take back their wives[16] at the risk of incurring the anger of the supernatural agencies that were believed to have enjoined the observance of these practices. Thus at every turn the shocked people found themselves forced to do those things which they ought not to have done, and to leave undone those things which they ought to have done. The result was that both in the minds of individuals and in society at large there raged an intense and disturbing conflict between the new and the old amongst a people most of whom still believed that any deviation from the traditional ways could only be made at the risk of divine punishment.

At the same time as the government was engaged in these acts of 'vandalism' against the people's cultural heritage, the influence of the missions as well as the diffusion of other Western influences from the urban centers which sprang up in response to the activities of the Government and European traders were also undermining society at many vital points. The advent of the missionaries had meant the end of the ideological unity of the village. In consequence, the elders ceased to be for all their people the unquestioned authorities in social and religious dogma, which they had hitherto been. The emergent Christians, usually in a hopeless minority but always over-confident, aggressive, vociferous and intoxicated with their newly-imbibed, but as-yet-undigested, Christian doctrines and attitude to life, even out-did their European masters in laying 'sacrilegious' hands on many ancient and sacred institutions and usages. Where the Government made a vague distinction, but nonetheless a distinction, between 'barbarous' and 'non-barbarous' institutions and practices and ear-marked all the former for destruction, the new converts often equated 'pagan' society to the devil with whom, their Bible clearly told them, they were engaged in a mortal combat. It was generally the case that the farther from white control these new converts were, the more frequently altercations and violent brawls occurred between them and the 'pagan' majority. A few examples will help to illustrate the nature of this conflict. The Opobo Division was notorious for clashes between Christians and 'pagans'. In 1918, for example, the schoolboys of one of the villages in this division forcibly prevented a 'pagan' from burying his dead mother. This was because the schoolboys objected to the noise, which accompanied 'pagan' burials, and because the woman had indiscreetly died on a Sunday! In the course of the conflict, the schoolboys destroyed one of the shrines of the village and appropriated for their own use all the valuables they founded therein.[17]

But the most fruitful source of conflict between the two groups in this division was the contempt with which the 'Christians' treated ancient secret societies like the *Ekpo*, which in pre-colonial days formed one of the main pillars of society. Among the Qua of Opobo division, for example, the *Ekpo* had the right to regulate the fishing seasons and to exclude non-members of the society from the enjoyment of the right to fish during the open season. As soon as a number of Christians came into being among the Qua they rebelled against this ancient practice because, they argued, "our conformity to the demands of this law will involve disloyalty to the faith of the Christian religion for at baptism we swore to have no other god but the true God and joining *Ekpo* means going back to the idolatrous practices which we have forsaken." They also maintained that the law took away from them "the common rights of the individual." In this controversy, the Government upheld the stand of the Christians.[18] It was for Government decisions such as that that Etak Eto, the village head of Ukam who was also a Warrant Chief told a political officer in 1921: "In plain words we are dissatisfied with British rule and want the Government to leave us so that the country may be governed by *Ekpo* and like societies. We shall then once more gain complete control over our people. I repeat my statement that the British are not fit to govern this country." For this statement, Etak Eto was charged with sedition and deprived of his warrant.[19]

Aiding the disintegration caused by the missions and their schools was the growth of general sophistication deriving from increased opportunities for travel created by new roads and by the economic attractions of urban centers. Young men who were conscripted for work on the roads or the railway or for head porterage traveled through hitherto unfamiliar villages and towns and came back with new and often revolutionary ideas. "There is no doubt," noted Resident James Watt of Owerri Province in 1920, "that the enlisting of labor has had a disturbing effect on social and political conditions in the province."[20] Young men who earned money and became economically independent of their fathers, or who had acquired some of the white man's 'magical' feats like driving cars or riding bicycles, often considered themselves wiser than their fathers and consequently grew arrogant and unamenable to control. "Rapid development," asserted the District Officer at Okigwe 1921, "has caused the youth of today to become as complete an anachronism as it is possible for him to be."[21] Migrations to urban areas, which in this period were fast becoming the centers of economic opportunity, the fact that a headman's cap or a Court member's warrant conferred more visible authority than the highest indigenous title, the fact that men now wanted to invest their money in new economic ventures: all these helped to reduce the number of those who sought admission into the age-grades, title lodges and secret societies and thus undermined the sway formerly wielded by these institutions. The overall effect of the impingement of these alien and disruptive forces on indigenous society was that rival passions and tensions were set up in almost each cell of the social organism. "In every area, in every village, and one might safely say in every family," wrote Colonel Moorhouse, the Lieutenant-Governor in 1921, "there are now two divisions, the 'primitives' who cling to the old superstitious beliefs and customs; and the 'progressives' who with a smattering of book learning, a wider experience of the outside world and their new-found 'Christianity' refuse to follow slavishly the old customs and beliefs. At the present the 'primitives' are the majority, but the 'progressive' minority is clamorous, growing in numbers . . . It is inevitable that eventually the 'progressives' will sweep the country."[22]

If the slightest transgression of the established ways and traditions of the elders was regarded as fraught with the direst consequences for society as a whole, the dawn of the era, which Colonel Moorhouse anticipated in the quotation above, it was widely believed, would be the end of civilization as known and appreciated by the conservative majority of the people. Oral tradition is rich in the fact that in most Eastern Nigerian villages, the advent of the first white man had been followed by stringent warnings from diviners and oracles to the effect that any attempt to accede to the demands of the new comers would inevitably lead to departure from the injunctions of the ancestors and the gods, a situation that would equally inevitably call down divine vengeance.[23] Since the imposition of British rule speedily led to the fulfillment of the first part of this prophecy, the fulfillment of the second part was equally expected by those who refused to embrace the new ways, but who nonetheless never ceased to do what they could to bring their erring brethren back to what they considered the path of sanity.

1918 was the year of the famous influenza epidemic that swept away a large section of the population. From all indications it would appear that this was regarded as the most widespread and most fatal plague in the people's history or at least in their remembered past. The devastation wrought by this plague was such that, as always happens during a great disaster, men and women became more emotional and mystical than rational and explained the events in terms of magico-religious causes. Christians were said to have ransacked their Bibles and to have announced with every sureness that it was the God of the Old Testament who was abroad. Just as Yahweh in days of yore had visited Egypt with great plagues because she refused to listen to the words of Moses and Aaron, the Christians were said to have claimed, so in 1918 He was visiting Eastern Nigerians who is spite of the efforts of the newly converted went on unheedingly along 'pagan' ways. This explanation of the epidemic did not appear absurd to the

'Christians' in spite of the fact that though Yahweh in the earlier example had spared his chosen, in 1918. He seemed to have forgotten which camp He supported: Christians and 'pagans' competed with each other in succumbing to the ravages of the plague. 'Pagans' on their side had no doubt that it was their insulted and outraged gods and ancestors who visited society for entertaining the new ways.[24]

Ultimately, it was the colonial regime, which made it possible for people to backslide from the traditional mode of life that was specially held responsible. In many places, anti-British activities designed, the people say, to drive the white man into the sea started but could make no headway because people were either dead or too sick to fight. In some places, it is said the plan was to prepare 'medicines' which would make the land too 'hot' for white men. However, in one or two places, especially in Calabar Province, serious upheavals nearly developed. Among the Ibibio of Ikot Ekpene, for instance, the 'eyei', a call to arms in this case,[25] was passed round to all neighboring groups with the message that all villages should meet in their respective market places and pass resolutions to the effect that an absolute return should be made to the pre-colonial *stats quo*. More especially it was urged that no one should attend Native Courts, that Court Messengers and police men should be expelled, that schools and churches should be destroyed and not allowed to reopen, that twin children should be killed and twin mothers driven out as before and that the British Government should be resisted in everything. In a number of villages, definite attempts were made to carry out this program.[26] The real reason behind the disturbance, said the Resident of Calabar Province, "would appear to be that under the exceptional conditions (caused by epidemic) the chiefs and the elders saw their opportunity and wanted to resume their old authority."[27]

Popular tradition has it that this epidemic led to a great deal of re-thinking amongst some would-be adherents of the new ways and forced some of the erring flock to turn back to the 'right path'. But it did not succeed in stemming the swelling tide of the new forces. Among the conservative majority, this continued and growing transgression of the time-honored ways meant that another, and perhaps the final, visitation was imminent. In 1925, one of such expectations reached fever pitch in portions of Owerri, Onitsha and Ogoja provinces and led to the so-called *Nwaobiala* or Dancing Women Movement, which, though non-violet, was all the same a protest against the colonial regime and an invitation to the British to withdraw since they had proved their inability to govern the land.

The exact politico-economic background to this movement remains obscure. The administrative records are silent on it, while oral tradition will not go beyond the assertion that it came as a result of divine inspiration and was anti-British. Nor is there any precise information on how and when and where it started. But it would seem that sometime between the last week of October and the first week of November 1925, what had been described as a 'miraculous birth' occurred somewhere on the Umuahia-Okigwi boundary. No doubt, a diviner or an oracle was consulted for an explanation and the diviner or oracle must have seized the opportunity to attribute the birth of the monstrosity to the intrusion of the new ways of thought and deed, and in conclusion urged a return to ancestral ways. In any case, whatever the details of the origin of the movement were, the fact remains that by the end of the first week of November 1925 the British administration found itself confronted with an all-women movement, which spread in relay fashion throughout the greater portions of Owerri, Onitsha and Ogoja provinces. The women generally arrived without any warning at the premises of a local Warrant Chief or dignitary and proceeded to sweep his compound and perform a special dance. This usually caused a stir in the visited village and rallied round a huge crowd. It was only then that the message was delivered with great solemnity and appropriate ceremony 'Chineke' (Almighty God) had appeared at Okigwi, the message ran, and ordered that all should return to the old customs and shun English ways. In particular, it was claimed He had ordered that people should stop the use of English currency, boycott the Native Courts, stop giving their children in marriage to Christians, reopen the old roads and routes and use them in place of the new ones, that all girls should go about nude until they had had babies, that bride price should be reduced to the old rates as also the prices of foodstuffs. All prominent men who heard the message were ordered to visit Okigwi for an interview with *Chineke*, and anybody to whom the dance was brought had to pay the women who brought it ten shillings.[28]

The movement assumed serious proportions in a number of places. "The dance and the chant," reported the Acting Divisional Officer at Awgu (Onitsha Province), "created a strong impression in the Division through which it spread in three days ... so great was the awe with which it was regarded – this song from the unknown, with its peremptory demand to be passed on and its personal expenses to the chief – that in the Owelli (court) district the chiefs absolutely ignored the order of the Divisional Officer not to pass it on, subsequently excusing themselves by saying they were afraid and hastened to pass it on as they were bid. The spirit was universal,"[29] In Ogoja Province converts to the movement were promised the extermination of the British. In Nkalagu and Izzi clans of Abakaliki Division serious breaches of the peace occurred in which even men took part. When the

Divisional Officer tried to hold a meeting with the Izzi at Inyimagu to counteract the influence of the revolt, he was expelled by an armed mob and we are told, "He was happy to escape with his life."[30] However, insufficient co-ordination amongst the villages involved, as well as Government action soon caused the movement to collapse by the beginning of 1926; but it left a deep impression on the minds of many.

It was while men and women were still pondering the import of this movement that they saw sprung upon them a new measure which they did not understand but which they saw as economically burdensome and above all believed was unethical. By 1924 the Colonial Government had finally made up its mind to introduce direct taxation into the portion of Southern Nigeria lying east of the Niger and into the Warri Province West of the Niger. The main reason for this decision was the desire to strengthen the Warrant Chief System through the establishment of Native treasuries after the true Lugardian fashion.[31] This aspect of the question, however, does not concern us here. The important fact is that in 1927 eastern Nigerians were for the first time in their history confronted with the demand for tribute by an alien power.

The economic implication of direct taxation was quite clear to all and was one of those considerations, which determined people's attitude to the innovation. In June 1927 the Resident of Calabar reported that "relief from corvee labor," the most attractive concession the Government had made to the people in the wake of the decision to impose monetary tribute, "did not seem to appeal to the peasantry if they were to pay money in lieu of this old form of taxation"; nor did the promise to pay 10% rebate to all village heads who lent assistance prove a never-falling bait.[32] Even the argument that the money was for local development had no magic appeal. One 'chief' pointed out that to whomsoever the money went the important thing was that it had left the people's pocket. During the period of propaganda designed to convince people as to the necessity for the tax, political officers found themselves confronted in many places with the complaint that there was no money in the country. In one Native Court area in Ikot Ekpene Division the 'chiefs' told William Edgar Hunt, Resident charged with the tax campaign, that people had been impoverished since the advent of the British and that taxation would merely revive the sale and mortgage of children. At Itu, Mr. Hunt was asked to give an undertaking that the Government would not prosecute people who pawned their children to get money with which to pay tax.[33] The economic side of indigenous objection to taxation was thus important and should not be played down, but it was by no means the only important factor that determined the reaction of the conservative majority of the people.

Other aspects of the measure which disturbed most people equally seriously, but which have never been emphasized, dealt with a number of religio-ethical questions and then with the question of sovereignty. During the Government tax campaign bewildered interpreters who labored to translate 'taxation' into indigenous languages and dialects which had no word for the institution, rendered it in such a way that it came to the people as either 'tax on head' or 'tax on land' which with further amplification meant 'ransom' or 'rent' respectively. Seen in this light taxation raised the question of how a *free man* could be required to pay a ransom on his head or how a stranger could ask for rent on land from the sons of the soil. This was a question that nobody could answer but the conservatives were sure that such a demand as taxation that has these implications was irreligious and unethical. It is said that in many places some old men died of heart-break rather than see what their fathers never saw, that is rather than pay ransom on their heads or rent on their own patrimonies to strangers. The second point, which shocked many people, was the census of population that accompanied the assessment of taxation. Throughout the four Eastern Provinces, the counting of human beings, especially of free men, was con-trary to custom. In traditional belief and philosophy, a man could count that which is his own, for instance his slaves, livestock, yams and the like. Again, the counting of human beings was believed to cause death. Count-ing, it was believed, reminded evils spirits that a particular kin-group had multiplied beyond a certain point and that the time had come to prune it down. But the taking of census was part of assessment for it was necessary to obtain the number of taxable males in each unit in order to know the net tax to be expected from it. It was this need for an accurate census and all the obscure ruses to which political officers resorted to attain it which made tax all the more obnoxious. The question, which perplexed elders, asked was: In taking a census of eastern Nigerians, was the Administration saying that the people had become its slaves or property or was it out to decimate them? [34]

Then there was the consideration that payment of direct taxation implied acceptance of British sovereignty. It is difficult to understand in what light the people had hitherto seen British occupation, but one of the nagging questions, which taxation raised was the right of the British to impose the measure in the first instance. In most places, the elders con-tended that taxation was contrary to their custom and therefore invalid. This attitude meant that the elders still regarded their customs and tra-ditions rather than British legislation as the supreme body of law and source of morality. But in places, the people did not stop at this vague assertion of the inviolability of their sovereignty. At Onitsha and Okigwi angry Warrant Chiefs and elders pointed out to Hunt that while it was understandable that the British should tax the 'Hausa' whom they had conquered, it was utterly bewildering to hear that they also planned to tax Eastern Nigerians whom they had never conquered. The people claimed that it was they who out of their munificence leased to the British the land on which to settle.[35]

In spite of all these objections by the people, the first collection was effected in 1928 without any grave breach of the peace – thanks to the effective use the administration made of the police, the army and the law courts in dealing with agitators. But the second collection was not so peaceful. In September 1929 Captain John Cook, Assistant District Officer, was sent to Bende as Acting District Officer to hold the Division until the return of Captain Hill from leave in November. On taking over the Division Captain Cook found the nominal roll of adult males, which was prepared for taxation purposes very unsatisfactory since it did not show to what ward or compound each payer belonged. He therefore decided on a more detailed and scientific nominal roll prepared on these lines. Against each payer were to be inserted details of the number of his wives, children, goats, sheep, fowls and the like. Captain Cook called round his warrant Chiefs in October, told them they were to conduct this new count and, rather irrelevantly, added that "it had no connection with any tax on women."[36]

The very mention of women in connection with taxation gave rise to the rumor that the Government had a plan to tax them. What made Cook's denials very unconvincing was the fact that in 1926 the Government had practiced deception on many villages and clans. In Oloko and Ayaba clans of Bende, for instance, the assessing officer, Mr. A. L. Weir, had told the people that the counting of heads was a 'mere count' not 'a census' and had nothing to do with taxation. But 1927 had shown that the reverse was the case. To make matters worse the Warrant Chiefs now amplified Captain Cook's injunction as they understood, or rather as they were ready to understand, it. Chief Ananaba of Umuala in Oloko, for instance, solemnly declared before a meeting of the elders of his village that the Government had ordered him to count women and domestic animals "so that they would be taxed." He did not stop there but instead proceeded to remind his elders of the devious methods by which they were counted at the inception of taxation.[37]

The women reacted swiftly to the news. People were already complaining bitterly of the economic burdens of the first payment done only by men. If women were also roped in, the reasoning ran, the financial consequences for the people would become unbearable. "Since the taxing of male adults started," said one Moses of Umuala in Oloko to the Donald Kingdom Commission of Inquiry into the subsequent riot, "there has been no peace in the land. A lot of men are in bondage in the hands of the chiefs. They pawn themselves in order to get the 5/- to pay their tax. Women have reason to be annoyed. They realized that as their husbands become slaves in order to obtain 5/- to pay their tax, the situation will be worse if women have to pay tax."[38] But above all the religio-ethical question regarding taxing and counting free men came up again in a very poignant way. To the people the taxing of women raised the whole question of the continued survival of society. Since counting was believed to cause death, and women could not be taxed without a census, taxation thus threatened a heavy mortality on women, if not the total extinction of women. "What have we women done to warrant being taxed?" asked one perplexed woman before the Commission of Inquiry. "We women are like trees which bear fruit. You should tell us why women who bear seed should be counted."[39] Anybody who understands indigenous thought on the matter will see the implication of this pointed question. It is therefore not surprising that the women of the various villages in Oloko Court area held tumultuous rallies at which they immediately resolved, "to wait patiently until anybody made a move to count them and then they would make trouble."[40]

This was the state of men's, or rather of women's, minds when in November Warrant Chief Okugo of Oloko, proceeded to count the people under his charge, through his agent Mark Emeruwa, a Christian mission school teacher. Somehow, the count went well until Emeruwa came to the compound of one Ojim where he confronted the woman Nwanyeruwa, one of Ojim's wives, preparing palm oil. The details of what happened are extremely obscure, but in all probability, Mark Emeruwa addressed himself to the woman whom, perhaps, he told to count her people and livestock. "Are you still counting?" replied this elderly woman. "Last year my son's wife who was pregnant died.[41] What am I to count? I have been mourning the death of that woman. Was your mother ever counted?"[42] By the time the dialogue got to this point both parties had thoroughly lost their tempers and gone for each other's throat in earnest – Nwanyeruwa clutching the mission school teacher, who was no doubt smartly dressed,[43] with her oily hands.[44] Unfortunately for Emeruwa, Okugo, Capt. Cook and the Government there was a mass rally of women in a neighboring compound which the women said met to discuss issues unconnected with taxation, but which the Donald Kingdon Commission said met to discuss the tax question. In any case whatever the purpose of the rally, Nwayeruwa ran to it in a frenzied state to announce to her fellow women the highly explosive news that the awaited enumerator of women had arrived. The women did not hesitate to act. They went at once to Emeruwa's house on the mission compound, and since they had come to regard counting as synonymous with taxation, proceeded to put words into his mouth by asking him why he said, "women should pay tax." From there they went to Okugo's compound. They also sent women armed with *omu*[45] to the women of neighboring villages inviting them to come to Oloko.[46] Thus began Women's Riot of 1929. The British in Nigeria by a series of untraditional measures had turned the world upside down and it came crashing on their heads.

It remains to emphasize that this movement was essentially anti-Government and that in fighting for the old political and moral order the women were asking for the exodus of the British. One or two examples of the types of sentiments expressed by the women during the Riot and before the commission into the Riot, which comprised four Europeans and only two Africans, will serve to show the depth of the anti-Government feeling that lay at the root of the trouble.[47] The women of Ohuhu told Chief Nwatu who tried to dissuade them from rising that "they would go to Owerrinta to demolish the Native Court; that they did not want the native Court to hear cases any longer; and that all white men should return to their country so that the land in this area might remain as it was many years ago before the advent of the white men." When Chief Nwatu tried to argue with them and point out to them the benefits of British rule and mentioned especially the railway which he said could carry them to anywhere at cheap rates, they told him that "after driving away everybody (every white man) they would remove the rails."[48] One woman, Nwoto of Okpala, told the Commission: "Our grievances are that the land is changed—we are all dying. Our object of coming here is that the news we heard last year has never been heard before … we said we thought white men came to bring peace to the land … All the towns were opened so that people might enjoy peace and now you suggest that tax should be paid—is that the old practice… When white men were coming to this country Bonny people tried to stop them from coming. They managed to come and we thought that when they came we should be very happy. Since the white men came our oil does not fetch money. Our kernels do not fetch money. If we take goats or yams to the market to sell, Court Messengers who wear a uniform take all these things from us."[49] In short, the people had been disillusioned and the British should go.

In practice the anti-Government sentiment took the form of attacks, often savage, on the agencies of local government —on Warrant Chiefs, Native Courts and their staff, that is to say on those men and institutions who and which brought British rule home to the people. The Oloko women who started the Riot had not only succeeded in securing the arrest of Chief

Okugo who precipitated the trouble, but had also seen him uncapped and imprisoned.[50] This set the pattern for the attack on the Warrant Chief regime for many of the Court areas affected by the Riot. At Owerrinta, the women started by stopping the proceedings of the Native Court, then proceeded to chase the chiefs away and ended by looting the houses of the Court Clerk, and damaging those of the Court Messengers.[51] Overall nine Native Courts were burnt, three destroyed and four damaged.[52]

An accident that occurred at Aba on 11 December 1929 made the Riot take a very savage turn. On that day bands of demonstrating Ngwa women were passing through Aba to Eke Akpara on the Aba-Owerrinta road when the car of the Medical Officer at Aba, Dr. Hunter, ran down two of them. The doctor, to escape from the mob that got infuriated at the fate of the two women, took shelter in the factory of the Niger Company. This was the signal for the looting, in revenge, of the property of the Company, which gave shelter to their quarry.[53] It was after the Aba incident that other women at Imo River, Utu Etim Ekpo, Omuoba, Mbawsi, Okepedi and Ntan, who did not want to be surpassed in their demonstration of exasperation with the colonial regime, proceeded to loot or to attempt to loot European factories and shops.

The Riot started on 18 November 1929 and was brought under control in January 1930 using the army and police. In Owerri Province, it swept through the four most populous of the six divisions, while in Calabar Province, it covered two of the three divisions. It also succeeded in intruding into Afikpo Division of Ogoja Province. Only Onitsha Province was left completely immune, though, it is asserted by the people that it was rumors of the merciless slaughter of women by the Government forces that prevented the women in Onitsha Province from joining in the movement. By the time the Riot ended, the women, according to the official figures lost fifty-five of their companions and fifty others wounded by machine gun and rifle fire. The highest slaughter took place at Opobo where thirty-two were killed and thirty-one wounded.[54] The women had started their movement in the naïve belief that white men would not shoot women,[55] but they ended it with the sad realization that a colonial power would stop short of nothing to meet any threat to the security of its tenure of power.

The Women's Riot of 1929 was the last of the conservative revolts against the colonial regime in Nigeria and for that it is an important landmark in the history of the nationalist movement. It was, for Eastern Nigeria at least, the culminating point of the protracted clash between two conceptions of progress- the indigenous and the British. To the people at large real progress, good government and ultimately the good life were best realized by walking along the path clearly laid out in the wisdom and traditions of the ancestors and which was believed to enjoy the sanction of the gods. But with the British progress, good government and so on were to be realized in a different way which Eastern Nigerians did not understand and could not appreciate. The Riot was an assertion by the people that no cultural group, no matter what high notions it might have about its civilization, could be good enough to rule another cultural group. The British were therefore invited to go back to their country so that the people would resume the control of their own destiny. After 1929, the movement for independence in Nigeria passed completely into the hands of the educated elements, and the program of a complete return to the pre-colonial *status quo* was abandoned as untenable and undesirable.[56] From then on, the only important programme came to be the achievement of a cultural synthesis, which combined the best in the old and the new. But this new synthesis was not to be received as a gift from a paternalistic regime, but was to be the work of Nigerians.

Equally important was the fact that the Riot stormed the ramparts of Indirect Rule, one of the main pillars on which the colonial regime rested. It undermined the complacency with which a particular interpretation of that system of local government had come to be uncritically accepted as the most successful method of ruling dependent peoples. In Nigeria, especially in the South-Eastern Provinces, Indirect Rule was remarkable for the fact that it was applied without any previous serious inquiry into the true nature of indigenous political systems. This shortcoming had led in the Yoruba areas to the exaggeration of the powers of the Obas and in Eastern Nigeria to the creation of artificial 'chiefs' and 'paramount chiefs.' "It is clear from the Report of the Commission, as well as from the evidence", noted the Secretary of State for the Colonies, Lord Passfield in 1931 while commenting on the Report, "that comparatively little is known, even now, of large portions of the South-Eastern Provinces . . . in my opinion the South-Eastern Provinces call for a degree of attention which has perhaps not been adequately realized in the past, and which I trust will be carefully kept in view in the future."[57] In the light of this opinion, it is not surprising that three months or so later Lord Passfield appointed Sir Donald Cameron, the man who had based his introduction of Indirect Rule into Tanganyika on detailed researches into indigenous society, as the Governor of Nigeria in succession to Sir Graeme Thomson.

Sir Donald Cameron's governorship in Nigeria was remarkable for the fact that it caused a liberalizing wind to sweep through the whole system of, and approach to, Indirect Rule in Nigeria. With him much desired emphasis was laid on the fact that even in the field of local government the wishes of the governed should be taken into serious consideration. Consequently, the emphasis shifted from the structure of the system *per se*, to whether the system was in harmony with the needs of the people for whom it was instituted. As a result of the new spirit, many necessary reforms were introduced. Throughout the Southern Provinces, exhaustive inquiries were carried out into the nature of the indigenous political system of each group of people. After this, it was also "ascertained" that a revival of the traditional machinery of government would enjoy the support of the people concerned. "If the latter (the people)," Donald Cameron warned, "are not prepared to accept the orders of the so-called chief unless we compel them, the administration is not indirect and the Native Authority set up on such a basis is a sham and a snare."[58] Donald Cameron went further to break with the tradition of portraying Indirect Administration as a mysterious cult in which neither the Legislative Council in Lagos nor the general public should have any say and from which, the educated elements should be vigorously excluded. The importance of these and many other innovations which Cameron introduced into the system and practice of Indirect Rule lay in the fact that Indirect Rule, even in Northern Nigeria, lost that air of mystery which hitherto had made it more or less untouchable.[59] Once the system was subjected to tinkering there was no saying where the process would stop.

It is intellectually stimulating but not necessary to speculate on whether or not and how soon this outburst of liberalizing reforms in local government would have come without the Riot. What is known is that it is this Riot that shattered the complacent British belief that their rule was welcome to the over-whelming majority of Nigerians. It also closed the era in which it was confidently, though unjustifiably, held that the hope of Nigerians lay in the political education of their traditional rulers for ultimate self-government rather than in listening to the so-called detribalized minority.[60] A few years before the Women's Riot the franchise had been introduced into Lagos and Calabar in a bid to satisfy the educated elements. Now after 1929 the reform of the local government was undertaken to satisfy the conservatives. The dawn of this period of adjustment on two fronts indeed marked the earliest beginnings of the end of the colonial regime in Nigeria. Here we may see the place of popular reaction to British rule in Eastern Nigeria in the movement for Nigerian independence.

NOTES

1. OW. 122/16, Memo on Native Courts by Dr. J. C. Maxwell.
2. It is for instance popularly believed that with the advent of the British it became very difficult to secure justice in the courts. This view is clearly illus-

trated in the following quotations taken from the statements of some of my informants in the field: Mr. F. O. Iwuchukwu (A member of Orizu ward in Nnewi, Onitsha, and a former police constable): "Since the white men came there has been no justice in the courts." Mr. P. O. Onwughgalu (An Onitsha man and a former District Interpreter): "There was more justice in pre-British days in Ibo land than under the Warrant Chief System or the systems that have followed it. With the advent of the British, judgments began favouring the highest bidder." It is necessary to point out that in the production of this article documentary sources have been supplemented with oral information, which I collected during fieldwork in Eastern Nigeria between 1962 and 1964. For information on the area covered in this field work as well as for the names of the people interviewed and details about them the reader should consult appendix II of my thesis: "*The Warrant Chief System in Eastern Nigeria 1900-1929*" (Unpublished Ph.D. thesis, University of Ibadan, 1964). This appendix, which runs into 44 pages of typescript, is an essay on the nature of the oral evidence collected and the method used in dealing with it.

3. The documents dealing with the famous Aro Expedition of 1901-1902 give a good account of the methods used by the British in imposing their rule on Eastern Nigeria. C.S.O. 1/13 of 1901 No. 381 of 24/11/1901 and the documents attached. C.S.O. 1/13 of 1902, copy of a letter from Officer Commanding the Aro Field Force. See also Conf. 21/05 (Enugu Archives) for the way the British dealt with the Ezza—Calprof 9/1 Vol. 1 Letter dated 19/10/1900 from Galwey to Moor for comment on the results of British high-handed treatment of the indigenous people.

4. Afigbo, *The Warrant Chief,* 357-64.

5. Ibid., 137-242.

6. C.S.O. 26/4 No. 30192, 192.

7. Afigbo, *The Warrant Chief,* 345-411.

8. C. 176/19 Report from Howard marked "C".

9. C.S.O. 20/1 No. 09098 Vol. II, 225.

10. C.S.O. 20/3 No. 27002, 54.

11. Afigbo, *The Warrant Chief,* 121-2, 379-381.

12. Based on information collected from different people in the field, see Appendix II of my thesis already cited.

13. E.P. 755/6, 4, 14-16.

14. Calprof. 10/3 Report No. 14 of 5/8/1902 from Central Division.

15. Intelligence Book A. Onprof 5/1 Entries of 26/8/1903 and of 20/4/1907.

16. Government Gazette Supplement of 13 November, 1907, vi-vii.

17. Calprof 14:C.271/18 No. 311/45/18 of 27/3/1918 from F.S. Purchas to Resident Calabar.

18. Calprof 14: C. 271/18. See petitions to Resident dated 26/6/1918 and the Resident's Comment dated 2/7/1918.
19. Calprof 14: C.35/1921 – The whole file.
20. E. P. 1308/7, 9.
21. E. P. 1308/8, 1.
22. E. P. 1308/8 Comment by H. C. Moorhouse dated 28/10/1921.
23. cf. Chinua Achebe, *Things Fall Apart,* (London: Heinemann, 1958), 123. After my tours of different sections of Eastern Nigeria and a comparison of my field notes with the novel, I came to the conclusion that Chinua Achebe's book contains reliable historical information on indigenous reaction (in thought and deed) to the "catastrophe' of European advent. It must however be used critically. cf. also C.S.O. 26/4 No. 30192.
24. Calprof 14: C. 100/9, 1. According to the Resident of the Calabar Province, it was in Opobo that non-Christians attributed the cause of the epidemic to the transgressions of the Christians. The Government, of course, did not conduct any inquiry into what the people thought about the disaster. My own fieldwork between 1962 and 1963 revealed that the attribution of responsibility for the plague by both Christians and pagans to each other was widespread.
25. The 'eyei' are young folded palm leaves and, according to the occasion, could symbolize different things. It could serve as a warning of danger, or a call for help, a call to arms and at times could symbolize peace, especially if accompanied with white clay.
26. Calprof 14: C. 100/19, 1.
27. Ibid.
28. O. P. 319/1925: The whole file.
29. O. P. 319/1925: Memo. No. 124/M.P. 62/1925 from Political Officer at Awgu to the Resident, Onitsha.
30. C.S.O. 26/4 No. 30192, 102.
31. C.S.O. 9/1/8 file No. 35, The whole entries.
32. C.S.O. 26/2 No. 18417. Memo on taxation dated 8/6/27 from the Resident of Calabar Province.
33. C.S.O. 26/2 No. 18417: Memo on direct taxation by W. E. Hunt.
34. Based on information collected from the field. See Afigbo, *The Warrant Chief,* Appendix II for my informants and the method by which I tested the validity of their statements.
35. C.S.O 26/2 No. 18317, 5, 7, 9.
36. *Aba Commission of Inquiry Reports* (hereafter referred to as A.C.I.R.) (1930), 11.
37. Ibid., 11-12.

38. *Aba Commission of Inquiry Notes of Evidence* (hereafter referred to as A.C.I.N.E) (1930), para. 1782.
39. Ibid.
40. *A.C.I.N.E.*, para. 1607. The comparison between *women and fruit-bearing trees* lies at the root of certain aspects of indigenous social and ethical philosophy. First, just as one cannot in the interest of human beings joke with the survival of fruit-bearing trees one could not play with the fate of women. Secondly, it was believed that there was a type of psychic union amongst all things –animals and trees which bring forth young ones, and that you could not treat them in certain ways without offending their *chi* – the supernatural element that is supposed to superintend over their interests either singly or as a group with special interests.
41. *A.C.I.R.*, 11-12.
42. I have a feeling that the interpretation here has obscured the woman's meaning or line of thought. In all probability, she saw a connection between the first count and the death of her son's wife, or the statement about the death would be highly irrelevant. Also the use of the present continuous: "Are you still counting?" implies that in view of all the disaster which were believed to have followed the first count, all counting should have stopped.
43. *A.C.I.R.*, 363.
44. White shirt on a pair trousers or shorts was very popular with the products of the schools in this period and for many years after.
45. *A.C.I.R.*, 12-13.
46. The same things as the Ibibio 'eyei.' See footnote 2 on page 548.
47. *A.C.I.R.*, 13-14.
48. The impressive point is that the women, even after their rising had collapsed, were bold enough to say some of the things they said before a commission dominated by white men. It is difficult to say what they would not have asked for if they had met with success in their demonstration.
49. *A.C.I.N.E.*, 9769-9770.
50. *A.C.I.N.E.*, 15470.
51. *A.C.I.R.* 14-17.
52. Ibid., 38-9.
53. Ibid. See enclosed map on the area affected by the Riot.
54. Ibid., 44-50.
55. *A.C.I.R.*, Appendix III (15).
56. *A.C.I.N.E.*, Paras. 15188-16087.
57. There is no attempt to say that there were no nationalists before 1929 who had a program that differed markedly from that of the conservatives. The point I have in mind here is that after 1929 the desirability for a return to the

life of pre-colonial times did not receive any further vociferous expression, though it continued to linger on in many conservative minds.

58. Despatch of the Secretary of State to the Officer Administering the Government of Nigeria dated February 1931.

59. *Supplement to Extraordinary Gazette* of 6.3.33, 8. Ibid., 5-26; M. Perham, *Native Administration in Nigeria* (Oxford: Oxford University Press, 1937), 325-44.

60. With the onset of the reforms of Cameron, the Government came to give attention to the question of what part educated elements could play within the frame-work of Native Administration.

Chapter 12

Igbo Women from 1929 to 1960

John N. Oriji

The 1929 Women's Revolt was one of the most significant events that occurred in Nigerian history during colonialism.[1] It was for example, the first major revolt of its type that was organized and led by rural women of Owerri and Calabar Provinces which contained a population of two million people, located in a total land mass of about 6,000 square miles.[2] Like other major events of its magnitude, the revolt has continued to attract much scholarly inquiry and discourse, unparalleled in Igbo history until the Nigeria-Biafra war.

The historiography of the revolt itself is revealing in terms of the methodological problems it has raised and the conflicting interpretations scholars and feminists have offered to explain its underlying roots, the organization of women, and their overall achievements.[3] While some of these themes will be covered in this essay, I hope to address different aspects of the revolt that have received little attention by attempting to answer the following questions: What type of women led the revolt, and how did their leadership enhance their social status during and after the revolt? What legacies did the revolt leave in Igbo society before Nigerian independence in 1960, and how have the legacies helped women to attain a better social standing in modern Igbo society?

METHODOLOGICAL PROBLEMS: SOURCES

Most of the primary sources used in studying the revolt were compiled by colonial officers who were largely concerned with finding its causes to establish a more functional and practical way of implementing the policy of indirect rule in southeastern Nigeria. The orientation of the colonial officers, which in the first instance, was meant to justify colonialism, affected the reports they compiled in varying ways. For example, the Women's Revolt was known in official circles as the Women's riots, to create the impression that they were "disturbances" caused by inarticulate, irrational, and disorderly women who woke up one morning on the wrong sides of their beds. But modern historiography has shown that the women were well organized and had leaders who clearly articulated their grievances during what they saw as "Ogu Ndem" (Women's War). That is why their movement is captioned in this paper as a revolt instead of "riots."

One can also raise issues about the linguistic difficulties some of the colonial officers who did not speak Igbo encountered. Their reports, which were compiled through interpreters who were barely literate in English, are subject to misinterpretations and distortions. The Igbo dialect is complex, and to an outsider, it could be perplexing. It is then not surprising that when Captain John Cook, a District Officer who had mastered the Onitsha dialect was transferred to Bende District during the genesis of the Women's Revolt, he confessed that he did not understand the Igbo language spoken in his new area of jurisdiction.[4]

The major primary source for studying the revolt is the Report of the Aba Commission of Inquiry (1930). The report itself is problematic since all those who testified took an oath and the hearings were regarded as formal court proceedings. Women in many communities retained lawyers who briefed them on what to say and what to withhold. Under the circumstance, it is unlikely that some of the testimonies represented the actual feelings and views of the women.[5]

My own field experience shows that people were still afraid of being interviewed by colonial officers many years after the Women's Revolt. In 1933 for example, J. G. C. Allen who wrote monumental intelligence reports on the Ngwa clan, visited the Amavo community to interview its elders on their local history and culture. Those who saw him simply took to the bush, fearing that he came to ask them implicating questions about the Women's Revolt. Allen frustratingly left Amavo without saying much about its history in his report.

The primary sources, however, are valuable, especially if they are compared and used along with the numerous works written on the Women's

Revolt by professional anthropologists, historians, feminists and others. The historiography of the Women's Revolt will also be enriched when the findings of some of the recent research projects are published. As discussed below, all the sources constitute one of the major legacies the Women's revolt has left in Igbo studies.

ACHIEVEMENTS OF THE WOMEN'S REVOLT

Renaissance in Igbo Studies

Igbo studies experienced a remarkable renaissance as a result of the Women's Revolt. The colonial administration, which was taken by surprise by the revolt, realized that it knew little about the Igbo whom it had ruled for almost three decades. The administration then took various measures that helped in promoting Igbo studies. For example, it asked District Officers to submit "intelligence reports" on the history and culture of Igbo societies. The administration also set up a Commission of Inquiry in 1930 to determine the causes of the revolt and commissioned in the 1930s, anthropologists like M. M. Green and S. Leith-Ross to study Igbo culture, paying particular attention to the varying roles of women in their societies. These and other works which constitute the primary sources for studying Igbo history and culture have enabled modern researchers and feminists to embark on more detailed and scholarly analyses of the Women's Revolt. The Women's Revolt, no doubt, provided an incredible stimulus to Igbo studies, comparable to the Nigeria-Biafran War of the 1960s.

Enrichment of Igbo Folklore and Rituals

Igbo folkloric songs and dance were greatly enriched during the Women's Revolt. Women composed songs embodying their grievances, as they danced and "sat" on the Warrant Chiefs, or marched to the District Officer to present their petitions. In Aba-Ngwa area, women chanted traditional war songs sang by male warriors while marching to battle entitled: "*Nzogbu, Enyimba Enyi*" (literary meaning: We are like elephants, marching to battle, crushing obstacles on our way). Some even sang saying that women were as strong as the elephant: "*Ndem mbu Enyi, Enyi, Ndem Mbu Enyi.*" Interestingly, these songs were quite popular in Biafra, revealing the extent to which the folkloric songs of the Women's Revolt influenced Igbo "martial songs and music" during the Nigerian Civil War.[6]

As for the rituals, my recent trip to Nigeria was quite insightful. During the trip, I happened to have gone to Union Bank, Aba, for some transactions on August 12, 1999. During my discussion with the accountant, the Senior Manager, whom I had not met before, was passing by, and the accountant introduced him to me. The Manager politely invited me to his office, looking quite excited. While in his office, he told me of an event that would take place shortly and appealed to me as an educated Ngwa man living in the U.S. to spend a few minutes and watch it with him and the other bank officers. The Manager then gave me a gist of what was happening: there was a large tree, which posed a threat to the bank building, and the yardmen refused to trim its branches because they believed it was a sacred tree where 25 women killed in Aba during the Women's Revolt were buried. According to the yardmen, any time one of them trimmed the branches, the individual got mysteriously sick, and in one instance, they remembered one of their crewmembers died after cutting the branches. The only remedy, the yardmen claimed, was to invite the traditional ruler of the town to pour libations and perform rituals around the tree before anybody could touch it. That was why the Manager wanted me to wait, and happily, within a few minutes, the Traditional Ruler arrived with some elders, and in a solemn mood, he paid tribute to the "unknown soldiers" buried under the tree and performed the rituals necessary for cutting its branches. This rare event reminded me about the significance of the Women's Revolt in traditional Igbo religious values and ideas and the important place it continues to occupy in their rituals practices.[7]

THE EMERGENCE OF POWERFUL AND HEROIC LEADERS

It is a well-known adage in history that heroes and heroines are born during a crisis. The Aba Women's Revolt produced many heroines who emerged as distinguished and courageous leaders of the movement in their communities. Interestingly, while the names and varying roles of these heroines were recorded in the Collective Punishment Inquiry, and the Commission of Inquiry held in 1930, oral traditions conducted recently in parts of Igboland have revealed the towering influence some of them acquired during and after the Revolt. A broad analysis of the heroines beginning with the community where the Revolt started is insightful.

Nwanyeruwa and the Crisis that Sparked off the Revolt in Bende District

The Women's Revolt of 1929 was sparked off by a scuffle between Nwanyeruwa, a woman of Ngwa ancestry married in Oloko, and an enumerator, Mark Emereuwa, who was asked by Okugo, the Warrant of the town, to help in obtaining an accurate census of his people as mandated by the District Officer. In Oloko and others parts of Igboland, census was associated with taxation, especially, as the colonial administration had taken a similar census in 1926 without revealing the fact that it would be used in imposing tax on men in 1928. In addition, there was widespread rumor that fueled the fears of women claiming that both men and their wives would be taxed after the next enumeration. Thus, before the counting began, women had decided in their meetings to wait and see who would tax them during the hyperinflation of the 1920s when family incomes were declining rapidly.[8]

Emeruwa never expected that task he was asked to perform would trigger a massive revolt of Igbo women when on that fateful day, November 18, 1929, he went to late Ojim's compound, his first place of call, and asked his widow, Nwanyereuwa, to "count her goats, sheep and people." In anger, the woman retorted, "Was your [late] mother counted?" In other words, why do you want me to pay tax? Don't you know that women don't pay tax in traditional Igbo society? The violent encounter and verbal exchanges between the two infuriated Nwanyeruwa who then rushed to the town square to report the incident to women who were incidentally holding a meeting that day to discuss how they would respond to the "tax problem."[9]

Oloko women, after hearing Nwanyeruwa's account, went into action, believing that women would be taxed. They sent leaves of palm-oil tree (a symbol of invitation) to women in other parts of Bende District, nearby Umuahia and Ngwa areas and other places, and within a few days, about 10,000 women were said to have assembled in Oloko, "sitting" on Warrant Chief Okugo and demanding his trial and resignation.[10]

Nwanyeruwa: An Apostle of Non-Violence and the Heroine of Heroines

Nwanyereuwa not only played a major role in precipitating the revolt but also emerged as a leading advocate of non-violence during the protest marches. As an elderly woman, her words of wisdom were often heeded by more youthful women in her community who led the revolt and started "sitting" on Warrant Chiefs, singing, and dancing around their houses until they surrendered their insignia of office and resigned. Although Nwanyeruwa's influence was largely confined to her community, it is note-worthy that the revolt in many parts of Igboland took a similar pattern, as women first massed in their village squares and then moved to sit on their Warrant Chiefs. Perhaps, without the influence of Nwanyeruwa and others to be discussed, the revolt would have led to more bloodshed and casualties.[11]

Women from Oloko, Umuahia, and northern Ngwaland in the then Bende District, as well as other parts of Igboland, saw Nwanyeruwa as their heroine who courageously fought for their cause and "prevented women from paying tax." It is noteworthy that when the revolt spread, leaders of the revolt from various places came to Nwanyeruwa, requesting her to put in writing the assurances she had received from the District Officer that women would not be taxed. She complied, and a letter written on her behalf stated that the District Officer "said women will not pay tax till the world ends [and] Chiefs were not to exist any more."[12]

It is also significant that women from Bende, Ngwa and other places rallied round Nwanyeruwa during the revolt and gave her donations of ten shillings per village. The money was used partly to entertain the large number of women who visited Oloko and partly to defray the transport expenses of Oloko women who travelled to Umuahia, Nbawsi and Port Harcourt to cool the tempers of women in those towns and reassure them that they would not pay tax.[13] Members of the Aba Commission of Inquiry were then right when they noted that: "Nwanyeruwa became and still remains a name to conjure with . . . [and the Oloko trio] cleverly used her as the symbol of womanhood rising against oppression."[14]

Emissaries of Peace, and Apostles on Non-Violence: The Oloko Trio: Ikonnia, Mwannedia and Nwugo

The influence of Nwanyeruwa on the Oloko trio is yet to be studied. But as the oldest, the trio who probably listened to her appeal for non-violence, are celebrated today as the most outstanding "emissaries of peace" during the revolt. The Oloko trio was selected as the spokespersons of Oloko women due to their youthful vigor, intelligence and oratory. The District Officer, Captain John Hills who paid tribute to their leadership qualities, often sent them to "hot spots" during the revolt to ensure that the protests did not escalate and lead to violence. In Oloko for example, tempers ran high among women on November 30, 1929 when the District Officer who assumed duty that day refused to accede to their demand for the immediate trial of Warrant Chief Okugo who had been arrested for allegedly assaulting some of them during the revolt. The women continued to follow the District Officer wherever he went from morning till evening, kind of "sitting on him" until his wife got in touch with the trio and reached an agreement with them. The trio promised to get the women out the District Officer's way if he granted their request. Although the

District Officer doubted the ability of the trio in controlling the women who had become increasingly restless, he was surprised that as soon as he announced that Okugo would be tried the next day, the women quietly dispersed. The women, however, returned on the day of the trial, and when Okugo was found guilty and jailed two years, they all jubilated.[15]

The District Officer, realizing how powerful the trio was, used them to prevent violence in other areas. In Umuahia for example, women had massed in the town to begin protest against the Warrant Chiefs. As the District Officer feared that the protest might get out of control and endanger European factories and government establishments, he quickly contacted the trio to dissuade the women from embarking on their protest. The trio addressed the women, and to the amazement of the District Officer, the protest march did not take place.[16]

It is noteworthy that the District Officer was also greatly concerned about the situation in Aba where women had started to burn government offices and European factories after two of them were killed in a car accident by a reckless British driver. The District Officer invited the trio to send a telegram to Aba women to eschew violence and carry out their protests peacefully. The telegram did not, however, appear to have had any significant effect since arson and looting continued in Aba until the police and army was dispatched to the town.[17]

HEROINE OF THE REVOLT IN ABA-NGWA AREA: THE POWER OF LITERACY

One of the most outstanding leaders of the Revolt in Aba-Ngwa area was Madam Mary Okezie (1906-99), the first Ngwa woman to gain Western education. She started to attend the Anglican Mission School at Opobo in 1915, and after her graduation, she became a teacher in her alma mater and other mission schools in Umuahia and Aba. Madam Okezie continued teaching till 1938 when she went to a nursing school at Aba and England and later served as a Health Visitor in the Ministry of Health until 1964.[18]

Madam Okezie was teaching at the Anglican Mission School in Umuocham Aba in 1929 when the Women's Revolt broke out. Although she did not as a civil servant participate in the Revolt, Madam Okezie was very sympathetic to the women's cause. It is not surprising that when some Ngwa women requested her to write a memo on their behalf to be submitted to the Commission of Inquiry in 1930, she willingly granted their request without charging them any money. Her memo is significant not simply because it was the only one written by a woman, but due to the fact that it clearly articulated the grievances of the women and gave some insight into the course and consequences of the revolt in Aba-Ngwa area where the most violent protests took place in Igboland.[19]

Madam Okezie clearly emerged as the most famous leader of Ngwa women after the revolt. She became a leading exponent of women's rights, calling for better health facilities for women, and their involvement in governance. Her influence towered in 1948 when she founded the Ngwa Women's Association to promote the education and welfare of women. Madam Okezie was continuously elected the president of the Association for over two decades, and her achievements have continued to be a source of inspiration for the younger generation of Ngwa women.[20]

Women Chieftains

Research in Mbaise folk tradition has shed some light on the towering height leaders of the Women's Revolt attained in their communities.[21] Among the women called "Eze Ndi-Iyom" (chief of women), was one Mary, the overall leader of the Women's Revolt in Onicha Ezinihitte, who was popularly known as "Mary Ogu Ndem" (Mary of the Women's War). According to an informant, Mary:

> Was treated as a V.I.P, and caused tremendous stir of excitement whenever she visited any village. Not only were all the village roads swept and weeded, but valuable sheep and goats would be killed for festive eating. All the women would stand along the road to watch and wait for [her]. She would come shaded by an umbrella and her deputy leaders would process behind her. She was the great mistress who laid down the rules.[22]

The Heroic Warrior

Similarly, the fame of the next woman, Ihejilemebi Ibe of Umuokirika, was very remarkable. She was a woman known for her incredible bravery and strength of character before and during the Women's Revolt. Ihejilemebi (meaning: may good things not end when it's my turn), had served as the head of women's spy team during local wars and a member of the war council before the revolt. It is not surprising that when the women's revolt broke out, she naturally emerged as a "warrior" who led women to "sit" on the Warrant Chiefs in various communities, burn the houses of those who refused to resign, and hand over their insignia office to her. Ihejilemebi took personal custody of the caps of the Warrant Chiefs who abdicated their office and probably displayed them as a symbol of women's power. She was so much feared by Warrant Chiefs that, in one instance, a Warrant Chief of Obohia, Eze Anyanwuagwu, is said to have secretly negotiated a truce with her by agreeing to resign and offer her two big goats and a huge sum of money to save his life.[23]

Some women who felt that they were violently abused by their husbands brought their cases before the "warrior" for arbitration. The men found guilty were disgraced by the "warrior," who selected younger women to beat them up and carry them shoulder-high around the village as a lesson to others.[24] Ihejilemebi was accorded the privileges powerful men enjoyed in her society. She dressed like a warrior during funeral ceremonies, slung a gun over her shoulder, and joined men of bravery in participating in dances and rituals reserved for them. Little wonder when Ihejilemebi died, the *ese* and *nkwa ike* music, meant exclusively for titled men and warriors respectively, were played in her honor during an elaborate funeral ceremony.[25]

ABOLITION OF THE WARRANT CHIEF SYSTEM, AND INVOLVEMENT OF WOMEN IN THE APPOINTMENT OF NEW COURT MEMBERS

Some critiques have attempted to underrate the achievements of women in the political arena, especially in terms of the various demands they made. But bearing in mind the hurdles they faced and the political climate during and after the Revolt, some of their achievements are quite impressive. As an example, in virtually all the communities, women complained about the oppressive and corrupt rule of the Warrant Chiefs, whom they described as usurpers, and called upon the administration to abolish the Warrant Chief system and involve them in governance. The administration acceded to these demands, and in many localities, women helped the government to identify the Ezeala or sacred authority holders of their communities. Some of the Ezeala were appointed to replace the Warrant Chiefs in Native Courts of the 1930s, called "massed benches."[26]

The administration, for the first time in its history, also appointed a few influential leaders of the Women's Revolt to serve as Native Court members, including Chinwe - the only female member out of the 13 members of the Nguru Mbaise Native Court. Similarly, in Umuakpo Native Court area, three out of 30 members were women, while one out of nine members of the Okpuala Native Court was a woman.[27]

Perhaps, the most prominent female member of the Native Courts during colonialism was Ahebi Ugabe (The Female Leopard) of Enugu-Ezike in Nsukka area. Ahebi who was appointed a Native Court member in

1930, was reputed for her spiritual prowess, and popularly called "Agamega" or "Female Leopard." Like the Warrant Chiefs, Ahebi was carried to the Native Court in a hammock, and the road she passed to the Native Court in Ogrute village is still called "Akpata Ahebi" (Ahebi's road). Because of her fame and spiritual prowess, Ahebi is the only woman known in remembered history who was permitted by the elders to watch the powerful Omabe masquerade and build an Omabe shrine in her compound.[28]

CONTINUATION OF THE LEGACY OF REVOLTS DURING THE 1930S & 1950S

It is tempting to speculate that, due to the high-handed manner in which the Aba Women's Revolt was suppressed, Igbo women were cowed down, and many retreated to their safe and peaceful village enclaves where they continued to live as second-class citizens. The fictional images of Igbo women, which portray them as marginalized and passive, do not reflect objective reality. Surely, policemen and soldiers were mobilized to suppress the Revolt in the "disaffected areas," and Igboland was occupied by the military to intimidate the people and prevent further "disturbances." But these severe measures did not stop women from revolting in future whenever they felt that their collective interests were threatened. The 1929 example showed women what could be achieved when they mobilize, and it served as an inspiration to them in organizing the revolts of the 1930s–1950s.

The Tax Protests of 1938

Unlike 1929, the tax protests of 1938 were confined largely to Okigwe and Bende Divisions of Owerri Province covering a total area of about 500 square miles. The protests, which in some places became violent, spread like wild fire from Isiukwuato, Uturu, Nneato, Isuochi, Umuchieze, Otanzu, and Otanchara communities of Okigwe Division to Alayi, Item, and Umuimenyi communities of Bende Division.[29]

As in 1929, the tax protests of 1938 were caused by a variety of factors, like inefficient and corrupt tax collectors and the rumor that the colonial administration had, during the Women's Revolt, promised to stop collecting tax from people after seven years. The global depression of the 1930s that led to a sharp decrease in the price of palm produce also contributed to the revolt. Men resented paying tax at a time when their annual income could hardly sustain their families. The grim economic situation in Okigwe Division partly explains why women got involved in the tax protests. Women throughout the Division were economically hard-hit when, in December 1938, troops of the Royal West African Frontier Force, who had become the major consumers of their foodstuffs, were relocated from Okigwe town to Enugu.[30]

Interestingly, the protests started in Okigwe Division where the police arrested some men who failed to pay their tax due in November 1938. Concerned about the situation, women began a massive anti-tax protest in Okigwe Divison from December 5-15, and in some places like Isuochi, they destroyed the Native Court house and released prisoners. The admin- istration forcefully suppressed the disturbances and failed to appoint a Commission of Inquiry to investigate its origins. In addition, the adminis- tration did not accede to any of the requests made by the women, including the demand that some of them be appointed tax collectors.[31]

Oil Mill Protests of the 1940s in Owerri and Calabar Provinces: The Example of Nsulu in Northern Ngwaland (1948)

Rural women continued their legacy of protests in the 1940s when- ever they felt their economic and social interests were undermined. As an example, in 1949, the colonial government decided, without consulting women, to set up agencies that would supervise the installation of oil mills to enhance the production of palm produce in the eastern region. Women correctly smelled a rat in the proposed oil mill project and quickly mobilized themselves to protest against it for varying reasons. They were, for example, concerned that women could not afford to buy the oil mills, costing 2,500 pounds each. In addition, women argued that the rich men who owned the oil mills bought palm fruits directly from their husbands and thereby deprived them of the income they derived from palm kernels.[32]

Even though the oil mill protests were quite widespread in parts of Owerri and Calabar Provinces, the Nsulu example is quite illustrative. Women of Ubaha village of Nsulu were infuriated when, on January 3, 1948, a woman in tears, reported to them that her cassava farm had been destroyed to make room for the installation of an oil mill purchased by the president of the Nsulu Group Council, Chief J. N. Wachuku. Within two days, hundreds of women from neighboring villages of Umuosu and those from Oloko in Bende bordering the Nsulu community embarked on a massive protest. They drove away the workers sent to install the oil mill and then moved to nearby Nbawsi town to burn down the Nsulu Native Court and free all the prisoners.[33]

Altogether 36 women were arrested and later fined five pounds each. But the Nsulu protests and others convinced the colonial government that it was necessary to take measures to allay the fears of women. The government, for example, instructed members of Group Councils to consult women and other people before oil mills were installed in any community within their jurisdiction. Interestingly, Nsulu people turned out in large numbers during a meeting of their Group Council summoned in January 12, 1948 to determine the fate of the oil mill. 90% or 3,000 out of the 4,000 people present voted against the oil mill project.[34]

Women and the Urban Revolts of the 1950s & 1960s: The Tax Revolt in Aba and Onitsha in 1956

Unlike earlier revolts, urban women dominated the protest movements of the 1950s- 1960s. The tax revolt of 1956 occurred in Aba and Onitsha, the leading commercial centers of eastern Nigeria where a large number of women were engaged in occupations such as teaching, nursing, retail trading and sewing. To raise money from the growing number of urban women professionals, the government of Eastern Region led by its premier, Dr. Nnamdi Azikiwe (Zik), passed in April 1956, a finance law which for the first time, imposed an income tax on urban and rural women whose total income exceeded 100 pounds per annum.[35]

The finance law was fiercely resisted by Aba and Onitsha women. In Aba, for example, more than a thousand market women marched to the Tax Authority to protest against the taxation of women. They then formed the Aba Women's Association to articulate their grievances, threatening to withdraw support for Zik and his party, the National Council of Nigeria and the Cameroon (NCNC), during the next election. Onitsha women took similar measures, and in consequence, the tax law was amended to the satisfaction of women.[36]

WOMEN IN PARTY POLITICS, 1950S -1960S

Women participated actively in the struggle for Nigerian independence, and some of them attended the constitutional conferences held in London to work out the modalities of governing the country. Their influence was very much felt in the women's wing of the major political parties, which they used in articulating their interests. But unlike the earlier movements that were concerned with the localized interests of women, urban and educated women led the women's wing of the NCNC. They used their position to address national issues that were of common interest to women.

Among the leading women of the NCNC was Mrs. Margaret Ekpo, an Efik who in 1936, settled in the town of Aba which she adopted as her home. Mrs. Ekpo was in 1953, elected to the National Executive Council or decision-making organ of the NCNC. She also served as a special member of the Eastern House of Chiefs in 1959 and the vice-president of the NCNC Women's Wing of Eastern Nigeria, which had over 200 branches. Similarly, Mrs. Janet Mokelu of Enugu, the secretary of the Eastern Region NCNC Women's Association, was appointed a special member of the House of Chiefs. She and Mrs. Ekpo were elected to the Eastern House of Assembly in 1961.[37] These and other women laid the foundation for the modern Igbo women engaged at the present time in a variety of professional activities as lawyers, high court judges and magistrates, medical doctors, and educationists. It is also noteworthy that some Igbo women are holding key cabinet positions at the federal and state levels, and a few serve as advisers and special assistants to heads of governments.[38]

CONCLUSION

The various revolts and women's movements discussed in this paper can be divided into two main categories. The first category, beginning with the Aba Women's Revolt untill the 1950s, was organized and led by rural women. The second category, which took place from 1950-1960, was associated with educated urban women. The Aba Women's Revolt, however, served as an inspiration to those who organized subsequent revolts and women's movements. The achievements of the Aba Women's Revolt and the legacies it left are noteworthy. The Revolt helped women to mobilize themselves, and change the existing political order during colonialism. It also enabled some of their leaders who emerged as heroines, to attain a privileged status in Igbo society comparable to those of titled men and warriors. The revolt contributed to the emergence of modern Igbo women who are currently engaged in diverse occupations. It ranks as one of the most outstanding primary resistance movements in Nigerian history.

NOTES

1. An earlier version of this paper was presented at the conference to mark the 70th Anniversary of the Aba Women's Revolt of 1929 and previously published in *West African Review* 2, no. 1 (2000). http://www.icaap.org/iuicode?101.2.1.14 [Accessed 2 April 2007]
2. Judith Van Allen, "'Aba Riots' or Igbo `Women's War'? Ideology, Stratification, and Invisibility of Women," in *The Black Woman Cross-Culturally, ed.* F. C. Steady (Cambridge, MA: Schenkman Publication Co, 1981), 60.

3.   The literature of the Women's revolt is quite rich, and it includes the works of Adiele E. Afigbo, *The Warrant Chiefs: Indirect Rule in South-Eastern Nigeria, 1891-1929* (London: Longman, 1972); H. A. Gailey, *The Road to Aba: A Study of British Administrative Policy in Eastern Nigeria* (New York: New York University Press, 1970); Nina Mba, *Nigerian Women Mobilized: Women's Political Activity in Southern Nigeria, 1900-1965* (Berkeley: Institute of International Studies, University of California, 1982); and John N. Oriji, *Ngwa History* (New York: Peter Lang, 1997).

4.   Proceedings before the Commission of Inquiry into Disturbances in Calabar and Owerri Provinces," *Gazette Extraordinary* 10 (February 7, 1930), 8-9, 11.

5.   Ibid., 1-2. For example, S. Macaulay represented Aba chiefs, the chiefs of Azumini, and the people of Opobo and Ameke, Messrs Benjamin and Etim represented the people of Umu koroshe and Utim Ekpo, while Mr. Rhodes represented the women of Aba and Azumini.

6.   Information obtained during my field works in Nigeria in 1975 and 1991 and my informants include the late Madam Ihuocha Ogbonna of Avo Ntigha, one of the leaders of the Women's Revolt in her community.

7.   The official reports are moot about what happened to women who died at Aba during the Revolt. It is likely that they were buried in a mass grave where the tree was planted. According to Judith Van Allen, a total of 50 women died, and 50 others were wounded during two encounters with the police and army. See Judith Van Allen, "Sitting on a Man: Colonialism and the Lost Political Institutions of the Igbo," *Canadian Journal of African Studies* 6, no. 11 (1972), 178.

8.   Oriji, *Ngwa History*, 90-97.

9.   Ibid. See also "Proceedings before the Commission of Inquiry," op. cit. 3-4.

10.   Ibid. See also Allen, "Aba Riots," 72.

11.   Mba, *Nigerian Women*, 81-8 and Allen, "Aba Riots," 72, and Nina E. Mba, "Heroines of the Women's War," in *Nigerian Women in Historical Perspective*, ed. Bolanle Awe (Ibadan: Sankore/Bookcrat 1992), 75-88.

12.   Ibid. cited by Mba, *Nigerian Women*, 82.

13.   The Aba Commission of Inquiry (1930), 9.

14.   Ibid.

15.   Ibid.

16.   Mba, *Nigerian Women*, 82.

17.   Ibid.

18.   Ibid., 80, 87, 91, 93 and 97. Information on Madam Okezie was obtained from Ihemakwa Nwamuo, retired administrative officer (90 years) who was interviewed at Aba on August 10, 1998.

19.   Ibid.

20. Ibid.
21 Ezi-Nwanyi Patricia Nwoga, "The Hero in Igbo Society," paper presented during on a conference on Institute of African Studies, University of Nigeria, Nsukka, 10 June 1986).
22. Ibid., 13- 14.
23. Ibid., 14-16.
24. Ibid., 18.
25. Ibid., 14.
26. "Proceedings before the Commission of Inquiry," 8.
27. Mba, *Nigerian Women*, 96.
28. C. K. Meek, *Ethnographical Report on the Peoples of Nsukka Division of Onitsha Province* (Lagos, 1930), 136-39.
29. Mba, *Nigerian Women*, 98.
30. Ibid. 99.
31. Ibid., 100-101.
32. Ibid., 107.
33. Ibid., 109.
34. Ibid.
35. Ibid., 102
36. Ibid.
37. Mba, *Nigerian Women*, 241-49. See also Allen, "Aba Riots," 82-3, and R. L. Sklar, *Nigerian Political Parties* (Princeton: Princeton University Press, 1963), 402-3.
38. For example, Dr. Kemafo Unegbu is the Federal Minister of Transport, and Mrs. Akanwa, a veteran politician and former member of the Imo State House of Assembly, serves as a cabinet member in Abia State. Every state government has at least a woman occupying a cabinet position.

ATLANTIC DIASPORA
CONNECTIONS

CHAPTER 13

IGBO IDENTITY IN AFRICA AND THE ATLANTIC DIASPORA

CHIMA J. KORIEH

The enslavement of Africans, which gave birth to the African Diaspora in the Atlantic world, scattered people who shared the same cultural and linguistic affinity but often lumped them together in identifiable regional patterns. A significant consequence of the pattern of trade was the emergence of identifiable "ethnic" and cultural patterns in the diaspora. Attention, therefore, has for a long time focused on the pattern of dispersion and the impact of the Atlantic slave trade on the emergence of New World cultures. This scholarly attention on the formation or otherwise of new identities in the new world has not merely added to our understanding of the genesis of contemporary American cultures but it has also added to the rich historical tapestry of African identities both in Africa and across the Atlantic.

Yet many questions and issues remain contested and unresolved. While ethnicity is a potentially powerful conceptual framework for analyzing the history and identity of African societies in Africa and the African Diaspora, at the same time, ethnicity is potentially problematic because of the tendency to essentialise and homogenize the essence of African groups whose histories and identities were often fluid, flexible, contested, and accommodating of other influences. Ethnicity wears many garbs, it seems.

Thus, the notion of ethnic identity is impossible to understand without a full sense of history, without a full sense of how identities are imposed, ascribed, and negotiated, to form, sometimes, imagined communities. A dynamic notion of ethnicity brings history, culture, and other interlocking variables that throw light on how people identity themselves and how they are identified by others.

This chapter addresses Igbo ethnicity and identity with a view to presenting a synthesis and a framework for understanding the essence of ndiIgbo in both Africa and the Atlantic Diaspora. The case of the Igbo suggests that identities are multi-layered, self imposed, as well as ascribed by others and as such require a critical analysis to avoid the essentialism that have bedeviled much of the discourse on African identity in the diaspora. The Igbo example is important for a number of reasons. First, the demographics of the Atlantic trade, as the *The Trans Atlantic Database* and other available records have shown, suggest that a large number of enslaved Africans from the Bight of Biafra were of Igbo origin in contemporary territorial terms.[1] Second, despite their large presence in the Americas, the role of enslaved Africans of Igbo origin in shaping the larger history of slavery, pattern of slavery, new identity formations in the Americas remain relatively unexplored. Third, the available literature on the Igbo Diaspora needs to be examined in the contexts of the larger Atlantic history and what constitutes Igboness in their African homeland.

Indeed, the unique tendencies exhibited by enslaved Igbos and the responses that differentiated them from other slaves in their attitude towards their servile position under slavery provide opportunity for a deeper understanding of their unique identity as defined by their actions and by slave traders and owners. These markers that differentiated slaves of African origins from one another can be aptly describes as "transitional identities." Although derived from African ones, these "transitional identities" were transformed or reconstituted in response to slavery, an institution that denied them their humanity and old world sense of who they are.

The first part of the paper is an overview of the debate regarding African ethnicities and identities in the Atlantic Diaspora. The aim is to situate the extent to which the African heritage was retained (or was able to be retained) by those who came under bondage as well as individuals and groups identities in a larger historical context. Second, the paper examines the historical background of enslaved Igbos in order to situate their diasporic identities within the broader framework of what constitutes Igboness in Africa. Third, the paper examines the stereotypes associated with Igbo slaves not only as a marker of an imposed New World identity but also a tool for reconceptualizing resistance and African response to slavery—an institution that ran counter to the republican ideals of their African world.

THE DEBATE IN HISTORICAL PERSPECTIVE

Scholars have traditionally been divided on the degree of African continuities in the diaspora. The debate's long and vigorous history has been characterized by the search for: African retentions in Atlantic cultures, the construction of African-Atlantic culture, and the notion of "hybridity" in the emergence of Black Atlantic. The debate dates back to the late 1930s, when sociologist Franklin Frazier, argued that African experiences and influences could not have survived the middle passage in any meaningful way to influence new world cultures.[2] Thus, it is their view that the formation or forging of the so-called African ethnicities and identities where in deed new world formations that evolved out of their experience of slavery.

The debate on the influence of enslaved Africans in the development of identifiable cultural markers and identities became a major theme in the 1940s amongst commentators on the early American past. The publication of Melville Herskovits' *The Myth of the Negro Past* in 1941[3] brought significant impetus to the debate. Herskovits had argued that it is possible to identify many broad similarities among the disparate cultures of Atlantic Africa. In other words, slaves were able to maintain an African culture that significantly influenced Afro-Atlantic culture.[4] This is a belief rooted in sociological theory. As Michael A. Hogg, Deborah J. Terry, and Katherine M. White have noted: "Individuals and groups have a social psychological "need to belong" and express this need through their social identities (or such categories as ethnic groups, nationality, or political identification."[5]

Sidney Mintz and Richard Price, Herskovits' opponents, *Afro-American Past* has influenced current thinking on the subject.[6] They stressed the numerous differences that emerged. For Mintz and Price slaves on the Middle Passage were a "crowd of disparate cultures rather than a grouping in any cultural sense."[7] The key elements in African-American culture according to this school of thought were forged in the New World and contained components that were not originally African. Indeed, John Thornton maintains that the cultural disorganization of slave society made slaves much more dependent upon the culture of the Europeans or Euro-American rather than the transmission of their African heritage.[8] For these groups of scholars, enslaved African arrived the New World without a common identifiable African culture, ethnicity and clearly defined identity.

The contemporary debate, largely influenced by Mintz and Price, who argued that there were major differences among the cultures of the Atlantic coast of Africa,[9] has not been a radical shift from the 1940s' debate. While the two main trends are indispensable for any broader syntheses, a regional and ethnically based approach in which African backgrounds are compared, analyzed, and contrasted, with New World identities makes for a more nuanced understanding of identity transformation in the diaspora. New data and critical historical analysis suggests that the above pictures are perhaps overdrawn.[10] Between the two extremes are perspectives that attempt to construct a much more fluid process of identity and ethnic formation in the new world.

Indeed, there is considerable agreement among scholars that see the transplanting of African ethnic identities that followed the strong regional pattern of enslavement from Africa and concentrated African people of particular ethnicities in identifiable regional patterns in the Americas. Herbert Klein argues that the slaves who arrived in America were mostly "illiterate, spoke a multitude of different languages, and had a few if any common ties." Nevertheless, their color and status, Klein argues, "soon bound them together, so they were able slowly to create a community and culture in the New World."[11] Philip Morgan argues along similar lines emphasizing that the "diverse and heterogeneous" parts of the Atlantic world "became one—a unitary whole, a single system,"[12] Morgan cautions, though, on premature conclusions and speculation that are not grounded in regional analyses of the patterns of trade and movement from African into the New World.[13]

Enslaved Africans did not arrive the new world as *tabular rasa*, yet they were ultimately influenced and were influenced by their new environment and condition in slavery beginning with the process of enslavement in Africa, transportation through the Middle Passage and inhumanity of slavery. Beyond the Atlantic, language, common worldview, and religion may have been important markers of ethnic identities, but their race and color and common experience became more important from the middle passage. Although the experiences of enslaved Africans bonded them together, their differing African backgrounds elicited different responses to slavery, the emerging identities in the Americas, and the perception of American slavers to different African groups.

It is important, therefore, to move beyond the homogenized and at times anachronistic characterization of Africans in the Atlantic world to consider specific regional, cultural, and historical experiences of the enslaved African brought to the Americas. That is, what do we know of their African background in relation to their identity as redefined in the Atlantic world? According to Paul Lovejoy, "sufficient information exists about individuals [and groups] taken as captives in the slave trade to allow historians to dispense with a generalized notion of a 'traditional' African background for New World blacks and, accordingly, to articulate the African-ness of the black Diaspora with ethnic and historical specificity."[14] Indeed, the regional approach is critical to transcend the narrow conceptualization of African continuities in the New World and appreciate the call for more focus on the role of particular individuals/ethnic group in the emergence of New World identities, continuities, and ethnic influences in the African Diaspora.[15] The individual backgrounds provide important new data, yet their stories are tangential to the societies from which they came. Indeed, they emphasize the fruitfulness of understanding the "interconnectedness of the histories of Africa and the colonial sites where Africans and their descendants lived on the other side of the Atlantic."[16]

The body of scholarship that has emerged despite its richness suggests exciting new ways of thinking about the field in trans-Atlantic and cross-cultural terms. The new perspective in the literature of African ethnicities highlight the possibility of centralizing Africa and cross-Atlantic narrative that follows the pattern of the initial movement itself—that is from Africa to the Americas rather than from the America's to Africa. A more nuanced approach to the discourse on African continuities in the Atlantic world can bring to light the trans-Atlantic connections between African history and African Diaspora history.[17] This model can historically link the history of the Diaspora to its African origins. Such a model is based on the notion that even though the Americas deeply influenced the formation of African identities in the new world, such identities were based upon functional ideas that enslaved African brought with them.

A secondary element of the new paradigm would support the understanding of the histories, identities, and influence of African experiences in relation to time and space. The discussion has largely ignored the African side of the equation. For example, what did it mean to be *ndi*Igbo in Africa? What was the nature of Igbo identity in the seventeenth and eighteenth centuries? What extrapolations into the diaspora are based on what did not exist, what was transitional, and fluid, or what was not uniquely Igbo? Certainly, African born captives and the immediate generations that followed had a greater capacity and need to retain their Africanness than those born in the Americas later on. For the American-born Africans, functionality (acquiring new identities and abandoning African ones) was perhaps more practicable in their adaptability in their environment. Their nostalgia about Africa or more appropriately, a "sense of place" was obviously different from the African generation of slaves. Stampp argues for example that more of the African continuities in America were evident in the eighteenth century when a large proportion of the slaves were native

Africans, than in the mid-nineteenth century when the great majority were second-and third-generation Americans.[18] Yet a collective perceptions of the self, community, and the "other," remained throughout the history of Africa's presence in the New World.

As new data provide opportunity to advance scholarship on both the African and early American past, it has become imperative to rely on historically-specific information of the political, social, and cultural backgrounds of the enslaved Africans to understand the worlds they came from and the worlds they (re)created in the America. As Gwendolyn Hall illustrates, "Atlantic slave trade ships did not meander along several African coasts collecting enslaved Africans and bringing them to many different places in the America."[19] Recent data from shipping records support a more harmonized sequence of movements between African coasts and different parts of the America.[20] The *Du Bois CD-ROM* database containing over 27,000 slave voyages and other data show that slave ships confirmed their ports of call, the pattern of ship movements and ports of disembarkation in the New World.[21] For example, the French ship, *The Diligent* obtained its slave cargo from a single port in the Guinea Coast and disembarked in Martinique during its maiden slave voyage of 1731-32.[22] Records of several other voyages follow similar patterns. The English ship *William* that sailed from London in December 1662 collected its cargo of 154 enslaved Africans from two ports, Rio Num and C. Lopez, and disembarked the 126 slaves but one that survived the journey in Barbados. Another English ship *Hope* that sailed in 1663 called only at Calabar where it began its journey to the Caribbean with 196 slaves. Of the surviving 159 slave, 138 disembarked in Jamaica while the remaining 21 disembarked in Barbados. The *Blackmore* discharged all but one of its 330 slaves in Jamaica in a voyage from Calabar in 1665. *Two Friends*, a Royal African Company slaver discharged all but one of 103 slaves from Gambia in Virginia in 1686.[23] As John Thornton argued, "although the process of enslavement, sale, transfer, shipment, and relocation on a plantation was certainly disruptive to the personal and family lives of those people who endured it, its effect on culture may have been less than many suggest."[24] While the slaves did not arrive into a cultural vacuum, they certainly were not *tabular rasa* on arrived to the New World. The struggle for survival in their new environment undoubtedly required adjustment and radical change, but slaves, Lovejoy argues also sought "connections with the past through language, religion, and cultural practices."[25] According to Kenneth Stampp "when the slaves left Africa, they carried with them knowledge of their own complex culture. Some elements of their cultures-or at least some adaptations or variations of them-they planted somewhat insecurely in America."[26] These surviving

"Africans" were evident in their speech, in their dances, in their music, in their folklore, and in their religion. In other words, Africans brought a cultural heritage in language, aesthetics, and philosophy that helped to form the cultures of the Atlantic world.[27]

Table 13.1: The Trans-Atlantic Slave Trade

Region	No	% of Total	Percentage (less unspecified)
Africa unspecified	2,281,660	28.70	–
West Central Africa	20,645,00	26.00	36.50
Bight of Biafra	941,463	11.90	16.60
Gold Coast	617,674	7.78	10.90
South-East Africa?	291,060	3.66	5.14
Senegambia	24,350	3.07	4.30
Sierra Leone	208,316	2.62	3.68
Windward Coast	16,529	2.03	2.85

Source: David Eltis, et al, *The Transatlantic Slave Trade: A Database.*

The manner in which the "slaves were captured and sold on the slave markets and confined in the slave pens in African ports had a more important effect upon the integrity of their cultural heritage." Such experiences and the ordeal of the "Middle Passage," Frazier argued did not destroy their African heritage. They were retained as memories of their home land, certain patterns of behavior and attitude towards their fellow men, and the physical world.[28] Many scholars are agreed, however, on the notion of what Lovejoy referred to as an Atlantic world that continued to be "fragmented, politically, economically, and culturally throughout the period of slavery."[29] Hence one can argue for continuity as much as adjustment for enslaved Africans in the new environment since the subsequent transfer of African to the New World was not a very randomizing a process.

THE IGBO AND THE ATLANTIC DIASPORA

As the evidence strongly indicates, a large number of the enslaved Africans from the Bight of Biafra were Igbo. David Eltis and David Richardson estimate that about one in seven Africans shipped to the New World during the whole era of the transatlantic slave trade originated from the Bight of Biafra.[30] This corresponds to the estimated 11.90 percent of the total number for which data is available via the Du Bois CD-ROM

database. Douglas Chambers suggests that of the 11.6 million people estimated to have been shipped to the New World between 1470 and 1860,
some 1.7 million were transported from the Bight of Biafra.[31] He estimates that 80 per cent of the people shipped from the Bight of Biafra were
Igbo-speaking and reached the Americas in British ships.[32]

As Table 2 shows, the vast majority disembarked in British Caribbean
and North American mainland, thus accounting for perhaps a third of all
slave arrivals in these colonies between 1700 and 1807.[33] If we accept these
estimates, then we should accept that such concentrations of Igbo exiles had
important consequences for the development of slavery and the slave society
in the British Americas.[34] We must also accept that other groups had originally arrived in the region prior the large-scale expansion of the Biafra trade
in the 18th century. The data indicates that between 1601 and 1700 most
of the slave came from the Gambia and a substantial number continued to
arrive from this region although the vast majority came from Calabar.

To situate enslaved Africans in the Americas in historical contest, it is
essential to understand the African background of the enslaved.[35] Recent
data have improved our knowledge of the origin of the slaves brought to the
Americas to the extent that we can identify African survivals.[36] Slave database has added numerical and regional specificity to the slave trade data.[37]
We now know that sourcing slaves was not a random process. We know
also that specific regional patterns existed in Africa that corresponded with
European regional possessions in the Americas. The number and regional
specificity are important in providing answers to immediate concerns for
slavers—people from particular parts of Africa with identifiable linguistic
and other characteristics concentrated/were demanded in certain parts of
the Americas. In mainland North America and the Caribbean, planters
had some knowledge of the regional or ethnic backgrounds of the slaves.
Planters in Brazil used specific terms to indicate vaguely the area in Africa
from which the slaves came.[38]

From a transatlantic perspective, when compared with the cultural
continuities and ethnic identities of other African groups, the Igbo seem
difficult to identify. The religious and linguistic influence of the Yoruba,
the Moslem identities of African slaves and indeed their material cultures
are more established in Diaspora Studies. It is no surprise that much are
made of the contribution of the Yoruba, the Akan, the Fon and the Ewe,
the Bakongo and so on to the neglect of the Igbo.[39] Why is the Igbo case
a neglected area in Diaspora studies considering the sheer size of Igbo
contingent to the New World? Does this mean that the Igbo adapted to
their new environment more than other ethnic groups? Does it mean that
the Igbo were more susceptible to change than others were? Answers to

Table 2. Summary of Slaves embarked from the Bight of Biafra and Principal port of disembarkation, 1601-1800.

Region	Number	Percent of total	Percent less unspecified
Jamaica	218,007	28.70	32.00
Not specified	79,158	10.40	--
Dominica	57,353	7.54	8.42
Barbados	51,982	6.84	7.63
Grenada	38,254	5.03	5.62
St. Kitts	35,923	4.73	5.62
Cuba	35,552	4.73	5.22
St. Dominique	30,436	4.00	4.47
Sierra Leone	29,937	3.94	4.40
Virginia	22,520	2.94	3.31
Antigua	21,569	2.84	3.17
Martinique	19,556	2.57	2.87
St. Vincent	18,692	2.46	2.74
Guianas	17,300	2.28	2.54
Virgin Islands	13,167	1.73	1.93
Carolinas	10,766	1.42	1.58
Trinidad	10,408	1.37	1.53
Guadeloupe	10,399	1.37	1.54
South-east Brazil	9,189	1.21	1.35
Bahia	6,485	0.85	0.95
Nevis	4,288	0.56	0.63
St. Lucia	3,670	0.48	0.54
Rio de la Plata	3,010	0.40	0.44
Tobago	2,994	0.39	0.44
Puerto Rico	2,865	0.38	0.42
Spanish America (main)	1,717	0.23	0.25
Bahamas	1,199	0.16	0.18
Dutch Caribbean	1,061	0.14	0.16
Northeast Brazil	816	0.11	0.12
Pernambuco	676	0.09	0.10
Montserrat	528	0.07	0.08
Maryland	310	0.04	0.05
Off-shore Atlantic	232	0.03	0.03
Gold Coast	144	0.02	0.02
Senegambia	81	0.01	0.01

Source: Calculated from David Eltis, et al, *The Transatlantic Slave Trade: A Database.*

these questions are difficult to provide because they involve the interrogation of the whole issue of a Pan-Igbo identity and to what extent this identity was created outside Igboland. Koelle, for example, had assertion that Igbo receptive in Sierra Leone had never heard of the name Igbo until they were sent away. Olaudah Equiano is often given as an example of the absence of an Igbo nation, hence an Igbo identity until recent times-for Equiano's Igboness only emerged during the Middle Passage and in the diaspora.[40] That was not unusual. Even in contemporary terms, notions of identity, territory is an on-going process in every society. This did not mean that people forgot where they came. Indeed notions of identity defined in territorial terms have always been an ongoing process in all societies. For many Africans in the pre-European contact era, the most important mark of identity was perhaps language and Equiano, like many other slaves in the Middle Passage was important quick to recognize it. Cultural life, economic, and social practices were equally more important marks of identity than territory. Indeed, Equiano's use of the term "our people" in describing the economic and social life of his village in the eighteenth century spoke beyond his immediate environment. "Our People" was recognition of a group of people who had certain things in common and embraced certain worldviews even if his knowledge of a pan-Igbo ethnic or cultural group was limited. Other slaves of Igbo origin emphasized similar traits often using the term "Our people," or "my people" as a metaphor for a specific group or nation.

The flexibility in the claimed identity of this single individual is reflected in Vincent Carretta's recent work questioning where Equiano was born based on Equiano's baptismal record at St Margaret's Church, Westminster dated 9 February 1759, which indicated that he was in 'Carolina'— thus challenging his claim to an Igbo and African identity.[41] Equaino described himself as African, Igbo but he was also American and European—and these identities were called upon at different times to achieve specific objectives. This is a constant individual and group dynamic. Several ethos were claimed as a marker of legitimacy and identity by enslaved Africans and Olaudah Equaino referred to several of these ethos. While some were universal to *Ndi* Igbo, other were status based symbols which ascribed a uniquely achievement based identity. Such claims were neither unique to Equaino; changing identities was an important phenomenon in the larger social context of early Americas and other societies in transition.

"Ethnogenesis did occur but in extremely complicated ways," Morgan argues. Morgan accepts the view that "many Africans from the Bight of Biafra who had never heard the name I[g]bo in their own lands and identified themselves instead by their villages or districts, yet came to accept—at least to some degree—the term abroad."[42] While the point at which Igbo consciousness and identification with the Igbo nation began cannot be pinned down easily, early European visitor to the Bight of Biafra the John Grazilhier writing in 1699 on Kalabari/Igbo relations noted of the people living north of Kalabari called "the Hackbous [Igbo] Blacks . . . In their territories there are two market-days every week, for slaves and provisions, which Calabar Blacks keep very regularly, to supply themselves both with provisions and slaves, palm-oil, palm-wine, etc. there being great plenty of the last."[43] William Baikie made reference to the Igbo in the 1850s. Both Grazilhier and Baikie reference to the Igbo was not generic but in terms of a particular ethnic group in the Biafra hinterland. According to Baikie, "In I'gbo each person hails . . . from the particular district where he was born, but when away from home all are I'gbos."[44]

The emergence or reinforcement of Igbo identity at least from the beginning of the twentieth century seem to have occurred in the context of increasing competition between the Igbo and other ethnic groups as colonialism opened opportunities for migration, commerce, and work in the emerging bureaucracy. It seems logical that once outside their homeland, a sense of cohesion, cooperation, and identification, at least based on a common language emerged. But such self-images (or 'internal identities') as Amartya Sen referred to it in the case of colonial India, were also much influenced - both collaterally and dialectically-by outside imagery ("external identity").[45]

The forces that determined the surge or otherwise of an ethnic consciousness has been addressed by Anthropologist Fredrick Barth who drawn parallels between ecological factors and the maintenance of ethnic identity/boundaries. It is their view that individuals downplay their ethnicity or seek incorporation into other groups because of ecological factors.[46] Rural Igbo migrants in Cameroon, Kleis argues were more conscious of their ethnicity than their urban counterparts were. The distinction between rural and urban based Igbo migrants in Cameroon or what Kleis calls "confrontational and incorporation ethnicity" only suggests that ethnic identity, as reflected in the Igbo case is often fluid in response to particular contextual issues.[47] The contextual space, in which, a particular people inhabit ecological niches and in relations to others may inform the exhibition or suppression of ethnic consciousness.

Unlike many other African groups, *Ndi* Igbo lack grand legends and myths of origin. Associated with this elusive cache through which historians have approached the history settlement, early migration and settlement patterns of the Igbo is the problematic of Igbo identity. The dual question of origin and identity has confounded Igbo scholars. But as

Elizabeth Isichei explained, "It is as if the question of origins contained, somewhere, a key to the elusive problem of Igbo Identity,"[48] a question she tried to unsuccessfully answer in her book, *A History of the Igbo People*.[49]

Similar and inaccurate representations surround our understanding of Igbo identity in the Atlantic Diaspora. The starting point for many scholars of the diaspora is to explain the patterns and the body of myths surrounding the Igbo that emerged from slavers and planters accounts. Despite the dangers associated with such anachronistic and essentialism, scholars of the Igbo diaspora till date have not done enough to dispel such myths or explained them with a great deal of historicity that takes full account of the African background. Interestingly some of the characterizations of the Igbo were based on physical characteristics rather than linguistic and cultural patterns. These descriptions have been expatiated with a sense of history. As we know however, the difficulties likely to be faced on the reconstitution of ethnic identity in the diaspora is that there are similar physical characteristics among the enslaved Africans than differentiated them, particularly among the Bantu groups.

The identity of the Igbo in the Atlantic diaspora can be critically shaped by a broader perspective that sees identity as a historically fashioned construct rather than a timeless continuum. Their African identity was an essential element in the construction of New World identities. To understand Igbo identity and situate it in the larger Diaspora history, we must understand the Igbo way of life, their cosmology and general outlook prior to enslavement. But what do we know from their African background? Early twentieth century and contemporary evidence may provide some answers to the "inherent" and ascribed markers of Igboness.

The Igbo have been described in historical and anthropological literature as a "stateless" or "segmentary" society consisting of autonomous village groups. The most important feature of this system is the perceived lack of a formalized leadership that Victor Uchendu described as "an exercise in direct democracy" and "representative assembly."[50] Cyril Onwumechili captures the essence of Igbo independence and their attitude to centralized authority.

Most Igbo governed themselves without giving power to chiefs or kings. They organized themselves into many independent village governments. . . . Every man could and did have his say on all matters under discussion. Nobody had any special privilege because of ancestry.[51]

Early twentieth century European description and characterization of the Igbo is informative on the broader stereotypical considerations of Europeans for the work ethic of different ethnic groups. Writing in 1913,

Major Darwin et al, based on little or no knowledge of both the Igbo and the Yoruba, wrote:

> As a race, the Ibo is not yet as advanced as the Yoruba is, but given equal opportunities and time, I think that under the beneficent rule it now enjoys it will prove to be the superior race. As far as my experience goes, Ibos have much stronger individuality, are more resourceful, energetic, artistic, musical and courageous than Yorubas, and they have deeper feelings. The Yoruba is a fine race, and in some respects—such as ease of control, and perhaps physique—it is better than the Ibo; but were I to need carriers or workmen for specially trying work requiring resources and self-reliance, and had to take men of one race only, I should choose Ibos before Yorubas from equal bodies of robust trained men of these races.[52]

Describing the political and organization of the Igbo and the failure of British Indirect rule policy, S. Cronje argued in *The World and Nigeria* that "In the East indirect rule failed altogether. There were no big chiefs, emirates or empires, which could be adapted to the needs of British administrators. The Eastern people lived in village groups administered by councils which were presided over by senior men who held office by virtue of their personal ability as much as by age or lineage."[53] Commenting on the decentralized nature of the Igbo political system, G. I. Jones notes that: "The usual patterns is for public matters to be discussed at a general meeting at which every able bodied male who is a full member of the community has a right to attend and to speak if he so wishes . . . the community particularly in the I[g]bo area is not prepared to surrender its legislative authority to any chiefs, elders or other traditional office holders."[54] Obafemi Awolowo spoke of the Igbo and Ibibio as people who "cannot tolerate anyone assuming the authority of a chieftain over them."[55] Jack Shepherd, senior editor of *Look* had this to say of Igbo during Biafra war 'Ibo aggressiveness and ambition in commerce, public utilities, and the civil service made them a hated people. They were called the "Jews of Black Africa." [56] Describing the different qualities and identities of the major ethnic groups in Nigeria during the civil war, *Times* characterized the Igbo as:

> Ambitious and clever. . . . Within their tribal culture lay unique seeds for Western-style self-improvement. Unlike many other tribes, they had no autocratic village chiefs. Instead, they were

ruled by open councils of what sociologists called high achievers
... successful yam farmers, warriors, public speakers. The titles
a man earned were buried with him and his sons were forced
unlike most Africans to make their own reputations. [57]

Edward C. Schwarzenbach writing in the *Swiss Review of World Affairs*
spoke of the Igbo thus: "To the Igbo with their egalitarian society, [are]
free of hierarchical structures."[58] Michael Mok quoting a Reverend Father
in Biafra during the Nigeria-Biafra War notes: "The Igbo man never begs.
He is much too proud. He wants to pay for what he gets."[59]

The societies of Eastern Nigeria were not highly stratified along class
and gender. On Igbo women, Frederick Lugard, first colonial governor of
Nigeria described them as "ambitious, self-reliant, hardworking, and independent. She claims full equality with the opposite sex and would seem
indeed to be the dominant partner.[60]

Yet, the absence of a formalized political structure did not mean
the absence of traditional intellectuals or stable political institutions
and culture.[61] Traditional intellectuals derived their power and authority
through an elaborate status conferring mechanism—age, lineage head-
ships, powerful titled and secret societies as well as possession of certain
spiritual powers. Others are based on individually achieved status and purchasing power.[62] Thus, traditional intellectuals included the native doctors,
the *ozo* and other title holders, oracular priests and priestesses, ritualists,
diviners, custodians of sacred shrines, men and women elders, griots,
women leaders, fortune tellers and interpreters of dreams, among others
who had the knowledge and power to read and interpret socio-political
and economic phenomenon and advance practical or spiritual solutions to
perceived notions of wrongs affecting their society. These skills and com-
petencies were applied in the new world.

STEREOTYPES AND MARKERS OF IGBO IDENTITY

New and expanding knowledge of the African side provide some
answers to several concerns including how the Igbo respond to slavery.
How enslavement and slavery contrast with the socio-political context of
their African environment and how did "the shame" of slavery affect the
formation of new identities and denial of old African identities, merge
with new ones. In a society characterized as stateless and where the notion
of *Igbo enweghi eze* (Igbo have no king) is widely accepted, the slave society
presented a great contrast to the republican ideals of traditional Igbo
society.

History and memory in Africa provide new possibilities for a better understanding of Igbo question in the formation of natal (nascent) ethnicities. Martin Klein has shown how slave descendants in West Africa and North Africa responded different to their post-abolition experiences. There was a dominant tendency for African of slave descent to "forget" their slave origin. Self-identification is important but it also raises the broader issue of denial when certain ascribed characteristic are not helpful. How did this apply to the Igbo, evidently perceived as a bad investment under slavery in different parts of the Atlantic world?

It is evident that many myths and stereotypes were associated with people from the bight in general and the Igbo in particular. Although the Igbo contribution to British trade in slaves was disproportionately high, Gomez and others have shown that "the demand for them in the New World was by no means consistent."[63] Slavers attitudes towards *ndi*Igbo slaves have helped magnify the identity of this relatively forgotten Diaspora. Indeed certain planters, Gomez has shown, were "particularly loath to accept captives from the bight, associated as they were with tendencies inimical to the enterprise of slavery."[64] Some North American colonies/ states preferred not to import Igbo captives.[65] Hall agrees that "it is a truism in the historical literature that Igbo, especially Igbo males, were not at all appreciated in the America, mainly because of their propensity to run away and/or commit suicide."[66] South Carolina planter "expressed an abiding preference for Senegambia and Gold Coast captives but were "disdainful" of the Igbo/Biafra and "short people" in general."[67] Daniel Littlefield explains that Africans who were "small, slender, weak and tended towards a yellowish colour, were less desirable. Calabar people or Ibo (sic) slaves, with whatever justice, seemed to epitomize these qualities."[68]

A part of the myth surrounding the Igbo throughout the slave era was their tendency to run away or commit suicide. Igbo were loathed in North America primarily for what Gomez and others have identified as the frequency by which they "choose the way of self-destruction (suicide)." But how did a practice so despised in Igboland become very much associated with them in the disapora. The Igbo abhorred suicide in their traditional society. Victims were not given normal burial but were thrown into the "evil forest." Special rituals are often performed by the priest of *Amadioha* (the god of thunder) before victims of suicidal death were buried.

Amid the inhumanity of slavery, the Igbo, like many other slaves responded in unique ways, sometimes taking their own lives. The myth about Igbo suicidal tendencies proved remarkably resilient—and the identity of Igbos as trouble makers crystallized on a wider scale and inspired by racist stereotypes, even among slaves. Like other slaves, the Igbo employed old strategies including revolts and escape, but they devised new strategies in their struggle including suicide.

To explain their propensity for suicide as groups and as individuals, one has also to understand the cosmology of the Igbo and their attachment to the land of their birth. The Igbo have a real attachment to the land (*ala*) literarily and symbolically. The unit of production was the family, made of a man, his wife or wives, and their unmarried children. The production unit had access to land for production, rituals, burials, etc. land was not just a factor of production, but it remained a link with the ancestors. For instance, the umbilical cord of a new born child is buries in ancestral land—that way the Igbo can make connection between the living and the land and between the land and the ancestors. Uprooted from the connection with the land and the ancestors which was vital to their Identity, the Igbo responded emphatically by committing what may be describes as "acceptable abomination." In the context of slavery, suicide was perhaps a justifiable evil and one that the ancestors would be willing to accommodate. This rationality was of course lost to New World scholars, a fact that scholars have failed to link to Igbo cosmology, attitude towards death and the fundamental belief in life after death.

Those from the Bight of Biafra, however, were largely accepted in the Chesapeake.[69] In contrast to the Akan and others, Gomez argues, there are relatively numerous accounts of runaway Igbo women. Littlefield confirms that "it is remarkable that Ibos as a group and the Bight as an area had a greater proportional representation of women among runaways that were produced by the native populace of South Carolina. In this they differed from all other African entities."[70] Elizabeth Donnan has shown however, that it was because Virginian planters were uninterested in the ethnic origins of the Africans that they imported a large number from the Bight of Biafra, a reflection of their dominant representation in the British slave pool as a whole.[71] In fact, James Rawley argued that the divergence between Virginia and South Carolina in their receptivity to the Igbo was such that the formers importation of the Igbo between 1710 and 1760 constituted some 38 percent of its total importation of Africans, a figure that mirrors precisely the British export trade from Africa.[72] The Igbo were purchased in high percentages in Virginia, Hall argues, "because the poverty of slave owners left them no alternative."[73]

Ironically, some deeply rooted qualities that some planters found attractive were the same qualities that drove them toward suicidal tendencies. The Igbo shared unique ethnic identity and characteristics that made them attractive to certain planters. Colin Palmer described the Igbo as a group that: ". . . were considered tractable and hence were highly sought after by some of the slaveholders in the Americas."[74] Malcom Laing writing to William Philip Perrin on 10 January1773 noted: "the new negroes that have been imported lately are what we call Windward Negros . . . the worst kind . . . imported here for labour except the Angolas . . . to buy such negros for sugar works is throwing away money"; will try to buy Gold Coast men and Ibo women."[75] As Moreau de St-Mery notes, some St. Dominque planters hesitated to buy Igbo slaves because of their suicidal tendencies, others preferred them because they were very attached to each other and "the newly arrived find help, care, and example from those who have come before them."[76] This ethos is deeply rooted in the traditional humane living among the Igbo.[77]

What emerges from these descriptions and stigmatization of the Igbo in South Carolina, Georgia, and other parts of the Atlantic world is a group of people who responded to their victimization in very emphatic, decisive, and irreversible ways. The conditions of slavery and victimization explain their prominence in suicide accounts despite their small number in South Carolina. In contrast, among Virginia and Maryland planters, Gomez notes, that there was relative absence of comparable traditions concerning Igbo behavior and response although both the Igbo and non-Igbo groups must have resisted their subjugation.[78] Anthony de Verteuil suggests that the Igbo, the largest group in Trinidad adjusted well to slavery because of the relatively benign system in Trinidad when compared to Jamaica, where Igbo rate of suicide and rebellion were high.[79] Indeed, the sense of inequality that characterized slave societies was at odds with the libertarian tendencies of their African homeland. But this body of mythology surrounding enslaved Igbo had not universal application in the diaspora.

Igbo response had much to do with their identity, unconventional response to slavery and unconformity with the stereotypes and perception of slaves by planters. The Igbo lacked the strategy of accommodation, compromise, and docility that endured slavers with other ethnicities. The republican ideals of the Igbo was obviously at odds with the institution of slavery; their attitude towards masters and the institution itself drew heavily from an identity formed and derived from the African background.

However, there are difficulties in simplifying these processes or avoiding reductionism. Obviously, there were differences between the process of identity formation and the resulting product. Functionality was key to their perception of their environment and adaptation to it. Why for example did the Igbo respond different to slavery in Jamaica and Trinidad? Why was the perception about the Igbo different from one part of the Atlantic world to the other?

The case of the Igbo raises important questions including the "fungibility of identity," and suggests that identities were neither static in Africa or the Atlantic world but rather flexible but shaped by previous experiences. This was particularly influential in shaping whatever new tendencies in the new world. The extent to which the dislike for the Igbo captives generally affected the creation of a new identity (whether to identify as Igbo or not) may provide more evidence to explain the relative absence of Igbo culture in the diaspora despite their numbers. Much emphasis has been placed on the seeking evidence of preservations but with no attempt to acknowledge what Cohen has termed "retribalization" either by Africans themselves of by the slave holders.[80]

Igbo consciousness and the negative stereotypes that scholars have outlined highlights the social and symbolic value of freedom and independence in the African world and helps explain Igbo resistance.

CONTINUITY AND CHANGE IN THE ATLANTIC DIASPORA

The scholarship and general commentaries on the Igbo is instructive about the influence of the Igbo cosmology in shaping their identity and suggests that certain elements and stereotypes associated with the Igbo were new World developments that emerged from the specific ways the Igbo responded to enslavement. Indeed, contrary to common assumptions, the lack of a pan-Igbo identity did not derive from unswerving loyalty based on sentimental attachment to a local community. Indeed, a cursory examination of their African origin explains Igbo uniqueness. Igbo self-identification among contemporary societies is not markedly different from how the Igbo diaspora identified themselves during slavery. While the Igbo language was a force that defined a pan-Igbo identity, many other forces upon which African identities were built have often lacked homogeneity among the Igbo. In many African societies, name and common identity was sometimes forged by the creation of a new powerful state.

Let us consider the case of the Yoruba. The Igbo lacked such centralized political and religious institutions, which brought large populations together and created a universal identity for groups such as the Yoruba. Second, unlike the Yoruba, where religious deities have a pan-Yoruba influence; Igbo communities worshiped several deities that often lacked any influence beyond their immediate locale, although the reputation of a select few such as *Kamalu* of Ozuzu, and *Ibini Ukpabi* of Arochukwu spread beyond the immediate communities that were custodians of these deities. Among the Igbo also, there are no universal myth of origin, or legendary progenitor of the Igbo, such as the Oduduwa myth and the greatest symbol of pan-Yoruba identity. Thus, religion and political institutions provided the consciousness of a common Yoruba identity before the arrival of the Europeans in the nineteenth century. But while the Igbo may have shared a common language, a common sense of origin and identity and developed much later on because locality formed the basis of religious, political, and social interaction was destroyed by the pattern of slavery. Like their kin in the Atlantic diaspora, the Igbo forged, in the wake of slavery (for those in the diaspora), and European encounter (for those in Africa), a new sense of identity based on a common language and new historical experience.

It is strongly believed that the way Igbo exiles related to their new environment and enslavement was influenced by their African experience. Unlike the Igbo, the legacies of the various ethnic cultures from where slavers drew remained ingrained as they are moved across the Atlantic. From the West African coast, most other groups had traditions of centralized authorities, kingship and aristocratic tendencies most of whom welded both political and religious powers over subject peoples. Thus, slaves from Benin, Huasaland, and Yoruba land had traditions of overseers, conformity to authority and control. The Igbo are very individualistic. This is very important in understanding the attachment to locality rather than to a Pan-Igbo identity within Igboland. Once outside, Igboland, however, this individual identity and strong loyalty to the locality transformed to make the new and unfamiliar environment meaningful. That Equiano, for example, continued to use a generic name 'country' to designate his homeland did not necessarily mean that there was not an Igbo nation. Although generalization are dangerous at this stage until further research is made, one can trace Igbo identity from their distinct set of behavior (social and ideological) that marked them not only as a peculiar group to slave owners but also the special ways by which they adapted to their environment.

Largely, the perceived cohesion and Igbo identity that developed in the diaspora can be traced to the strong identification with the local community. In other words, the Igbo were not creating a new identity, but rather rebuilt a community to reinforce the identity of their old world. Within the structure of the slave society, which largely reduced individual autonomy, the Igbo must have attempted to strike a balance between individual autonomy and servitude with community identity. Writing on the Igbo susceptibility to change in another context, John C. Merriam, notes that the Igbo "in Nigerian history were a relatively insignificant tribe, but their society had achievement based norms that adapted quickly to Westernization.[81] The Igbo of the eighteenth century were primarily loyal to their respective village and village groups, but they were very much aware of their shared qualities and identities as Igbo. This "latent potential of Igbo ethnicity, according to Gomez "matured very rapidly under the pressure of North American slavery."[82] Largely, therefore, the distinct political institutions, religious and ideological perspective of the Igbo informed the behavior of those enslaved in the Americas and must have left their mark on the New World cultures.

Despite the fragmentary nature of information on the Igbo Diaspora, some tentative conclusions can be made. In mainland North America, the discriminatory tendencies of planters throughout the colonies resulted in distinct patterns of ethnic distribution. Such patterns Gomez argues assist immensely in any analysis of subsequent sociocultural development, operating under the premise that black life and culture in a given area evolved out of and in creative tension with norms associated with specific ethnic groups imported via the slave trade.[83] Gomez argues for example that Virginia and Maryland developed a servile population largely out of Igbo (in majority) and Akan antecedents. Both groups were largely rural, their diet equally dependent upon root crops.

Douglas Chambers also identifies evidence of what he calls Igboisms in Anglophone American slave societies, which includes Igbo dietary habits. *Okoro* for example a staple in slave diet and "one pot" cooking practices is identified as Igbo in origin. "The vegetal part of the basket of African-American "soul food" indicates a strong Igbo presence in Anglophone slave food ways. Most important were yams, black-eyed peas, and greens."[84] These were the basic food crops in nineteenth and early twentieth century Igbo society. In the Diaspora, the Igbo continued to grow yams and maintained nearly all the secondary subsistence crops of their ancestral village agriculture.[85]

There is also clear evidence of Igbo influence in power ways, which Fischer has defined as "attitudes towards authority and power" and "patterns of political participation."[86] Slaves in the Americas drew on similar social resources to order their individual and collective lives. Though there was no major slave rebellion in areas such as the Chesapeake and western Jamaica were there was a strong Igbo presence, Igbo slaves tended to resort more to resistance either suicide, escape or to get some concession. Such political consciousness was also important in the way Igbo women featured largely amongst runaways in America.[87] The collective identity of the Igbo, like many other African ethnicities, was fundamental in their response and recreation to their new world in the Americas. Their sense of independence can be traced to Igboland itself where they were prominent in the political, economic and social arrangements of society. Igbo society had established a high regard for women, reflected by such evidence as the veneration and popularity of the earth mother (*ala*), the perfection of gender balance and the independent spirit exhibited by Igbo women in their new environment.[88]

At the cosmological level, the Igbo like other African groups seemed to have retained a lot of their spiritual world view. The Igbo slaves drew on their African institution to recreate the world familiar to them and to maintain contact with the spirit world and their personal god (*chi*). Two institutions in Igboland that were recreated include the *ahiajoku*, yam spirit cult and *Okonko* society. It is likely, Chambers argues, that diasporic Igbo combined these essentially shared traditions into a Creole institution in the *jonkonu* masquerade.[89]

This speculation is problematic for a number of reasons. First, *ahiajoku*, and the ritualized nature of the festival is directly associated with the planting and harvesting of yams. In the absence of large-scale yam cultivation, the ritual importance of *ahiajoku* would have diminished. Second, *Okonko* was not a pan-Igbo phenomenon and masquerading wide-spread throughout sub-Saharan Africa.

Chambers has also drawn attention to other evidence of Igbo continuities as can be found in the system of "doctoring" called 'obeah.' According to Chambers, Igbo slaves drew on ancestral ideological resources to make sense of their new environment and in the process "Igboized" slave religious tradition throughout British America. Chambers identifies a strong link between the function of *obeah* men and women in the diaspora to the functions of *dibia* (medicine men) in Igboland.[90]

CONCLUSION

African agencies were central to the formation of identities in the Atlantic world. Yet African identities saw important transformations in response to New World cultures, the institution of slavery and demographic characteristics of specific African groups in locations in the Americas. Such New World cultures and identities were influenced by several forces including location, the functioning of specific slave societies, the attitude of slave holding society, and the immediate influence of the dominant African culture in specific regions of the America.

NOTES

1.   See for example, David Eltis et al, *The Transatlantic Slave Trade: A Database on CD-ROM* (New York: Cambridge University Press, 1999).

2. E. Franklin Frazier, *The Negro Family in the United States* (Chicago: University of Chicago Press, 1939). See also Franklin Frazier, *Negro Church in America* (New York: Schocken, 1974).
3. Melville J. Herskovits, *The Myth of the Negro Past* (Boston: Beacon Press, 1941).
4. Ibid.
5. Michael A. Hogg, Deborah J. Terry, and Katherine M. White, "A Tale of Two Theories: A Critical Comparison of Identity Theory with Social Identity Theory," *Social Psychology Quarterly* 58 (1995): 255-69. Cited in Neal G. Jesse and Kristen P. Williams, *Identity and Institutions: Conflict Reduction in Divided Societies* (Albany: State University of New York Press, 2005), 4.
6. Sidney Mintz and Richard Price, *An Anthropological Approach to Afro-American Past: A Caribbean Perspective* (Philadelphia: Institute for the Study of Human Issues, 1976).
7. Mintz and Price, *An Anthropological Approach*, 3-26. See also Morgan, "Cultural Implications of the Slave Trade," essentially making the same argument, and Paul E. Lovejoy, "Situating Identities in the African Diaspora: Islam and Slavery in the Americas," Harriet Tubman Seminar, York University, 1998. Lovejoy essentially argues for Old World influences on the New.
8. John Thornton, *Africa and Africans in the Making of the Atlantic World, 1400-1680* (Cambridge: Cambridge University Press, 1982), 183.
9. Mintz and Price, *Afro-American Past*, 5-8.
10. David Eltis, "Ethnicity in the Early Modern Atlantic World," paper presented at the Harriet Tubman Seminar, York University, 26 January 1999.
11. Herbert S. Klein, *African Slavery in Latin America and the Caribbean* (New York: Oxford University Press, 1986), 163.
12. Philip D. Morgan, "The Cultural Implications of the Atlantic Slave Trade: African Regional Origins, American Destinations and New World Development," *Slavery and Abolition* 18, no. 1 (1997), 122.
13. Philip Morgan, "Rethinking American Slavery," cited in Lovejoy, "Situating Identities." See also, Thornton, *Africa and Africans.*
14. Paul E. Lovejoy, "The African Diaspora: Revisionist Interpretations of Ethnicity, Culture and Religion under Slavery," *Studies in the World History of Slavery, Abolition and Emancipation* II, 1 (1997), <21 January 2002>. http://www2.hnet.msu.edu/~slavery/essays/esy9701love.html <9 October 2002>.
15. For more recent scholarships see for example Paul E. Lovejoy and David V. Trotman, eds., *Trans-Atlantic Dimensions of Ethnicity in the African Diaspora* (London and New York: Continuum, 2003).
16. Paul E. Lovejoy and David V. Trotman, "Introduction: Ethnicity and the African Diaspora," in Paul E. Lovejoy and David V. Trotman, eds., *Trans-*

Atlantic Dimensions of Ethnicity in the African Diaspora (London and New York: Continuum, 2003).

17. Lovejoy and Trotman, "Introduction," *Trans-Atlantic*, 1-8.

18. Stampp, "Between Two Cultures." See also Thornton, *African and Africans*, 129.

19. Gwendolyn M. Hall, *Slavery and African Ethnicities in the America: Restoring the Links* (Chapel Hill: University of North Carolina Press, 2005), 56.

20. See, David Eltis, et al., *The Transatlantic Slave Trade: A Database*.

21. For some analysis, see Paul Lovejoy, "Identifying Enslaved Africans: Methodological and Conceptual Considerations in Studying the African Diaspora," *Identifying Enslaved Africans: The "Nigerian Hinterland" and the African Diaspora*, proceedings of the UNESCO/SSHRCC, Summer Institute, York University, 1997; Thornton, *Africa and Africans*, especially 192-205; David Eltis and Stanley L. Engerman, "The 'Numbers Game' and routes to Slavery," *Slavery and Abolition* 18, no. 1 (1997): 1-15; David Richardson, "Slave Exports from West and West-Central." See also more recent data from *The Trans-Atlantic Database* and Eltis, "Ethnicity in Early Modern Atlantic World."

22. Robert Harms, *The Diligent: A Voyage through the Worlds of the Slave Trade* (New York: Basic Books, 2001).

23. See Eltis, *The Atlantic Slave Trade Data Base*. See also Public Record Office/ CO 388/10 for information on the slave ship, *Two Friends*.

24. Thornton, *Africa and Africans*, 204-5.

25. Lovejoy, "The African Diaspora." See also Thornton, *Africa and Africans*, 205. Thornton argues that slaves although no longer surrounded by their familiar home environment, were nevertheless not in a cultural wilderness when they arrived in America as they could easily find others who spoke their language and shared common norms in the new environment especially if they were on a large estate.

26. Kenneth M. Stampp, "Between Two Cultures," in Peter I. Rose ed., *Americans from Africa: Slavery and its Aftermath* (New York: Atherton Press, 1970), 56.

27. Thornton, *African and Africans*, 129.

28. Unlike many other parts of the New World, conditions in what became the United States and conditions of life destroyed the significance of their African heritage and caused new habits and attitudes to develop to meet new situations. See E. Franklin Frazier, "The Significance of the African Background," in, *Americans from Africa: Slavery and its Aftermath* ed. Peter I. Rose (New York: Atherton Press, 1970), 37-8.

29. Lovejoy, "Situating Identities."

30. See David Eltis and David Richardson, "West Africa and the Transatlantic Slave trade: New Evidence on Long Run Trends," *Slavery and Abolition* 18, no. 1, (1997): 18-21.

31. See Douglas B. Chambers, "'My own nation': Igbo Exiles in the Diaspora', *Slavery and Abolition* 18 no. 1, (1997): 72-97. For African export figure for 1470s-1699, see Paul E. Lovejoy, "The Volume of the Atlantic Slave Trade: A synthesis," *Journal of African History*, 23 (1982), especially, 478-481; for 1700-1809 see Richardson, "Slave Exports from West and West-Central Africa, 1700-1810: New Estimates of Volume and Distribution," *Journal of African History* 30 (1989), 3, 6-17; and 1811-1870, see David Eltis, *Economic Growth and the Ending of the Transatlantic Slave Trade* (New York, 1987), 249, 250-2. Chambers based his estimate for Igbo numbers on these sources. See note 17.

32. Chambers, "'My own nation,'" 75-7.

33. Ibid., 77.

34. Ibid.

35. Paul E. Lovejoy, "Situating Identities in the African Diaspora."

36. On several slave voyages, see Eltis, et al., *The Trans-Atlantic Slave Trade: A Database.*

37. An important data that sheds light on the demographics and regional character of the trade include Eltis, Transatlantic *Slave Trade Database.*

38. Frazier, "The Significance of the African Background," 39. Cf. the term, "Red Ibo" to designate fair skinned African slaves in Jamaica a term still in use today.

39. Thornton, *Africa and Africans*, 114.

40. Olaudah Equiano, *The Interesting Narrative of Olaudah Equiano, Written by Himself* (ed.) Robert J. Allison (original edition, 1789; Boston, 1995 edition).

41. Vincent Carretta, *Equiano, the African: Biography of a Self-Made Man* (Athens: The University of Georgia Press, 2005).

42. Philip D. Morgan, "Trends in the Study of Early American Slavery of Potential Interest to Archaeologists," presented at the Digital Archeological Archives of Chesapeake's Slavery Steering Committee Workshop, Charlottesville, 6 October 2000, 3. See also David Northrup, "Becoming African: Identity formation among liberated slaves in nineteenth-century Sierra Leone," *Slavery and Abolition*, 27, no.1 (April 2006): 1-21.

43. "Mr. John Grazilhier's voyage from Bandy to New Calabar," in John Barbot, *A Description of the Coasts of North and South Guinea* (Vol. V in Churchill's *Voyages and Travels* (London, 1746), 380-1. Cited in Elizabeth Isichei, *Igbo Worlds: An Anthology of Oral Histories and Historical Descriptions* (Philadelphia: Institute for the Study of Human Issues, 1978), 10.

44. William Balfour Baikie, *Narrative of an Exploring Voyage up the River Kwora and Binue* (1856, London, 1966 edition), 307.
45. Amartya Sen, "Indian Traditions and the Western Imagination," *Daedalus* 216, 2, (1997), 2.
46. Fredrik Barth, "Introduction," 9-38 in F. Barth (ed.) *Ethnic Groups and Boundaries* (Boston: Little, Brown, 1969).
47. Gerald W. Kleis, "Confrontation and Incorporation: Igbo Ethnicity in Cameroon," *African Studies Review* 23, no. 3 (Dec., 1980) 89-100.
48. Elizabeth Isichei, *A History of the Igbo People* (New York: St. Martin's Press, 1976), 3.
49. New York: St. Martin's Press, 1976.
50. Victor Uchendu, *The Igbo of Southeastern Nigeria* (New York, 1965), 41-46. There were exceptions. Some Igbo communities like Onitsha, Oguta and Nri had chieftaincy institutions in pre-colonial times.
51. Cyril Agodi Onwumechili, "Igbo Enwe Eze: The Igbo Have No Kings," The 2000 Ahiajoku Lecture (Owerri: Ministry of Information, 2000).
52. Major Darwin; Walter Egerton; Dr Falconer; A. E. Kitson, "Southern Nigeria: Some Considerations of Its Structure, People, and Natural History: Discussion," *The Geographical Journal* 41, no. 1 (Jan 1913): 34-38.
53. S. Cronje, *The World and Nigeria* (London: Sidgwick and Jackson, 1972). Cited in Ekwe Nche Organization, "Leadership in Igbo Society: Analysis, Challenges and Solutions," http://www.biafraland.com/leadership_Igbo%20Identity.rtf. <12 December 2004>.
54. G. I. Jones, *Report on the Position, Status and Influence of Chiefs and Natural Rulers in the Eastern Region of Nigeria* (Enugu: Government Printer, 1957).
55. Obafemi Awolowo, *Path to Nigerian Freedom* (London: Faber and Faber, 1947).
56. *Look*, November 26, 1968.
57. *Time*, August 23, 1968.
58. Ekwe Nche Organization, "Leadership in Igbo Society." http://www.biafraland.com/leadership_Igbo%20Identity.rtf.< 12 December 2004>.
59. Ibid.
60. Ibid.
61. Translated literally, the term "intellectual" (*inwe ugugu isi,*) or "to posses brain power or be knowledgeable" defined traditional intellectuals among the Igbo and other Eastern Nigerian societies.
62. Traditional tittles in Igbo society can be grouped into four main categories: (i) symbolic titles or those emanating from acquisition of wealth; (ii) those awarded due to heroic achievement, (iii) honorary awards and (v) ascribed or titles of institutionalized social force origin. The *Duru* and *Ozo* titles are example of status symbols among the Igbo. Its legitimacy was enhanced if

conferred by the Nri since they are the direct descendants of Eri (a legendary figure regarded as the creator of the earth). An *ozo* title holder was revered and possessed a kind of diplomatic immunity that is respected throughout Igboland.

63. Michael A. Gomez, *Exchanging our Country Marks: The Transformation of African Identities in the Colonial and Ante-bellum South* (Chapel Hill and London: The University of North Carolina Press, 1998), 115.

64. See, Gomez, *Exchanging*, 114. See also David Brion Davis, *The Problem of Slavery in the Age of Revolution 1770-1823* (Ithaca: Cornell University Press, 1975). The Igbo reputation as 'bad' slaves who tended to run away, shrink work or commit suicide instead of facing perpetual servitude must have contributed to the social relation of slavery in the areas where there were substantial numbers of Igbo. See Chambers, "Igbo Exiles," note 21.

65. Chambers, "Igbo Exiles in the Diaspora," note 21.

66. Hall, "The Igbo," *Slavery and African Ethnicities*, 139.

67. Donnan, in Gomez, *Exchanging our Country Marks,* 115.

68. See Daniel C. Littlefield, *Rice and Slaves: Ethnicity and the Slave Trade in Colonial South Carolina* (Baton Rouge: Louisiana State University Press, 1981), 10 in Gomez, *Exchanging our Country Marks,* 115. While these stereotypes may not indicate Igbo origin, Jamaican folklore also refers to people with a yellowish skin as 'Red Ibo."

69. See James A. Rawley, *The Transatlantic Slave Trade: A History* (New York: W.W. Norton, 1981), 334-35.

70. Littlefield, *Rice and Slaves,* 143-55, in Gomez, *Exchanging our Country Marks,* 121.

71. Donnan in Philip D. Curtin, *The Atlantic Slave Trade: A Census,* (Madison: University of Wisconsin Press, 1969), 156-57; Elizabeth Donnan, "The Slave Trade into South Carolina before the Revolution," *American Historical Review* 33 (1927-28): 816-17. Cited in Gomez, *Exchanging our Country Marks.* See also Douglas Chambers, "Eboe, Kongo, Mandingo: African Ethnic groups and the Development of Regional Slave Societies in Mainland North America," International Seminar, "The History of the Atlantic World," Harvard University, 3-11 September 1996.

72. Cited in Gomez, *Exchanging our Country Marks,* 115. In contrast to Virginia, it has been estimated that South Carolina may have imported only 2 percent of its African captive population from the Bight of Biafra from 1733 to 1807.

73. Hall, *Slavery and African Ethnicities,* 139.

74. Colin Palmer, *Human Cargoes: The British Slave Trade to Spanish America, 1700-1939* (Urbana: University of Illinois Press, 1981), 29.

75. Derbyshire Record Office, D239 M/E 16753-16754, "West Indian papers," Plantations of William Perrin and William Philip Perrin, Correspondence of the Jamaican Attorneys, 10 January 1773.
76. Cited in Hall, *Slavery and African Ethnicities*, 126.
77. See Chieka Ifemesia, *Traditional Humane Living among the Igbo: An Historical Perspective* (Enugu: Fourth Dimension Publishers, 1979).
78. Gomez, *Exchanging our Country Marks*, 124.
79. Anthony de Verteuil, *Seven Slaves and Slavery: Trinidad, 1777-1838* (Port of Spain, Trinidad: Scrip–J Printers Limited, 1992).
80. Abner Cohen, *Custom and Politics in Urban Africa* (Berkeley: University of California Press, 1969), 1.
81. *The Harvard Crimson*, Nov. 12, 1968. Cited in Ekwe Nche Organization, "Leadership."
82. Gomez, *Exchanging our Country Marks*, 126.
83. Ibid., 146.
84. Chambers, "Igbo Exiles in the Diaspora," 85.
85. Ibid.
86. David Hackett Fischer, *Albion's Seed: Four British Folkways in America* (New York: Oxford University Press, 1989), 9. Cited in Chambers, "Igbo Exiles," 85.
87. Gomez, *Exchanging our Country Marks*, 126.
88. Cf. the 1929 Women's revolt in Eastern Nigeria during the colonial period and the part played by women in the post-emancipation slave revolts in Trinidad.
89. Chambers, "Igbo Exiles," 87.
90. Ibid. See also P. Amury Talbot, *Tribes of the Niger Delta: Their Religions and Customs* (London: The Sheldon Press, 1932); M. M. Green, *Ibo village Affairs* (New York: Frank Cass, 1964), 54, for the functions for *dibia* in Igboland. Compare also with Equiano, *The Interesting Narrative*, 12.

CHAPTER 14

IGBO WOMEN IN THE EARLY MODERN ATLANTIC WORLD: THE BURDEN OF BEAUTY

DOUGLAS B. CHAMBERS*

INTRODUCTION

Throughout the Atlantic world Igbo Africans had a reputation as 'bad' slaves. Stereotyped as lazy and despondent, ornery and obstreperous, and tending to bolt (and even commit suicide) rather than to revolt outright, Igbo resisted slavery in ways that confounded their masters.[1] As a German traveler to Bonny on the Calabar coast in 1840 learned, even after generations of slaving the Ibani still spoke of Igbo "as they would speak of sharks, 'Iboman wawa too much,' 'Ibo people are very wicked'." In other parts of the Atlantic littoral, like the Carolina lowcountry in the 1770s, other Africans berated Igbo as rogues. As a visitor to a late-colonial South Carolina rice plantation in the 1770s noted, slaves there would tease each others' African nationalities, especially 'Gulli' (Gullah, i.e., Ngola) and 'Iba' (Igbo) slaves. Barclay wrote that, "The one will say to the other, 'You be Gulli Niga, what be the use of you, you be good for nothing'. The other will reply, 'You be Iba Niga; Iba Niga great 'askal [rascal]'."[2]

Ironically, however, Igbo women had a surprisingly 'good' reputation. They were generally thought to be hard workers, industrious and diligent. And Igbo women were one of the few Atlantic Africans whom white men generally saw as beautiful.[3] In 1788 a major Bristol merchant trading to the West Indies wrote that, unlike females from the Gold Coast, "Eboe Women (from Bonny & New Calabar) are very fine and may be had."[4]

As Captain Hugh Crow, who traded extensively at Bonny from 1791 to 1808 wrote of enslaved Igbo at the coast, "many of their women are of remarkably symmetrical shape, and if white, would in Europe be deemed beautiful." A generation later (ca.1830), the Lander brothers, having come down the Niger from the north via Nupe, noted (and presumably in contrast to other Africans) that in riverain Igboland "the women are generally pretty."[5] A late-antebellum American (USA) evocation of this trope of the 'very fine' Igbo woman, a fictional "beautiful Eboe mulattress," exists even in the novels of Harriet Beecher Stowe.[6]

Within this circum-Atlantic white male gaze, this burden of beauty, enslaved Igbo women and their immediate descendants resisted slavery in distinctive ways. As with Igbo in general one could enslave the bodies of Biafran women, but not their minds. And in the Black Atlantic, it seems that enslaved Igbo women used their own bodies at times as sites of resistance. This paper will explore a central 'burden' of Igbo female beauty; strategic reproduction.

Jennifer L. Morgan's recent sweeping book on the significance of enslaved women in the emerging plantation societies of pre-1750 Anglophone America (in particular Barbados and South Carolina) provides new ways of thinking about gender and slavery in the Black Atlantic.[7] She argues that white male assumptions about black women and their sexuality in the construction of racism, and the reality of commercial consequences of childbirth for the slave master, as well as the centrality of slave women in actual work, and their laboring as cultural actors in the creolization of the slave population over time, all suggest that the study of slavery must *account* for women, not simply *include* them. This is especially true for Africans, particularly when their numbers were proportional to those of men, such as in the Anglophone Atlantic before ca.1750. In the slave-trade era and beyond, the depth of white stereotypes about African sexuality and the sexuality of African-American women in particular, underscores the importance of gender in understanding both slavery and the construction of racism.

I am also reminded of a traditional Igbo proverb, evocative of the patriarchal past (and still wielded in the present): "Do this, do that, does not allow a woman to grow a beard."[8] And yet, in the era of the slave-trade, Igbo women in particular bore the burden of a peculiar stereotype, a burden of beauty in a multi-veiled system of oppression (gender, race, status) within which they had to negotiate as best they could. For many, perhaps, the body and its reproductive potential was a means of agency, if at times a tragic one. As Morgan suggests, in the end what most directly distinguished enslaved women from men was the female body and its potential for reproduction; how it was represented, appropriated, exploited (and resisted), defended, and deployed. Given the peculiar stereotype of Igbo women as "very fine," perhaps they and their daughters may well have been the historical image which the distorting mirror of American racism shaped into the plantation myth of 'the Jezebel'.[9]

GYNEOLOGICAL REVOLTS

Many enslaved women, Igbo or otherwise, clearly rebelled by refusing to bear children, by self-restraining their "reproductive capacities...to damage the wealth and power of the slaveowner."[10] Sometimes others refused to raise those who *were* born, choosing infanticide over the bringing up of new children into the hellish conditions of slavery. In general, the very low birth rates that characterized enslaved populations in world history may well constitute, in the words of Orlando Patterson, a kind of generalized 'gynecological revolt'. Writing specifically of Jamaica after ca.1750, Patterson noted that at the height of the slave-trade, "all the available data suggest that not only was the mortality rate abnormally high but, more extraordinarily, slave women absolutely refused to reproduce - partly out of despair and outrage, as a form of gynecological revolt against the system, and to a lesser extent because of peculiar lactation practices."[11] In 1818, for example, Matthew Lewis noted that on his plantation in western Jamaica he held 330 slaves, with more women than men, and yet in the previous year no more than twelve or thirteen children were born, which was even fewer than the year before.

When considering Igbo women in particular, however, one perceives another kind of woman-centered resistance, what I will call 'gyneological revolt'. In this section of the paper I will use a series of stories, from the late-20th century backward in time to the early 18th, to suggest a line of female-reasoning, or *gyneo-logos*, which may be termed Igboesque. In effect, Igbo slave women sought to bear children as a form of resistance to their social and cultural marginalization.

IN IGBOLAND

In Obé village of the Nkanu village-group ('clan') of present-day Enugu state in north-central Igboland, in the two generations since

Nigerian independence the female descendants of slaves systematically increased their birth-rates as a means of resisting the continuing marginalization by the *Amadi* (free-born descendants). The idea has been to have more and more children in order to increase the proportion of the *Ohu* (or *Awhia*, slave descendants) in the immediate village-group. And this strategy of strategic reproduction has succeeded dramatically. Whereas the *Ohu* were about 2 or 3 percent of Obé's population in the 1950s, by the turn of the century they were between one-quarter and one-third. This local gyneological revolt was part of a larger history of struggle against their masters, stretching back to the 1920s.[12] However, in Obé the *Amadi* did not formally renounce their 'ownership' of the *Ohu* until 1988. Since then, the slave-descendants have demanded a new collective name, *Amaoji* ([people from] 'Big Tree Land'),[13] and are asserting their right to self-representation. However, the strict ban on inter-marriage and the refusal to recognize *Amaoji / Ohu* seniors as structural elders have been largely maintained by the *Amadi*. The *Amadi* justify their coerced endogamy (enforced by threats of banishment, 'excommunication', and even death) by claiming that the *Amaoji* have 'bad blood'; selective gerontocracy rests on the same essentialist ideology.

In the early 1980s, my narrator also saw the flip-side of this gyneologos. He had graduated from university and returned to Nkanu, an educated and ambitious but poor *Amadi*. One night at a party he fell in lust with a beautiful girl, who also wanted to befriend him, but she was *Ohu*. She was beautiful but a 'slave.' When her cousins saw what was happening, they became angry because they knew the two could never marry, and thus that this *Amadi* must simply want to "use-less" her. As it turned out, my narrator did not have sex with her, because he was afraid that if she were to become pregnant that this would ruin his life. As my narrator explained:

> In primary school I had seen this happen to my star teacher who had sexed around with *Ohu*. And if there was a child, it belonged to the father of course, but would still be *Ohu* because the mother was *Ohu* and would have passed on her bad blood. In the past a father would have claimed such a child but then would have sent it away, or to another town, or simply sold it, or even put it out in the Bush because it was a useless thing. The girl could never expect to marry or would have been ruined, as would the father among his fellow *Amadi*.

In this case, the *Amaoji* cousins then sought to punish my narrator for having played around with the girl. And they did so by trying to poison him. A few days later he was invited to come drinking and they all had Guinness beer and they all used a glass but kept wanting my narrator to drink straight from a bottle which they had previously opened and given him. But he said to them, 'if a man is in a place where the people slit their ears then the man should also have his ear slit' (i.e., 'when in Rome') and so they gave him a glass and when he poured his glass the poison thing fell out into it, and my narrator did not take it. Later he found out from the girl and her friends that indeed those *Amaoji* boys had tried to poison him; the girl apparently had known about the plan but did not warn him.

Now let us shift backward in time to the 1920s. Throughout Igboland, indeed throughout the eastern provinces of recently amalgamated colonial Nigeria, people had been living under a "reign of terror." The failing Warrant Chief system (instituted ca.1903) had become increasingly corrupt, and since the pronouncement of the 1916 Native Authorities Ordinance there had been a fierce "scramble for warrants."[14] As well the world-wide Influenza Pandemic of 1918-19 ravaged Nigeria, causing perhaps a quarter-million deaths in the southern provinces out of an estimated population of 9 million. In some towns, the panic of the pandemic was marked by naming the ca.1919-21 age-grade after the disease (*Ogbo Ifelunza*). In others, the calamity in part sparked a rejection of even the deepest traditional practices, such as *mgburichi* facial scarification at Nri, the 'Jerusalem' of the Igbo; the ca.1918-20 male age-grade at Nri (*Ifedioranma* or *Ifediora*) was the first to generally not take the ennobling *ichi* scarification, which for a millennia had been the physical sign of Nri ritual royalty. Stopping *ichi* was taken as a mark of the men's embrace of "modernity."[15]

While the men, as a kind of *andro-logos* were abandoning certain ancient traditions to assert their modernity, at this time in Owerri Division women responded to the chaos of 'government time' by demanding a return to tradition. In the same year (1925) that the colonial divisional officer tried to manipulate the most basic form of traditional authority (the *ofo*) by making some men Warrant Chiefs simply because they were *ofo*-holders, women in the region organized an anti-colonial and anti-modernist movement.[16] They argued that Chukwu (God) demanded a return to ancient customs, and as proof of their opposition to 'government time' the women sought to increase their birth-rate. Strategic reproduction became their tactic of resistance to the chaotic 'reign of terror' of early colonialism. Four years later (1929) thousands of women in Owerri Division resorted to violence, incensed by rumors that the colonial state (through the Native Courts) was going to start taxing them directly. By the time the 1929 'Women's War' was bloodily suppressed, it had spread to coastal Opobo and into Ibibioland (Calabar Province); rioting women physically attacked 16 Native Courts and actually destroyed 12 of them.[17]

In both of these twentieth-century cases (1920s, 1970-80s), Igbo women initially responded to oppression by strategic reproduction, by moving to have more children. The *Amaoji* women of Obé self-consciously sought to increase their numbers even as the men continued to threaten with poison (as well as social sanctions) those who crossed the divide of slave and free status. The women in Owerri in the 1920s launched a cultural-revivalist movement, one that was explicitly anti-modernist as well as anti-colonial, by calling (in the wake of the catastrophe of the coming of the white man and the *ifelunza* and the warrant chiefs) for having more children. As the vice tightened they then turned to outright violence.

IN THE ATLANTIC WORLD

Let us now turn to the western landfall of the Atlantic, in the era of the slave trade. One small if notable corner of the Anglophone Americas with a sizeable presence of Igbo was the Chesapeake (Virginia and Maryland). Of the 63,500 Africans landed in the first half of the eighteenth century, well over half came from the Bight of Biafra. For Virginia, which always dominated the Chesapeake trade, after figuring percentages of percentages,[18] at least 25,000 Igbo wound up there, mostly in one wave, in the generation from ca.1710s to the 1740s.

The Chesapeake was also unusual for the relatively early and sustained growth of the slave population. From the 1730s, and especially after 1740, the slave population was able to reproduce itself. The numbers of slaves in Virginia more than doubled between 1720 and 1740 (from 26,500 to 60,000) and then doubled again (to 120,000) by 1755, and by 1760 there were over 140,000 black people in the colony.[19] Beyond the fact of a crude annual growth rate of about 3 percent (1730-1770), the most remarkable aspect was that the fastest population growth occurred in the decades of the most intensive importation of Africans (1730-1750), the height of the transatlantic slave trade to the colony.[20]

The 'natural increase' of the Chesapeake slave population was in stark contrast to the general case throughout the Americas, where the slave-trade suppressed population growth, as enslavement and the Middle Passage and plantation regimes all damaged the reproductive health of African women, many of whom also resisted 'gynecologically'.

The accepted explanation for the unusual demographic success of the slaves in 18th-century Virginia was the growing number, by about 1740, of native-born or creole slave women.[21] Creole women tended to have more children, and to have them earlier and at shorter intervals. In Virginia, wrote Alan Kulikoff, "While the black population may have barely replaced itself in the 1710s and 1720s, substantial natural population growth began in the 1730s, and the rate of growth probably increased in the 1740s and 1750s as the proportion of native women in the population rose."[22] What is most curious, however, is that this demographic breakthrough occurred at the precise historical moment when Africans (and often Igbo) were flooding the colony.

In fact the basic argument that creole population growth derived from creolization begs the question. Given that slaves in Virginia began to physically reproduce themselves during the very height of the slave-trade, when the proportion of African-born women in the slave population was likely increasing (rather than declining), one wonders whether there was also an ethnic cultural influence involved? As early as 1702 a Virginia merchant-planter wrote that African slaves "can be selected according to pleasure, young and old men and women. . . . Both sexes are usually bought, which increase afterwards."[23] The relatively balanced sex ratio of the slave trade to the Chesapeake meant that children of African-born parents were abundant. Given the centrality of the belief in reincarnation, for an Igbo woman, even (or especially) one torn from her village and thrown down half a world away into slavery, each birth required attending to the question of who was being (re)born. Or conversely, she would have had to reckon with the possibility that the child was an 'abomination', that is, something totally and utterly new.

In other parts of North America, at Pointe Coupée in Louisiana in the last quarter of the eighteenth century (1771-1802), for example, Gwendolyn Midlo Hall has found (from a quite small sample) that in this plantation outpost in the lower Mississippi Valley, Igbo women tended to have the highest birth-rate among African women. Like other Africans in this area, they also tended to marry within their nation. In this sample of 35 Igbo women, they had had at least 23 children.[24]

The issue would have been complicated when the father was a non-Igbo, or a white man. Another possibility is that some Igbo women sought out relations with non-Igbo men in the crucible of slavery, perhaps to counter the cultural assumption of carrying 'bad blood'. Relations with white men also carried the potentially bittersweet promise of eventual freedom.

We can perhaps see the Janus-face of this burden of beauty in two 'events' in 1730s Virginia. Again this was when the Virginia trade was utterly dominated by Bristol merchants and slaves from 'Calabar', the great majority of whom would have been Igbo.[25]

The first involved the unnamed African grandmother of Sally Hemings of Monticello, whom I will call 'Mother Gran' (for convenience). She was born ca.1710/1715 and would have been taken to the colony in the late-1720s or early 1730s. The family story is that 'Mother Gran' was a "fullblooded African," the slave of John Wayles (1715-1773) of Charles City County, in the lower peninsula between the York and James rivers.[26] In 1734/35 Mother Gran, who was likely in her late-teens or perhaps early twenties, had sex with an English ship captain named Hemings, and became pregnant, and in 1735 gave birth to a daughter whom she named Elizabeth (Betty).[27] Though certainly the threat of rape was always real, in this case it seems clear that this was a consensual relationship, or at least that Capt. Hemings is remembered as claiming his paternity and indeed he sought to first buy, then to steal away, this mixed-race child. Here is the distilled family oral history, from Madison Hemings (1873):

> Capt. Hemings happened to be in the port of Williamsburg at the time my grandmother was born [1735], and acknowledging her fatherhood he tried to purchase her of Mr. Wales, who would not part with the child, though he was offered an extraordinarily large price for her. She was named Elizabeth Hemings. Being thwarted in the purchase, and determined to own his own flesh and blood he resolved to take the child by force or stealth, but the knowledge of his intention coming to John Wales' ears, through leaky fellow servants of the mother, she and the child were taken into the 'great house' under their master's immediate care. I have been informed that it was not the extra value of that child over other slave children that induced Mr. Wales to refuse to sell it, for slave masters then, as in later days, had no compunctions of conscience which restrained them from parting mother and child of however tender age, but he was restrained by the fact that just about that time amalgamation began, and the child was so great a curiosity that its owner desired to raise it himself that he might see its outcome. Capt. Hemings soon afterwards sailed from Williamsburg, never to return. Such is the story that comes down to me.[28]

In the mid-1730s, then, a young African Arrivant woman apparently had consensual sex with a white ship captain, who cared enough (apparently) about the child she bore that he tried to buy his daughter, and then thwarted by the master's refusal to sell even schemed to steal her away. One can reasonably assume that Capt. Hemings would have carried the girl out of Virginia, and likely out of slavery; perhaps this was Mother Gran's intention too? The African Arrivant had created a 'white folk' of her own, as well as a 'curiosity' of a child. But the white father sailed off and abandoned Mother Gran, who then had the added burden of becoming a house-slave to a young master (and one who did not marry for another ten years).[29]

At this point and place in time, when mixed-race children were still "so great a curiosity," for an enslaved Igbo woman such a child would also have been an ontological anomaly. But if Mother Gran was Igbo and gambled on the 'good blood' of a white man, creating a new line of part-Igbo/part-white 'ancestors', the burden of her beauty eventually paid off. Her daughter grew up to have a relatively privileged life, and created 'white folk' and mixed-race children of her own, including with her master Wayles. The family story is that Elizabeth had "seven children by white men and seven by colored men - fourteen in all." Lucia Stanton has documented twelve children by at least three fathers, two of whom were white; four were born 1753-1761, then six by Wayles (1762-1773), and finally two born after Wayles had died (1776, 1777), one by a white man named Nelson.[30]

By 1773, Betty Hemings lived at a place called 'Guinea,' a 6 500-acre tract straddling Cumberland and Amelia counties, with six of her children and an infant grandson. At Guinea lived three families, which included Abram a carpenter, Barnaby (b.1760) a young blacksmith, and Phill a shoemaker. The other two households were Aggy and her two children, and Sall and her two children (one named Aggy, b.1769). With the interesting overlap of names (Betty and Sall both had sons named Jemmy, born 1765 and 1771, respectively; and the year the master died Betty named her new daughter Sally), and the privileged occupational status of this slave Quarter, it seems likely that these three families were closely related. This is all in stark contrast to another Wayles quarter called 'Angola', also in Cumberland County, which had no tradesmen; all five of the adults living there were field-slaves.[31]

One of Betty Hemings' daughters (Sally, 1773-1835), a product of that 'Guinea' (figuratively as well as literally), would in 1789 specifically trade her sexual being for the pledged future freedom of her children by Thomas Jefferson. In the end, Jefferson largely upheld his end of the infamous bargain (which Sally Hemings negotiated when pregnant with her first child in Paris, which ironically was not actually Jefferson's). The reputedly beautiful creole grand-daughter of the African Mother Gran had six or seven children with white men, of whom four lived to adulthood; Jefferson allowed two of his slave children (Beverley and Harriet) to escape to their freedom, and then manumitted the other two (Madison, Eston) by his will in 1826. Sally went to live with these two sons in Charlottesville as a nominally free woman, and in 1830 Sally, Madison and Eston were all listed in the federal census as white.[32]

Of course this added burden of being mixed-race, or of being a beautiful creole, did not necessarily mean 'becoming white.' In fact in Virginia in the 1780s, there is a record of a runaway slave woman described as 'a likely mulatto wench' (meaning an attractive mixed-race woman), but who otherwise was seen as decidedly African. In the summer of 1784 in Charlotte County in the southern piedmont, this woman ran away. She was born ca.1749 and as a 'mulatto' was probably creole (though perhaps she had been born on the slave ship, that is, was a 'saltwater creole'). She carried several physical burdens with her, having been "much whipped by her former master." But most remarkably, she was described by her current master as "outlandish" (the standard metaphor in Virginia for being a 'new Negro', that is, for acting African) and "has some of her country marks on one of her cheeks."[33]

The 'burden of beauty' could also result in collective violence against the master. In the 1730s, on another backcountry piedmont Virginia plantation, in a district settled by a series of chain migrations from the York River, that epicenter of the colony's trade in Igbo slaves, the *Ohu* (slaves) successfully poisoned the *Ézè Amadi* (free-born master). And one of the conspirators was a young slave woman.

In 1732 Ambrose Madison (ca.1696-1732), the grandfather of the future president James Madison, moved his family to join a community of slaves (most probably African, therefore likely Igbo, and their several creole children) in what was then western Spotsylvania County. These slaves had been 'seating' this new plantation (later called Montpelier) for perhaps a half-dozen years before the master arrived. Within six months he was poisoned in an apparent conspiracy among some of his slaves, no doubt in revenge.[34]

The conspirators were a young woman named Dido and another Madison-owned adult man named Turk, and a third slave Pompey who was owned by a neighbor. Madison apparently was poisoned in the summer and languished until dying in late-August. In September his planter peers tried the three slaves on "Suspition of Poysoning Ambroes Madison." The outsider Pompey was executed, probably because he supplied the poison (because he was a *dibia* or "conjureman"?), but quite surprisingly the two Madison-owned slaves were convicted only of misdemeanors. The court declared that they were "Concerned in the said ffelony, but not in Such a Decree as to be punished by Death," and instead were ordered to be whipped with 29 lashes "on their bare back at the Common Whiping post, and thereafter to be discharged . . . to their said Mistris [Mrs. Madison]."[35] As this was the first recorded use of poison to kill a master in Virginia, presumably the justices saw some exculpatory or extenuating circumstances in the case, or perhaps Dido and Turk really were not centrally involved, though that seems highly unlikely.

Instead, there is just a hint that this deadly conflict, which was resolved by the slaves in an extreme (and thoroughly Igbo) way, that is, by poisoning the master, had a sexual context. Though it can never be 'proved', it seems likely that Madison had either raped, or had tried to force, young Dido. And certainly in the emerging plantation world of the eighteenth-century Anglo-Atlantic, there were masters who became quite vicious serial rapists, such as Thomas Thistlewood (1721-1786) of western Jamaica, another heavily Igbo-influenced region.[36]

Nearly a century later in the 1820s an aged slave woman at James Madison's Montpelier, Granny Milly (b.ca.1721), hints at a historical connection. The prized possession of this remarkable slave woman, who lived to over 100 years and thus bridged the time of the Africans with the last decade of President Madison's life, was a bound copy of the Greek myth *Telemachus*.[37] She proudly pulled the book from her trunk and showed it off to visitors, including to Lafayette (and Dolley Madison) during his visit to Montpelier in 1825. She also apparently spoke French, and perhaps her copy was a French version of Fénelon's stridently anti-monarchical *Avantures de Telemaque*, which certainly would have pleased the old revolutionary Lafayette. Or perhaps the book had a deeper significance, one intimately connected with the charter event of Montpelier (the poisoning of old master by his 'African' slaves), to which Granny Milly was old enough to testify. Perhaps the book was in fact a *lieu de mémoire*, or site of memory. I imagine a series of symbolic associations with the Telemachus myth among the Madison slaves (with Granny Milly as the keeper of the tale); an epic story which culminated in an extreme act of violence over a burden of beauty; of how a son helped his long-lost father (Odysseus) slaughter the many unwanted suitors of the beautiful Penelope. It is a primordial story of revenge for 'rape' (or dishonor).[38] In any case, the collective burden at Montpelier was that the slaves killed Old Master Madison, and they did so through the classically African (and in particular, Igbo) technology of 'poison', and quite possibly in revenge over a wrong done by the master to a slave woman.

CONCLUSION

The irony for many enslaved Igbo women throughout the Atlantic world is that the cultural-physical markers of female beauty in what Equiano called "Eboan Africa," that is, inscribing the female body through cicatrisation, tattooing, teeth-filing (and excision or clitoridectomy, which was probably universal), as well as through ritual fattening for marriage, were 'outlandish' in their new world. In Igboland, women without those markers would have been dishonored, their beauty highly contingent, or else they would have been seen as slaves with 'bad blood'. And yet in the diaspora, such 'country marks' defined them as slaves, and their creole daughters would have been that much more beautiful without them. Perhaps this is why the "likely mulatto wench" who ran away in Charlotte County, Virginia was given "some of her country marks on one of her cheeks." Perhaps her mother, no doubt an African, marked this girl as *her own*, consciously subverting the mark of her mixed parentage, denying in the starkest way, in the flesh of the girl's face, the *burden* of her beauty.

Others carried their burden, seeking to produce children as a form of resistance, of gyneological revolt. In Igboland, as among *Amaoji* in Nkanu and women in general in colonial Owerri, having children was part of a larger strategy to confront marginalization. In the diaspora in the era of the slave trade, one may also see examples of strategic reproduction in regions such as the Chesapeake of North America, in particular Virginia, where Igbo slaves were numerous. The burden of beauty could cut both ways, as "very fine" Igbo women sought to resist dehumanization in the oppressive circumstances in which they found themselves. Their own bodies could be sites of resistance; that some slave women may have utilized themselves to counter the supposed 'bad blood' of slavery by producing children with their masters, or other white men, may be seen as a form of strategic reproduction.

NOTES

1. For summaries of these stereotypes in the secondary literature, see Ulrich Bonnell Phillips, *American Negro Slavery: A Survey of the Supply, Employment and Control of Negro Slavery* (1918; repr. Baton Rouge, LA, 1966), 43-4; Darold D. Wax, "Preferences for Slaves in Colonial America," *Journal of Negro History* 54, 4 (1973): 391-398; Johannes Postma, "The Origin of African Slaves: The Dutch Activities on the Guinea Coast, 1675-1795," in Stanley L. Engerman and Eugene D. Genovese, eds., *Race and Slavery in the Western Hemisphere: Quantitative Studies* (Princeton, 1975), 36; Daniel C. Littlefield, *Rice and Slaves: Ethnicity and the Slave Trade in Colonial South Carolina* (Baton Rouge, LA, 1981), 10, 72, 127, 150-151; Michael Mullin, *Africa in America: Slave Acculturation and Resistance in the American South and the British Caribbean, 1736-1831* (Urbana, Ill., 1992), 27; Michal A. Gomez, *Exchanging Our Country Marks: The Transformation of African Identities in the Colonial and Antebellum South* (Chapel Hill, NC, 1998), 116-17.

2. Hermann Koler (1840), quoted in Elizabeth Isichei, ed., *Igbo Worlds: An Anthology of Oral Histories and Historical Descriptions* (Philadelphia, PA, 1978), 15; James Barclay, *The Voyages and Travels of James Barclay, Containing Many Surprising Adventures and Interesting Narratives* (Dublin, Ireland, 1777), 26.

3. Phillips, *American Negro Slavery*, 43. See also 'Considerations on the Present Peace' (1763), in Elizabeth Donnan, ed., *Documents Illustrative of the History of the Slave Trade to America* (1931; repr. New York, 1969), II, 516-517. On the issue of European male conceptions of African female beauty, French men in eighteenth century Senegal also were said to be attracted to Wolof women because of their 'lustrous black skin' (beau noir lustré); Gwendolyn Midlo Hall, *Africans in Colonial Louisiana: The Development of Afro-Creole Culture in the Eighteenth Century* (Baton Rouge, LA, 1992), 40.

4. That is, may be purchased, or were available for sale at the coastal slave-trade entrepots; one should not assume that the author meant, in modern parlance, that Igbo women were "easy" or particularly "promiscuous." James Jones to Lord Hawksbury, in Littlefield, *Rice and Slaves*, 72. Jones (d.1795) was a prominent slave-trade merchant in the last quarter of the 18th century, who concentrated on the Bight of Biafra trade (and secondarily in the Gold Coast). He was the principal owner 60 slave shipments in the 1780s and 1790s, of which 31 were between 1789 and 1793. Of the 60 known shipments (involving some 17,600 slaves), nearly 70 percent were embarked in Biafra (with another 16 percent at the Gold Coast); two-thirds were disembarked at Jamaica, with the rest in smaller Caribbean islands, especially St. Vincent and Grenada; after David Eltis, et al., eds., *The Trans-Atlantic Slave Trade: A Database on CD-ROM* (Cambridge, 1999) [hereafter *TSTD*], query, 25-year period=1776-1800 and (First owner of venture=James, Jones AND Port of departure=Bristol); See also David Richardson, ed., *Bristol, Africa and the Eighteenth-Century Slave Trade to America*, 4 vols. (Bristol, UK, 1986-96), in particular *Vol.4: The Final Years, 1770-1807* (1996), xxx-xxxvii.

5. Quotations are from, respectively, Hugh Crow, *Memoirs of the late Captain Hugh Crow, of Liverpool* (1830; repr. London, 1970), 199; Richard Lander and John Lander, *Journal of an Expedition to Explore the Course and Termination of the Niger*, 2 vols. (New York, 1832), II, 233. Two other 1840s English sources, one on the Niger and the other on the Cross river, evoke the beauty of Igbo women: Capt. William Allen, *A Narrative of the Expedition Sent... to the River Niger in 1841* (London, 1848), I, 238; Capt. Becroft and J. B. King, "Details of Explorations of the Old Calabar River, in 1841 and 1842," *Journal of the Royal Geographical Society* 14 (1844), 271. Becroft and King had traveled up the Cross River beyond Old Calabar to see the slave-worked plantation of a local big-man (Anna), and when there met "several Eboes,

who were come to visit Anna, one of whose wives residing here, *a remarkably fine-looking woman*, is of their country" [my emphasis].

6. The mother of the novel's slave protagonist, Harry, who was also the son of his master Colonel Gordon; *Dred; A Tale of the Great Dismal Swamp*, 2 vols. (Boston, 1856), quote from I, 45.

7. *Laboring Women: Reproduction and Gender in New World Slavery* (Philadelphia, PA, 2004).

8. F. C. Ogbalu, *Ilu Igbo (The Book of Igbo Proverbs)*, 2nd ed. (Nigeria, 1965), 119. The subtextual meaning, of course, is "does not allow a woman to grow a [penis]."

9. For the 'Jezebel' myth of the oversexed female slave see Deborah Gray White, *Ar'n't I a Woman? Female Slaves in the Plantation South* (New York, 1985), 27-46.

10. Morgan, *Laboring Women*, 11.

11. Orlando Patterson, *Slavery and Social Death: A Comparative Study* (Cambridge, Mass., 1982), 133, 407-408 n3. Matthew Lewis, *Journal of a West India Proprietor* (1834; ed. Judith Terry, Oxford, 1999), 202. Part of the issue no doubt was that the women tended to breastfeed children for two years or more; Lewis tried to command that they wean their infants at 15 months (251). Snelgrave (1734) reported that at Old Calabar ca.1713 that women "generally suckle their Children till they are above two years old"; Ibid., xiii. In the 1920s, Talbot reported that mothers generally breastfeed children for two to four years; P. Amaury Talbot, *The Peoples of Southern Nigeria* (London, 1926), II, 378-381.

12. In the southern areas of UmuNkanu, such as Agbani, slaves had been much more numerous, and in the 1920s in some villages they were a majority. Nigeria Field Notes 2005, Interview with Anayo Enechukwu, Esq., (b.1961), at Obé, Nkanu West, Enugu State, Nigeria (5 March 2005). Throughout the Nkanu region slavery had been particularly oppressive; Carolyn A. Brown, "Testing the Boundaries of Marginality: Twentieth-Century Slavery and Emancipation Struggles in Nkanu, Northern Igboland, 1920-29," *Journal of African History* 37, 1 (1996): 51-80. For a general history of this region see Anayo Enechukwu, *History of Nkanu* (Enugu, Nigeria, 1993).

13. Replacing the previous self-asserted name of *Awbia* ('strangers') which came out of the slave insurrection of 1922-23 in the Agbani area to the south of Obé; Brown, "Testing the Boundaries," 77.

14. A. E. Afigbo, *The Warrant Chiefs: Indirect Rule in Southeastern Nigeria 1891-1929* (New York, 1972), quotations from, respectively, 272, 174.

15. D. C. Ohadike, "The Influenza Pandemic of 1918-19 and the Spread of Cassava Cultivation in the Lower Niger: A Study in Historical Linkages," *Journal of African History* 22, 3 (1981), 384, 386. The town referenced is

Igbuzo in Anioma (Ika Igbo), originally settled by people from Isuama; Don C. Ohadike, *Anioma: A Social History of the Western Igbo People* (Athens, OH, 1994), 17-19. Only 8 of the 100 members in *Ogbo Ifedioranma* of Nri, born on either side of the 1918-19 pandemic, eventually took *ichi*; Prince P.N. Mebuge-Obaa II, "Age Grade/Group (Oral History Project)" (TMs., December 2003). Most refused to do so as a sign of their modernity; Nri Field Notes 2003, Interview with Wilson Abana (b.ca.1910), Nri, Anambra State (December 2003). Today in Nri, only about four *mgburichi* are still alive; Nri Field Notes 2003, Nigeria Field Notes 2005, Interviews with Ichie Okoye Mmefu, who is one of the four (December 2003, March 2005). For dating of *Ogbo Ifedioranma*, see 'Tradition and Modernisation in Nri', vol.2 (pamphlet, n.d. [post-1989]); though Michael Onwuejeogwu dates the age-group as 1915-17; idem, *An Igbo Civilization: Nri Kingdom & Hegemony* (London, 1981), 139.

16. The 1925 Owerri women's movement is noted in C. K. Meek, *Law and Authority in a Nigerian Tribe* (1937; repr. New York, 1970), 201-202. *Ofo* was (and is) the ancestral staff of authority, bestowed on heads of families, the symbol of truth and justice, and a staff of office: see John N. Oriji, "Sacred Authority in Igbo Society," *Archives de Sciences Sociales des Religions* 68, 1 (1989), 118; A. E. Afigbo, "Prolegomena to the Study of the Culture History of the Igbo-speaking Peoples of Nigeria," in B. K. Swartz and Raymond E. Dumett, eds., *West African Cultural Dynamics* (The Hague, The Netherlands, 1980), 316.

17. Afigbo, *Warrant Chiefs*, 237-248. The British responded by sending troops and firing on the crowds of women; in Calabar Province 53 women were killed and 50 wounded (and of these 32 and 31, respectively, were at Opobo). These women groups generally attacked Warrant Chiefs and Native Courts.

18. Some 57 percent of the estimated 56,369 disembarked, of whom 75-80 percent were likely to be Igbo; after *TSTD*; see also Douglas B. Chambers, *Murder at Montpelier: Igbo Africans in Virginia* (Jackson, MS, 2005), 77-78, 193-197.

19. Douglas B. Chambers, "'He Is an African But Speaks Plain': Historical Creolization in Eighteenth-Century Virginia," in Alusine Jalloh and Stephen E. Maizlish, eds., *The African Diaspora* (College Station, TX, 1996), Table I, 110.

20. Allan Kulikoff, "A 'Prolifick' People: Black Population Growth in the Chesapeake Colonies," *Southern Studies* 16, 4 (1977), 393.

21. Kulikoff, "'Prolifick' People," 406-409, 412-413. The basic demographic variables included black birth rate, adult death rate, infant/childhood mortality, sex ratio (396-406).

22. Ibid, 412.

23. Quoted in Donnan, ed., *Documents*, IV, 68. Twenty years later (1723) another noted that Calabar Africans were "one of the sorts usually carried to Virginia" (107).

24. Hall, *Africans in Colonial Louisiana*, 294, 299. In a larger sample of 462 creole and African mothers, with some 327 children under age 15, creole women were twice as 'fertile' as African women, with child/woman ratios of .665 and .313, respectively; that is, the 203 creole women had 195 children whereas the 259 African women had 132 children (297).

25. There were 43 recorded shipments of slaves to the York River between 1726 and 1735, carrying some 11,000 African slaves; nearly 60 percent originated in the Bight of Biafra, or more than twice as many as the next most numerous provenance (West-Central Africa); *TSTD*.

26. What little is known of her is from the published memoir of her great-grandson Madison Hemings (1805-1877), which were published in an Ohio newspaper in 1873; reprinted in Annette Gordon-Reed, *Thomas Jefferson and Sally Hemings: An American Controversy* (Charlottesville, VA, 1997), 245-248. John Wayles, the father-in-law of Thomas Jefferson, remains a relatively little-known character as his papers were largely lost, as were the records of Charles City County (in the Civil War); but see the various manuscript and typescript materials in the John Wayles Files, International Center for Jefferson Studies Research Center [ICJS], at Monticello.

27. Betty Hemings (1735-1807); see genealogical tables in Lucia Stanton, *Free Some Day: The African-American Families of Monticello* (Charlottesville, VA, 2000), opp. 192.

28. Gordon-Reed, *Jefferson and Hemings*, 245.

29. In 1746 Wayles married Martha Eppes (1721-1748), of Eppington (Bermuda Hundred), who was a young widow; he would marry twice again (ca.1750, 1760); Wayles Files, ICJS.

30. Madison Hemings Memoir, in Gordon-Reed, *Jefferson and Hemings*, 248 (quotation); Stanton, *Free Some Day*, opp. 192.

31. Edwin M. Betts, ed., *Thomas Jefferson's Farm Book* (1953; repr. Charlottesville, VA, 1976), 9; on provenance of 'Guinea' tract see [James Bear], The Wayles Estate, n.d., TMs, Wayles File, ICJS. Of the 6 adults, only Sall was a field-slave; Ibid, 9.

32. Gordon-Reed, *Jefferson and Hemings*, 2.

33. *Virginia Gazette or American Advertiser* (April 1785), in Lathan A. Windley, ed., *Runaway Slave Advertisements* (Westport, Conn., 1983), I, 374. Cf. a captured runaway woman named Bessy in Jamaica (1816), who "formerly said she was an Eboe, but now found out to be a salt-water creole"; Douglas B. Chambers, ed., "Jamaican Runaways 1718-1817: A Compilation of Fugitive Slaves" (TMs, 2003), 467.

34. For a full account of this event, and sources for it, see Chambers, *Murder at Montpelier*, 5-9; to be available in a revised (and affordable) Nigerian edition, published by Jemezie Associates, Enugu, in 2008.

35. Quoted in Ibid., 8-9.

36. Douglas Hall, *In Miserable Slavery: Thomas Thistlewood in Jamaica 1750-86* (Kingston, Jamaica, 1999); Trevor Burnard, *Mastery, Tyranny, and Desire: Thomas Thistlewood and His Slaves in the Anglo-Jamaican World* (Chapel Hill, NC, 2004). In the end, though, Thistlewood did manumit his principal slave mistress Phibba and their mixed-race son John, and provided a small plot of land for them; Hall, 313-314.

37. Chambers, *Murder at Montpelier*, 96-97, and 222 for a brief biographical note on 'Granny Milly'. This may well have been an English copy of François de Salignac de la Mothe-Fénelon's much reprinted *Avantures de Telemaque, fils d'Ulysse: ou, Suite de quatrième livre de l'Odysse* (1699); English editions were published regularly from 1720 onward. A revised and corrected 16th edition of Fénelon's *Telemachus* was published in English in 1759 in London, and Martha Jefferson (1748-1782) apparently owned at least seven copies. It may well have been privately published, as the WorldCat digital database shows seven libraries worldwide currently own a copy of the edition under this heading: Fénelon, Isaac Littlebury, Abel Boyer, and Martha Jefferson [former owner], *The adventures of Telemachus, the son of Ulysses: in XXIV books*, 2 vols., rev. 16th ed. (London: for W. Meadows . . . [and 12 others], 1759) [LCCN no.2002-555068]. Presumably this 1759 edition, which apparently was arranged to mirror the 24 'books' (chapters) of *The Odyssey*, comprised the Telemachy (first four books of Homer's *Odyssey*), and material in books 15-19, 21-24; see for example Samuel Butler, *The Odyssey, rendered into English Prose for the use of those who cannot read the Original* (London: Longmans, Green, 1900).

38. *Telemachus* is as much an account of how a young man goes in search of his famously absent father, and in fact was driven on his quest by threats against his life by the same 'unwanted suitors' who were harassing his mother. The story of an 'abandoned' youth, driven from his home by the impending violence of a host of adult men to go on a quest for a wandering father, and once finding him then returning home to avenge the honor of the wife/mother would also likely have resonated among diasporic Igbo and their children. On a more proximate level, one wonders whether there was a father-son relationship (or a fictive one, as between shipmates) between the two male slaves involved in Madison's murder (that is, Turk and Pompey)?

CHAPTER 15

AFRICAN CULTURAL VALUES: THE SIGNIFICANCE OF IGBO ORAL FORMS IN SELECTED CARIBBEAN POETRY*

HANNAH N. EBY CHUKWU

I have crossed an ocean
I have lost my tongue from the root of the old one a new one
has sprung.[1]

I am constantly amazed at how much of Africa still remains in
the Caribbean, considering the disruption caused by slavery and
the European colonizing experience.[2]

Africa has survived in the Caribbean in terms of culture, language, and
music but its survival in literature accounts for the vibrant, functional, and
strong assertion of national identity present in the Caribbean's literary production. Edward Kamu Brathwaite in *History of the Voice*[3] has described Caribbean
speech as a continuum beginning with the ancestral root, which root is rightly
called African. Literary scholars in Africa and the diaspora have concerned
themselves with the question of African presence and representation in dia-

sporic literature. For instance, Richard D. E. Burton supports the view that the Caribbean have re-created African culture to form an essentially unique Caribbean culture. He argues "that the passage from African to Afro-Creole, [. . .] involved at the same time cultural loss, cultural retention and reinterpretation, cultural imitation and borrowing, and cultural creation."[4] In *Reggae International*, Stephen Davis and Peter Simon reiterate that same point by quoting Eric Roach: "We give history its due and correctly approach the problem of 'building creatively on what we have because of who we are.'"[5] O. R. Dathorne poses the questions: "How did Africa come into Caribbean literature and what precisely has the Caribbean environment taught its writers to mean when they write about Africa?"[6] He argues that there are both "the authentic" and "modern revivals" that have shaped the "imaginative concept of Africa in the minds of the West Indians."[7] In terms of cultural retention and borrowing, Caribbean oral poetry is replete with Igbo oral forms as the authentic presence of some empowering African cultural values. Caribbean culture has undergone some recreativity and hybridity, but with regard to some oral features and language use in its earlier poetry, a strong connection to its ancestral root—Africa, and in particular, Igbo—is evident. This paper examines the African category of work-songs in Caribbean oral poetry and the nature and functions of two key features, call-and-response and proverbs in the poetry of Louise Bennett and Bruce St. John. The paper presents evidence of work-songs in Igbo culture and the significance of the two key features, identified as Igbo oral forms, for Black people in the diaspora.

Some contemporary Caribbean poets have also responded to the issue of Africa in Caribbean poetry through direct reference to Africa. For instance, Edward Brathwaite traveled to and lived in Ghana, which journey he articulates as a journey back to his roots that has contributed to shaping his Caribbean identity, as he explores in his first trilogy *The Arrivants*.[8] Lorna Goodison, in her poem "Africa on the Mind Today"[9] presents her relationship to a specific African location, which is also authenticated by her continuous identification with her great-grandmother whom she refers to as "the Guinea woman."[10] Although Louise Bennett's satirical poem "Back to Africa"[11] is a counter response to Marcus Garvey's Back to Africa Movement,[12] it paradoxically demonstrates some aspects of Caribbean's ambivalent attitude toward Africa and specific Caribbean national identity with its roots in Africa. Most Caribbean writers acknowledge the fact that Africa has survived in the new world in both language usage and in literature with specific examples in consonance with Brathwaite's claim about the ancestral root, Burton's argument of a synthesis of culture, and Grace Nichols's psychic connection to Africa "as a kind of spiritual homeland."[13] It is easier for Black people in the diaspora to refer to Africa in a collective term because of the conglomeration of different African cultures in the diaspora, but further investigation shows that both the category of work-songs and the two key oral features in the poetry of Louise Bennett and Bruce St. John are distinctly Igbo oral forms.

Caribbean poetry from its beginning owes much to African cultural values whether in terms of (1) its composition, (2) its mode of transmission, and (3) its performance, which three aspects Ruth Finnegan writes are what make a work of poetry oral.[14] Both oraliture and written literature will likely continue to exist in the society to give a complete and communal expression of the society's social, political, cultural, religious, and historic experiences. A communal identity, unique to a particular people, reverberates in oraliture. Scholars have identified up to sixteen categories of oral poetry,[15] among which is work-songs. This category of oral poetry often manifests the key features of call-and-response and the use of proverbs.

Work-songs abound in Caribbean oral poetry. They are songs that are chanted according to the rhythmic movement of work so as to lighten the burden and monotony of work as well as to offer some pleasure to the workers, and even make them work faster, depending on the rate of the rhythmic beats. Finnegan asserts that "Songs to accompany rhythmic work seem to occur universally in African societies. They are extreme examples of 'special purpose' poetry in that they have a direct connection with a specific occasion and with action itself."[16] They are task-bound and may differ from task to task. Most books that discuss the literary history of Caribbean poetry trace its beginning to work-songs and music leading on to the more complicated forms of contemporary poetry.[17] It is significant that Caribbean poetry, beginning with work-songs and music, demonstrates Igbo sense of community, which sense of community has the prevalent feature of call-and-response. Igbo people are known for their commitment to maintaining ancestral homesteads, and in their songs and music, their sense of community is evident. For instance, Gentleman Mike Ejegha, Obili Igbo, Okonkwo Asaa, and Prince Emeka Morocco Maduka are famous for their story-in-music, *akuko-na-egwu* or *egwe ekpili*, which features prominently the Igbo oral form of call-and-response. Their music and songs can be used as work-songs; however, music being part of Igbo people's daily life provides for the continuous creation of work-songs by even amateurs during any task. For instance, one can hear schoolchildren, during compound work, sing:

Ayi jeko ibu okwute	We are going to carry stones
Onye nwuru ozuru ike	If you die, you will rest
Iyaa, oru oyibo	Iyaa, white-collar job

Iyaa, oru oyibo   Iyaa, white-collar job

They can also sing:

Lebra toro toro e dey   Three pence, three pence for a Laborer
Onye isi nii nii e dey   Nine pence, nine pence for the overseer[18]

These work-songs function to give pleasure as well as create rhythm and hasten the completion of a task. At the same time, the two songs are protests couched in subtle terms. They comment on some existential problems, such as colonial disintegration of Igbo society and the dull, repetitive, impersonal work associated with white-collar jobs. Detailed analysis of the literary significance of work-songs as well as the key Igbo oral forms are presented in the examination of some Caribbean poetry later in the paper.

Song in the context of Black Caribbean and North American cultures also signals the resilient spirit of the Black slaves that helped to keep their hopes and identity alive through the middle passage and in the so-called New World. Black slaves, no doubt, continued the practice of singing, carried from their ancestral homeland to the diaspora. Dennis Osadebey's description of Black people as a singing race presents a significant connection to Afro-Caribbean's ancestral origins because singing was one of the tools the slaves used to rarefy the pain of the chattel form of slavery and to keep their culture alive. He writes: "We sing when we fight, we sing when we work, we sing when we love, we sing when we hate, we sing when a child is born, we sing when death takes a toll."[19] Osadebey shows evidence that work-song is an Igbo cultural means of creation of meaning, assertion of identity as a people and as individuals, despite the challenges in life. According to Paula Burnett, "to the enslaved, exiled and abused blacks it was an important tool for survival: to sing of suffering and sorrow was to commute their pain."[20] The act of singing metamorphosed in the so-called New World for the purpose of maintaining identity, preserving history and culture. Burnett's view suggests the inevitable ancestral empowerment through creating a sense of community, and dealing with and surviving the chattel form of slavery. Nelly Uchendu, who released "Best of Igbo Blues in "80s," started out with call-and-response form of music and later, by addressing some existential problems, began to sing the blues as a means of purging strong emotions.

Okumba Miruka on discussing the social functions of oral poetry, as used in work-songs, shows how it can be used to give pleasure, which may emanate from the play on words and humor and to "derive some information intended to cultivate in us the sense of the social fabric from which the poetry is created."²¹ He gives an example with a woman's pounding song entitled "Eyes of Hunger:"

You made me marry a man with a bald head
You could spread flour on it to dry
If you put a penny on it, it falls down;
Eyes of hunger, e-e
You made me marry a man with a bald head.²²

The poem is a pun on the implications of poverty, which are related to both lack of money (even a penny cannot be found with the poor), and lack of hair to protect the head (baldness offers the head no protection from the heat of the sun).

The fluidity of some of these work-songs and their function as embodiments of the daily experiences and aspirations of the people are obvious from their analysis because they transcend the easing of the monotony of the physical work to become tools for survival and resistance by the slaves. For instance, in one of the "Work-songs" anthologized by Paula Burnett in *The Penguin Book of Caribbean Verse in English*²³ we read:

Tink dere is a God in a top,
No use me ill, Obissha!
Me no horse, me no mare, me no mule,
No use me ill, Obissha. (1-4)

The self-consciousness of the persona is made obvious as he appeals to the faith of the master or overseer, and uses that to draw attention to the unjust treatment the master metes out to the slave. In the poem "Freedom a Come Oh!" we see evidence of orality in the formulaic nature, repetition, and improvisation in a fixed music framework of the ideophone "Talla ly li oh," which provides the rhythmic movements and which synchronizes with the hoe or farming implements in each stanza of the poem:

Talla ly li oh
Freedom a come oh!
Talla ly li oh
Here we dig, here we hoe.

Talla ly li oh
Freedom a come oh!

Talla ly li oh
Here we dig, here we sow! (1-4, 21-24).

From the chanted rhythm of the song the words "dig" and "hoe" are regularly repeated in the five stanzas of the poem, but the last lines introduce a different idea about sowing, which may connote planting or sowing the seed of resistance. The spirit of resistance is obvious in the work-song "Song of the King of the Eboes": "Buckra in this country no make we free: /What Negro for to do? What Negro for to do? /Take force by force! Take force by force!" (4-6). Then the chorus says, "To be sure! To be sure! To be sure!" Eboes in this song is most likely a variant spelling of Igbos, and the message of resistance in the song is obvious. Selwyn Cudjoe discusses the hidden nuances of the slaves' field songs and how the slaves employ these songs as instruments of resistance and as affirmation of their humanity and selfhood.[24] The transcendent function of these work-songs supports the idea that they function as literature in that context and are far from shallow utterances of illiterate people, which disdainful attitude to oral poetry Finnegan warns against in *Oral Literature in Africa*.[25] Therefore the nature and function of work-songs call for a closer study and analysis even in our contemporary preoccupation with written literature. Embedded in work-songs are the key features, call-and-response and proverbs, which features strongly suggest their literary qualities.

The idea of call-and-response implies audience involvement during composition, performance, and transmission. An audience presence is an imperative for oral poetry, a feature which strongly distinguishes oral poetry from the written form. That involvement is not simple; rather it influences and affects both levels of composition and performance, and directly involves the whole community in creativity. Burnett observes: "The call-and-response structure of the choral singing which came from Africa and is still found in Caribbean folk-songs differs from the European ballad-and-chorus, which have much longer units."[26] Miruka describes it as "antiphony" and writes, "The classic example of an antiphonal delivery is the existence of a soloist who calls the tune and the rest chorus the response. But there are variations in this structure where for example, the two parties are complementing one another rather than the soloist dominating in calling the tune."[27] A complementary example prevails in the Igbo story-in-music where the soloist begins by first greeting his music team, addressing them with their special titles; the different responses from the team form part of the meaning and significance of the song, showing that meaning is communally created.

Bruce St. John's poem entitled "Bajan Litany" exemplifies call-and-response, with a soloist calling out while the others respond alternatively with "Yes, Lord" and "O Lord." The poet uses a parallel structure to present a strong sense of nationalism, balanced with the use of proverbs:

Follow pattern kill Cadogan	Yes, Lord
America got black power?	O Lord
We got black power	Yes, Lord
Wuh sweeten goat mout 'e tail	O Lord
Bermuda got tourism?	Yes, Lord
We got too	O Lord
De higher monkey go, de more 'e show 'e tail Yes, Lord (1-7)	

Burnett, commenting on the poem and on its use of call-and-response structure, says that "the chiming of assent in such phrases as 'Yes, lord' or 'True, true' is mirrored in everyday speech, and has been adapted to the oral poetry." She also remarks that St. John's poem is "witty just because it cheats the expectation of that chiming assent; where the litany should be ritualistic, his suffers a rebellion in the ranks and makes its satiric point with delicious humour."[28] This feature of call-and-response in oral poetry is documented evidence of the immediacy of the people's life and conveys a powerful feeling of the audience's involvement as opposed to the distance often conveyed by written poetry. Even apart from poetry performance, call-and-response assumes an indispensable status in most public discourse in Igbo societies. For instance, Chinua Achebe in *Things Fall Apart* illustrates its use in a town people's meeting. He describes how the powerful orator, Ogbuefi Ezeugo, standing in the midst of the people "bellowed four times, '*Umuofia kwenu,*' and on each occasion he faced a different direction and seemed to push the air with a clenched fist. And ten thousand men answered '*Yaa!*' each time. Then there was a perfect silence."[29] The silence and the appeal to their nativity as "Umuofia people" and the antiphonal response of "Yaa" illustrate the transformative effect of call-and-response and its inevitability in oral discourse for it provides mutual pleasure and identity for the people.[30]

The response can take the form of choric refrain, music, repetition, questions and even challenges. Challenges can come from the audience even surprisingly during composition, which sometimes is also public, a fact which strongly suggests the extemporaneous quality of oral composition. Burnett acknowledges that feature, writing that "The ability to compose extempore and wittily was highly valued in the West African cultures and its esteem continued in the Caribbean."[31] The ability to speak well is still one of the qualities of good leaders in Igbo society. Judith Van Allen in "Sitting on a Man" writes about Igbo women's pre-colonial political power. She goes on to show how political discourse is built on the ability to use proverbs, parables, and metaphor: "Influential speech was the creative and skillful use of tradition to assure others that a certain course of action was both a wise and right thing to do. The leaders of Igbo society were men and women who combined wealth and generosity with 'mouth'—the ability to speak well."[32] Creativity is invested in the orality, politics, and spirituality of the society; hence, creativity is the effect of living and participating in social, political, and spiritual affairs in the society. Ogbuefi Ezeugo, in Achebe's account, did not have to prepare his speech ahead of time, or to read from a script. The sense of community makes the ability to compose extemporaneously an imperative so that there will be no barrier between the performer and the audience. Finnegan makes an interesting observation that "extemporization or elaboration are often more likely to be to the fore than [...] memorization"[33] and then connects extempore feature of composition to the imperative of the presence of the audience. She writes:

> An audience of some kind is normally an essential part of the whole literary situation. There is no escape for the oral artist from a face-to-face confrontation with his audience, and this is something which he can exploit as well as be influenced by. The close connection between artist and audience can almost turn into an identity. Members of the audience too need not confine their participation to silent listening or a mere acceptance of the chief performer's invitation to participate—they may also in some circumstances break into the performance with additions, queries, or even criticisms.[34]

This interesting relationship between the artist and the audience can extend to illustrate the fluid and complementary qualities of different categories and features of oral poetry. The fact is that there is no static dichotomy between the nature and function of one feature and the other; neither can their contexts be compartmentalized.

These empowering African oral forms are intertwined and function for totality of effect in the society in the same way that the artist and the audience can assume a singular identity in some contexts. Likewise, the feature of call-and-response can give rise to the feature of proverbs, and composition, performance, and transmission are similarly dynamically interconnected. Brathwaite has observed that "The oral tradition [...]

demands not only the griot but the audience to complete the community: the noise and sounds that the maker makes are responded to by the audience and returned to him."[35] Therefore in a community where oral poetry is functional, it can be argued that the individual performer and the community (audience) are involved in an unlimited productivity, and because of the rapport between them they can have a wholly-shared full aesthetic experience. Life is not so solitary; interactions, agreements, and disagreements are part of life. Igbo culture is various; the various parts are its different communities strung together by Igbo oral forms and sociopolitical organizations. Therefore, this feature of oral poetry helps to recapture the totality of life experiences in Igbo society and in the diaspora.

Another empowering African cultural value present in Igbo oral form is the use of proverb. Proverb illustrates the richness of the oral tradition and its creativity because the proverb arises from the context of a given circumstance and functions as an integral part of the community experience. No performer or user of proverb deliberately sets out or determines to use proverb; rather proverb is extemporized and contextualized in usage, which is a strong indication of its autochthonous creative quality. The relevance and suitability of proverb both for the user and for the context are weighed against its adaptability or applicability in a particular context and its effectiveness for the advancement of a discourse. Use of proverbs is not usually determined by age, though older people may tend to use more proverbs than younger people because of their greater linguistic experiences and authority in the language. Use of proverbs, to an extent, also indicates one's admittance into the culturally enlightened class, according to an Igbo proverb, *Aturo omara omara, aturo ofeke ofenye na ohia.* This means that, according to Igbos, it is only a fool that would ask for a proverb to be explained, or assume that a proverb has a literal application. In Igbo culture, proverbs are not taught, but they arise out of the contexts of social interactions. Proverbs are acquired as part of the language and are not necessarily learned. The proverb, according to Finnegan, may then be referred to as an "African linguistic symbol" because it can be used to give order or direction, broach a difficult subject, expound a concept, invite interpretation and elaboration on a subject and, sometimes, function as a vehicle for satire and humor. Finnegan writes that the "Proverb is a vehicle particularly suited to give depth and elegance through its allusive, figurative and poetic mode of expression."[36] The fact that Caribbean poetry is replete with proverbs is an example of African cultural value in Igbo oral form, and that fact is indicative of its ancestral roots. Igbo culture has survived in the diaspora in terms of figurative language markings and usage, and through even direct reference.

I shall illustrate the ancestral roots of Caribbean poetry as Igbo cultural identity with the use of an Igbo proverb, and another version of the proverb in Swahili, and use the proverb to demonstrate the general function and symbolic importance of proverbs in oral literature, and, in particular, the significance of Igbo oral forms as a tool of identity and vehicle for literary language in Caribbean poetry. The Igbo proverb *Anya fue azu na mmiri, oburu nni* (When a fish loses its way of life, it becomes a captive) and the Swahili proverb *Mwacha mila ni mtumwa* (One who leaves one's culture is a slave)[37] are applicable to Caribbean poetry in two ways—symbolically and literarily. Its symbolical application points to its ancestral roots, which fact Finnegan accentuates by stating that "Proverbs seem to occur almost everywhere in Africa, in apparent contrast with other areas of the world."[38] Louise Bennett demonstrates how proverbs function as a means of the transmission of wisdom and the mastering of difficult or unpleasant situations in the Caribbean just as in Africa. In the poem "Dutty Tough," Louise Bennett employs proverbs in order to present powerfully, in a para-doxical combination of proverbial words, perennial problems of Caribbean social and economic existence. She writes:

> Sun a shine but tings noh bright;
> Doah pot a bwile, bickle noh nuff;
> River flood but wata scarce, yah;
> Rain a fall but dutty tough! (1-4).

The poem is based on proverbs and makes use of antithesis and parallel grammatical structure. Miruka defines parallelism, which is a feature of the proverb, as "the use of two balancing units within a literary form. It is quite a common feature in proverbs. Many proverbs exist in two parts usually of equal length, separated by a convenient punctuation mark. Parallelism makes the proverbs poetic and creates rhythm."[39] Bennett's poem pres-ents a contrast between expectations and realities in people's lives. Bennett makes significant use of proverbs in many of her poems and even has a poem entitled "Proverbs."[40] In another poem entitled "Independance" she also employs proverb to make strongly the point about the psychologi-cal, political, and social adjustments the people needed to make with the advent of independence. In stanza eight, she writes:

> Dog wag im tail fe suit im size/An match im stamina-
> Jamaica people need a /Independence formula!" (29-32).

By introducing proverbs in the first two lines of the poem, she is importing the wisdom of the elders, in order to help Caribbean people's political situation. Though the poet did not attribute the saying to the elders, the attribution is implied in the sense of what Miruka refers to as "Wellerism," which "establishes objectivity,"[41] force, and aesthetic distance in the use of proverbs, and can also be achieved with the use of animals and inanimate or abstract figures.

The second application of the Igbo and Swahili proverbs in the literal sense comes from an analogy which can be drawn from the literal meaning of the proverb and shows that a people's way of life or culture is an authenticated identity of the people as opposed to slaves who have no autonomous identity and consequently no culture of their own because they are in bondage. So when a people strive to represent their culture, or to maintain their way of life, they are invariably claiming their roots and the rights of autonomous identity and representation. Even though the slaves are physically in bondage, psychologically and spiritually they are free because physical bondage may not have as much adverse effect on individuals as the bondage of the mind and spirit may have. Therefore, the attempts by Caribbean poets to reconstruct their unique culture and affirm their national identity make them draw from the ancestral roots of their cultural heritage. Slaves have no culture, so through their attempts to create a unique cultural identity as Africans in the diaspora, they are pointing to their roots and culture and thus denying the oppressive naming of slaves and affirming their own cultural identity. In essence, the use of proverb in Caribbean poetry is foremost an indication of ancestral background and an assertion of Caribbean people's own authentic culture, apart from the nadir of slavery. It is liberation from cultural superficiality into deeply rooted cultural consciousness, reinterpretation, and re-assessment of a people's experience in order to create a holistic existence. Interestingly, Obioma Nnaemeka in discussing feminism in Africa relies on an Igbo proverb to make African women's fight for equality with their men distinct from Western women's fight for equality with their own men. In her article "Feminism, Rebellious Women, and Cultural Boundaries" she advocates for what she calls "negofeminism" as a term suitable to describe Black women's liberation struggles, inscribes her ideology of Black women's personhood and movement into the primacy of communality located in the Igbo cultural philosophy about negotiation, partnership, and cooperation. In her exposition of the idea she quotes E. N. Njaka in *Igbo Political Culture*, "The Igbo believes he [sic] can negotiate anything"; an Igbo proverb says, "*Ife kwulu, ife akwudebie* (When something stands, something else stands beside it)."[42] Nnaemeka's negofeminism relies on Igbo thought embedded in the use of proverb as a way of creating reality in human context. Igbo proverbs in Africa and in the diaspora suggest the art of rhetoric that is the quintessence of meaning, order, identity, and nationhood.

Proverbs are closely interwoven with other forms of linguistic and literary forms and social and cultural behavior. Both Finnegan's further description of proverb as "a saying in more or less fixed form marked by 'shortness, sense, and salt' and distinguished by the popular acceptance of the truth tersely expressed in it"[43] and Achebe's affirmation that "proverbs are the palm-oil with which words are eaten"[44] show the terseness or brevity, pithiness, and economy of words in the use of proverbs, just as in poetry. These qualities foreground the seriousness of this feature of Igbo oral forms and call for greater attention in the study of proverbs as a representative symbolic language, which abounds in the use of simile, metaphor, hyperbole, paradox and antithesis. Therefore Achebe's metaphoric reference to proverbs as "oil" and Finnegan's reference to them as "salt" foreground the use of proverbs as that which adds spice to life by not only giving taste to creative language but adding essential nourishment and sustenance to the poetic creative experience.

These Igbo oral forms and features examined with reference to selected Caribbean poetry demonstrate an interconnectedness and transcendence from their physical context to make statements about national identity and offer deep reflection upon life experiences. These Igbo oral forms are significant, but they are like wealth locked up in oral literature and are yet to be fully explored, appropriated, and appreciated, even in the modern times.

NOTES

*   A version of the paper was first presented during the Association of Canadian College and University Teachers of English (ACCUTE) Annual Confrence of the Humanities and Social Sciences Federation of Canada held at Dalhousie University Halifax, Nova Scotia, May 28-31, 2003. Thanks to Susan Gingell, University of Saskatchewan for her useful insight and comments on earlier drafts of this paper. Thanks to Janice Fiamengo, University of Ottawa for her comments and encouragement in the writing of this paper. Thanks to Ike Oguocha for his suggestions of proverbs in the course of revising this paper.

1.   Grace Nichols, "Epilogue," 303, in E. A. Markham, ed., *Hinterland: Caribbean Poetry From the West Indies & Britain* (New Castle: Bloodaxe Books, 1989).

2. Grace Nichols, "The Battle with Language," 283, in Selwyn R. Cudjoe, ed., *Caribbean Women Writers* (Massachusetts: Calaloux, 1990), 283-89.

3. Edward K. Brathwaite, *History of the Voice* (London: New Beacon, 1984), 49.

4. Richard D. E. Burton, *Afro-Creole: Power, Opposition, and Play in the Caribbean* (Ithaca: Cornell University Press, 1997), 5.

5. Eric Roach, in Stephen Davis and Peter Simon, *Reggae International* (New York: Rogner & Bernhard, 1982), 26.

6. O. R. Darthorne, *The Black Mind: A History of African Literature* (Minneapolis: University of Minnesota Press, 1974), 433.

7. According to O. R. Dathorne there are significant survivals of African culture in Haitian voodoo and among the maroons of Jamaica, the "Bush Negroes" of the Surinam, and the Yoruba of Brazil. Other significant influences on the theme of Africa in Caribbean literature include folklore and language survivals. A typical example of folklore is the Caribbean Anancy tales, some of which P. M. Sherlock, Louise Bennett, and Andrew Salkey have collected. There are obvious linguistic survivals in the usage and application of words. For even in language usage there is a surprising retention of African forms as we see in the example of the use of certain words "foo-foo" (pounded food), "pickney" or "pickin" (small child), and "obissha" (overseer). Another striking linguistic connection is in the use of " 'e," which according to Richard Allsopp in *Dictionary of Caribbean English Usage* (Oxford: Oxford University Press, 1996), is the third person singular pronoun, which functions for the subjective, objective and possessive cases for both masculine and feminine genders, which function is observable in most African languages. For instance, Yoruba uses "o", Igbo uses "ya", and Efik uses "enye" (210). Dathorne further relates some "modern revivals" of Africa in the Caribbean to "popular modern movements" and influence in the Caribbean such as the "The Black Muslims in the United States, . . . the Rastafarians in Jamaica, the Jordanites and the Coptics in Guyana, and the Shouters and the Shango cult in Trinidad," (434).

8. Edward K. Brathwaite, *The Arrivants: A New World Trilogy* (London: Oxford University Press, 1973).

9. Lorna Goodison, *Turn Thanks* (Urbana: University of Illinois Press, 1999), 37.

10. Ibid, 21.

11. Louise Bennett, "Back to Africa," 31-2, in Paula Burnett, ed., *The Penguin Book of Caribbean Verse in English* (Harmondsworth: Penguin, 1986).

12. Marcus Mosiah Garvey was the founder of Universal Negro Improvement Association (UNIA), African Communities League (ACL), and *Black Man* magazine (Kingston, Jamaica 1933-35, London, England 35-40). Motto

for UNIA is "One God, One Aim, One Destiny." Provisional President of African Republic was elected at 1920 UNIA convention. UNIA promoted Garvey-inspired program of collective self-help for racial uplift. Just like the Rastafarians, he envisioned Africa as the promise land for Black people in the Diaspora. (Source: "The Marcus Garvey and UNIA Papers Project, UCLA," www.isop.ucla.edu/mgpp/lifeintr.htm 5). [Accessed 5 May 2007].

13. Grace Nichols, "Home Truths," 296, in E. A. Markham ed., *Hinterland: Caribbean Poetry From the West Indies & Britain* (New Castle: Bloodaxe Books, 1989), 294-98.

14. Ruth Finnegan, *Oral Poetry: Its Nature, Significance and Social Context* (Cambridge: Cambridge University Press, 1977), 17.

15. Okumba Miruka as well as Ruth Finnegan has classified oral poetry as (a) Birth or Cradle songs (b) Circumcision songs (c) Marriage /Wedding /Nuptial songs (d) Dirges or Elegiac poetry (e) Work songs (f) Hunting poetry (g) War poetry (h) Love songs (i) Political songs (j) Lyric (k) Panegyric (l) Court poetry or Official poetry (m) Epic or Heroic poetry (n) Hortatory poetry (o) Satirical poetry (p) Elocutionary poetry (95-6). These categories are sometimes connected to each other because there is often no rigid division between songs and poetry since both are related in the oral tradition.

16. Ruth Finnegan, *Oral Literature in Africa* (Nairobi: Oxford University Press, 1970), 230.

17. Paula Burnett begins her anthology, *The Penguin Book of Caribbean Verse in English*, with the oral tradition and lists work-songs first. Stephen Davis and Peter Simon in *Reggae International* trace the evolution of Caribbean music from the African communal feature of work songs to Afro-Christian continuum of myalism and Jonkonnu (ritual beliefs and dances), to Afro-Christian Kumina and Pukkumina, to Zion Revival or Zionism, to Buru, and to Rastafarian. A synthesis of these forms of music evolved into Jamaican Mento, (but in Trinidad it is Calypso, which is popular and has a clear influence from Jonkonnu) into Ska, into Rock Steady, and into Reggae. Even some accomplished Caribbean poets employ music in their poetry. For instance, Brathwaite uses Reggae music to give form and meaning to some of his poems. E. A. Markham, for his own part, begins his anthology, *Hinterland: Caribbean Poetry From the West Indies & Britain*, with Louise Bennett, who is reputed to be "the pioneering figure of the century in the oral tradition of Caribbean poetry," (44).

18. These songs are not collected or published in books, as far as I can tell. Work-songs pervade the Igbo society.

19. Dennis Osadebey qtd. in Okumba Miruka, *Encounter with Oral Literature* (Nairobi: East African Educational Publishers, 1994), 87.

20. Paula Burnett, ed., *The Penguin Book of Caribbean Verse in English* (Harmondsworth: Penguin, 1986), xxxiv.
21. *Encounter with Oral Literature*, 118.
22. "CHISENA—Malawi" Ibid, 119.
23. *The Penguin Book of Caribbean Verse*. All references to quoted poems are to this anthology and the lines appear in parentheses in the text.
24. Selwyn R. Cudjoe in the "Introduction" to *Caribbean Women Writers* makes the point about the connection between the routine activities of the slaves with their struggle for freedom and affirmation of their identity as humans. His succinct observation about work-songs shows that their function as poetry is as good as that in any society. He writes, "Cultural resistance cannot be defined too narrowly as the transmission of language and /or songs to succeeding generations. It also involves the everyday activities of work and physical efforts of all the slaves as they struggled to liberate themselves from the oppressor class" (10). Cudjoe further quotes Barbara Bush, who on discussing the role of slave women in resistance says: "Women field hands were experts in the use of the rich creole language which, with its *double entendres* and satire, was frequently employed as subtle abuse of whites. Through such channels women helped to generate and sustain the general spirit of resistance," (9).
25. Finnegan warns against dismissing oral literature as being "inherently crude." She offers some insight towards appreciating the import of oral literature and its function in the society. She writes, "With this type of literature a knowledge of the whole literary and social background, covering these various points of performance, audience, and context, is, however difficult, of the first importance. It is at least necessary to be aware of these problems from the outset, rather than, as so commonly happens, substituting for an awareness of the shallowness of our *own* understanding an imaginary picture of the shallowness in literary appreciation and development of the peoples we are attempting to study" (15).
26. *The Penguin Book of Caribbean Verse*, xxx.
27. *Encounter with Oral Literature*, 89.
28. *The Penguin Book of Caribbean Verse*, xxxvi.
29. Chinua Achebe, *Things Fall Apart* (Oxford: Heinemann Educational Books, 1989), rpt., 10.
30. Call-and-response is part and parcel of most public gatherings in Igbo societies, and in Caribbean poetry we see its resources being harnessed for the purpose of poetry. In the instance given with Chinua Achebe's *Things Fall Apart*, in the context of a town gathering, we see the feature employed for the following purposes: (a) calling the gathering to order, and (b) appealing to the town people's communal sense of belonging and identification with a

common cause. One might argue that since antiphonal chanting of psalms and liturgy is part of Christian culture, and that also during sport events that cheer-leaders lead in the call-and-response, so that feature might not be unique to Igbo oral forms. The fact is that in those contexts the feature is restricted to those occasions, unlike its prevalence as part of African cultural values.

31. *The Penguin Book of Caribbean Verse,* xxxii.
32. Judith Van Allen, "'Sitting on a Man': Colonialism and the Lost Political Institutions of Igbo Women," *Canadian Journal of African Studies* 6.2 (1972), 167.
33. *Oral Literature in Africa,* 10.
34. Ibid., 10-11.
35. *History of the Voice,* 18-9.
36. *Oral Literature in Africa,* 416.
37. This proverb was supplied to me during telephone and personal interviews with Josiah Obiero on the use of proverbs in Kenyan culture, 17 & 21 Sept. 2002. A similar version of the proverb is *Bila asili utumwa* (One who knows not one's origin is doomed to servitude), which Gay Wilentz (*Binding Cultures: Black Women Writers in Africa and the Diaspora,* Bloomington: Indiana University Press, 1992, 116) uses in her discussion of shared culture in Africa and diasporic women's writings.
38. *Oral Literature in Africa,* 389.
39. *Encounter with Oral Literature,* 64.
40. Louise Bennett, "Proverbs," in *Hinterland: Caribbean Poetry From the West Indies & Britain* ed. E. A. Markham (New Castle: Bloodaxe Books, 1989), 61-2.
41. Miruka on discussing the structure of proverbs refers to "wellerism." He describes its use in proverb as "the aspect of attributing the saying to some actual or fictional person with an introductory tag to authenticate the quotation. Sometimes the tag comes after the proverb. An example of wellerism is: 'It has been said, Marriage is rib-rib, it has no eyes' (i.e. marriage is a matter of luck). Whoever is saying the proverb attributes it to someone else and thus withdraws from the responsibility of its meaning. It is like saying: 'I am not responsible for this but it is the truth that . . .'" (63-4).
42. Obioma Nnaemeka, "Feminism, Rebellious Women, and Cultural Boundaries: Rereading Flora Nwapa and Her Compatriots," *Research in African Literatures* 26, 2 (1995), 106.
43. *Oral Literature in Africa,* 392-3.
44. Achebe, *Things Fall Apart,* 6.

CHAPTER 16

AFRICAN ORIGINS OF IGBO SLAVE RESISTANCE IN THE AMERICAS

DANIEL KLOZA

INTRODUCTION

Slavery is the most abhorrent condition in which human beings have been subject to live. Awarded virtually no rights and extremely limited freedoms, the enslaved Africans resisted the institution of slavery often and in clever ways. From outright insurrection to something as basic as breaking the tools owned by their masters, the slaves were not simply victims in a prostrate condition; they were reactive and responded to their circumstances with an active physical, social, and cultural resistance. These notions are essential to the understanding of slavery in the historical past. Additionally, it is important that we examine the indigenous cultures from which enslaved Africans were taken during the period of the Trans Atlantic slave trade. To understand the scope, methods, and existence of resistance to the institution of slavery in the Americas, one must look to social institutions, political institutions, interpersonal relations, and religious beliefs of the indigenous Africans. This paper will be specifically examining the case of the Igbo Africans, who originated in the eastern portion of present day Nigeria, and came primarily from the region known as the Bight of Biafra.

Over the course of roughly three hundred and fifty years, according to Paul E. Lovejoy, the Trans Atlantic slave trade saw the export of over ten million enslaved Africans from various regions in Africa.[1] The most predominant numbers of Africans came from four regions of the trade including West Central Africa, accounting for 36.5 percent, the Bight of Benin, 20 percent, the Bight of Biafra, 16.6 percent, and the Gold Coast, with 11 percent.[2] A large number of Africans who embarked on the slave ships, however, did not make it to the intended destinations. According to the data presented in *The Trans-Atlantic Slave Trade Database* of the 7,943,600 Africans who embarked from their homeland between 1527 and 1866, 6,757,654 Africans arrived at the shores of the New World and entered the slave system. This data reflects a loss of roughly 1.1 million Africans, about 15 percent, who never even completed the trans-Atlantic journey due to the dreadful conditions faced on the slave ships.[3]

This is the overall context of the Trans Atlantic Slave Trade and ultimately the African Diaspora that came with the displacement of millions of people. The study of the Diaspora itself is a broad based study of the African people who had, one way or another, been dispersed to various places throughout the world. For the purposes of this chapter, I will only provide a brief overview of the African Diaspora as it relates to Igbo Africans. In general, a majority of this dispersion occurred during the forced removal of Africans during the Trans-Atlantic slave trade, as shown above in the sheer volume of numbers of Africans that were taken from their homeland. The study of the Diaspora concerns itself with the history, culture, and impact these Africans had on their new places of residence. Michael A. Gomez distinguishes the study of the African Diaspora with a primary focus on two major issues; the first being the "ways in which preceding African cultural, social or political forms influence African-descended persons in their new environment, and how such forms change through interaction with non-African cultures," and the second being "comparisons and relationships between communities of African-descended people who are geographically separated or culturally distinct."[4] The main concern of this paper is within the first goal outlined by Gomez. By detailing and examining the indigenous culture of the Igbo peoples of Africa one can achieve a much better understanding of why and how slaves responded the way they did in the Americas.

Next, the discussion will turn to a description and examination of the concentrations of Africans in the Americas. As the sources indicate, the African people that would be dispersed into the Americas came primarily from four regions, including the Bight of Biafra. The Bight of Biafra is located in the Niger Delta and Cross River Valley, what is now southeastern

Nigeria. Based on the available data, throughout the entirety of the Trans-Atlantic slave trade, 941,463 Africans embarked from the Bight of Biafra, with a total of 760,242 Africans disembarking at their destinations in the Americas.[5] According to this data, the total number of Africans from the Bight of Biafra accounted for nearly one fourth of the total number of Africans imported into North America.[6]

Destinations of Africans from the Bight of Biafra, 1527-1866

Destination	Number of Africans	Percentage of total
Jamaica	266,191	25%
Virginia	28,159	28%
Dominica	70,000	58%
Barbados	60,000	15%
Grenada	46,475	32%
St. Kitts	44,000	32%

Source: David Eltis, et al eds. *The Atlantic Slave Trade: A Database on CD-ROM* (New York: Cambridge University Press, 1999).

The table above shows the various significant areas of concentrations of Africans that embarked from the Bight of Biafra. The first of these is Jamaica, which was the destination where the greatest number of Biafran Africans disembarked. Here roughly 25 percent of the enslaved Africans originated from the Bight of Biafra throughout the years of the slave trade, which is the highest concentration of any place of African origin for Jamaica. In addition, the database shows that the destination of the majority of Africans from Biafra between the years of 1726 and 1825 was Jamaica.

In mainland North America, disproportionately high numbers of Biafran Africans ended up in Virginia. The period where their concentration was greatest was between 1701 and 1725, but considerable numbers of Africans from Biafra continue to disembark in Virginia until the abolition of the Virginian slave trade in 1775, with about 30 percent of the Virginian slave population originating from the Bight of Biafra. Other significant concentrations of Biafran Africans include Dominica, Barbados, Grenada, and St. Kitts.[7] Clearly, the raw data suggest that a substantial number of Africans from the Bight of Biafra concentrated in certain areas.

With significant concentrations of Africans coming from specific areas of Africa, a definitive sense of identity and cohesiveness emerged. Many scholars have concluded that a strong Igbo cultural presence was prevalent in the Americas. Michael A. Gomez reports that the Bight of Biafra was a "very homogeneous region." Given that southeastern Nigeria is the cultural origin of the Igbo people, it can safely be asserted that the majority of Africans from the Bight of Biafra were, in fact, Igbo.[8] Reporting on the significance of the Biafran contribution to the slave trade, Gomez stresses the sheer number of Africans as well as its small geographic size, leading to a much more homogeneous grouping of the captives who were taken from there.[9]

Gwendolyn Midlo Hall makes the same argument, stating that pioneer Nigerian historian Kenneth Dike has argued convincingly of the Igbo cultural domination of the Biafran region by citing significant evidence gathered by Captain John Adams between 1786 and 1800. She cites recent work from American scholars such as Douglas B. Chambers and Lorena Walsh, that the amount of Africans in the New World who were self-identified as Igbo was impressive.[10] E. N. Njaka also states that the Igbo have always managed to preserve their customs and practices, ensuring the retention of social unity and cultural traditions of a national group, even without the existence of a central Igbo state.[11] Indeed, Chambers has estimated that 80 percent of the Africans shipped from the Biafran region were Igbo speaking peoples.[12] Overall, there will always be uncertainties because it is simply impossible to pin point the exact number of Igbo Africans taken captive and transported to the New World. However, given the available scholarship, a solid consensus exists that the majority of Africans taken from the Bight of Biafra had an Igbo cultural background and therefore transferred their Igbo culture to the American landscape.

A considerable amount of research has also focused on how well the African identity and culture endured and affected life in the Americas. The question of how creolized the African slaves and their children became has been debated extensively by scholars.[13] Overall, it is clear that one must move beyond the notion of complete homogeneity of African slaves in the Americas and begin to look more closely at specific regions of origins and how these concentrations affected their new places of residence. Accordingly, Lovejoy has called for a more focused look at the cultures, ethnicities, and the historical contexts from which the Africans of the Atlantic Diaspora were taken in order to achieve a better understanding of their cultural impact.[14]

Indeed, specific concentrations of fairly homogenous populations were taken to the New World. The slave traders did not randomly collect Africans and ship them to various localities in the Americas. In fact, quite the opposite occurred, as demonstrated by the extensive documentation of patterns of population movements between the African coastline and the shores of the Americas. These concentrations must be put under the historical lens for examination. For the Igbo, as Douglas B. Chambers argues, the "historical world the creolizing slaves created in Virginia seems to have developed largely from a diasporic Igbo base."[15] Thus, the knowledge, practices, and traditions of the indigenous Africans remained "meaningful in succeeding generations."[16] Although the degree to which African culture was retained by slaves in the New World cannot be discerned with precision, many elements of African culture are evident in the slave cultures of the Americas; cultures that were influencing and being influenced by the dramatic cultural change of continental relocation.

ROOTS OF RESISTANCE: THE CULTURE OF THE IGBO

Given the overview of the numbers of Igbo Africans dispersed into the New World and an examination of the endurance of their cultural identities, the discussion will turn now to the Igbo culture itself and its relationship to the resistance of the institution of slavery in the Americas. Ultimately, the indigenous culture of Igbo Africans encouraged a vigorous and varied resistance to slavery. In examining Chinua Achebe's novel *Things Fall Apart*, one can see how the pre-colonial Igbo Africans were indeed a well-organized people, with complex political and social institutions. Diana Rhoads states that the indigenous Igbo had "achieved the foundations of what most people seek today – democratic institutions, tolerance of other cultures, capacity to change for the better or to meet new circumstances, a means of redistributing wealth, an effective system of justice, striking and memorable poetry and art."[17] "The intensely individualist character of the people of the Eastern Provinces would not permit the setting up of one man as "bigger" than another," a colonial officer wrote of the Igbo.[18] Clearly, the Igbo, like other enslaved Africans, were taken from an organized society with a rich cultural heritage and thrown into a system that hostilely opposed their traditions, institutions, and their fundamental way of life.

Let us first explore the function of leaders in the Igbo political institutions and society. The leadership structure that did exist in the indigenous Igbo world was one of culpability for ones actions and a responsibility towards the people, the exact opposite of that in the context of slavery in the Americas. As Victor C. Uchendu states, "Domination by a few powerful men" in the Igbo society is "deeply resented."[19] There is a strong sense of accountability, responsibility, and reciprocity that exists in Igbo society, which dominates their relationships with their leaders. This idea of accountability is seen in the "transparency" of the Igbo lifestyle. This "transparency" held that the Igbo lived in a society where all people, including leaders, are responsible for their actions.[20] The notion that leaders should be accessible to all in the society is an idea that is alien from slave societies.

In addition, one-sided relationships, either in obligation or in reward, do not last a long time among the Igbo. In the eyes of the Igbo, leadership must be earned, achieved, and consistently re-validated in order for it to be retained. "Authority," Njaka states, "in the way it is understood by the West, shocks the Igbo, just as the Western concept of power eludes him. An authority in which he has no share is suspect and intolerable."[21] Heritage and family ties also have little to nothing to do with the making of a leader. Leaders are not born into a position of power or a predetermined societal status. Leaders, in the Igbo worldview, "emerge."[22] In addition, leaders must also create opportunity for others in their village and provide chances for other Igbos to advance within their society.

On the relationship of the Igbo people to their leaders, Njaka tells of a folk tale about the tortoise (*mbe*). In the story, all species of birds were invited to a feast that was going to take place in the sky. One bird thought they should bring the *mbe* with them because he was universally respected for his intelligence and wisdom. Knowing this, all the birds agreed and donated a feather to the tortoise so that he could fly and attend the feast. Upon arrival, the tortoise suggested that the birds call him "All the Birds" stating that this would be a good name given the source of his feathers. At the feast, however, when the host presented the congregation with any food or gifts, he would address "all the birds." The tortoise then took advantage of this and claimed the gifts and best portions of the food for himself. Taking notice of this, the birds became quite angry and devised a plan to take back the feathers they had given to *mbe*. After resting at a tree, the birds took back their feathers, leaving him stranded and alone. *Mbe* finally fell from the tree, breaking his shell into many pieces. This is the reason why tortoises walk extremely slowly and why their shells are patched-up.[23]

This folk tale is an entertaining story about the origins of the tortoises' physical features. However, it is a more telling example of how the Igbo reacted within their political system to leadership and abuses of power. Clearly, *mbe* represents a leader who has taken advantage of their given situation in order to claim benefits for him alone. The birds, recognizing this exploitation, take back the "power" they had awarded him, eliminating his status and his authority. The tale reinforces the basic tenet that a dictatorial leader in the Igbo society is inherently inconceivable. This principal foundation of the Igbo society is the polar opposite to the environment of slavery that Igbo Africans were thrust into in the system of slavery in the Americas. Plantation owners and masters were the ultimate authority in the lives of enslaved Africans. They did not earn their position through hard work, were not expected to validate their position through achievements, and certainly did not create real opportunities for slaves to attain a position of authority. These contradictions with the Igbo worldview, not to mention the horrid conditions of slavery itself, generated a real source of discontent and resentment for the institution and formed a breeding ground for slave resistance.

The story above also represents another basic principle within the Igbo society—the right of the people to elect and depose leaders as they see fit. To be sure, the Igbo were "averse and sensitive to outside authority" and molded their political powers and institutions in such a way that places them among the "democrats of the world."[24] Without a doubt, the indigenous political institutions of the Igbo closely resemble that of modern democratic societies. As Adiele Afigbo reports, the accepted practice of the Igbo system of governmental organization at the lineage and village level was that of a direct democracy. On the level of groups of villages, the Igbo then practiced a form of representative democracy.[25] Furthermore, political participation was allowed for all the males in an Igbo village. Every villager who had something to say or had something to contribute to a hearing or discussion on village policy was allowed speak up. Public matters and issues were kept open for village discussion and were not confined to a king, elder or any single man's sole discretion.[26] This idea of political democracy within the Igbo society has its roots, according to Afigbo, in the basic ideal of equality and equivalence among the Igbo. In the Igbo society "all men are equal" and "each must have its fair share of work and reward."[27] In turn, all must be permitted to participate in governmental affairs and be afforded the opportunity to participate in the decision-making.[28]

Another characteristic of the Igbo political organization was decentralization. Each village was an autonomous unit of legislative, judicial, and executive affairs. As Uchendu states, "The Igbo are jealous of their legislative authority and are not willing to surrender it to another group."[29] Matters that were taken to the legislative body of the Igbo villages were the control and regulation of economic affairs within the village, questions of going to war, reconciling peace, and of preparing defense. The people who made these laws also executed them, tried them, and delegated orders to others to enforce them as well.[30] In addition, as Afigbo affirms, the Igbo felt an extreme sense of community within their political groups. The group itself is not there to simply uphold law, order, and promote social welfare. It functions as a "union of blood relatives – a sort of spiritual commonwealth."[31] Furthermore, it is interesting to note that Igbo did not deal in matters of capital punishment. They felt that the village has no right to take the life of another human being. According to Uchendu, "No social group or institution has this power."[32] Clearly, the Igbo had a profound respect for the life of individual human beings and their community as a whole; a phenomena that is quite foreign to the institution and leadership structures of slavery in the Americas.

In relating all these characteristics of Igbo political organization to the institution of slavery, one can see a stark contrast. It is not as though the Igbo were an oppressed population under a dictatorial rule, with no individual power or voice. The Igbo were accustomed to participating in the decisions of the village and holding an open dialogue with others in order to reach solutions that would attempt to benefit everyone in the village. The institution of slavery, especially on the local and plantation level, was a highly centralized power structure specifically designed to make slaves powerless and degrade the rights of the Africans in order to maximize work output and obedience. Echoing this sentiment, Njaka states, "To the Igbo, a government that does not afford him an opportunity to participate actively is not parademocratic and cannot be countenanced. All means, implicit and explicit, overt and covert, should be employed to get rid of such a government."[33] This usurpation of the Igbo's basic human and democratic rights under slavery lends an important insight and explanation for why Igbo slaves resisted the institution and employed "overt and covert" means in order to combat and overthrow it.

The next aspect of the Igbo that played an important part in their society was existence and prevalence of a real and valued social mobility. This basic concept is rooted in the fact that the people have the option to work hard, gain respect, and ultimately change their destiny in life through their own accord. The Igbo feel that they are the masters of their social destiny and that they are able to choose their own roles in society. By likening to their own free will, persevering, and working hard any Igbo can set out to make a success of their social position and career. Even though this quest can sometimes be dangerous or hazardous to an individual, it should not deter them from trying their hardest to overcome the problems that they face in achieving success.[34] Also tying into the idea of social mobility and interaction in Igbo society is the function of competition among the Igbo. Afigbo places a high premium on the idea of competition within Igbo society, stating that the nature of Igbo competition was to "place a premium on achievement" and to keep individuals and social groups functioning in the most efficient ways possible; basically, an African cultural version of Adam Smith ideology.[35] Additionally, social mobility is reinforced through the Igbo belief structure. It is reflected in the Igbo belief of reincarnation and it "rationalizes the individual's ability to improve his status in either the world of man or after his reincarnation, in the world of ancestors."[36] Much more will be said about the belief structures of the Igbo later on, as it plays an important role in the discussion and argument presented here.

To draw again from Achebe's *Things Fall Apart*, the character Okonkwo is the perfect example of the Igbo person's constant attempt to improve his stature in the society. Okonkwo fears, more than anything, to be like his lazy father; squandering his resources and ultimately becoming a joke to the rest of the village. In response to this, Okonkwo vows to work harder, longer, and more efficiently in order to achieve titles, yams, wives, and to build up his compound in order to be viewed as a respected member of his village. In response to his efforts, Okonkwo is appreciated by his community and elected to the position of a prominent clan leader.[37] His financial and social success is directly attributable to his own decision and dedication to move up the social ladder in his village; a decision that clearly reflects the Igbo's ideals of personal freedom and social mobility.

Another portion of Igbo culture that relates to this idea of social mobility is the fact that the Igbos based their society on the principles of relative equalitarianism. As Uchendu states, "Equality or near equality ensures that no one person or group of persons acquires too much control over the life of others."[38] Providing relatively equal opportunities for the village ensures that the people will achieve success, happiness, a higher feeling of security in the town, and a strong, pervasive community spirit. Obviously, this notion of social mobility was entirely absent from the systems of slavery in the Americas. To be sure, some enslaved Africans were eligible to work for extra money in hopes of buying their way to freedom. However, this practice is definitely in the minority of experiences that the slaves endured. The concepts of hard work, competition, gaining respect, improving one's own social destiny, and even the slightest inkling of free will were void in the lives of the enslaved.

Stemming out of their political organization and the existence of social mobility in the Igbo society are a set of related characteristics, which describe the unique nature of the Igbo and shed some light on several other aspects of their lives that help to explain Igbo resistance in the Americas. The first of these is individualism. This individualism is rooted within the personal sphere of the Igbo, however. This can be seen in the communal spirit and the attention paid by the Igbo to improving and helping the entire group. The individualism of the Igbo is not selfish; it is set in the vein of social mobility and belief of independence. This deeply personal sentiment employs the Igbo to improve his own life, accumulate wealth, and ultimately contribute to the prestige and well-being of the entire group.

In addition to its personal and social features, the pervasive individualism of the Igbo extends into the realm of the political as well. Thus, each individual has the right to independence and would "fight to the last man rather than bow down to forcible control."[39] In fact, "The concept of one dominating or ruling another is strictly un-Igbo."[40]

Another factor borne out of the Igbo's political and social freedoms is the ability to negotiate. This key attribute is apparent in multiple aspects of their society, including their local political organization, trading markets, inter-village communications and resolutions, and personal relations with one another. The Igbo proverb "Tomorrow is pregnant, nobody knows to what it will give birth," testifies to the persistent nature of uncertainty and negotiation that penetrate the life of the Igbo.[41] This process of negotiation is clearly missing from the interactions that are evident in a system of slavery. The institution of slavery strips away the processes of negotiation and democratic debate and replaces it with that of an ultimate and oppressive authority. Igbo Africans view this with suspicion and contempt.

The final aspect of Igbo life that will be examined here is the religious structures and belief systems that are prominent in their society. The beliefs of the Igbo people saturate numerous other aspects of their life including their political and social systems. Therefore, it is impossible to completely understand these systems without a thorough discussion of the Igbo religion. The religion itself is not aggressive and deals with both the world of living men and the world of spiritual ancestors, and involves the principles of freedom, obligation to the people, and tolerance. The Igbo people do not attempt to convert or recruit others into believing exactly as they do, because there are variations within the Igbo belief system itself. Their religion holds that people should be guaranteed their own right to practice customs, rituals, and beliefs as they see fit. As we can see, a strong sense of acceptance and tolerance is rooted directly in the manner in which the Igbo practice their religion.[42]

In the realm of what or who the Igbo actually worship, the simplest answer is that they have many gods. There is a host of different gods, with different functions. One of the most important is *Ala*, the earth-goddess, being perhaps the closest to an Igbo individual. However, hosts of other spirits are worshiped as well, two examples being *Anyanwu* the sun god, and *Igwe*, the sky god, among several others. There is also a "Supreme Being," named *Chukwu*, but it is quite different from anything conceptualized by Western religions or beliefs. This "high god" is not worshiped directly, unlike the Christian religion. As stated in a lecture by Professor Michael J.C. Echeruo, "Our god is not the one towards whom all creation aspires . . . he has no troop of angels and saints ministering to him. He has promulgated no Decalogue, and he has not appointed a day when he will judge the living and the dead."[43] Instead, the Igbo see *Chukwu* as an entity that does not require direct worship because he is all-powerful and essentially not concerned with the actions of individuals.

Furthermore, *Chukwu* is the source of the Igbo's *chi*, which is, according to Echeruo, "one of the most complex theological concepts ever devised to explain the Universe."[44] Chi is a spiritual entity that resides within an Igbo at all times and is their very essence of individual life. All Igbo have a unique *chi* assigned to them and they are in constant negotiation with their chi in order to empower themselves as much as possible. This is the beginnings to understanding what Christian's would consider "prayer" in the Igbo belief system. In Christian religions, the objective of prayer is apologize to God, repenting what one has done wrong, and ultimately winning your way back into God's graces by confession. In the Igbo belief however, prayer functions as an attempt to "exhort chi to action." Thus, prayer acts as an inspiration to a person's *chi* in order to change his or her own destiny.

Even in this mere overview of the Igbo belief system, one can see various influences on the Igbo political, social, and personal outlook on life that deeply contrast with the attributes and forces that exist when living a life under slavery. First, the overriding principles of tolerance and acceptance in the Igbo religion are obliterated under slavery. The enslaved are subject to the worst conditions a human can endure and are treated as a uniform group with little to no room for difference and inclusion. Second, the Igbo's tradition of belief in many gods is not only in direct conflict to the religions of their slave masters, but in opposition to the system of slavery itself. This idea of worshipping multiple gods, and not one, all powerful being can be related to the concept of obeying under enslavement. Slavery holds that one person, the master, holds all power over a group of people. If the Igbo did not even feel that the gods had this power, how could they accept it from another human being? Third, the concept of *chi* in the Igbo religion encourages action to be taken on the part of the individual when you wish to improve your own social standing or position in life. As Njaka states, "A *chi* does not help an individual who fails to help himself."[45] This emphasis on taking action, not simply praying for better fortunes, is indicative of the culture and spirit of resistance that the Igbo were known for in the Americas.

A fourth factor that was not stated above is the Igbo concept and belief in "living" ancestors and reincarnation in the Igbo society. Reincarnation will be discussed in depth later on in this essay, as it plays an extremely large role in the Igbo religion and in the rationalization of slave resistance.

RESISTANCE IN THE AMERICAS

Possibly more than any other concentrated group from the shores of Africa, the captives taken from the Bight of Biafra received special attention to their characteristics and were subject to numerous stereotypes. Various locations across the Americas, including South Carolina, simply refused to accept imports from the Bight of Biafra, and held an intense prejudice toward these captives. The Igbo were seen as "lazy, despondent, suicidal, melancholy, superstitious, and sickly" and planters in South Carolina preferred slaves from Senegambia or the Gold Coast regions.[46] Other areas, including Haiti, viewed the Biafran slaves as prone to suicide and in Jamaica the popular perception of Igbo slaves was that they were "manageable but deceitful" and also suicidal if they were mistreated.[47] The effects and importance of these stereotypes can be seen as the discussion of how the Igbo Africans resisted the institution progresses.

Evidently, slave insurrections and resistance began even before the voyage from Africa was completed. As Gomez asserts, this resistance has something to do with the conditions on the slave ships themselves, but also has links to the Biafran people on board the boat.[48] One example of this is from an article in the *Maryland Gazette* from November 1750 detailing a slave insurrection on a slave ship en route from St. Kitts, a place of significant Igbo concentration. The resistance was enacted by fifteen slaves on the ship and ended in killing five crew members, the captain, and throwing nine more white men overboard. Upon acquiring control of the boat, the slaves requested to sail to various locations, among them being Calabar, in the Bight of Biafra. In the end, the decision was made to sail for a nearby island with no whites although the ultimate fate of the Africans who resisted is not reported.[49]

Another example of resistances on slave ships themselves is an instance involving slaver Captain Barbot who reported that the Igbo were violent on the crossing from the Bight of Biafra to the Americas. He stated there was evidence of choking, fighting, and murdering one another on board the slave ships. Despite even meticulous precautions, as Barbot reported taking, resistance was still common. Describing one mutiny among the slaves on his ship, Barbot stated that the Africans "premeditated a revolt, had broken off the shackles from several of their companions feet, which served them, as well as billets they had provided themselves with, and all other things they could lay hands on, which they imagin'd might be of use for this enterprize. Thus arm'd, they fell in crowds and parcels on our men."[50] Without question, there is a lively and industrious spirit of resistance that surrounds the Igbo slaves, even before they disembarked at their destinations in the New World. The stereotypes of their character, reluctance to deal with the Biafran Africans by slave ship captains and plantations owners, and the accounts of resistance onboard the ships themselves liken to this fact.

Running away was perhaps the most common method of resisting the institution of slavery throughout the Americas. It is certain that slaves ran away from their masters in every setting and location in which the institution existed. The Igbo are no different and in countless cases they were either specifically identified by the name itself or by specific character traits that were commonly used to identify slaves during this era. The plethora of runaway slave advertisements from the colony of Virginia easily reveals the Igbo presence and ultimately the significance of their running away. The slave advertisements often report the basic characteristics and circumstances of the runaway, such as their height, hair color, skin tone, posture, other distinguishing physical features, and whether or not they ran away alone, with a group, and their family.

The Igbo incidences of flight can be found within the database of advertisements by doing a little bit of detective work. In one online database, there are only nine instances of the word "Ibo" and "Eboe" represented in the advertisements themselves. This, however, is to be expected because slave owners often did not know the race or ethnicity of their slaves and the newspaper advertisements in turn rarely catalogue this fact. On the other hand, the advertisements did often record the observable features of the runaways. Looking to Littlefield and revisiting the stereotypes of Igbo Africans, the planters of the North American colonies referred to Igbos as "small, slender, weak and tended toward a yellowish color. Calabar or Ibo slaves, with whatever justice, seemed to epitomize these qualities."[51] After this realization, one can comb through the database of advertisements and by reading the descriptions carefully there are numerous references to slaves of "yellow complexion," "yellowish complexion," "yellow hue," "yellowish hue," and "yellow colour."[52] On querying the entire online database of advertisements again, this time adding the descriptive adjectives previously listed, 467 advertisements appear in total.

Within these advertisements, there is a great degree of diversity. Some refer to a single slave who has escaped, others to a pair of slaves, and even some describing groups of slaves who have taken flight together. Furthermore, I queried the database in order to weed out any advertisements that refer specifically to mulattos, who could also be characterized by "yellow" features. Interestingly, only six advertisements refer to both yellow complexioned individuals and mulattos. However, within these six, three of them refer to "yellowish" complexioned individuals who look "much like a mulatto" or "almost like a mulatto." Therefore, although characteristics of Igbo runaways and mulattos are similar, the slave advertisements show that these two groups are represented independently from one another in the language of the advertisements. Thus, concluding that Igbo runaways are well represented in the slave advertisements.

So what can be deduced from these hundreds of instances of Igbo slaves appearing in hundreds of runaway advertisements from the Chesapeake region? For one, it tells that the Igbo were not absent from the runaway population. Indeed, they appear quite often in the available documentation. Synthesizing this information with other sources, one can see that the phenomenon of the Igbo runaway was quite common. As Philip Morgan reports, "Igbos were the one group to produce a marked divergence between their known proportions among immigrants and runaways."[53] Data from South Carolina immigrant runaways show that Igbos only represented 5 percent of the known immigrants in this area, out roughly 62,000, but were represented as 10 percent of the total runaways, out of roughly 1,200.[54] John Brown, a fugitive slave, recalled distinctly in his narrative of slave life in Georgia that his father was of the "Eboe" tribe.[55] Furthermore, Gomez has reported the high proportion of Igbo women who appear in the runaway population, attributing this fact to the various freedoms that women expressed in several arenas of Igbo society, such as their ability to participate in battle, their dominance in the local exchange of goods, the ability to grow their own store of crops, and even sell these at the market in order to accumulate personal wealth.[56] If we accept Gomez's interpretation, one can associate the existence and prevalence of Igbo runaways to the freedoms, democratic institutions, and social mobility enjoyed in their indigenous African culture.

Another form of resistance is the incidents of suicide in the New World. The Igbo were specifically stigmatized in the Americas as slaves who committed suicide often. At first glance, one might retort by claiming that suicide does not have a real place in the realm of resistance; that it is basically a giving up by the slaves, a last gesture to end their misery. However, by looking at the deeper connection of the Igbo to their indigenous culture and beliefs it seems quite conclusive that suicide was not simply a way out. It was a way back to their homeland. Gomez reports numerous accounts in slave narratives claiming to see "flying Africans." Indeed, these Igbo Africans were actually committing a form of ritual suicide, attempting to "fly" back to their homeland. Another instance is a group of Igbo slaves in nineteenth century Georgia who marched towards the sea, singing ritual songs of their culture and ended their lives by drowning themselves off St. Simon's Island.[57]

In relation to suicide in the New World is the firm Igbo belief rooted in reincarnation and returning home to their ancestors at death.[58] Looking again at the notion of the Igbo's concept *chi*, one can see another source of encouragement for suicide. The *chi* of a man leaves upon his death and does not return with his reincarnation. At reincarnation, the Igbo believe a new *chi* is assigned to each person, changing their fortunes, their social outcomes, and chances in life.[59] Combining this information with Gomez's argument, and the sheer numbers of Igbo who committed suicide, it does indeed seem that suicide could actually be the "ultimate form of resistance, as it contained within it the seed of regeneration and renewal."[60] In its rawest form, it would seem as if the Igbo belief in reincarnation and returning to the home of their ancestors was a primary motivating factor in their decision to commit suicide. Even though suicide was seen as an abomination in the eyes of the Igbo, one must take into account the deplorable and humiliating conditions of slavery. It is quite understandable that the Igbo would reach a conclusion of hopelessness, make a decision based on their circumstances, and commit suicide, praying this would be a way home.

A third form of resistance was the use of poison and murder. Douglas Chambers discusses this phenomenon in relation to a famous event in which three Igbo slaves poisoned and ultimately murdered their master, Ambrose Madison, the paternal grandfather of future President James Madison. Chambers argues that this event was in direct relation to the indigenous culture of the Igbo slaves, claiming that the use of poison is related to the phenomena of conjuring in both Virginia and the Caribbean, which were both primarily comprised of Igbo slaves. He relates the poisoning to the Igbo word "Obeah," a word that was used for the practices of doctoring, herbalism, and spiritual as well as supernatural powers. The word also has associations to resolving conflicts and the punishment of enemies.[61] Furthermore, this case documents the first known case of slaves murdering their master and the first known use of poison in doing so. The fact that this is the first case tells us that the slaves were clearly not following any previously set precedent. They were being creative and using what they knew in order to resist slavery. This resistant inspiration was drawn directly from their indigenous Igbo culture. As Chambers states, the "enslaved Africans throughout the Atlantic relied on ancestral cultures to make sense of their new lives" in the Americas.[62]

The Igbo were involved in several instances of slave rebellions and insurrections in the New World. Some of the most famous of American slave rebellions took place right in Virginia, a known concentration of the Igbo. There was a total of seven planned insurrections in the colonial history of

Virginia, three of these being Gabriel Prosser's failed insurrection, which was a planned raid on the city of Richmond, Virginia, and Nat Turner's rebellion, the most vigorous and violent instance of slave resistance in the pre-Civil War era of American history, and the raid on Harper's Ferry led by white abolitionist John Brown.

Another insurrection took place in South Carolina in 1822 and has connections to the Igbo. The plot involved an Igbo man named Monday Gell, who was instrumental in the plotting and coordinating of the insurrection. He owned a shop that was a center for holding meetings and providing aid for the conspirators. Also of note in this plan is the fact that there is a group referred to as the "Ebo Company." Whether or not this group of slaves was all of Igbo origin is disputable, but the fact that the slaves had a resistance group "who are going to fight the white people" named after the Igbo is notable in its own right.[63] Other insurrections and plots from areas of Igbo concentration consist of 39 instances of planned rebellions in Jamaica, including one in 1815 where a major conspiracy was discovered involving about 250 "Ibo" slaves, 9 instances in Barbados, and 1 in both Grenada and St. Kitts.[64]

Although the question of how involved Igbo Africans were involved in the numerous slave rebellions and insurrections cited above still remains, it is quite significant that so many occurred in areas of large Igbo concentrations. Their resistant spirit has been specifically seen by name in various instances but the other occasions demand further research and sources to make any concrete connections.

In conclusion, it seems that when the basic premises of Igbo society are juxtaposed with that of the components of slave society, the distinction becomes clear. The Igbo's fundamental ideals and view of the world is in direct opposition to a system of slavery. Their political systems, social structures, religious beliefs, and cultural norms are all indicative of an equalitarian and democratic society. When taken out of this context, the enslaved Igbo Africans from the Bight of Biafra were forcefully positioned into a world of overt dominance, violence, and dictatorship of lifestyle. Given their previous life choices and norms, the Igbo slaves reacted with a determined and varied resistance; a resistance that can be traced from the slave ships on the Atlantic Ocean, to the plantation master's home, the trails of hundreds of runaways, and to the secret plots of rebellion that flooded the New World.

NOTES

1. Paul E. Lovejoy, *Transformations in Slavery: A History of Slavery in Africa* (New York: Cambridge University Press, 2000), figures taken from Tables 1.1, 3.2, 3.4, 4.1 and 7.4.

2. Michael A. Gomez, *Reversing Sail: A History of the African Diaspora* (New York: Cambridge University Press, 2005), 65.

3. David Eltis, David Richardson, Stephen D. Behrendt, and Herbert S. Klein, eds., *The Atlantic Slave Trade: A Database on CD-ROM* (New York: Cambridge University Press, 1999). The figures presented here represent a query of the entire database and a summary of the data therein.

4. Gomez, *Reversing Sail:*, 2.

5. Eltis, et al. The figures here represent a query and summary of the number of Africans who disembarked from the Bight of Biafra during the full time period provided by the database, 1527-1866.

6. Michael A. Gomez, *Exchanging Our Country Marks: The Transformation of African Identities in the Colonial and Antebellum South* (Chapel Hill, NC: The University of North Carolina Press, 1998), 115.

7. Eltis, et al. The figures in this paragraph represent a query of where the Africans had disembarked and examination of the numbers in the database. It is important to note that within the records there is a degree of anonymity for the origins of Africans who disembarked at various destinations. Within the database, significant numbers of slaves originate from "Africa Unspecified." For example, St. Kitts and Barbados report that roughly 40 percent of Africans came from "African Unspecified."

8. Gomez, *Exchanging Our Country Marks*, 114.

9. Ibid., 115.

10. Ibid., 130-131.

11. E. N. Njaka, *Igbo Political Culture* (Evanston: Northwestern University Press, 1974), 22.

12. Douglas B. Chambers, "My Own Nation: Igbo Exiles in the Diaspora," *Slavery and Abolition* 18 (1997): 72-97.

13. See for example, Melville J. Herskovitts, *The Myth of the Negro Past* (Boston: Beacon Press, 1941); Franklin E. Frazier, *Negro Family in the United States* (Chicago: University of Chicago Press, 1939); and Franklin E. Frazier, *Negro Church in America* (New York: Schocken Books, 1974).

14. Paul E. Lovejoy, "The African Diaspora: Revisionist Interpretations of Ethnicity, Culture, and Religion under Slavery," *Studies in the World History of Slavery, Abolition, and Emancipation II*, 1 (1997). http://web.archive.org/web/20010606194224/www2.h-net.msu.edu/~slavery/essays/esy9701love.html [Accessed 10 March 2007].

15. Douglas B. Chambers, *Murder at Montpelier: Igbo Africans in Virginia* (Jackson, MS: University Press of Mississippi, 2005), 12.

16. Ibid., 15.

17. Diana Akers Rhoads, "Culture in Chinua Achebe's *Things Fall Apart*," *African Studies Review* 36 (September 1993), 61.

18. Rhodes House, Oxford University: Mss Afr. s. 546. Carr Frederick Bernard (Sir), "Reminiscences of Sir F. Bernard Carr—Administrative Officer, Nigeria 1919-1949."

19. Victor C. Uchendu, *The Igbo of Southeast Nigeria* (New York, NY: Holt, Rinehart and Winston, 1965), 15.

20. Ibid., 17.

21. Njaka, *Igbo Political Culture*, 59.

22. Uchendu, *The Igbo*, 20.

23. Njaka, *Igbo Political Culture*, 50.

24. Ibid., 22.

25. Adiele Afigbo, "The Indigenous Political Systems of the Igbo," in *Igbo History and Society: The Essays of Adiele Afigbo* ed. Toyin Falola (Trenton, NJ: Africa World Press, 2005), 157.

26. Uchendu, *The Igbo*, 41.

27. Afigbo, "The Indigenous," 163.

28. Ibid.

29. Ibid., 42.

30. Ibid., 42.

31. Ibid., 162.

32. Uchendu, *The Igbo*, 43.

33. Njaka, *Igbo Political Culture*, 55. The uses the word "parademocracy" in this quotation is used to describe the characteristics of the Igbo political organizations. Njaka avoids the "overused term 'democracy'" because the word parademocracy includes the "attitudinal, behavioral, conceptual, moral, and valuational judgments which are part and parcel of any political decision" in which the Igbo believe that they have a natural right to participate.

34. Uchendu, *The Igbo*, 19.

35. Afigbo, 164.

36. Uchendu, *The Igbo*, 94.

37. Chinua Achebe, *Things Fall Apart* (New York: Mcdowell and Oblensky, 1959).

38. Uchendu, *The Igbo*, 19-20.

39. Njaka, *Igbo Political Culture*, 62.

40. Ibid.

41. Ibid., 66-67.

42. Ibid., 28.

43. Michael J.C. Echeruo, "A Matter of Identity," 1979 Ahiajoku Lecture. *IgboNet: The Igbo Network*, http://Ahiajoku.igbonet.com/1979/.
44. Echeruo, "A Matter of Identity."
45. Njaka, *Igbo Political Culture*, 32.
46. Gomez, *Exchanging our Country Marks*, 115-17.
47. Ibid., 116.
48. Ibid., 115.
49. *Maryland Gazette* (Green), Annapolis, November 14, 1750. *The Geography of Slavery*, http://www.vcdh.virginia.edu/gos/news.html. [Accessed March 10, 2007].
50. Barbot's complete narrative can be found in Elizabeth Donnan, *Documents Illustrative of the History of the Slave Trade to America,* (Washington, D.C., 1930). However, this reconstruction and synthesis of his narrative was taken from various sources, including Gomez, *Exchanging Our Country Marks,* Corey Malcom, "Iron Bilboes of the Henrietta *Marie" A Slave Ship Speaks.* http://www.melfisher.org/henriettamarie/ironbilboes.htm, [Accessed 15 March 2007] and Harvey Wish, "American Slave Insurrections Before 1861," *The Journal of Negro History* 22 (July 1937), 300-3.
51. Gomez, *Exchanging Our Country Marks*, 115. The quote is taken from within Gomez, who is referring to the work of Daniel C. Littlefield, *Rice and Slaves: Ethnicity and the Slave Trade in Colonial South Carolina* (Baton Rouge: Louisiana State University Press, 1981).
52. Tom Costa, *The Geography of Slavery*, 2005. http://www.vcdh.virginia.edu/gos/index.html. [Accessed 15 March 2007]. This quotation is in reference to numerous slave advertisements that can be found on this website, not any one in particular.
53. Philip D. Morgan, *Slave Counterpoint: Black Culture in the Eighteenth Century Chesapeake and Lowcountry* (Chapel Hill, NC: University of North Carolina Press, 1998), 67.
54. Morgan, *Slave*, 68.
55. John Brown, "Slave Life in Georgia: A Narrative of the Life, Sufferings, and Escape of John Brown, a Fugitive Slave, Now in England," *Documenting the American South*, http://docsouth.unc.edu/neh/jbrown/jbrown.html. [Accessed 15 March 2007].
56. Gomez, *Exchanging Our Country Marks*, 126-127.
57. Morgan, *Slave Counterpoint*, 590.
58. Gomez, *Exchanging Our Country Marks,* 118-120.
59. Njaka, *Igbo Political Culture*, 30-32.
60. Gomez, *Exchanging Our Country Marks*, 120.
61. Chambers, *Murder at Montpelier*, 14.
62. Ibid., 15.

63. James Hamilton, "Negro Plot. An Account of the Late Intended Insurrection among a Portion of the Blacks of the City of Charleston, South Carolina," *Documenting the American South*. http://docsouth.unc.edu/church/hamilton/hamilton.html.

64. Living Easton, "Slave Revolts, Rebellions, Revolutions, Rebels, Conspiracies & The Maroon Wars," http://www.cems.uwe.ac.uk/~rstephen/livingeaston/local_history/slavery.html. [Accessed 10 March 2007].

CHAPTER 17

EDITING RACE: THE MEDIATION OF EQUIANO'S *INTERESTING NARRATIVE* AND THE CORRELATING BLACK AESTHETIC

RON MILLAND

SLAVE NARRATIVE: A BRIEF EXPLICATION

Slave narratives remain a source of insight into the institution of bondage as well as scholarly analysis and debate. Their conception, however, was contextualized by the abolitionist movement and the emergence of new perspectives regarding humanity and the black aesthetic. This polemic of abolitionism was often employed by those who edited the slave narratives so that the completed works would suit the preconceived notions of a potentially racist readership. Accomplishing this in a way that would persuade the reading public to rally for an end to bondage required the editors to design works that both elicited sympathy for the enslaved and confined them with this new rhetorical framework – a formulaic structure that was intended to ideologically truncate their freedom and even their expressed humanity. Through a detailed examination of the slave narrative of Olaudah Equiano, this paper asserts that, despite the efforts of editors to envelope the voices of such authors in multiple layers of authentication,

Equiano successfully relays a sense of his Igbo origins, the substantial difficulties of racial integration in the West Indies, and the social and legal limitations of curtailing or abolishing slavery and enforcing freedom – thus serving to allude to the need for subsequent struggles such as desegregation and the Civil Rights movement.

According to scholars, *The Interesting Narrative of the Life of Olaudah Equiano* is an example of a slave narrative where the author was in a position to do most if not all of his own editing. Through an analysis of letters and other evidence demonstrating Equiano's ability to read and write, Paul Edwards concludes that Equiano was more than sufficiently educated to both write and proofread his own narrative.[1] A ghostwriter would have therefore been unnecessary. However, Equiano had accumulated a considerable network of friends and allies, many of whom he surely consulted for advice and suggestions as he compiled his narrative. He was familiar with numerous texts that preceded his own, including those written by Africans living in England like Gronniosaw and Cugoano. Equiano's religious conversion meant that his narrative could also be regarded as a spiritual autobiography, as he includes quotations and passages from the Bible for added emphasis at key moments throughout his narrative. In short, Equiano knew what the readership would accept, and in addition to being literate, Equiano was a sufficiently resourceful and savvy author as well.

Functioning as his own editor, Equiano employs his strategy right from the very start of his narrative. The inclusion of the author's portrait at the beginning serves to authenticate the author as a real person in the mind of the reader, who can use it to put a face to the story being told. However, the stance in the portrait is more noteworthy than the portrait itself. It is dignified and stately, and in the mind of the reader may conjure the image of an intellect or revolutionary hero like Benjamin Franklin or George Washington. It is not the image of a downtrodden slave, but of a free man who appears to be an established and productive member of white society. Any hint of defiance or arrogance in his stance would have been downplayed, of course, but Equiano has certainly been painted to appear as a spiritually enlightened figure prepared to fight oppression with a corrective sense of religion and morality. The notion of the underdog, opposed by seemingly insurmountable odds, who manages to overcome enslavement by his own diligence and cleverness, would have been quite appealing to the reader.

However, not everyone thought Equiano's narrative wore "an honest face." Two reviewers asserted that Equiano was not born in Africa, but in the West Indies. While this allegation would not have negated his existence or rendered him subordinate to a dominant ghostwriter, allowing it to spread and gain credibility among the readership would have proved damaging. This would particularly apply to the initial sections of his Narrative where he describes in some detail the context of growing up in Africa, and makes comparisons with European cultures and customs. If it came to be believed that these areas were fabricated, the authenticity of the entire narrative would soon be called into question, as well as the genuine motivations of the author himself. Consequently, Equiano did what was necessary to validate his narrative and its author in the minds of readers by including testimonials in the form of letters in his 1792 and subsequent editions.

In and of themselves, these letters of recommendation are not particularly unusual. But in the context of Equiano's Narrative, they hold special significance. For one, they are all written by or to the "friends of humanity."[2] This is a direct reference to the polemic context for which his Narrative was originally intended, for it implies that anyone who opposed the abolitionist cause or denounced Equiano's narrative was not a "friend of humanity." It also implies, though perhaps more subtly, that slaves should be treated with humanity since they were humans who were unjustly held in bondage and cruelly treated by those who claimed ownership over them. Bringing an end to this system would be the only humane thing to do, and if you did not believe so, you were not a "friend of humanity."

This appeal to the humanity of the readers proved to be an effective tactic in the abolitionist cause and Equiano's role therein. Many of the more distinguished readers endorsed his Narrative and called for its continued circulation, as well as the expansion of Equiano's network of influential contacts and friends. There lies another interesting feature these letters predominantly share: the assertion that Equiano is a person of good character and honorable intent. Fully legitimating a free black man as an author would seem to first require that his peers of distinguished standing in society attest to his humanity, intelligence, and honesty.

In the initial pages of his narrative, Olaudah Equiano describes in considerable detail the particulars of daily life in his native village in Africa. Even though he characterizes these recollections as little more than a crude summary, the detail is vivid and qualitatively meritorious. He includes descriptions of daily life pertaining to everything from food preparation to clothing to the construction of houses and the sort of furniture they contain. Also described are customs of his people pertaining to the rules of marriage, the execution of laws, and the means by which wars are fought. This information is simply too comprehensive to have been fabricated by the author, and has clearly been generated by someone who has lived in this context for some time and was a participant (as opposed to a mere eyewitness) in this society. Those critics who accused Equiano of being born in the West Indies, therefore, may have derived their erroneous claim from elsewhere in his narrative.

Indeed, one would hope that those who supported the continuation of the slave trade would have no solid basis for their accusations. The accusing reviewers in this case, however, may have used Equiano's own words against him. Late in the first chapter of this narrative, he cites the example – which he hoped would "not be deemed impertinent . . . to insert"[3]– of a poisoned virgin whose body was being carried to the grave, whose bearers, being apparently possessed, uncovered the murderer's identity in that moment of seizure. Equiano contextualizes this example in a broader explanation of the beliefs of his people as regards medicine, magic, superstition, and the related priests and wise men. But, like any diligent author, Equiano clearly states that this example is cited by inhabitants of the West Indies, and that he was in the West Indies when he witnessed the incident in question, a fact the author made certain to include in a footnote, along with a date that clearly indicates it occurred well after his removal from his village in Africa. In following the protocols of good authorship, Equiano may have inadvertently supplied the anti-abolitionists with something they might use against him, which they immediately seized since delegitimating evidence against him was as hard to find as it was to fabricate.

If the pertinence of inserting the aforementioned incident was questionable, the author's observations on the matter of race near the end of the first chapter are far from it. Serving as his own editor proves quite fruitful here, as a white editor or ghostwriter might have excluded this section that, rather than detailing the abuses of slavery, demonstrates the manner in which race-based distinctions and debasements are invalid as evidenced by legitimate and respected scholars. Equiano very logically outlines this evidence, taking care to claim no scholarly credit for it. Instead, he credits contemporary scholars – "men of both genius and learning"[4]– who would have already earned the respect of his readership. Therefore, his discussion of the cultural parallels between Eboan Africans and Jews, and the ways in which geographical context undermines judgments based on race or skin pigmentation, is duly authenticated. Operating as his own editor, Equiano recognized the need for this level of authentication in this discussion, since many of his allies in the abolitionist cause may not have believed that the minds of most Africans were intellectually capable beyond the mechanically repetitive labor that characterized much slave work. The abolitionists wanted to end the slave trade and the abuse of those it exploited. In choosing to include this potentially controversial analysis, Equiano demonstrates that true freedom for enslaved blacks would require more than mere emancipation, for if they continued to be regarded as inferior, their disadvantageous status in society would endure.

Equiano viewed the world through the peculiar disadvantage of slavery in the first volume of his narrative. His initial encounter with whites was when he came to fully realize this subservient status, and taken from the point of view of a young man in completely alien surroundings, was indeed quite terrifying. On board the slave ship, he thought his captors were the most "savage" (71) people he had ever seen, and based on their mannerisms and the way they treated each other (let alone the way they treated him and the other kidnapped Africans), he truly thought that they were planning to eat him. In a metaphorical sense this was not far from the truth, since Equiano and his fellow victims were being forced into a system that would essentially consume their individual identities, family ties, and links to native culture and homeland. What humanity they had was indeed about to be eaten, and in its place they were granted the low status of property. Equiano's captors had no plan of eating him in the literal sense, however, and the author was greatly relieved when he learned that he was to work for the whites. It should be noted that regarding the crew of the ship as "savage" proves an interesting editorial inclusion, as Africans were initially deemed savage by whites who sought to enslave them, and blacks in Africa, as well as many enslaved in the Americas, were probably deemed savage by some of Equiano's white readers. Such an inclusion might be taken as an indication, by his more astute readers, that "savage" is more a matter of perspective than of race.

Fortunately, not all of the whites Equiano encountered were brute savages. One in particular named Richard Baker, befriended Equiano and was kind enough to tutor him. As the author relates it, Baker was one who, at a young age, "found a mind superior to prejudice" (80), for he did not shun or otherwise ill-treat Equiano on account of his race. This inclusion clearly serves as an example of the sort of tolerance that all whites should exhibit toward blacks. His diction here indicates that whites as well as blacks would benefit from this tolerance since a prejudiced attitude, once surpassed, leads to something "superior." Equiano is characterizing prejudice as a vice, and he surely hoped that such inclusions would have a moralizing effect on his readership.

Equiano complements his appeal to the moral sensibilities of some of his readers with an appeal to the financial sensibilities of his slaveholding readers. He makes certain to note that one of his masters, a Quaker named Robert King, treated him with much civility and acknowledged that Equiano was of "more advantage to him" (119) than some of his paid employees. King recognized Equiano's diligence and value by refusing to sell him despite numerous offers, and by treating him not luxuriously, but not cruelly abusing him either. This actually earned King some criticism, to which he responded that slaves who received better treatment were better workers (120). Consequently, King got a better return on his initial investment in Equiano as compared to his more abusive counterparts, who might beat their slaves to such a merciless extent as to impede their ability to work effectively. Obviously, Equiano was not advocating the continuation of slavery in any form. But the author rather artfully makes the point that abuse of slaves is not just immoral and unjust, but financially unsound. Thus, even those readers who deemed slaves to be unfeeling brutes would now have an alternate reason to think twice before subjecting their slaves to cruel forms of punishment.

Unfortunately, King was more the exception than the rule. The greater number of slave owners, at least in the West Indies, treated their slaves very much like property, and many were abusive to great excess. In detailing these atrocities, Equiano chooses to do some selective editing, and spares the reader from having to peruse some of the more graphic descriptions. The author claims that these details are "too shocking to yield delight to either writer or reader" (129). Not only does he wish to spare the sensibilities of the reader, but the details of these various torments are so gruesome that Equiano himself is hesitant to resurrect them from memory! A genuinely artless tale bereft of creativity or any other individually derived persuasion might coldly include an exact catalog of all abuses witnessed, key participants, and injuries incurred or losses suffered. But this author did not set out to compile an empirical taxonomy of slave abuses; rather, his is a personalized account, one that is subject to the unique sensibilities of the writer. This is evidenced in Equiano's own assertion that a detailed catalog of abuses would be "tedious and disgusting" (129). To disgust the reader would prove counterproductive with regard to the polemic intentions of those backing the narrative, for this might inhibit their desire to read further. The goal, therefore, would be to design a narrative that conveys the odious condition slaves endured without compiling a text that is itself as hideous in content as the system it describes. The effective execution of such a task would require the writer and editor to be quite resourceful.

Equiano recognized a need to be resourceful long before endeavoring to publish a narrative. This was particularly true in the West Indies, where it seemed that an overwhelmingly prejudiced hegemony reigned supreme. The author was lucky (or so he thought himself) to have been spared from ownership by masters who were notoriously abusive. Nevertheless, the context in which he conducted himself was fraught with dangers. He cites, for example, the incident of a mulatto, one Joseph Clipson, who was married to a free woman and had a child. This fellow was widely known as being free, and remained unmolested for the duration of his travel aboard Equiano's vessel. That is, until it anchored in the West Indies and a Bermudas captain claimed him as property and forcibly removed him. As he was never before handled as such, Clipson responded with shock at first, and then produced a certificate attesting to his free birth. Unfortunately, this proved as futile as his pleas for due process, and he was dragged into slavery "insulted and plundered without the possibility of redress" (137). Clearly, the letter of the law in the West Indies was enforced along racial lines.

It did indeed seem that a racist consciousness permeated this region. Race is even a determinant in the validity of evidence in court since a "free negro's evidence" is inadmissible (137). While the legal system was designed on the perceived untrustworthiness of blacks, the author found that many whites could not be trusted, especially regarding business transactions. On several occasions, Equiano would sell fruits or other goods at ports his vessel visited, and his white customers were sometimes inclined to take his goods and not pay the full cost or even nothing at all. There was little that a black person in the West Indies could juridically do to right such a wrong, but Equiano was resourceful enough to know a fair number of influential whites whom he could turn to for assistance. His experiences in the West Indies clearly exemplified that there was "no law for free men" (176) regardless of manumission.

It is at the halfway point of his narrative that Equiano describes the process of legally purchasing his freedom, something for which he had saved diligently. The author chooses to include, at full length, his certificate of manumission at this juncture, and from an editorial standpoint, it serves as a suitable divide in his text delineating a socially recognized change in his status. But the more profound implications of this document can be gleaned from its intricate wording, the importance of which is not lost to the author who sees in it "the absolute power and dominion one man claims over his fellow" (157). It verbosely sets forth just how much a slave *does not* have before gaining freedom, and sounds almost as if it contains the power to bestow existence itself. Essentially, this document employs the language of ownership as it describes all of the ways in which Equiano is to be liberated, "manumitted, emancipated, enfranchised, and set free . . . *for ever*" [my italics]. The sense of eternity implied here is proportionally complemented with rhetoric that could be used to describe the dissolution or creation of a nation-state, or a shift in borders or territory. Ownership is certainly changing hands, for it sounds as if the "giving, granting, and releasing unto" Equiano is in reference to the overturning or termination of a prison sentence, especially if prisoners are deemed the property of the state. But in reality he is getting something much greater: "all right, title, dominion, sovereignty, and property, which, as lord and master over the aforesaid Gustavus Vassa, I had, or now I have, or by any means whatsoever I may or can hereafter possibly have over him the aforesaid negro, for ever." The "lord and master" would seem to far outrank any mere jailor, for he controls not just confinement, but the ownership of a life, or even a destiny. Indeed, one simply cannot deny the connotation that some divine entity is permanently relinquishing possession and control over a vastly inferior creature. It is ironic that a document that represents freedom and, essentially, ownership of oneself, should also convey so thorough a notion of the power held by slave owners and the hegemony of slavery itself.

Despite the comprehensive way in which his freedom was bestowed, the author remained subjected to the hegemony of prejudice even after manumission. As the wording of the author's manumission certificate implied, freedom was never enforced with the same zeal as ownership. But after gaining his freedom, it was the culture that continued to oppress Equiano, though the law no longer had any legitimate basis for doing so. He experienced this in quite a violent way at the hands of an unreasonable captain. The author declined to fulfill his request to work aboard another vessel, a refusal that incensed the captain who had Equiano "hung, without any crime committed, or without any judge or jury" (228). As previously stated, his race combined with his location – the West Indies – resulted in his being readily denied any form of due process. Anyone who did not know he had been freed and saw him at that moment, hung by the wrists and bound by the ankles, would have assumed that he was a slave suffering a punishment for a misdeed at the hands of his master. His only crime (which, again, could not be acknowledged under the letter of the law) was that he dared to exercise a glimmer of individualized thought and desire, and did not behave in the compliant manner expected of him.

Expressions of ideological noncompliance with the oppressive status quo have been included by the author throughout the narrative. He is never belligerent in his assertions, or even very angry, though he does express frustration at the persistence of inequities, and the lack of civility with which supposedly good Christians deal with Africans, free or enslaved. He recognizes that while the practices of prejudice and racism remain prevalent, the rights of freedom remain undefended, and in a context like the West Indies where subjugation by race is the norm, freedom is almost completely unenforceable. Equiano counters this system by reporting what he has seen and relating the experience of living under the racial hegemony. But he is also his own editor,[5] and as he very astutely fulfills this role, he includes commentary and criticism that culminate in suggestions for change. His ultimate goal, and that of his sponsors, is the abolition of the slave trade altogether. But as this may be only a distantly achievable reality at the time he first publishes his narrative, he advocates improving the situation of Blacks by other means in the short term, namely by ending the cruel punishments that slaves suffer, a barbarity which he describes at some length while still managing to spare the reader the full magnitude of gore. It is the slave owner who the author portrays as barbaric and savage, and the ugliness and lack of civility previously attributed to enslaved Africans[6] he very effectively transfers to the cruel master. This reconfiguration of the black aesthetic is the result of a very specific elegance with which Equiano tells his story of incident and adventure, poetry and religious enlightenment. The enslaved African is the oppressed victim, whose status in society only suffers further degeneration under a system of cruel beatings and racial prejudice. In contrast, it would take only education and religious edification, according to Equiano, to turn emancipated slaves into productive members of society who can live with the socially validated sense of humanity that they innately possess. The cruelty is irrational, the racism is unjustified, and the hegemony of prejudice can be undermined, a fact to which the multiple editions and republications of Equiano's narrative stand as an irrefutable testament.[7]

ADDENDUM

There has been recent, scholarly inquiry into the accuracy of Equiano's assertion that he was of African birth. Many of these scholars rightly point out that evidence in either direction on this issue is, at best, circumstantial. However, there is a matter of more immediate relevance here. If he did falsify in his narrative the truth with regard to his birthright, why would he make such a choice?

Acting largely as his own editor, there are a number of reasons for this. For one, he needed to sculpt an effective story. His *Interesting Narrative* was not written merely for his own personal sense of satisfaction; if it could be used to further the cause of the abolitionists, then so much the better. Since it was contextualized in that framework, he had to mold the story of his life for a particular audience[8] that would hopefully be convinced to appreciate both a well-told life story and the injustices of slavery. And that notion of being taken away from one's homeland (especially a geographically distant one) made the whole that much more compelling and facilitates the foregrounding of added dimensions of slavery and its related injustices – namely, the Middle Passage. That was itself a brutal and shocking beginning for the enslavement of countless Africans, and for the abolitionist's cause to seem all the more justified, it had to be real for those reading Equiano's book. For all those who did not fully know what the Middle Passage was like, it surely proved an eye-opening experience to read the words of one who lived it.

The slave narratives had a sort of power of their own – a power that transcends the impact of works written in many other genres of literature. They were designed to exercise this power in polemical ways, and if that meant compromising what might ordinarily be considered aesthetically essential, then that was deemed a justifiable sacrifice for a far greater cause. In this sense, one might feel justified in disparaging an author who includes falsehoods in a work that strictly qualifies as non-fiction literature or autobiography, especially when claiming to be speaking simply, plainly, and truthfully.[9] However, few or no scholars disparage Equiano at all, or at least not on these grounds, partly because (one might safely assume), it is generally accepted that Equiano was not strictly designing a mere autobiography, and that polemical causes are often deemed to necessitate a blurring of the distinction between fiction and non-fiction for the sake of enhancing or even just enabling effectiveness.

If Equiano deemed such measures necessary, his reasons for doing so are hardly concealed from at least a cursory analysis. Much of his reading audience was composed of individuals who probably had no real problem with slavery, and probably even regarded blacks as grotesque creatures who on some level even benefited from the forced labor and cruel forms of discipline that often accompanied enslavement. This stereotype of blacks is one that these members of the public had come to regard as a truth that essentially embodied a form of racism that abolitionists needed to fight if they had any hope of furthering their cause. While this seemed apparent to them, they also recognized that completely eradicating slavery and racism was probably more than could be accomplished at the time, and perhaps even much more than the abolitionists themselves wanted.

The compromised and watered-down (as compared to the black power movement that occurred a century later in the United States) solution was not to empower blacks in any way, but rather to save them from the cruel planter. So instead of seeming embittered by unjust enslavement, slaves had to seem victimized and pitiful. Virtually anything that could be done to make the reader feel a little sorrier for the "poor African" was done. Equiano *knew* that even with the use of truly artful (while claiming artlessness) rhetorical measures, his power to shift public opinion was limited: not by his ability to write well (which was considerable), but by the steadfast belief by many members of the public in the eternal and irrevocable inferiority of enslaved blacks. The most he could probably hope for, in that day and age, was to portray blacks as children that white readers could feel sorry for. Additionally, his portrayal of his own youth and Igbo origins served to illustrate an inherent innocence – the sort of innocence that one associates with nascent time and place – that was destroyed by slavery and the colonizing forces behind it. While readers would have found these components relatable, any attempt on the author's part to demonstrate even greater parallels between enslaved blacks and the reading audience – especially relating to their shared equalities - would run the dangerous risk of overtly disparaging his readers (if only in their own minds) and perhaps alienating or inadvertently closing their minds to hearing anything further.

Ultimately, the scholarship surrounding the slave narratives should be shifted in its focus, regardless of whether Equiano falsified his birthright in his narrative. Slave narratives *must* be studied by scholars at all levels from three perspectives: the literary, the political, and the sociological with regard to race. These works stand as a testament to the hegemony's attempt to solve a problem by essentially burying it in new legalities that only partially helped slaves. It did not so much matter what the ruling entities wanted, for even their magnanimous attempts to litigate a solution were countered by the racist opposition, and the ideologies of the anti-abolitionists so thoroughly corrupted the systems and social contexts that emancipatory measures became subjugating constrictions that confined blacks in insidiously less visible ways long after manumission. Only by analyzing these contexts – and the aspects slaves revealed artfully in their narratives – can students and scholars begin to fully appreciate the design of the slave narratives, the naturalization of racist sentiment in white society, and the incompleteness and imperfection of emancipation that made subsequent social upheavals like the Civil Rights movement necessary and just.

NOTES

1. Werner Sollors, ed., *The Interesting Narrative of the Life of Olaudah Equiano, or Gustavus Vassa, the African, written by himself* (New York: Norton, 2001), 308.
2. Ibid., 183.
3. Angelo Costanzo, *Surprizing Narrative: Olaudah Equiano and the Beginnings of Black Autobiography* (New York: Greenwood Press, 1987), 57.
4. Ibid., 59.
5. Charles T Davis, *The Slave's Narrative* (NY: Oxford University Press, 1985).
6. Leonard Cassuto, *The Inhuman Race: The Racial Grotesque in American Literature and Culture* (New York: Columbia University Press, 1997).

7. James Green, "The Publishing History of Olaudah Equiano's *Interesting Narrative*," *Slavery and Abolition* 16. 3 (1995): 362-375.
8. Marion Wilson Starling, *The Slave Narrative: Its Place in American History* (Washington DC: Howard University Press, 1988).
9. Frances Smith Foster, *Witnessing Slavery: The Development of Ante-bellum Slave Narratives* (London: Greenwood Press, 1979).

Selected Bibliography

Achebe, Chinua. *Things Fall Apart.* London: Heinemann, 1958.

Acholonu-Olumba, Catherine. *The Igbo Roots of Olaudah Equiano: A Linguistic and Anthropological Search.* Revised edition. Abuja: Afa Publications, 2007.

Adiele, Afigbo E. *The Abolition of the Slave Trade in Southeastern Nigeria, 1885-1950.* Rochester, NY: The University of Rochester Press, 2006.

_____. "Of Men and War, Women and History." Valedictory lecture delivered at the University of Nigeria, Nsukka, 1992.

_____. *The Warrant Chiefs: Indirect Rule in South-Eastern Nigeria, 1891-1929.* London: Longman, 1972.

Allison, Robert J. ed. *The Interesting Narrative of the Life of Olaudah Equiano.* Boston: Bedford/St. Martins Press, 1995.

Amadiume, Ifi. *Male Daughters, Female Husbands: Gender and Sex in an African Society.* London: Zed Books Ltd., 1987.

Ivan Van Sertima. "Death Shall Not Find Us Thinking That We Die." In *African–American Humanism: An Anthology,* ed Ivan Van Sertima, and Norm R. Allen. New York: Promotheses Books, 1991.

Appiah, Kwame A. *In My Father's House: Africa in the Philosophy of Culture.* Oxford: Oxford University Press, 1992.

Armah, Ayi Kwei. *Two Thousand Seasons.* London: Heinemann, 1972.

Asad, Talal. "Ethnography, Literature and Politics: Some Readings and Uses of Salman Rushdies The Satanic Verses." *Cultural Anthropology* 5, no. 3 (Aug. 1990): 239-69.

_____. *Anthropology and the Colonial Encounter.* London: Ithaca Press. 1973.

Awolowo, Obafemi. *Path to Nigerian Freedom*. London: Faber and Faber, 1947.

Baikie, William Balfour. *Narrative of an Exploring Voyage up the River Kwora and Binue*. London, 1856; repr. 1966.

Barbot, John. "A Description of the Coasts of North and South Guinea." In *Voyages and Travels*, ed Thomas Astley and John Churchill, London, 1746.

Barth, Fredrik. ed. *Ethnic Groups and Boundaries*. Boston: Little, Brown, 1969.

Bland, Sterling Lecater, Jr. *Voices of the Fugitives: Runaway Slave Stories and Their Fictions of Self-Creation*. London: Greenwood Press, 2000.

Blyden, E. *Christianity, Islam and the Negro Race*. Edinburgh: University of Edinburgh Press, 1967.

Bontemps, Arna, ed. *Five Black Narratives: The Autobiographies of Venture Smith, James Mars, William Grimes, The Rev. G. W. Offley, and James L. Smith*. Middleton: Wesleyan University Press, 1971.

Bonvillain, Nancy. *Women and Men: Cultural Constructs of Gender*. Upper Saddle River, NJ: Pearson/Prentice Hall, 2007.

Boulukos, George E. "Olaudah Equiano and the Eighteenth-Century Debate on Africa." *Eighteenth-Century Studies* 40, 2 (2007): 241-55.

Brown, Carolyn. "Testing the Boundaries of Marginality: Twentieth Century Slavery and Emancipation Struggles in Nkanu, Northern Igboland, 1920-1929," *Journal of African History* 37 (1996): 51-80.

Byrd, Alexander X. "Eboe, Country, Nation, and Gustavus Vassa's Interesting Narrative." *The William and Mary Quarterly* 63, 1 (2006): 123-48.

Carretta Vincent. *Equiano, the African: Biography of a Self-Made Man*. Athens GA: The University of Georgia Press, 2005.

_____. "Defining a Gentleman: The Status of Olaudah Equiano or Gustavus Vassa." *Language Sciences* 22 (2000): 385-99.

_____. ed. *Equiano, Olaudah. The Interesting Narrative and Other Writings*. New York: Penguin Books, 1995.

_____, Clifford, J. and Markus, G. E. *Writing Culture: The Poetics and Politics of Ethnography*. Berkeley: University of California Press, 1986.

Cassuto, Leonard. *The Inhuman Race: The Racial Grotesque in American Literature and Culture*. New York: Columbia University Press, 1997.

Chambers, Douglas B. *Murder at Montpelier: Igbo Africans in Virginia*. Jackson: University Press of Mississippi, 2005.

_____. "'My Own Nation': Igbo Exiles in the Diaspora." *Slavery and Abolition* 18 (1997): 72-97.

_____. "Eboe, Kongo, Mandingo: African Ethnic groups and the Development of Regional Slave Societies in Mainland North America." Paper presented at International Seminar, "The History of the Atlantic World," Harvard University, 3-11 September 1996.

Christophe, Marc A. "Changing Images of Blacks in Eighteenth Century French Literature." *Phylon* 48 no. 3 (3rd. Qtr. 1987): 183-89.

Cohen, Abner. *Custom and Politics in Urban Africa*. Berkeley: University of California Press, 1969.

Corley, Ide. "The Subject of Abolitionist Rhetoric: Freedom and Trauma in 'The Life of Olaudah Equiano.'" *Modern Language Studies* 32. 2 (Autumn 2002): 139-56.

Costanzo, Angelo. *Surprizing Narrative: Olaudah Equiano and the Beginnings of Black Autobiography*. New York: Greenwood Press, 1987.

Cronje, S. *The World and Nigeria*. London: Sidgwick and Jackson, 1972.

Curtin, Philip D. *The Atlantic Slave Trade: A Census*. Madison: The University of Wisconsin, 1969.

_____. *The Image of Africa: British Ideas and Action, 1780–1850*. Madison: The University of Wisconsin Press, 1964.

Dangarembga, Tsitsi. *Nervous Conditions*. Seattle: Seal Press, 1988.

Darwin Major, Walter Egerton, Dr Falconer, Kitson, A. E. "Southern Nigeria: Some Considerations of its Structure, People, and Natural History: Discussion," *The Geographical Journal* 41, no. 1 (Jan 1913): 34-8.

David Kpobi. "African Chaplains in Seventeenth Century West Africa." In *African Christianity: An African Story*, ed. Ogbu U. Kalu, 140-169. Pretoria: University of Pretoria Press, 2005.

Davis, Charles T. *The Slave's Narrative*. NY: Oxford University Press, 1985.

Davis, David Brion. *The Problem of Slavery in the Age of Revolution 1770-1823*. Ithaca: Cornell University Press, 1975.

de Verteuil, Anthony. *Seven Slaves and Slavery: Trinidad, 1777-1838*. Port of Spain, Trinidad, Scrip – J Printers Limited, 1992.

Derbyshire Record Office, D239 M/E 16753-16754, "West Indian papers," Plantations of William Perrin and William Philip Perrin, Correspondence of the Jamaican Attorneys, 10 January 1773.

Dietrich R. F. and Roger H. Sundell. *The Art of Fiction*. New York: Holt, Rinehart and Winston Inc, 1967.

Donnan, Elizabeth. "The Slave Trade into South Carolina before the Revolution," *American Historical Review* 33 (1927-28): 804-28.

Ebron, Paula. *Performing Africa*. Princeton, N.J. Princeton University Press. 2002.

Echeruo, Michael J. C. "A Matter of Identity." 1979 Ahiajoku Lecture. Owerri: Ministry of Information and Culture, 1979.

Edwards, Paul, ed. *The Life of Olaudah Equiano of Gustavus Vassa the African*. New York: Longman, 1996.

Ekejiuba, F. I., "The Aro Trade System in the 19th Century." *Ikenga, Journal of the Institute of African Studies* 1, no. 1 (1972): 10-21.

Elder, Arlene A. *The "Hindered Hand": Cultural Implications of Early African-American Fiction*. London: Greenwood Press, 1978.

Eltis, David. *Economic Growth and the Ending of the Transatlantic Slave Trade*. New York: Oxford University, 1987.

_____ and David Richardson. "The 'Numbers Game' and Routes to Slavery," *Slavery and Abolition* 18, no. 1 (1997): 1-15.

_____ and Stanley L. Engerman. "Ethnicity in the Early Modern Atlantic World." Paper presented at the Harriet Tubman Seminar, York University, 26 January 1999.

_____, David Richardson, Stephen D. Behrendt, and Herbert S. Klein, eds. *The Atlantic Slave Trade: A Database on CD-ROM*. New York: Cambridge University Press, 1999.

Equiano, Olaudah. *The Interesting Narrative of the Life of Olaudah Equiano, Gustavus Vassa, the African, Written by Himself*. London, 1789.

Favor, Martin J. *Authentic Blackness: The Folk in the New Negro Renaissance*. Durham: Duke University Press, 1999.

Fischer, David Hackett. *Albion's Seed: Four British Folkways in America*. New York: Oxford University Press, 1989.

Fishburn, Katherine. *The Problem of Embodiment in Early African American Narrative*. London: Greenwood Press, 1997.

Forde, D. and Jones, G. I. *The Ibo and Ibibio-Speaking Peoples of South-Eastern Nigeria*. Oxford: Oxford University Press, 1950.

Foster, Frances Smith. *Witnessing Slavery: The Development of Ante-bellum Slave Narratives*. London: Greenwood Press, 1979.

Frazier, E. Franklin. *Negro Church in America*. New York: Schocken Books, 1974.

_____. "The Significance of the African Background." In *Americans from Africa: Slavery and its Aftermath*, ed Peter I. Rose, 37-54. New York: Atherton Press, 1970.

_____. *The Negro Family in the United States*. Chicago: University of Chicago Press, 1939.

Frye, Northrop. *The Anatomy of Criticism*. Princeton: Princeton University Press, 1957.

Gailey, H. A. *The Road to Aba: A Study of British Administrative Policy in Eastern Nigeria*. New York: New York University Press, 1970.

Gakwandi, S. A. *The Novel and Contemporary Experience in Africa*. London: Heinemann, 1977.

Gates, Henry Louis, Jr. *Figures in Black: Words, Signs, and the "Racial" Self*. Washington, DC: Civitas Counterpoint, 1998.

_____. and William L. Andrews, ed. *Pioneers of the Black Atlantic: Five Slave Narratives from the Enlightenment, 1772-1815*. Washington, DC: Civitas Counterpoint, 1998.

Geertz, Clifford. *The Interpretation of Cultures*. New York: Basic Books, 1973.

Gomez, Michael A. *Reversing Sail: A History of the African Diaspora*. New York: Cambridge University Press, 2005.

_____. *Exchanging our Country Marks: The Transformation of African Identities in the Colonial and Ante-bellum South*. Chapel Hill, NC: The University of North Carolina Press, 1998.

Goodman, Jane E. "The Proverbial Bourdieu: Habitus and the Politics of Representation in the Ethnography of Kabylia." *American Anthropologist* 105, 4 (2003): 782-93.

Gould, Philip. "Free Carpenter, Venture Capitalist: Reading the Lives of the Early Black Atlantic." *American Literary History* 12, 4 (2000): 659-84.

Green, James. "The Publishing History of Olaudah Equiano's *Interesting Narrative*." *Slavery and Abolition* 16, 3 (1995): 362-75.

Green, M. M. *Igbo Village Affairs*. London: Frank Cass & Co. Ltd, 1947.

Hall, Gwendolyn Midlo. *Slavery and African Ethnicities in the Americas: Restoring the Links*. Chapel Hill and London: University of North Carolina Press, 2005.

Hallett, Robin. "The European Approach to the Interior of Africa in the Eighteenth Century." *Journal of African History* IV, 2 (1963): 191-206.

Harms, Robert. *The Diligent: A Voyage Through the Worlds of the Slave Trade*. New York: Basic Books, 2001.

Harrow, Kenneth W. *Thresholds of Change in African Literature: The Emergence of a Tradition. Studies in African Literature*. Portsmouth NH: Heinemann, 1994.

Hartman, Saidiya V. *Scenes of Subjection: Terror, Slavery, and Self-Making in 19th Century America*. New York: Oxford University Press, 1997.

Hegel, G.W.F., *The Philosophy of History*. New York: Willey Book Co., 1944.

Herskovits, Melville J. *The Myth of the Negro Past*. Boston: Beacon Press, 1941.

Hinds, Elizabeth Jane Wall. "The Spirit of Trade: Olaudah Equiano's Conversion, Legalism, and the Merchant's Life." *African American Review* 32, 4 (1998): 635-47.

Hodgson, Dorothy L. "In Focus: Indigenous Rights Movements Introduction: Comparative Perspectives on the Indigenous Rights Movement in Africa and the Americas." *American Anthropologist* 104, 4 (2002): 1037-49.

Hogg, Michael A., Deborah J. Terry, and Katherine M. White, "A Tale of Two Theories: A Critical Comparison of Identity Theory with Social Identity Theory," *Social Psychology Quarterly* 58 (1995): 255-69.

Horton, Robin. "The Ohu System of Slavery in a Northern Ibo Village-Group." *Africa: Journal of the International African Institute* 24, no. 4 (Oct., 1954): 311-36.

Hountondji Paulin. *Introduction to African Philosophy: Myth and Reality*. London: Hutchison & Co., 1976.

Ifeka-Moller, Caroline. "Female Militancy and Colonial Revolt: The Women's War of 1929, Eastern Nigeria." In *Perceiving Women*, ed Shirley Ardener, 128-32. New York: John Wiley & Sons, 1975.

Irele, Abiola. *The African Experience in Literature and Ideology*. Ibadan: Heinemann. 1981,

Isichei, Elizabeth. *Igbo Worlds: An Anthology of Oral Histories and Historical Descriptions*. Philadelphia: Institute for the Study of Human Issues, 1978.

Jacques, T. Carlos. "From Savages and Barbarians to Primitives: Africa, Social Typologies, and History in Eighteenth-Century French Philosophy." *History and Theory* 36, 2 (1997): 190-215.

Jesse Neal G. and Kristen Williams P. *Identity and Institutions: Conflict Reduction in Divided Societies*. Albany: State University of New York Press, 2005.

Johnston, G. *Of Maxim and Guns: Presbyterianism in Nigeria, 1846-1966*. Ottawa: Wilfrid Laurier University Press, 1988.

Jones, G. I. *Report on the Position, Status and Influence of Chiefs and Natural Rulers in the Eastern Region of Nigeria*. Enugu: Government Printer, 1957.

Kalu, Ogbu U. *Embattled Gods: Christianization of Igboland, 1841-1991*. Trenton NJ: Africa World Press, 2003.

_____. ed. *A Century and Half of Presbyterian Witness in Nigeria, 1846-1996.* Enugu: Presbyterian Church in Nigeria, 1996.

_____. "*Nsibidi*: Pictographic Communication in Pre-Colonial Cross River Basin Societies."*Cahiers D'etudes des Religions Africaines* XII, 23, 4 (Jan/Juill, 1978):97-116.

_____. "Battle of the Gods: Christianization of Cross River Igboland, 1903-1950."*Journal of the Historical Society of Nigeria* 10, 1 (1977): 1-18.

_____. "Waves from the Rivers: The Spread of Garrick Braide Movement in Igboland, 1914-1934." *Journal of the Historical Society of Nigeria* 8, 4 (June 1977): 95-110.

Kawash, Samira. *Dislocating the Color Line: Identity, Hybridity, and Singularity in African-American Narrative.* Stanford: Stanford University Press, 1997.

Klein, Herbert S. *African Slavery in Latin America and the Caribbean.* New York: Oxford University Press, 1986.

Kleis, Gerald W. "Confrontation and Incorporation: Igbo Ethnicity in Cameroon." *African Studies Review* 23, no. 3 (Dec., 1980): 89-100.

Kollman, Paul V. *The Evangelization of Slaves and Catholic Origins in Eastern Africa.* Maryknoll, NY: Orbis, 2005.

Korieh, Chima J. "Yam is King! But Cassava is the Mother of All Crops: Farming, Culture, and Identity in Igbo Agrarian Economy." *Dialectical Anthropology* 31, nos. 1-3 (2007): 221-32.

Landsman, Gail and Ciborski, Sara. "Representation and Politics: Contesting Histories of the Iroquois." *Cultural Anthropology* 7, no. 4. 9 (1992): 425-47.

Leith-Ross, Sylvia. *African Women: A Study of the Ibo of Nigeria.* London: Routledge & Kegan Paul Ltd., 1965.

Littlefield, Daniel C. *Rice and Slaves: Ethnicity and the Slave Trade in Colonial South Carolina.* Baton Rouge: Louisiana State University Press, 1981.

Lovejoy, Paul E. "Autobiography and Memory: Gustavus Vassa, Alias Olaudah Equiano the African." *Slavery and Abolition* 27, no. 3 (2006): 317-47.

_____. and David V. Trotman eds. *Trans-Atlantic Dimensions of Ethnicity in the African Diaspora.* London and New York: Continuum, 2003.

_____. *Transformations in Slavery: A History of Slavery in Africa.* New York: Cambridge University Press, 2000.

_____. "The Volume of the Atlantic Slave Trade: A Synthesis." *Journal of African History* 23 (1982): 473-501.

Magubane, Zine. *Postmodernism, Postcoloniality and African and African Studies*. Trenton: Africa World Press, 2005.

Mandel, Barret J. "Full of Life Now." In *Autobiography: Essays Theoretical and Critical*, ed James Olney, 49-72. Princeton: Princeton University Press, 1980.

Marren, Suzan M. "Between Slavery and Freedom: The Transgressive Self in Olaudah Equiano's Autobiography." *PMLA* 108, 1 (Jan, 1993): 94-105.

Mazola, D. A. *African Philosophy in Search of Identity*. Indiana: Indiana University Press, 1994.

Mazrui, Ali. "European Exploration and Africa's Self-Discovery." *The Journal of Modern African Studies* 7, no. 4 (1969): 661-76.

Mba, Nina. "Heroines of the Women's War." In *Nigerian Women in Historical Perspective*, ed B. Awe, 75-88. Ibadan: Sankore/Bookcrat 1992.

_____. *Nigerian Women Mobilized: Women's Political Activity in Southern Nigeria, 1900-1965*. Berkeley: Institute of International Studies, University of California, 1982.

Mbefo, L. N. *The Reshaping of African Traditions*. Enugu: Snaap Press, 1988.

Mckay, Nellie Y., and Frances Smith Foster, eds. *Incidents in the Life of a Slave Girl* by Harriet Jacobs. New York: W.W. Norton, 2000.

Meek, C. K. *Law and Authority in a Nigerian Tribe: A Study of Indirect Rule*. Oxford: Oxford University Press, 1937.

_____. *Ethnographical Report on the Peoples of Nsukka Division of Onitsha Province*. Lagos, 1930.

Mintz, Sidney and Richard Price. *An Anthropological Approach to Afro-American Past: A Caribbean Perspective*. Philadelphia: Institute for the Study of Human Issues, 1976.

Misch, Georg. *A History of Autobiography in Ambiguity Vol. 1*. London: Routledge and Kegan Paul, 1960.

Morgan, Philip D. "The Cultural Implications of the Atlantic Slave Trade: African Regional Origins, American Destinations and New World Development," *Slavery and Abolition* 18, no. 1 (1997): 122-45.

_____. *Slave Counterpoint: Black Culture in the Eighteenth Century Chesapeake and Lowcountry*. Chapel Hill, NC: University of North Carolina Press, 1998.

Mutiso, D.C.M., & Robio, S. W. eds., *Reading in African Political Thought*. London, Ibadan, Nairobi, Lusaka: Heinemann, 1975.

Njaka, E. N. *Igbo Political Culture*. Evanston: Northwestern University Press, 1974.

Nkrumah, Kwame. *Consciencism Philosophy and Ideology for Decolonization with Particular Reference to the Africa Revolution.* London: Heinemann, 1970.

Northrup, David. "Becoming African: Identity Formation among Liberated Slaves in Nineteenth-century Sierra Leone." *Slavery and Abolition* 27, no.1 (April 2006): 1–21.

Nzimiro, Ikenna. *Studies in Ibo Political Systems: Chieftaincy and Politics in Four Niger States.* London: Frank Cass & Co. Ltd., 1972.

Ogede, O. S. "The Igbo Roots of Oladah Equiano." *Journal of International African Institute* 61, no. 1 (1991): 138–41.

Oguejiofor, J. O. *The Influence of Igbo traditional Religion on the Socio-Political Character of the Igbo.* Nsukka: Fulladu Publishing Company, 1996.

Ohadike, Don. "The Decline of Slavery among the Igbo People." In *The End of Slavery in Africa,* eds., S Miers and R.Roberts, 437-61. Madison: University of Wisconsin Press, 1988.

Okonjo, Kamene. "Women's Political Participation in Nigeria." In *The Black Woman Cross- Culturally,* ed.. E. C. Steady, 79-106. Cambridge, Mass: Schenkman Publication Co, 1981.

Olney, James. ed. *Autobiography: Essays Theoretical and Critical.* Princeton, NJ: Princeton University Press, 1980.

_____. *Tell Me Africa: An Approach to African Literature.* Princeton: Princeton University Press, 1973.

Onwujeogwu, M. A., "Evolutionary Trends in the History of the Development of Igbo Civilization in the Culture Theatre of Igboland in Southern Nigeria." *1987 Ahiajoku Lecture.* Owerri: Ministry of Information, 1987.

Onwumechili, Cyril Agodi. "Igbo Enwe Eze: The Igbo Have No Kings." The 2000 Ahiajoku Lecture. Owerri: Ministry of Information, 2000.

Onyewuenyi, I. C. *The African Origin of Greek Philosophy.* Nsukka: University of Nigeria Press, 1993.

Orban, Katalin. "Dominant and Submerged Discourses." *The Life of Oaludah Equiano (or Gustavus Vassa?). African American Review* 27, no. 4 (1993): 655-64.

Oriji, J. N. *Ngwa History.* New York: Peter Lang, 1997.

Ortner, Sherry B. "On Key Symbols." *American Anthropologist* 75, no. 5 (Oct., 1973): 1338-46.

_____. and Hariet Whitehead. *Sexual Meanings: The Cultural Construction of Gender and Sexuality.* Cambridge: Cambridge University Press, 1981.

Ottenberg, Simon. *Boyhood Rituals in an African Society: An Interpretation.* Seattle: University of Washington Press, 1989.

_____. "Oedipus, Gender and Social Solidarity: A Case Study of Male Childhood and Initiation." *Ethos* 16, no. 3 (1988): 326-52.

Palmer, Colin. *Human Cargoes: The British Slave Trade to Spanish America, 1700-1939.* Urbana: University of Illinois Press, 1981.

Pascal, Roy. *Design and Truth in Autobiography.* Cambridge, MA: Harvard University Press, 1960.

Patterson Orlando. *Slavery and Social Death: A Comparative Study.* Cambridge, MA: Harvard University Press, 1982.

Paton, Diana ed. *A Narrative of Events, since the First of August, 1834, by James Williams, an Apprenticed Laborer in Jamaica.* Durham, NC: Duke University Press, 2001.

Perbi, Akosua Adoma. *A History of Indigenous Slavery in Ghana. From the 15th to the 19th Century.* Accra, Ghana: Sub-Saharan Publishers, 2004.

Peterson, Carla. *"Doers of the Word": African-American Women Speakers and Writers in the North (1830-1880).* New York: Oxford University Press, 1995.

Rawley, James A. *The Transatlantic Slave Trade: A History.* New York, 1981.

Rhoads, Diana Akers. "Culture in Chinua Achebe's *Things Fall Apart.*" *African Studies Review* 36 (September 1993): 61-72.

Richardson, David. "Slave Exports from West and West-Central Africa, 1700-1810: New Estimates of Volume and Distribution." *Journal of African History* 30 (1989): 1-22.

Ricouer, Paul. *Hermeneutics and the Human Sciences: Essays on Language, Action and Interpretation.* Cambridge: Cambridge University Press, 1981.

Rose Peter I. ed., *Americans from Africa: Slavery and its Aftermath.* New York: Atherton Press, 1970.

Rushdy, Ashraf H. A. *Neo-Slave Narratives: Studies in the Social Logic of a Literary Form.* New York: Oxford University Press, 1999.

Sabino, Robin, and Jennifer Hall. "The Path Not Taken: Cultural Identity in the Interesting Narrative of Olaudah Equiano." *MELUS* 24, 1 (1999): 5-19.

Said, Edward. *Orientalism.* New York: Vintage Books, 1979.

Samuels, Wilfred D. "Disguised Voice in *The Interesting Narrative of the Life of Olaudah Equiano or Gustavus Vassa, the Africa.*" *Black American Forum.* 19, 2 (1985): 64-9.

Scupin, Raymond. *Cultural Anthropology: A Global Perspective.* 6th edition. Upper Saddle River, NJ: Prentice Hall, 2007.

Sen, Amartya. "Indian Traditions and the Western imagination." *Daedalus,* 216, no. 2 (1997): 1-26.

Sklar, R. L. *Nigerian Political Parties.* Princeton: Princeton University Press, 1963.

Sollors, Werner, ed. *The Interesting Narrative of the Life of Olaudah Equiano, or Gustavus Vassa, the African, written by Himself.* New York: Norton, 2001.

Starling, Marion Wilson. *The Slave Narrative: Its Place in American History.* Washington DC: Howard University Press, 1988.

Thiongo Wa, Ngugi. *Writers in Politics.* Ibadan: Heinemann, 1981.

Thornton, John. *Africa and Africans in the Making of the Atlantic World, 1400-1680.* Cambridge: Cambridge University Press, 1998.

Uchendu, Victor C. *The Igbo of Southeast Nigeria.* New York: Holt, Rinehart and Winston, 1965.

Van Allen, Judith. "'Aba Riots' or Igbo `Women's War'? Ideology, Stratification, and Invisibility of Women." In *The Black Woman Cross-Culturally.,* ed F. C. Steady. Cambridge, Mass: Schenkman Publication Co, 1981.

_____. "Sitting on a Man: Colonialism and the Lost Political Institutions of the Igbo." *Canadian Journal of African Studies* 6, 11 (1972): 165-81.

Wallman, Sandra. *Social Anthropology of Work.* London: Academic Press. 1979.

Wish, Harvey. "American Slave Insurrections before 1861." *The Journal of Negro History* 22 (July 1937): 299-320.

Wonham, Henry B. ed. *Criticism and the Color Line: Desegregating American Literary Studies.* New Brunswick: Rutgers University Press, 1996.

Zafar, Rafia. *We Wear the Mask: African Americans Write American Literature, 1760-1870.* New York: Columbia University Press, 1997.

NOTES ON CONTRIBUTORS

Catherine Acholonu holds a doctorate degree in English and American Language and Literature and Germanic Linguistics. Her doctoral thesis was on "Igbo Literature and Oral Tradition." She was a lecturer in the Department of English Language and Literature, Alvan Ikoku College of Education, Owerri, Nigeria for 16 years, where she rose to the position of Associate Professor/Reader. Between 1990 and 1991 she was a visiting professor of African Studies and African Women Studies at the Westchester Consortium for International Studies, New York, USA. In the same period (1990-1991) Acholonu was Fulbright Scholar-Writer-in-Residence at the Manhattanville College, Purchase, New York. Acholonu is the author of 16 books on poetry, drama, essays, and children's literature including *The Igbo Roots of Olaudah Equiano; Motherism: The Afrocentric Alternative to Feminism; and The Gram Code of African Adam.*

Adiele E. Afigbo is an authority on the history and historiography of Africa, particularly Igbo history and the history of Southeastern Nigeria. He spent many years of teaching and research at the University of Nigeria, where he rose to become the Head of the Department of History and Archaeology and the Dean of the Faculty of Arts. He is currently a professor in the Department of History and International Relations at Ebonyi State University, Nigeria. His recent book is *The Abolition of the Slave Trade in Southeastern Nigeria, 1885-1950* (The University of Rochester Press, 2006).

Douglas B. Chambers is an expert on the Igbo Diaspora in the early modern Atlantic world. The author of *Murder at Montpelier: Igbo Africans in Virginia* (2005), and numerous articles and book chapters, including

"The Links of a Legacy: Figuring the Slave Trade to Jamaica" (2007) and "The Black Atlantic: Theory, Method, and Practice" (Indiana University Press, 2008). In 2005 Chambers was honored with a chieftaincy title bestowed by the founding royal clan of Nri, a 1,000-year old Igbo civilization in Nigeria. He was raised in Virginia and earned three degrees at the University of Virginia, including his Ph.D. in History in 1996. Chambers has conducted research in Jamaica, Cuba and Nigeria, and currently consults with several museums, including The Frontier Culture Museum of Virginia for its new permanent 'West African Farm' exhibit.

Hannah Ngozi Eby Chukwu (Ph.D.) is with the Department of English, University of Saskatchewan, Saskatoon where she works as a Research Assistant on Samuel Taylor Coleridge Project. She is also a faculty member at the University of Nigeria, Nsukka. She is currently working towards her CERTESL, teaching ESL classes, and working with immigrants sometimes. Her essays and review have been published in *African Literature Today, Ariel,* and in *The Newsjournal of the Canadian Association for Commonwealth Literature and Language Studies.* She has also published poems in *inmedias res.*

Maureen N. Eke has a Ph.D. in Comparative Literature from Indiana University, Bloomington. She is Professor of English and former Vice President for Diversity and International Education at Central Michigan University, where she teaches Postcolonial Literatures and Theory, African American Literature as well as African Literatures and Cinema. She is the co-editor of *Gender and Sexuality in African Literature and Film* (2007); *African Images: Recent Studies in Cinema and Texts* (2000). Her articles have appeared in *SATJ, Callaloo, Research in African Literatures,* and *Visual Anthropology.*

Felix K. Ekechi is Professor Emeritus of African History and Coordinator of African Studies Program at Kent State University. He has published extensively on different aspects of Igbo social, economic, political and cultural life and history. His publications include the following: *Missionary Enterprise and Rivalry in Igboland, 1857-1914* (London: Frank Cass & Co., 1972), which was nominated for the prestigious Herskovits Award of the African Studies Association; *Owerri in Transition* (Owerri: Imo Newspapers, 1985); *Tradition and Transformation in Eastern Nigeria: A Sociopolitical History of Owerri, 1902-1947* (Kent, Ohio: Kent State University Press, 1989), and *African Market Women and Economic Power: The Role of Women in African Economic Development,* co-edited with Bessie House-Midamba

(Westport, Connecticut/London: Greenwood Press, 1995). Professor Ekechi's numerous articles have appeared in professional journals. In addition, Professor Ekechi has contributed numerous chapters in books. He is currently completing the biography of the Rev. M. D. Opara of Nigeria, MP and *Transformations in the History of the Igbo People*.

Ogbu U. Kalu is the Henry Winters Luce Professor of World Christianity at McCormick Theological Seminary, Chicago. He studied History at the University of Toronto, Canada and University of London, UK, obtaining BA Hons, M.A., Ph.D. (University of Toronto). He graduated Master of Divinity (M.Div) from Princeton Theological Seminary, New Jersey, winning the Grier Davis Award. He was awarded Doctor of Divinity (DD) *honoris causa* in 1997 by Presbyterian College, Montreal, Canada. Dr. Kalu taught as a full professor at the University of Nigeria, Nsukka, where he served as Dean of the Faculty of the Social Sciences, and Director of Institute of African Studies. He has served as a visiting professor at New College, University of Edinburgh, Faculty of Arts McGill University, Emmanuel and Knox Colleges, University of Toronto, Harvard Divinity School, University of Bayreuth, Germany and Presbyterian Theological Seminary and College, Seoul. He has published 18 books including *Divided People of God: Church Union Movement in Nigeria* (New York, 1978); *The History of Christianity in West Africa* (London: Longman, 1980); *African Church Historiography: An Ecumenical Perspective* (Berne, 1988); *Embattled Gods: Christianization of Igboland* (Lagos/London, 1996); *Power, Poverty and Prayer: The Challenges of Poverty and Pluralism in African Christianity* (Frankfurt, 2000); *African Christianity: An African Story* (University of Pretoria Press, 2005); *African Pentecostalism (*2008); *Clio In A Sacred Garb: Christian Presence and African Responses, 1900-2000* (2008); and over 180 articles in journals and as book chapters.

Daniel Kloza graduated from the Department of History, Rowan University, Glassboro, New Jersey. He received several awards for academic achievement, including the Deans Outstanding Graduating History Major award in 2007 and Best Paper Award in the History Department of Rowan University. He also received a certificate and medallion award for Excellence in African American Studies. His interests include music.

Chima J. Korieh teaches African History at Marquette University, Milwaukee, Wisconsin. He holds a Ph.D. in African History from the University of Toronto, Canada. Prior to joining Marquette, he was associate professor of African history at Rowan University in New Jersey. He recently completed a prestigious fellowship as a British Academy Visiting Fellow at Oxford University, Oxford, UK (2007/2008). He has authored many articles and essays in journals, books, and encyclopedia. His publications include the following co-edited volumes: *The Aftermath of Slavery: Transition and Transformation in Southeastern Nigeria* (Trenton, NJ: Africa World Press, 2007); *Missions, States and European Expansion in Africa* (New York: Routledge, 2007); *Gendering Global Transformations: Gender, Culture, Race, and Identity* (New York: Routledge, 2008). He was associate editors (Africa) of *Encyclopedia of Western Imperialism and Colonialism since 1450* (New York: Macmillan Reference USA, 2006). He is the founder and editor of *Mbari: The International Journal of Igbo Studies*.

Ron Milland holds a Master's Degree from the Department of English, Queens College of the City University of New York, USA. Ron Milland has analyzed numerous slave narratives through a literary and historical lens, with particular interest paid to the methods used to edit these works. His research has linked these editorial strategies to the dynamics of the larger slave system as well as colonial rule, which is of personal interest to Milland given his descent from a former British colony in the Caribbean. The correlating post-emancipation codification of race informs Milland's interest in legal history regarding attempts to *humanize* people formerly classified as *property*.

Raphael Chijioke Njoku, a first class honors graduate of University of Nigeria Nsukka, is an Associate Professor of African History. He received a Ph.D. in African History from Dalhousie University, Canada, 2003, and another Ph.D. in African Politics from Free University Brussels, 2001. Before his current appointment in the Department of History, and Department of Pan African Studies at the University of Louisville in 2003, Njoku taught at the Department of History, Alvan Ikoku College of Education, Owerri, Nigeria. He is the author of *Culture and Customs of Morocco* (Greenwood, 2005), and *African Cultural Values: Igbo Political Leadership in Colonial Nigeria 1900-1966* (Routledge, 2006), and co-editor of *Missions, States, and European Expansion in Africa* (Routledge, 2007). Njoku has also published 20 articles in scholarly journals, edited volumes, and encyclopedias. His most recent awards include Victor Olurunsola Endowed Research Award (2007) and a research fellowship from the New York based Schomburg Center for Research in Black Culture (2006-07). Njoku is currently working on a book manuscript entitled *African Masks and Masquerades and Carnival of the Diaspora*.

J. Akuma-Kalu Njoku has a Ph.D. from Indiana University. He is an associate professor in the Department of Folk Studies and Anthropology at Western Kentucky University where he teaches courses in Peoples and Cultures of Africa, African American Folklore, World Folk Music, and Community Traditions and Corporate Culture in the Global World. His current research interest is Slave Journeys and Settlements in the African Diaspora.

John Oriji teaches African History, Comparative World History, and Modern Political Economy at California Polytechnic State University, San Luis Obispo. He is the author of two books: *Traditions of Igbo Origins* (New York: Peter Lang, 1994, revised edition) and *Ngwa History* (New York: Peter Lang 1998, revised edition). He also published over 30 articles in journals and edited books.

Elizabeth Onogwu teaches African Literature in the Department of English, Benue State University, Makurdi, Nigeria. Her areas of interest include literary criticism. Her scholarly essays have appeared in a number of journals including *FAJ*, *The Ker Review*, *Zajola* amongst others. She has a handsome collection of yet to be published short stories.

Ogbo Ugwuanyi is a senior lecturer in Philosophy and pioneer Head of the Department of Philosophy, University of Abuja, Abuja, Nigeria. He obtained his Ph.D. from the University of Ibadan in 2003. He was formally a lecturer in Philosophy at Ambrose Alli University Ekpoma (1994-2003) and senior lecturer in Philosophy at Delta State University Abraka, Nigeria (2003-2006). Ugwuanyi has over 21 publications in journals and anthologies and has presented papers at more than 10 international conferences. He served as a visiting scholar at the University of South Africa in 2005.

Dorothy Ukaegbu is a cultural anthropologist of Igbo descent. She obtained her Ph.D. from the University of Massachusetts at Amherst. Her main areas of specialization are interpretive anthropology, political anthropology, African historiography, and grassroots participatory development (rural development). Her research interests include gender studies, folklore, the anthropology of film, contemporary African immigrant populations, and the trans-Atlantic slave trade. Before joining the College of Southern Nevada in 1995, she was a visiting professor at Virginia Commonwealth University in Richmond, Virginia (1992-1994). She is the author of *Writing in Anthropology: The Summary and the Critique Paper. A Handbook* *for Beginners* (Upper Saddle River, NJ: Pearson/Prentice Hall, 2004). She co-edited, *Faces of Anthropology: A Reader for the 21st Century* with Kevin Rafferty (Upper Saddle River, NJ: Pearson/Prentice Hall, 2007). She is on the editorial board of *Mbari: The International Journal of Igbo Studies.*

INDEX

Aba Commission of Inquiry 274
Aba Women's Riot 165
Abakaliki 249
Abakaliki Division 256
Abam 169
Abiriba 167, 199
Aboh 4
Abrahams, Peter 122
Achebe, Chinua 57-8, 61, 63, 101,
    104, 105, 122, 136, 207, 220,
    339, 343, 353
Achebe, Nwando 240
Acholonu, Catherine 7, 25, 30, 70,
    84, 101, 102, 108, 113, 114–15,
    120-22, 131
Adams, John 109, 112, 114, 351
Adams, Russel L. 120
Afigbo, Adiele 13, 159, 181, 355,
    357
Afikpo 122
African Americans, 62
African Diaspora xii, xiii, 14, 15,
    17, 67, 288, 291, 350
Africanity xii
Afro-American, xi, 51
Afro-British, xi

Agbala 170
agency 88
Aguleri 161
Akokwa 194
Akwete 168, 233
ala 72, 165
Alayi 278
Allen, J. G. C. 270
Allison, Robert J. 29
Aluko, T. M. 122
ama 87
amaala 161
Amadi 318
Amadioha 90
Amadiume, Ifi 113
American National Assembly for
    the Advancement of Colored
    People 133
Americas 290, 349-50
Amo, William 124
Angola 52
anti-racism 7, 51
Appiah, Kwame 129, 134
Armah, Ayi Kwei 122

Aro 11, 161, 166, 168-69, 180, 184-85, 189, 190-93, 198, 211
Arochukwu 211, 238, 246, 304
Arochukwu Expedition 233
Arondizogu 194
arusi 111
Asaba 225
Asad, Talal 110, 124-26
Atlantic Diaspora xiii, 5, 288, 289
Atlantic slave trade 203, 206, 210
Atlantic World 3, 4, 14, 17
Awka 97, 167, 170, 199
Awolowo, Obafemi 299
Azikiwe, Nnamdi 131, 280

Back to Africa Movement 344
Baker, Richard 387
Balogun, Odun 88
Barbados 292, 316
Basso, Kenneth 82, 86
Beidelman, T. O. 228
Bende 229
Bende Division 278
Benin 83, 92, 168, 221, 246
Bennett, Louise 334
Beti, Mongo 122
Bight of Biafra 2, 5, 7, 10, 11, 68, 350-51, 360, 350
Bini 1, 2
Bjornson, Richard 122
Black Caribbean 336
Black Diaspora xiii
Blyden, Edward 119, 127
Bonny 64, 84
Boulukos, George E. 40
Bourdieu, Pierre 125
Brathwaite, Edward Kamu 344

Breeches 109, 110, 126
Brewer, H. G. 195
British 123, 124, 127
Brown, John 362, 364
Brown, Paula 161
Brown, William Wells, 27
Bunyan, John 153
Burnett, Paula 337
Byrd, Alexander 79, 85, 92, 93, 96, 99, 109, 123

Calabar 264, 297, 301, 321, 361
Calabar Province 12, 254, 270, 279
Calvinists 10, 160
Cameron, Sir, Donald 263-64
Cameroon 1, 297
Capuchins 18
Caribbean 7, 15, 31, 51, 129, 294, 233, 334-36, 338-39, 341-44.
Carolina low country 316
Carolinas 6, 89
Carretta, Vincent 6, 7, 8, 25, 34, 36, 53, 60-3, 65, 68-71, 81, 83, 84, 85, 87, 94-6, 103-04, 110-13, 143, 145, 152-53
Cesaire, Aime 125-26
Chambers, Douglas 15, 294, 306-7, 363, 352-53, 64
chi 77
Chineke 4, 77
Christianity 13, 180, 197, 228
Christians 252-3, 376
Christophe Marc A. 28, 29
Christopher, John 184
Chuku, Gloria 166
Chukwu 4, 81, 359

city-states 223
Civil Rights Movement 16, 370, 379
clan 86, 95, 99
Clarkson, Thomas 50
Clipson, Joseph 374-5,
Connah, Graham 204
Consciencism 125
Cook, John 259
Coomarswamy, Radhika 165
Corley, Ide 26
Cowper, William 148
Crafts, Ellen 27
Cronje, S. 299
Crow, Hugh 62, 63, 64
Crowder, Ajayi 167, 184, 231
Cudjoe, Selwyn 338
Cugoano, Ottabah 50
Curtin Philip x, 34, 38-40, 42

da Sorrento, Girolamo Merolla 181
Dafoe, Daniel 153
Dathorne, O. R. 334
de Montaigne, Michel 142
Dedalus, Stephen 144
Demanet, Abbé 36
Dennis, Archdeacon, Tom 221
Dietrich, R. F. 145
Dike Kenneth 123, 159
dimkpa 96-100, 105-9
Diop, Cheik Anta 123-24,
Dodds, Fred 193
Donald Kingdom Commission of Inquiry 260
Donnan, Elizabeth 302
Doran, Captain, James 143

Douglas, H. M. 237-8
Douglass, Frederick 26
Du Bois, W. E. B 119, 134
Dutch 50

Ebo Company 365
Eboe, 85, 89, 92, 93, 94, 95, 100, 338
Ebron, Paula 94
Echeruo, Michael J. C. 3, 205, 358
Economic Community of West African States (ECOWAS) 167
Edda 169
Edwards Paul 27, 31, 42, 56-8, 91
Efik 159
Ejidike, Okey Martin 164
Ekechi Felix 12
ekpe 172, 188, 189, 252-3
Ekumeku 225
Elese, 98, 99, 233
Eliot T.S. 142
Eltis David 293
embrenche 52, 110, 111
Emeruwa, Mark 260
Enlightenment x, 31
Equatorial Guinea 1
Essaka 68, 81, 82, 83, 85, 90, 96, 131, 143
European Union (EU) 167
Evans-Pritchard, E. E. 161

Falk, Edward 4
Feld Steven 82, 86
Ferguson, Adam 205
Fortes M. 161
Foster, Frances Smith 27

Franco, Francisco 163
Franklin, Benjamin 370
Frazier, Franklin 289
French 33, 50
Frye, Northrop 148

Galston, William 161
Gambia 292
Garvey, Marcus 334
Gates, Henry Louis 56, 57
Geertz, Clifford 126
Georgia 362
Gobolo War 182
Gold Coast 301
Gomez, Michael 15, 306, 334, 350, 362
Goodison, Lorna 334
Goodman, Jane 111
Gray, Richard 181
Grazilhier, John 5
Green, M. M. 271
Grenada 365
Grevisse, F. 213
Guerin, Mary 59, 70
Guinea 32
Gullah 315
Gusdorf, Georges 147

Habeas Corpus 31
Hall, Gwendolyn Midlo 15, 292, 321, 352
Hallett, Robin 29, 33
Harlem Renaissance 52, 119-21
Hausaland 305
Heebo slaves 109, 126
Hemings, Betty 323

Hemings, Madison 322
Hemings, Sally 322
Henderson, Richard 220
Herostein, Richard 134
Herskovits, Melville 289
Heywood, Linda 204
Hitchcock, J. W. 191
Hills, John 274
Hochschild, Adam 26
Hogg, Michael A. 289
Hogson, Dorothy L. 126
Horton, W.R.G. 118
Hugh Crow 84
Hughes, Langston 120
human agency 7
Hume, David 120
Hunt, William Edgar 257

ibe 87
Ibibio 245
Ibibio 97, 159
Ibini Ukpabi 169-70, 246, 304
ichi 53, 63, 82, 85, 96, 109, 110, 117, 118, 119, 120, 121
identity 3, 50, 75, 89-90, 102, 120, 288, 305
Idoma 1, 2, 159
Igala 1, 2
Igbo Ukwu 4
Igwe-ka-ala 170
Ijaw 84, 97
Ikenga 98-100, 111, 171
Ikot Ekpene 251, 257
Ikot Obong 251
Ikwuano 83
Indirect Rule 12, 239
International Monetary Fund 158

Irele, Abiola 119
Isichei, Elizabeth 224
Isiukwuato 278
Israel 94
Isseke 7, 53-4, 56, 58, 81, 82, 83, 88, 94, 116, 119, 120, 126, 143
Isuochi 194, 278
Item 278
Izzi 256-7

Jacques, T. Carlos 31, 32, 36
Jaja (King of Opobo) 64
Jamaica 303
Jamaica 6
Jewish 80
Jews 35, 36, 80, 94, 299, 386
John Holt 212
Jones, G. I. 185, 299
Jones, Simon 183

Kalabari 84
Kamalu 304
Kant, Immanuel 120
King, Robert 373, 387
Klein Martin 301
Klein, Herbert 290

La Guma, Alex 122
Langford, Jean M., 112, 126, 127
Leith-Ross, Sylvia 12, 157, 271
Leonard, Karen 75, 89, 90
Leonard, Major, A. G. 158
Lewis, Matthew 317
Lijphart, Arend 163

Littlefield, Daniel 15
Loghod, Abu 91
Lopez, C. 292
Lovejoy, Paul 9, 59, 62, 64, 70, 81, 84, 109, 123, 290, 292-93
Lugard, Frederick 159, 300

MacDonald, Claude 222
Madison, President, James 363
Mandel Barret J. 148
manumission 390
Marren, Suzan M. 40
Maryland 320
Maxwell, James Crawford 245
Mazrui, Ali 33
McKay, Nellie Y. 27
Merriam, John C. 305
mgburichi 319
Middle Passage 5, 25, 36, 290, 293, 320, 377-78
military alliance 169
Milly, Granny 325
Milton, John 152
Mintz, Sidney 289
Miruka, Okumba 336
Misch, Georg 142-43
Monteath, Archibald 6
Monteath, John 6
Moor Ralph, 184
Moor, Ralph 221
Morgan, Jennifer L. 316
Morgan, Philip 290, 296, 317
Morovians 6
Mosaic Law 80
Mphahele, Ezekiel 152
Mudimbe, V. Y. 213
Munonye, John 122

Murray, Charles 134

nation 85, 86, 95, 97, 99
National Council of Nigeria and the Cameroon (NCNC) 280-81.
Native Administration System 14
Native Court 14, 247, 249, 251, 277-78
ndi-ichie 63
Negritude 125-26
New Calabar 316
New World 7, 14, 15, 31, 64, 71-2, 74-6, 184, 288, 289, 290-90, 294, 352, 361
New York 292
Ngwa 222, 229
Nichols, Grace 344
Niger Delta 223, 350
Niger Delta Pastorate 195
Nigeria, xiii, 1, 12, 14, 240
Nigerian Civil War 271
Nikkols, Robert Boucher 151
Nishida, Mieko 74, 88-9
Njaka, E. 95, 97, 111, 343, 352, 354
Nkalagu 256
Nkwere 167, 199, 227
Nneato 278
Norcom, James 27
North America 294
North American Free Trade Agreement (NA FTA) 167
North Atlantic Treaty Organization (NAT O) 169
Nri 63, 161, 168, 319
Nsugbe 227
Nsukka 240

Nsulu Native Court 279
Nwanyeruwa 260
Nwoga D. I. 130
Nyang, S. S. 123
Nzimiro, Ikenna 4

Obodo 194
Obohia 222
Obosi 227
Oduduwa myth 305
Oedipus complex 107
ogaranya 96-100, 105-9, 171
Ogbunike 227
Ogede, O. S. 30, 41
Ogidi 227
Ogoja 255-56
Ogude, Steven 83
Oguta 4, 161, 233
Ogwo 172
oha 73, 95
Ohadike, Don C. xiii, 181, 225
Ohafia 169, 208, 215, 229
ohu 103, 116, 117, 118, 318
Oil River Protectorate 130
Ojike, Mbonu 220, 228
Ojim 260
Okigbo, Pius 130
Okigwe 253, 256
Okigwe Division 278
Okonko 307
Okoro, Kanu 186
Okugo, Chief of Oloko 260, 273
Olaude 54, 85, 101
Old Calabar 169
Olney, James 142, 144
Oloko 260, 273-74, 279

Olu Oguibe 57
Onicha Ezinihitte 276
Onitsha 4, 58, 161, 182, 227, 230, 251, 255
Onitsha Province 262
Onwuejeogwu, M. A. 62, 198
Onwumechili, Cyril 298
Opara, Rev. M. D. 237
Opatam, D. U. 118
Opobo Division 253
Orban, Katalin 25
Oreri 161
Oriental 32
Orientalism 32
Orientalist 32
Orlu 52, 56, 58, 63
Ortner, Sherry B. 111
Osamiri 4
Otanchara 278
Otanzu 278
Ottenberg, Simon 104, 107
Ousmane, Sembene 122
Owerri 229, 233, 237, 247
Owerri Province 270, 279, 319
Oye Eboe 94
Oyewumi, Oyeronke 11
Oyono, Ferdinand 122
ozo 63, 112, 113, 120, 172, 300

Pacheco, Duarte 5
padroado system 181
Palmer, Colin 302
Palmer, H. P. 12, 13
pan-Igbo identity, 90
pan-Igbo, 3
Paris Club 158

Patterson Orlando 36, 317
Perrin, William Philip 303
Plato 142
polygamy 37
postmodernism 107
postmodernist 108
Praff, J. A. 191
Pratt, William 182
Price, Richard 289
primitive 159, 161
Prosser, Gabriel 364
Puritans 10, 160

Qua Iboe Mission 195-96
Quaker 7, 373

race 389
Racehorse 59
racism 118, 318
Raheja, Gloria 213
Ramsay James 50
Rawley, James 302
Read, S. O. Crew 238
representation 108, 125
Richardson David 293
Ricouer, Paul 81
rites of passage 120
Robinson, J. A. 228
Rodney, Walter 124
Roman Catholics 195
Rousseau, Jean-Jacques 142
Royal Niger Company 223, 225, 226

Saad-Filho, Alfredo 158

Said Edward, 32, 124
Santa Cruz 82
savage 31
Schwarzenbach, Edward C. 300
Second World War 240
Senegal 52
Senghor, Leopold 126
Seven Years War 143
Seventh Day Adventists 195
Sharp, Granville 29
Shaw, Rosalind 91
Shepherd, Jack 299
slave trade 4, 10, 11, 29, 151
slavery ix, 1, 2, 4, 6, 9, 10, 14, 50
    306, 349-50, 377
slaves 3, 6, 15, 182
Society of African Missions 225
South Africa 63
South Carolina 58-5, 62, 60, 67,
    71, 81, 301, 302, 303, 316, 365
Spacks, Patricia Meyer 148
St. John, Bruce 344, 339
St. Kitts 351, 360, 365
Stoller, Paul 126
Sundel, Roger H. 145

Talbot, P. A. 168
Taylor, John 222
Taylor, John Christopher 183
Terry, Deborah J. 289
Thomson, Sir Graeme 263
Thornton, John 289
Tinmah 64, 83, 97, 98
Tobin James 50
trans-Atlantic slave trade 50, 180
Trinidad 303
Ubani 180

Uchendu, Victor 73, 78, 87, 91, 92,
    112, 115, 118, 298, 353, 355-56
umu-afo 210
Umuahia 274
Umuchieze 278
Umuimenyi 278
umunna 95, 100
United African Company (UAC)
    212
United States of America 50
Upper Senegal 33
Uturu 278

Van Allen, Judith 340
Vassa, Gustavus xi, 6, 24, 27, 59,
    82, 94-5, 109, 375-6
Virginia 292, 320-21, 302, 321-23,
    363
Voice of America 57
Von Herder, Johann Goltfried 120

Wa Thiongo, Ngugi 144, 149-50
Waddell, H. M. 229
Wallman, Sandra 118, 119
Warrant Chiefs (System) 246-51,
    257-58, 271, 319
Washington, George 370
Watson, James Dewey 134
Weir, A. L. 259
Wesley, John 40
West Africa, 1
West Indies 68, 376
Weston, Gustavus 84
Wheatley, W. L. 196
White, Katherine M. 289
Wilberforce, William, 50

Wilson J. 63
Women's Revolt 14, 271-72, 277
Women's Riot 13, 261
Women's War 239, 246, 319
World Bank 158
Wormsley, William 101

Yacub, Zera 124
yam 4, 172, 207, 208
Yoruba 1, 2, 11, 81, 305

Zong 29, 49